THE ETERNAL GOD

God Revealing Himself to Us

WILLEM J. OUWENEEL

AN EVANGELICAL INTRODUCTION TO
REFORMATIONAL THEOLOGY
VOL II/1

PART II: GOD:
THE PERSONAL SOURCE BEHIND
EVANGELICAL THEOLOGY

AN EVANGELICAL INTRODUCTION TO REFORMATIONAL THEOLOGY

Part I: Scripture: The Revealed Source For Theology
    I/1 *The Eternal Word:* God Speaking To Us
    I/2 *The Eternal Torah:* Living Under God

Part II: God: The Personal Source Behind Theology
    II/1 *The Eternal God:* God Revealing Himself To Us
    II/2 *The Eternal Christ:* God With Us
    II/3 *The Eternal Spirit:* God Living In Us

Part III: Redemption: The Christ-Centered Heart of Theology
    III/1 *The Eternal Purpose:* Living In Christ
    III/2 *Eternal Righteousness:* Living Before God
    III/3 *Eternal Salvation:* Christ Dying For Us
    III/4 *Eternal Life:* Christ Living In Us

Part IV: Consummation: The Lived Shape of Theology
    IV/1 *The Eternal People*: God in Relation To Israel
    IV/2 *The Eternal Covenant*: Living With God
    IV/3 *The Eternal Kingdom*: Living Under Christ

Part V: Method: The Comprehensive Foundation of Theology
    V/1 *Eternal Truth:* The Prolegomena to Theology

THE ETERNAL GOD

God Revealing Himself to Us

WILLEM J. OUWENEEL

The Eternal God: God Revealing Himself to Us

This English edition is a publication of Paideia Press (P.O. Box 500, Jordan Station, Ontario, Canada L0R 1S0). Copyright © 2023 by Paideia Press. All rights reserved. Except for brief quotations in critical publications or reviews, no part of this book may be reproduced in any manner without prior written permission from Paideia Press at the address above.

Unless otherwise indicated, Scripture quotations are from the ESV® Bible (The Holy Bible, English Standard Version®). Copyright © 2001 by Crossway, a publishing ministry of Good News Publishers. Used by permission. All rights reserved.

Scripture quotations or references marked as NKJV are taken from the New King James Version®. Copyright © 1982 by Thomas Nelson, Inc. Used by permission. All rights reserved.

Scripture quotations or references marked as NIV are taken from the Holy Bible, New International Version®, NIV®. Copyright © 1973, 1978, 1984, 2011 by Biblica, Inc.™ Used by permission of Zondervan. All rights reserved worldwide. www.zondervan.com. The "NIV" and "New International Version" are trademarks registered in the United States Patent and Trademark Office by Biblica, Inc.™

Book Design by: Juan Esteban Clavijo

ISBN 978-0-88815-358-6

Printed in the United States of America

*The eternal God is your dwelling place,
and underneath are the everlasting arms.*

> Deuteronomy 33:27

*Even before the mountains came into existence,
or you brought the world into being,
you were the eternal God.*

> Psalm 90:2 NET

*Your throne was set in place a long time ago.
You are eternal.*

> Psalm 93:2 NOG

*Don't you know? Haven't you heard?
The LORD is the eternal God, Creator of the earth.
He never gets weary or tired;
his wisdom cannot be measured.*

> Isaiah 40:28 CEV

*[The mystery] has now been disclosed
and through the prophetic writings has been made known
to all nations,
according to the command of the eternal God,
to bring about the obedience of faith.*

> Romans 16:26

Table of Contents

Series Preface		i
Author's Preface		v
Abbreviations		ix
Chapter 1	The God Question	1
Chapter 2	The Science of Religion	49
Chapter 3	Apologetics and the Theistic Proofs	93
Chapter 4	The Being of God	121
Chapter 5	God and Time	163
Chapter 6	God's Attributes: Introduction	193
Chapter 7	God's Attributes (Natural Modalities)	213
Chapter 8	God's Attributes (Spiritive Modalities)	265
Chapter 9	The Doctrine of the Trinity	333
Chapter 10	The Development of Trinitarianism	371
Bibliography		411
Scripture Index		439
Subject Index		453

Table of Contents Expanded

Series Preface	i
Author's Preface	v
Abbreviations	ix
1 The God Question	1
1.1 The Development of the God Question	1
1.1.1 Beginnings	1
1.1.2 Faith Versus Philosophy	3
1.1.3 The Enlightenment and Afterward	5
1.2 Examples	6
1.2.1 The Atheists	6
1.2.2 The Theists	8
1.2.3 The Postmodernists	10
1.3 Theology Proper and Anthropology	12
1.3.1 The Human Question	12
1.3.2 A Reformational-Philosophical Approach	13
1.3.3 Related Views	15
1.4 True and Apostate Religion	16
1.4.1 Human Responses to Divine Revelation	16
1.4.2 Prolegomena to Theology Proper	17
1.5 Faith Knowledge of God	18
1.5.1 Knowledge Is Fellowship	18
1.5.2 Care and Praise	20

	1.5.3 The New Testament	22
1.6	Cognitive, Theoretical, and Existential Knowledge of God	24
	1.6.1 Theoretical and Practical	24
	1.6.2 Fellowship with God	26
	1.6.3 In Summary	28
1.7	Protestant Scholasticism	29
	1.7.1 Abraham Kuyper	29
	1.7.2 Herman Bavinck	30
	1.7.3 Divergent Views	31
1.8	Theoretical and Practical Knowledge of God	32
	1.8.1 Distinctions	32
	1.8.2 Theoreticalizing Everyday Thought	34
	1.8.3 A Basic Error	35
1.9	Concepts and Ideas	36
	1.9.1 Theoretical and Practical	36
	1.9.2 What Are Ideas?	37
	1.9.3 Consequences of Misunderstanding	39
1.10	Ideas and Metaphors Concerning God	41
	1.10.1 Again, Concepts and Ideas	41
	1.10.2 Metaphors	43
	1.10.3 A New Way	45
2 The Science of Religion		49
2.1	Religious Studies, Elenctics, Theology	49
	2.1.1 Boundaries	49
	2.1.2 No Basic Differences	51
2.2	Religiosity and Religion	53

	2.2.1 Immanent and Transcendent	53
	2.2.2 Forms of Religiosity	55
	2.2.3 More Recent Views	57
2.3	Some Views from the Psychology of Religion	59
	2.3.1 William James	59
	2.3.2 Sigmund Freud	60
2.4	Carl G. Jung	64
	2.4.1 Archetypes	64
	2.4.2 Conjunction	65
	2.4.3 Buber's Comments	67
2.5	Transcendental Critique	68
	2.5.1 True Self-Knowledge	68
	2.5.2 Knowledge of Self and of God	70
	2.5.3 The Religious Root of All Human Thought	72
2.6	What Is Religion?	74
	2.6.1 Various Descriptions	74
	2.6.2 Again, Concept and Idea	76
	2.6.3 Again, the Immanent and the Transcendent	78
2.7	Questions in the Field of the Science of Religion	80
	2.7.1 The Religious Variable	80
	2.7.2 Various Types of Religiosity	83
	2.7.3 Intrinsic and Extrinsic	85
2.8	Elements of Religiosity	87
	2.8.1 Intrinsic Religiosity	87
	2.8.2 Other Features	89

		2.8.3 Three Dimensions	90
3	Apologetics and the Theistic Proofs		93
	3.1	Theology Proper and Apologetics	93
		3.1.1 Types of Apologetics	93
		3.1.2 Problems in Apologetics	96
		3.1.3 The Central Problem	98
		3.1.4 Dooyeweerdian Anthropology	100
	3.2	Natural Theology and Its Problems	101
		3.2.1 Thomism	101
		3.2.2 Reformational Thought	103
		3.2.3 Romans 1	105
	3.3	An Evangelical Approach	107
		3.3.1 Norman L. Geisler	107
		3.3.2 Teleology, Ethics, Ontology	109
		3.3.3 The Cosmological Proof of God	112
	3.4	The Theistic Proofs and the Supra-Rational	114
		3.4.1 A False Dilemma	114
		3.4.2 Again, the Ontological Argument	116
		3.4.3 Supra-Rationality	118
4	The Being of God		121
	4.1	Introduction	121
		4.1.1 Image-Building	121
		4.1.2 The Term "God"	123
	4.2	The Personal God	124
		4.2.1 The Who-ness of God and Human Beings	124
		4.2.2 Rationality Over-Emphasized	126

		4.2.3 Modal Aspects of Personality	128
	4.3	Anthropomorphic? Supra-Personal?	130
		4.3.1 Terminology	130
		4.3.2 Concepts and Ideas	131
		4.3.3 The Idea of the Person	132
	4.4	Dangers for Theology Proper	134
		4.4.1 Hellenism	134
		4.4.2 Substantialism	136
		4.4.3 A Christian Philosophical Approach	138
		4.4.4 True Essence	140
	4.5	The Damage Created by Substantialism	142
		4.5.1 Dualism	142
		4.5.2 Prima Causa	142
		4.5.3 Idealism	143
	4.6	Scholastic Remnants	144
		4.6.1 Communicable and Incommunicable	144
		4.6.2 The Three Ways	145
		4.6.3 Divisions	147
	4.7	Concrete Dangers	148
		4.7.1 God's Self-Revelation	148
		4.7.2 Statements about God	151
	4.8	More on the Being–Appearance Dualism	153
		4.8.1 Negative Theology	153
		4.8.2 The Analogia Entis	156
		4.8.3 Further Explanation	158
5	God and Time		163

	5.1	The Eternity of God	163
		5.1.1 Lexicographical Aspects	163
		5.1.2 Is God Timeless?	165
		5.1.3 Greek Thought versus the Bible	168
	5.2	Ancient and Scholastic Views	170
		5.2.1 Earlier Views	170
		5.2.2 An Astonishing Continuum	172
	5.3	Bavinck's View	174
		5.3.1 A Traditional Approach	174
		5.3.2 A Biblical Basis?	175
	5.4	A New View of Eternity	177
		5.4.1 Eternal and Supra-Temporal	177
		5.4.2 Further Development	179
		5.4.3 (Trans-)Cosmic Time	180
	5.5	Pleni-Temporality	181
		5.5.1 Supra- or Pleni-Temporal	181
		5.5.2 Duality and Dualism	183
	5.6	A New View of God's Eternity	185
		5.6.1 Is God Timeless?	185
		5.6.2 Biblical Proof?	188
		5.6.3 Once More: Time, Eternity, and Ideas	190
6	God's Attributes: Introduction		193
	6.1	Attributes and Names: Philosophical Aspects	193
		6.1.1 "Open Windows"	193
		6.1.2 De-Hellenization	195
		6.1.3 The Term "Attribute"	195

6.2	The Modal Aspects	197
	6.2.1 Modal Analogies	197
	6.2.2 Analogies Within Analogies	198
6.3	Attributes and Names: Theological Aspects	199
	6.3.1 A Christological-Soteriological Approach	199
	6.3.2 Attributes As Soteriology	201
	6.3.3 No Separate Compartments	203
6.4	Other Theological Aspects	204
	6.4.1 Inherent Antitheses	204
	6.4.2 Too Little Attention?	205
6.5	Multiplicity of God's Attributes	207
	6.5.1 Examples of Classifications: Until 1950	207
	6.5.2 More Recent Examples of Classifications	209
	6.5.3 Summary	211

7	God's Attributes (Natural Modalities)	213
7.1	The Arithmetic Modality: God's Unity	213
	7.1.1 The Unity of Singularity	213
	7.1.2 The Unity of Simplicity	215
	7.1.3 Further Complications	217
	7.1.4 Names of God	219
7.2	The Arithmetic Modality: God's Infinity	220
	7.2.1 Two Kinds of Infinity	220
	7.2.2 Application	221
	7.2.3 Names of God	222

- 7.3 The Spatial Modality: God's Elevation — 223
  - 7.3.1 Supratemporal, Surpassing — 223
  - 7.3.2 The Spatial Modality: God's *Aseitas* — 224
  - 7.3.3 Names of God — 224
- 7.4 The Spatial Modality: God's Omnipresence — 225
  - 7.4.1 Historical Background — 225
  - 7.4.2 Conceptual Misunderstandings — 226
  - 7.4.3 Ambiguity — 228
  - 7.4.4 Names of God — 230
- 7.5 The Kinematic Modality: God's Transcendence — 230
  - 7.5.1 Transcendence and Immanence — 230
  - 7.5.2 Descending and Ascending — 231
  - 7.5.3 Names of God — 233
- 7.6 The Kinematic Modality: God's Immutability — 233
  - 7.6.1 Changeable and Unchangeable — 233
  - 7.6.2 Being and Becoming — 235
  - 7.6.3 Names of God — 237
- 7.7 The Physical Modality: God As *Causa Sui* — 238
  - 7.7.1 God's Independence — 238
  - 7.7.2 Names of God — 240
- 7.8 The Physical Modality: God's Omnipotence — 241
  - 7.8.1 Potentiality and Actuality — 241

	7.8.2	Power and Weakness	243
	7.8.3	Names of God	245
7.9	The Biotic Modality: God's Vitality		247
	7.9.1	The Living God	247
	7.9.2	God's Eternal Life	248
	7.9.3	Names of God	250
7.10	The Perceptive Modality: God's Spirituality		250
	7.10.1	God Is Pneuma	250
	7.10.2	Is God Incorporeal?	252
	7.10.3	Names of God	253
7.11	The Perceptive Modality: God's Invisibility		254
	7.11.1	The Contemplation of God	254
	7.11.2	Seeing God Through Christ	255
	7.11.3	Names of God	256
7.12	The Sensitive Modality: God's Emotionality		256
	7.12.1	Anthropopathisms?	256
	7.12.2	Pathos or Apatheia?	258
	7.12.3	Names of God	259
7.13	The Sensitive Modality: God's Beatitude		260
	7.13.1	Beatus and Benedictus	260
	7.13.2	Perfection, Knowledge, Love, Joy	262
	7.13.3	Names of God	263
8	God's Attributes (Spiritive Modalities)		265
8.1	The Logical Modality: God's Rationality		265

	8.1.1	Higher Thoughts	265
	8.1.2	Reasoning Together	266
	8.1.3	Names of God	268
8.2	The Logical Modality: God's Omniscience		269
	8.2.1	Knowing All, Yet Acquiring Knowledge	269
	8.2.2	Prescience in God?	270
	8.2.3	Divine Foreknowledge and Human Responsibility	272
	8.2.4	Logical Errors	274
	8.2.5	Names of God	276
8.3	The Historical-Formative Modality		277
	8.3.1	God's Sovereign Will and Arbitrariness	277
	8.3.2	God's Sovereign Will and Evil	279
	8.3.3	Bavinck's Example	281
	8.3.4	Names of God	284
8.4	The Lingual Modality: the Speaking God		285
	8.4.1	The Word and the Words	285
	8.4.2	Speech and the Trinity	286
	8.4.3	Names of God	288
8.5	The Social Modality (1)		289
	8.5.1	God Practicing Fellowship	289
	8.5.2	Names of God	291
8.6	The Social Modality (2)		292
	8.6.1	The Covenanting God	292
	8.6.2	Names of God	294

8.7	The Economic Modality	295
	8.7.1 God's Perfection	295
	8.7.2 God's Sufficiency	296
	8.7.3 Names of God	298
8.8	The Aesthetic Modality: God's Glory	299
	8.8.1 Splendor and Magnificence	299
	8.8.2 Goodness and Beauty	301
	8.8.3 Glory and Light	302
	8.8.4 Names of God	304
8.9	The Aesthetic Modality: God's Peace	305
	8.9.1 Harmony, Order, Rest	305
	8.9.2 Names of God	305
8.10	The Juridical Modality	306
	8.10.1 The Righteous God	306
	8.10.2 The Justifying God	309
	8.10.3 Names of God	311
8.11	The Ethical Modality: God's Love	312
	8.11.1 Love from Eternity	312
	8.11.2 Types of Love	313
	8.11.3 Agapē	315
	8.11.4 Names of God	317
8.12	The Ethical Modality: Other Features	317
	8.12.1 Lovingkindness, Patience, Mercy	317
	8.12.2 Grace	319
	8.12.3 Names of God	320
8.13	The Ethical Modality: God's Holiness	320

		8.13.1 Is Holiness a Divine Attribute?	320
		8.13.2 The Holy and Sanctifying God	322
		8.13.3 Names of God	324
	8.14	The Ethical Modality: God's Wisdom	324
		8.14.1 Moral Aspects of Wisdom	324
		8.14.2 Names of God	325
	8.15	The Pistical Modality	326
		8.15.1 God's Faithfulness	326
		8.15.2 God's Truthfulness	328
		8.15.3 Names of God	330
9	The Doctrine of the Trinity		333
	9.1	The Unitarian Challenge	333
		9.1.1 Introduction	333
		9.1.2 The Double Sense of "Father"	335
		9.1.3 A Spiritual Battle	337
	9.2	The Existential Background	339
		9.2.1 Practical and Theoretical	339
		9.2.2 A Confession of the Heart	341
	9.3	In Conflict with Scholasticism and Liberalism	343
		9.3.1 Ontology and Axiology	343
		9.3.2 Trinitarianism and Faith	344
	9.4	Positing the Theological Problem: Exegetical Ground-Questions	346
		9.4.1 Theoretical and Practical	346
		9.4.2 Main Theoretical Problems	348
	9.5	Trinitarian Problems	351

	9.5.1 An Introduction	351
	9.5.2 Is Further Theological Development Possible?	353
	9.5.3 Criteria	355
9.6	The One and the Three	357
9.6.1 Ancient Formulation		357
9.6.2 Analysis of the Terms Used		358
9.7	New Testament Use of Terms	360
	9.7.1 *Ousia*	360
	9.7.2 *Physis*	360
	9.7.3 *Prosōpon*	361
	9.7.4 *Hypostasis*	362
9.8	Trinitarian Tension	365
	9.8.1 Confusing Use of Terms	365
	9.8.2 One or Three Persons?	367
	9.8.3 Once More: Tradition	368
10 The Development of Trinitarianism		371
10.1 Divine Properties		371
	10.1.1 Introduction	371
	10.1.2 Mutual Relationships	372
	10.1.3 Some Comments	374
10.2 The Two Extremes		376
	10.2.1 Introduction	376
	10.2.2 Tritheism	376
	10.2.3 Modalism	378
10.3 Three More Models		380
	10.3.1 Arianism	380
	10.3.2 Socinianism	381

10.3.3	Subordinationism	383
10.4	Orthodox Trinitarianism	386
10.4.1	Features	386
10.4.2	Confusion	387
10.4.3	Intuition and Speculation	388
10.5	The Older Tradition	389
10.5.1	The Big Five	389
10.5.2	Comments	390
10.5.3	Trinitarian Terminology	393
10.6	Newer Examples	395
10.6.1	Who Is Orthodox Today?	395
10.6.2	Herman Bavinck	396
10.6.3	Lewis Sperry Chafer	399
10.7	Again, Tritheism and Modalism	401
10.7.1	The Golden Mean	401
10.7.2	The Term *Persona*	403
10.7.3	Further Considerations	404
10.8	The Three Hypostases	406
10.8.1	A First Pair of "Contras"	406
10.8.2	A Second Pair of "Contras"	407
10.8.3	A Third Pair of "Contras"	408
Bibliography		411
Scripture Index		439
Subject Index		453

Series Preface

BY MEANS OF THIS PREFACE, the editor and publisher of this series wish to help the reader both understand and process the content of these volumes.

The capacities and erudition of Dr. Willem J. Ouweneel need no demonstration or defense from us. His voluminous work and prodigious writing stand as a testimony to his love for the Lord Jesus Christ, God's Word, and God's people.

But these volumes present ideas that will surprise some, anger others, and possibly confuse still others. Both the editor and publisher disagree with some of Dr. Ouweneel's assertions and conclusions, but this is not the place for offering our counter-arguments. That requires an altogether different venue. Nevertheless, discerning readers will legitimately wonder why this editor and publisher invested effort and resources in putting these volumes into print.

At least three reasons justify that investment. Each of them is very sensitive.

The first reason is: *self-examination*. Some of our readers may conclude that, in presenting his exegetical, doctrinal, and historical case, Dr. Ouweneel is "coloring outside the lines" of what they have come to believe. He challenges deeply and firmly held convictions and beliefs, like those associated with Israel, with the law of God, with election and reprobation, with infant baptism, with covenant theology, and with justification. At each point, his challenges call us readers to self-examination, regarding our love for Scripture, for the God of Scripture, and for the Truth revealed and incarnated personally in Jesus Christ. One of Ouweneel's challenges is for us believers in Jesus Christ who are Reformed and Presbyterian church members to recognize that there are millions, even billions, of Jesus-believers who disagree with us *and are nevertheless genuine Christians*. And they ought to be acknowledged as such.

The second reason is: *repentance*. Coming, as they do, from one who lives and teaches outside the orbit of many of our readers, Dr. Ouweneel's observations about the state of our (numerous) churches and of our (interminable) doctrinal squabbles ought to embarrass us Reformed and Presbyterian church members. Our incessant polemicizing, our cantankerous stridency, and our offenses against the unity of Christ's church seriously compromise the gospel's witness to the watching world. Brothers and sisters, we must repent of these, for the sake of the gospel, for the sake of the church's witness, and for the sake of our children.

The third reason is: *ecumenicity*. This reason may indeed strike you as strange, but one of the salutary outcomes of reading Dr. Ouweneel's arguments can be this: not that you surrender your commitments and convictions that are being challenged, but instead that you come to respect and love those Jesus-believers who don't share them with you. These Christians are those whose spiritual pilgrimage and gospel-guided history have not brought them to the same place on the road, but who nonetheless are walking the same road as we.

You may well be asking: How, then, is this different from advocating doctrinal relativism? If these distinctive features of Reformed confession and theology are biblical, then why is Dr. Ouweneel being given a microphone for proclaiming his criticisms and rejections of these distinctive emphases of

Reformed teaching? The short answer is this: So that from this brother in Christ, this close cousin in the faith, this fellow pilgrim-soldier, we may learn how to lock arms with other Jesus-believers as we face unbelief in our day, even if we can't hold hands. So that we may learn what it means to be Jesus-believers *first*, Reformed or Presbyterian confessors *second*, and only then, *thirdly, theological advocates*.

So we leave you with this challenge: Why do you believe what you believe? What is your biblical warrant? Dr. Ouweneel presents fairly the various positions prevalent within Christianity. The reader will learn why others believe what they believe, and why they don't emphasize certain teachings in the same way that we do.

These books, then, are not for the faint of faith. But they are for those wanting to grow up and mature into the unity of faith in our Lord Jesus Christ (John 17: 20–23; Eph. 4:13).

Nelson D. Kloosterman, editor
John Hultink, publisher

Author's Preface

This is Volume II/1 in a systematic-theological series on the "unseen, eternal" things of God (cf. 2 Cor. 4:18). Whereas the previous two volumes dealt with bibliology, and more specifically with the Torah, the present one is the first of three volumes on the divine persons. The present Volume II/1 is on theology proper, the doctrine of God. Volume II/2 will deal with Christology, and Volume II/3 with pneumatology. The present volume deals with the subject of religious studies in general, with the being of God, with the question of God and time, with the many attributes of God, and with the subject of the Trinity. The latter subject is dealt with insofar as there is a certain overlap with theology proper; the more Christological and pneumatological aspects will have to wait until the next volumes.

This volume is a re-working and expansion of two parts of my Evangelisch-Dogmatische Reeks ("Evangelical Dogmatic Series," abbrev.: EDR, published in Dutch by Medema, located originally in Vaassen and later in Heerenveen, the Netherlands, consisting of twelve volumes in total; they will be quoted in the present volume as EDR 1 through 12). The one part consists of chapters 1–5 from Volume 12 (*De glorie van God*), the other part consists of chapter 2 from Volume 2 (*De Christus van God*). The titles of the volumes in the EDR all end with the words van God ("of God"). For the English series I have chosen the key term "Eternal" in each title.

As planned thus far, this series will contain thirteen volumes; the preliminary titles are as follows (in the present volume referred to by their prospective numbers):

I/1 *The Eternal Word*: A Christian Theology of God Speaking to Us

I/2 *The Eternal Torah*: A Christian Theology of Living under God

II/1 *The Eternal God*: A Christian Theology of God in Relation to Us

II/2 *The Eternal Christ*: A Christian Theology of Christ in Relation to Us

II/3 *The Eternal Spirit*: A Christian Theology of God Living in Us

III/1 *The Eternal Purpose*: A Christian Theology of Living in Christ

III/2 *Eternal Righteousness*: A Christian Theology of Living before God

III/3 *Eternal Salvation*: A Christian Theology of Christ Dying for Us

III/4 *Eternal Life*: A Christian Theology of Christ Living in Us

IV/1 *The Eternal People*: A Christian Theology of God in Relation to Israel

IV/2 *The Eternal Covenant*: A Christian Theology of Living with God

IV/3 *The Eternal Kingdom*: A Christian Theology of Living under Christ

V/1 *Eternal Truth*: A Christian Study of the Prolegomena to Theology

Bible quotations in this book are usually from the English

Standard Version.

I thank Dr. Nelson D. Kloosterman again very warmly for his expert editorial work on the manuscript of this book. And I am again deeply thankful to my publisher, John Hultink, for his constant encouragement in this entire project.

Willem J. Ouweneel
Spring 2019

Abbreviations

Bible Versions

AMP	Amplified Bible
AMPC	Amplified Bible, Classic Edition
ASV	American Standard Version
CEB	Common English Bible
CEV	Contemporary English Version
CJB	Complete Jewish Bible
DLNT	Disciples' Literal New Testament
ERV	Easy-to-Read Version
ESV	English Standard Version
GNT	Good News Translation
GW	God's Word Translation
HSV	Herziene Statenvertaling
ICB	International Children's Bible
ISV	International Standard Version
KJV	King James Version
LEB	Lexham English Bible
NASB	New American Standard Bible
NET	New English Translation
NIV	New International Version
NKJV	New King James Version

NLV	New Life Version
RSV	Revised Standard Version
TLB	Living Bible
WEB	World English Bible

Other Sources

CD	Barth, K. 1956. *Church Dogmatics*. Trans. by T. H. L. Parker et al. Vols. 1/1–4/4. Louisville, KY: Westminster John Knox.
CW	Darby, J. N. n.d. *The Collected Writings of J. N. Darby*. Kingston-on-Thames: Stow Hill Bible and Tract Depot.
DD	Kuyper, A. n.d. *Dictaten Dogmatiek*. Kampen: J. H. Kok.
EBC	Expositor's Bible Commentary
EDR	Ouweneel, W. J. 2007–2013. *Evangelische Dogmatische Reeks*. 12 vols. Vaassen/Heerenveen: Medema.
EHG	Kuyper, A. 1909. *Encyclopaedie der heilige godgeleerdheid*. 2nd rev. ed. Vols. 2–3. Kampen: J.H. Kok/Amsterdam: Wormser.
KD	Schilder, K. n.d. *Kompendium dogmatiek*. Kampen: Van den Berg.
KV	Korte Verklaring der Heilige Schrift
MEW	Marx-Engels-Werke
NC	Dooyeweerd, H. 1984. *A New Critique of Theoretical Thought*. Vol. 1: *The Necessary Presuppositions of Philosophy*

(1953). Vol. 2: *The General Theory of the Modal Spheres* (1955). Vol. 3: *The*

	Structures of Individuality of Temporal Reality (1957). Jordan Station: Paideia Press.
NICNT	New International Commentary on the New Testament
RD	Bavinck, H. 2002–2008. *Reformed Dogmatics*. Edited by J. Bolt. Translated by J. Vriend. 4 vols. Grand Rapids, MI: Baker Academic.
RGG	Galling, K. ed. 1986. *Die Religion in Geschichte und Gegenwart*. 6 vols. Tübingen: Mohr (Siebeck).
SBB	Cohen, A., ed. 1982–1985. *The Soncino Books of the Bible*. 14 vols. London: Soncino.
ST	Chafer, L. S. 1983. *Systematic Theology*. 15th ed. 8 vols. Dallas, TX: Dallas Seminary Press.
TCW	Tydskrif vir Christelike Wetenskap
TDNT	Kittel, G. et al., eds. 1964–1976. *Theological Dictionary of the New Testament*. Translated by G. W. Bromiley. 10 vols. Grand Rapids, MI: Wm. B. Eerdmans.
TI	Rahner, K. *Theological Investigations*. London: Darton, Longman and Todd.

Chapter 1
The God Question

The LORD is high above all nations,
and his glory above the heavens!
Who is like the LORD our God,
who is seated on high,
who looks far down
on the heavens and the earth?

Ps. 113:4–6

1.1 The Development of the God Question
1.1.1 Beginnings

IT IS QUITE UNDERSTANDABLE that textbooks of systematic theology usually begin with theology proper (Lat. *theologia propria*), that is, theology in the narrower sense, the doctrine of God (Lat. *locus de Deo*). In the present "Eternal" series (about the eternal Word, the eternal Torah, the eternal purpose, righteousness, salvation, covenant, kingdom) we now come to that which—or rather, he who—is *truly* eternal: God himself. Similarly, the "eternal Spirit" (Heb. 9:14) is truly eternal because he is God the Spirit. And "eternal life" is truly eternal because basically it is the life of God himself: Jesus is the true God and eternal life (1 John 5:20). In a derived sense, God's Word, God's purpose, God's righteousness, God's salvation, God's covenant, and God's kingdom are eternal. These are all works of God. Now, then, who is this God whose many works we are attempting to clarify in this series?

The task of systematic theology involves the theoretical analysis and systematization of Christian doctrine, including the doctrine of God. However, this discipline cannot ignore the fact that it speaks of a matter that, in our secularized, post-Christian times, has become an irrelevant side theme. God plays only a minimal role—if any role at all—in the natural and cultural sciences[1], in the arts, in the judicial order, in morals, in politics[2], in society and economy, in medicine, technology, and ecology. Why should we still write about God? For whom? Today, in the Netherlands, a country that since the early seventeenth century was thoroughly Calvinistic, fewer than fifty percent of the people confess belief in a personal God. Among university professors, this seems to be only seventeen percent; forty-four percent call themselves outright atheists (which goes much further than agnostics). Moreover, we should wonder in how many of the lives of that seventeen percent God plays an actual role

In a sense, the "God question" began with those ancient Greeks who made a sharp distinction between, on the one hand, the truth of God as based on philosophical thought and, on the other hand, the popular views concerning God as based upon experience and tradition (Parmenides, Xenophanes). It was the distinction between, on the one hand, philosophical concepts and ideas concerning the Godhead and, on the other hand, popular "myths" and "narratives" concerning the Godhead. The early Christians grew up with the great "narrative" of God in the Torah—the God of Abraham, Isaac and Jacob (Exod. 3:6, 15–16; 4:5; cf. Matt. 22:32; Acts 3:13; 7:32)—as continued in the prophetic books of the Old Testament, and the apostolic books of the New Testament. It was inevitable, however, that the early Christians, too, developed their own philosophical concepts and ideas concerning the Godhead

---
1. Cf. Ouweneel (2018).
2. Cf. Ouweneel (2017).

in what, since Origen, they called "theology." How did, and does, this "theology" relate to the great narrative of God in the Old and New Testaments?

1.1.2 Faith Versus Philosophy

In the strict sense of the terms, the prophets and the apostles never theorized and theologized about God. However, the apostles dealt with Hellenists, that is, those who had imbibed Hellenist thought, a mixture of Greek and various Middle-Eastern thought systems. In order to persuade these people, the early Christian apologists—defenders of Christianity—had to formulate the doctrine of God in the thought molds that the Hellenists had prepared: the "God of the philosophers," as French Christian apologist Blaise Pascal (d. 1662) called them (see below). The "narrative" of God was still told to the masses; but meanwhile the theologians endeavored to develop the "concept" of God by introducing Greek terms such as hypostasis (Lat. *substantia*, "substance") and *ousia* (Lat. *essentia*, "essence"), which, in their newly developed meanings, are foreign to, though not necessarily in conflict with, Scripture.

The God preached to the masses and the God of the philosophers clearly ran the risk of growing apart. Take the Athanasian Creed (ca. AD 500), which contains Latin terms such as *trinitas* ("Trinity"), *substantia, persona* ("person"), the Son *ante saecula genitus* ("begotten before the world") by the Father, *assumptione humanitatis in Deum* ("assumption of humanness into God") in the person of the Christ, the *anima rationalis* ("rational soul") of Christ, terms that are foreign to the Bible (though their contents are not necessarily unbiblical). This was not the language in which "common" believers spoke of God and thought of God and of Christ.

For a time, the two ways of representing God seemed to compete with each other. Then, with the rise of scholastic theology, with its inherent nature–grace dualism, each of the two received its own specific place. "The God of the philosophers" was assigned to the "lower story" of nature, that is, to "natural theology,"[3] whereas "the God of Scripture" was thought to belong to the "upper story" of grace (supernature). Natural reason was thought to rule in the domain of nature, just as revelation and faith were supposed to rule in the domain of grace. *Supernatural* theology may contain many difficulties in the doctrine of God—let me mention only the dogma of the Trinity—but rested at least on the stable foundation of *natural* theology with its theistic evidence (rational proofs for the existence of God) and its speculations about God's substance and his communicable and non-communicable attributes (see extensively §4.6.1).

At the outset of modern time, French Christian philosopher Blaise Pascal was the brilliant prophet who blew up this framework with the few words that, after his death, were found sewn into his clothes, and that began as follows: "FIRE. God of Abraham, God of Isaac, God of Jacob, not of the philosophers and scholars. Certainty, joy, certainty, feeling, view, joy. God of Jesus Christ. My God and your God, John 20:17," and so on.[4] Pascal made short work of the idea that the God of Scripture (with whom believers enjoy an intimate relationship) and the God of philosophy (who is nothing but a rational-theoretical, distanced abstraction) could ever walk together. This is the reverse of Amos 3:3, "Do two walk together, unless they have agreed to meet?" The two ideas of God will never agree to meet, and therefore they cannot easily get along. The God of the believers can be only the God of Scripture, never the God of the philosophers—at best the God of believing philosophers, but then in their quality of believers, not that of philosophers.

---

3. See Ouweneel (2019, §§2.10 and 4.1).
4. In French (and partly Latin): "FEU. Dieu d'Abraham, Dieu d'Isaac. Dieu de Jacob non des philosophes et savants. Certitude, joie, certitude, sentiment, vue, joie. Dieu de Jésus-Christ. Deum meum et Deum vestrum. Jean 20.17."

1.1.3 The Enlightenment and Afterward

Pascal's statement was a challenge to future generations to make a philosophical-theological, and even an existential, choice. However, in the scientific and rationalistic climate of Western thought, neither orthodox theology nor liberal theology managed to free itself of its strongly theoretical "concept of God," nor of its speculations about the divine "being" (Gk. *ousia*, Lat. *essentia*), the divine "substance" (Gk. *hypostasis*, Lat. *substantia*), and the divine "nature" (Gk. *physis*, Lat. *natura*).

If, therefore, theoretical thought would have to surrender one of the two ways of representing God, the choice could not be difficult. During the (pre-)Enlightenment, thinkers like René Descartes (d. 1650), John Locke (d. 1704), Gotthold E. Lessing (d. 1781), and Jean-le-Rond d'Alembert (d. 1783) did respect revealed theology (Lat. *theologia revelata*),[5] but the God whom they themselves presented was none other than the God of natural theology. This was the God of Descartes' ontological proof of God, Locke's proof that from eternity something had existed, Lessing's philosophical God, who ostensibly made the earlier biblical narratives concerning God superfluous, and d'Alembert's Supreme Being. Voltaire (François-Marie Arouet) and Jean-Jacques Rousseau (both d. 1778) came with their own proofs for the existence of the Supreme Being, and flatly denied the God of revelation, or any god of any revelation whatsoever.

Julien Offray de la Mettrie (d. 1751) was perhaps the most modern of the Enlightenment philosophers in the sense that, though prepared to accept the existence of a Supreme Being, he hardly showed any interest in him. Dutch philosopher Theo de Boer offered an interesting brief survey of the Enlightenment views of God.[6] In this, he suggested that it is nothing else than this Supreme Being of the Enlightenment, the God of the philosophers, whom we still find here and

---
5. A strange misnomer; at most we can speak of a theology concerning revealed things, not of a theology that itself would have been revealed.
6. De Boer (1989, 16–31).

there identified on Western currency (coins and bills), with phrases like "In God we trust," in the oaths that are sworn at inaugurations and in parliaments ("So help me God"), and in the "God bless you" (or "God bless America," and the like) that is so easily expressed at official public events.[7] This may be somewhat exaggerated, but this is certainly a God bereft of every recognizable Jewish-Christian element. This is a charming, safe God, not the dangerous God of the Bible (e.g., the God of Heb. 10:31; 12:29).[8]

As the God of revelation lost his impact, and the Enlightenment focused upon the God of natural reason, so that the views of David Hume (d. 1776) and Immanuel Kant (d. 1804), who swept the floor with the traditional theistic proofs, were even more devastating. Kant did argue that *pure* [i.e., theoretical] reason has no theistic proofs, but he continued to defend God's existence on the ethical grounds of *practical* reason. However, this could not slow down the philosophical developments in the nineteenth century with respect to the "God question." A totally new phenomenon arose in the Western world: atheism. This is either the conviction that there is no God (we might call this "ontic atheism"), or the experience of the absence of God (we might call this "existential atheism").[9]

1.2 Examples
1.2.1 The Atheists

Friedrich Nietzsche (d. 1900) was an example of the second attitude mentioned. His statement concerning the death of God[10] turned out to be a prophetic description of modern Western culture. As his Zarathustra says, we ourselves have killed God, that is, have made him superfluous; we have removed him from the public domain, and often also from the

---

7. Ibid., 20.
8. Cf. the words that C. S. Lewis (2009) says about Aslan the Lion: "'Course he isn't safe. But he's good. He's the King, I tell you."
9. Cf. the distinction by Durand (1985, §2.6) and Wentsel (1987, 123–33) between theoretical and practical atheism.
10. Nietzsche (1999, §§108, 125, 343).

private domain, as a *quantité négligeable*. Nietzsche attacked not only orthodox Christianity but also the *bourgeois* mentality of Enlightenment Christianity.

Others went further.[11] Pierre-Simon de Laplace (d. 1827) reduced God to an "unnessary hypothesis."[12] Ludwig Feuerbach (d. 1872) reduced him to a projection of the person's Ego (cf. his statement, "a man's heart is his God"[13]). The socialist Karl Marx (d. 1883) saw God and religion as merely the means to societal dominion (cf. his statements, "religion is opium for the people" and "an aromatic mist to cover up earthly misery" [14]). The psychoanalyst Sigmund Freud (d. 1939) reduced God to an infantile-regressive, narcissistic, and neurotic illusion.[15] In the wake of the poet Friedrich Hölderlin (d. 1843), the existentialist Martin Heidegger (d. 1976) spoke of "the absence of the god."[16] This is not God's absence as we often encounter it in the biblical psalms (e.g., 10:1, 4; 22:2-3; 42:4, 11; 63:2; 88:15), for in them, the psalmist always engages Someone with his lamentations. He remains a believer, who needs God, and therefore longs for him, and appeals to him. However, the modern absence of God is infinitely worse: modern people no longer need him. This is what Nietzsche foresaw when he announced the modern "afternoon" of nihilism. For where God is rendered superfluous, nothing (Lat. *nihil*) is left.

Such a practical atheist—in the figurative sense—was the prodigal son (Luke 15:11-32). He no longer needed his father, but enjoyed using the latter's property. Turning his back on his father led to "reckless living" (v. 13). Since the Enlightenment, people have put their trust in the autonomy of reason,

---

11. Cf. Pannenberg (1971, 347–60; 1988, 167–69); Wentsel (1987, 123–27).
12. Quoted in Rouse Ball (2003, section Pierre-Simon Laplace).
13. Feuerbach (1957).
14. Marx (Einleitung zur Kritik der Hegelschen Rechtsphilosophie, MEW 1.378, and elsewhere).
15. In Freud (2011), see *Totem and Taboo* (1913), *The Ego and the Id* (1923), *The Future of an Illusion* (1927), and *Civilization and Its Discontents* (1930).
16. See, e.g., Heidegger (2009, 183).

in the power of science and technology. But these powers are now coming to dominate them. We need think only of climate changes, nuclear technology, artificial intelligence, in order to see the perils of modern humanity-without-God. When nothing was left of the son's property, in which he had put his trust, he "began to be in need" (v. 14). But instead of immediately returning to his father, he "hired himself out to one of the citizens of that country." Seemingly, for modern people there are plenty of sources among the "citizens" around from which to draw life, as long as it is not the Father. There was no hope left for this man, unless he came home to the father—but for this to happen, he first had to come "to himself" (v. 17).

1.2.2 The Theists

That is the plight of non-theïsts.[17] Theists, too, were aware of God's actual disappearance from public life in the West. Amid the horrors of his Nazi captivity, the German theologian Dietrich Bonhoeffer (murdered in 1945) foresaw a Godless era—an era without even the Supreme Being of Enlightenment Christianity—in which believers, too, paradoxically enough would have to live *etsi deus non daretur*, "as if there were no God," but at the same time "before God":[18] "before God and with God we live without God." In my own words: before God, and with the God of Abraham, Isaac and Jacob, but without the traditional God of *bourgeois* Christianity, who in the meantime had died.

Leszek Kolakowsky (d. 2009) wrote that the absence of God became a constantly open wound in European thinking, even though people managed to intoxicate themselves in such a way that they forgot about it.[19] Jewish thinker Martin Buber (d. 1965) spoke in a powerful way about the "eclipse of God' (Ger.: *Gottesfinsternis*):[20] a God who is there but is withdrawn

---

17. Cf. the excellent analysis by Kasper (1983, chapters 2–3).
18. Bonhoeffer (1964, 241–42).
19. Kolakowsky (1981, 10).
20. Buber (1989).

from our eyes just like the sun during an eclipse.[21] There is a Jewish story about a rabbi's grandson who told his grandfather with tears, "We were playing hide-and-seek, and it was my turn to heed, and I have been waiting all the time, but nobody seeks me!' The grandfather answered, 'Do you know, my boy, that God must say the same? I have hid myself, and I wait, but there is nobody seeking me...."[22]

Actually, God having "hid" himself is one aspect of the "eclipse of God"; the other aspect is that people have driven him out. It is like Jesus having healed a man with a demon; when the people found out, "they began to beg Jesus to depart from their region" (Mark 5:17). Jesus indeed withdrew himself; he never imposed himself on the people. To say that the prodigal son "left" his father is the same as saying that people have "driven out" God in the sense of telling him, or Jesus, that they do not want him; as the citizens in another parable said, "We do not want this man to reign over us" (Luke 9:14).

On the whole, modern Western society no longer has room for God or Jesus, in terms of believing in him. However, he has become questionable both in the sense of doubting him, as well as in the sense of querying about him, as Heinrich Ott (d. 1982) has put it.[23] Thus, the discussion about God has definitely not disappeared. On the contrary, in the 1960s a number or writings were published with regard to the "God question" that drew worldwide attention, such as those by John A. T. Robinson (d. 1983), those from "Christian atheism" or the "God-is-dead theology," and those by Dorothee Sölle (d. 2003).[24]

In the Netherlands, thorough responses were published by Jan Sperna Weiland (d. 2011), Johannes L. Springer, Gerrit C. van Niftrik (d. 1972), Edward Schillebeeckx (d. 2009),

---

21. I have elaborated this topic elsewhere: Ouweneel (1994).
22. I found the story recounted by Steenbergen (1990, 27).
23. Ott (1974, 9).
24. Robinson (1963); Altizer (1966); Altizer and Hamilton (1966); Sölle (1967, with the subtitle: "An Essay in Theology after the 'Death of God'"; 1968).

Theo de Boer, and Cornelis Graafland (d. 2004).[25] In Germany, the "theology of hope" by Jürgen Moltmann constituted a response to the "God-is-dead theology." In the wake of Bonhoeffer, both Moltmann and Wolfhart Pannenberg (d. 2014) tried to overcome the antithesis between (traditional) theism and the new atheism ("Christian" or not). They did so by means of the idea of the suffering God, who has become entangled in the sinful history of humanity.[26] Despite this attempt, the "God question" is still very much alive today, although questions are being asked, and tentative answers are being given, that earlier generations could never have thought of.

1.2.3 The Postmodernists

In contrast to what many Christian thinkers seem to believe, postmodernism as such is not necessarily a threat to Christianity. On the contrary, a new movement known as Radical Orthodoxy (John Milbank, Catherine Pickstock, Graham Ward) does make use of postmodern philosophy, in a challenging way, as an ally against modernism.[27] As John D. Caputo stated, the undeniable result of the postmodern turn was to make it possible for the religious and theological discourse to pull rank. Even addressing God (not only arguing about God) can no longer be rejected on the basis of the argument that it involves a non-empirical hypothesis (the naturalist, positivist view), and it can no longer be reduced to ethics (Immanuel Kant). And if this holds for religious discourse, then it holds also for theology.[28] Even the alleged atheist Jacques Derrida (d. 2004), another leading postmodernist, wrote about his mother, who had raised him in the Jewish faith and was concerned about him, that she must have known that the constancy of God in his life was referred to by different names.[29]

---

25. Sperna Weiland (1966; 1971); Springer (1969); Van Niftrik (1971); Schillebeeckx (1974); De Boer (1989); Graafland (1990).
26. Moltmann (1993); Pannenberg (1971, 361–98).
27. Milbank et al. (1999); for a concise introduction, see Shakespeare (2007).
28. Caputo (2006, 53).
29. Quoted in ibid., 62 (referring to Derrida [1991], the latter's remarkable

In a summary of Caputo concerning postmodernism, he argued that, if his survey was correct, the old boundaries and high walls that modernity tried to build around reason, science, and philosophy, have fallen down. If this is the case, then the language of faith has regained respectability, and if faith has been restored to its legitimate place among the virtues, this gives a new opportunity for theology, in which things center on faith.[30] Whether faith is anything more here than just one of the virtues is questionable;[31] but the core is clear: in postmodern times, faith is acceptable once again — whatever the term "faith" may mean in such a statement. And yet we wonder whether this is truly a return to the Father, or whether it is only the prodigal son "hiring himself out to the citizens of the country." That is, is it the God of the Bible whom people are speaking about, or is it just another "God of the philosophers"?

Whatever the case may be, it is positive that speaking about God, about religion, is again allowed, even though this new speaking about God has its own problems. How do we speak about God after modernism, and perhaps (already) after postmodernism? In our day, there is a flood of publications about the question how, in a responsible way, we can do "God-talk" (if the reader will allow me this somewhat irreverent, but popular expression). God-talk is allowed, but today it seems less self-evident than ever *in what way* we can do God-talk.[32] One need think only of the discussion around so-called "open theism," or of the thesis of Dutch theologian

---

biography); see 59–67 for Caputo's treatise concerning the similarities and differences between Augustine and Derrida.
30. Ibid., 68.
31. See Vol. III/2 in this series, entitled Eternal Righteousness.
32. On this issue, see Van den Brink and Sarot (1995); Wolterstorff (1995); Houtepen (1997); Plantinga (2000); Loonstra (2003); Richards (2003); Kärkkäinen (2004); Lamont (2004); Caputo and Vattimo (2007); Plantinga and Tooley (2008); Plantinga and Wolterstorff (2009); see also Hauerwas (2001); Taylor (2007).

Klaas Hendrikse (d. 2018):[33] "God does not exist but occurs." In some way, this thesis fits into the same category as that of Dutch theologian Nico ter Linden (also d. 2018) concerning many biblical stories:[34] "They are true but did not really happen." In both cases, we are dealing with events (things that occur) but to which no existence in concrete reality can be attributed. It is positive that people speak of God again—but it is not yet clear how to handle a God who occurs but does not exist.

1.3 Theology Proper and Anthropology
1.3.1 The Human Question

Meanwhile, systematic theologians and others have steadily continued their work, including their studies concerning the doctrine of God, necessarily interacting with ongoing discussions involving the existence and the nature of God. Among Roman Catholics, we must mention here the masterly work by Hans Küng, *Does God Exist?*, and *Theological Investigations* (with many treatises on the "God question") by Karl Rahner (d. 1984).[35] Among the Protestants, *Systematic Theology* by Wolfgang Pannenberg, with his extensive treatise of the "God question," as well as *Divine Discourse* by Nicholas Wolterstorff, are excellent examples.[36] Despite the numerous theological objections one might have against such publications, we can observe that the "God question" is enjoying the focused attention of influential theologians and philosophers in our day.[37] The Second Vatican Council rightly remarked that atheism is one of the "signs of the times," and that it "must be counted among the most serious problems of this time."[38] Yet, millions of people today still wish to think about God.

---

33. Hendrikse (2007).
34. Ter Linden (1996–2003).
35. Küng (1978; Rahner (TI).
36. Pannenberg (1988, chapters 2–3); Wolterstorff (1995).
37. See more recently, Schwöbel (2006); Taylor (2007); Plantinga and Tooley (2008); Plantinga and Wolterstorff (2009).
38. Abbott (1966, 201, 216).

In my own contribution to the subject, I will try to avoid the traditional approach, which is heavily burdened under the scholastic idea of "scientific knowledge" about God. Such an approach rarely poses the following three questions:

(a) What *is* scientific knowledge of God?

(b) *Can* we have scientific, that is, systematic-theological, knowledge of God?

(c) And if so, *how* can we obtain scientific knowledge of God? How do we know that such knowledge really is genuine *knowledge* of God? What are the criteria for reliable knowledge of God?

No matter how we answer these questions, they show that, from the outset, theology proper (the doctrine of God) is intertwined with not only epistemology but also anthropology. *In concreto*, the first question is epistemological in nature, and in a certain sense so is the third one; but the second question is (also) anthropological in nature. It is preceded by another question: Can we have *pre-scientific* knowledge of God, or: Can we have *any* knowledge of God at all? The answer might be: Yes, for God has revealed himself.[39] But our counter-question could be, Why do animals not receive this revelation? In other words, what makes humans such special beings that, first, God takes the trouble of revealing himself to them; second, that these beings are capable of receiving this revelation; and third, that as a consequence they can enter into a relationship with this God?

1.3.2 A Reformational-Philosophical Approach

I have discussed the answer elsewhere:[40] humans have been created as *transcendent-religious beings*. Later, we will investigate the meaning of this description more closely; but at this point, we can observe that this implies the following. As the only beings in the empirical, created world, humans have a

---
39. See extensively, Ouweneel (2019, chapters 1–4).
40. See extensively, Ouweneel (*EDR* 3; cf. 2014a; 2014b; 2015).

deep urge—residing in their hearts, their deepest selves—to reach out beyond the immanent-finite to the transcendent-infinite, to some fixed, unshakeable Ground of their entire existence. This urge itself is transcendent in nature, that is, it surpasses the everyday, immanent world; and it is convergent in nature, that is, comprising people's everyday, immanent, inner and outer reality. This relationship between theology proper and philosophical anthropology is of great importance, not only for ontological reasons, but for existential reasons as well. Not only in relationship with God but, in close relationship with the "God question," *humans have become a problem to themselves.*

In 1960, Dutch Christian philosopher Herman Dooyeweerd (d. 1977) sharply analyzed the anthropological crisis.[41] First and foremost, the present crisis of Western humanity is a consequence of the total decline of the human personality, and the rise of the impersonal crowd, caused by the supremacy of technology and the over-organization of modern society. Human behavior is governed by an impersonal society, which is itself dominated by the computer and the threat of artificial intelligence, the bureaucracy, the power of fashion, and the mass media (today we should add the social media).

Second, the average secularized person has fallen into a spiritual nihilism, that is, has lost all faith—including faith in humanity and in the power of human reason—and has lost all ideals, except the satisfaction of their lusts. God is dead, and after two World Wars, the rise of the nuclear and ecological threats, and the decline of all ideologies, humanity is dead as well. Humans have lost not only God, but they have lost themselves, and feel overwhelmed by a meaningless and hopeless reality.

Dooyeweerd added this explanation:

---

41. Dooyeweerd (1960, chapter 8); for my update of the time, cf. Ouweneel (1986, 13–15).

[T]he symptoms of the spiritual decadence of this civilization, manifesting themselves in an increasing expansion of the nihilistic mind, cannot be explained by external causes. They are only the ultimate result of a religious process of apostasy, which started with the belief in the absolute self-sufficiency of the rational human personality and was doomed to end with the breaking down of this idol.[42]

1.3.3 Related Views

Neither the mystery of the human personality, nor the enigma of the decline of this personality in our present time, can be explained from human nature as such, but only from the human "eccentric" relationship to God (i.e., a relationship originating outside the human being), and the apostate loss of this relationship. As Roman Catholic Walter Kasper put it,[43] ". . . with the disappearance of the mystery of God, the mystery of humanity disappears as well. . . . The death of God leads to the death of humanity." Conversely, Jewish Martin Buber has indicated again how, in our earthly I-thou relationships, we catch glimpses of God's eternal Thou, which challenge humanity.[44] It therefore bears repeating: humans are finite, immanent beings, but with a deep, inner urge to reach beyond their immanent-finite environment to the transcendent-infinite, to the fixed and unshakable Ground of their very existence.

This Ground, this Origin, and this Goal of human existence are usually called God, whatever this term may imply to various people. As Thomas Aquinas (d. 1274) said at the end of each of his *quinque viae* ("five ways"), his five theistic proofs, after having arrived at a certain basic concept ("first mover," "necessary being," etc.): *quod omnes nominant Deum*, "what all people call God," or something similar[45]. There is

---

42. Dooyeweerd (1960, 178–79).
43. Kasper (1983, 11).
44. Buber (1989).
45. Aquinas, S. Theol. 1a, q. 2 a. 3 co; cf. extensively, Kreeft (1990).

an experience that is both rooted in our immanent-empirical world and points beyond this world to a state of affairs that, because of their natural sense of God, all people call God.[46]

1.4 True and Apostate Religion
1.4.1 Human Responses to Divine Revelation

The phrase used above, "or something similar," implies a prior, enormously significant question that is both ancient and modern: Why do people have such widely differing views of God? If there is only one (true) revelation of God, why are there so many varying responses to this one revelation? Why do people differ about what exactly does and does not belong to this revelation? The central answer that I defend, and will defend, in the present series is that, indeed, there is only one revelation of God, though in various forms: nature, Scripture, Christ—and that *all* religion, true and false, is a response, in some way or another, to this one and only divine revelation.[47] There are two basic but essentially opposite responses to this revelation:

(a) There is a response of believing subjection and obedience to the divine revelation in Scripture and in Christ, which is possible only through regeneration and the enlightenment of the Holy Spirit.

(b) There is also a response of apostasy, that is, being confronted with God's revelation and responding in a spirit of insubordination and rebellion, rejecting it in disobedience to follow one's own—by definition sinful—path.

It is the difference between true and false (or putative) religion. The phenomenon of false religion is quite interesting, since false religion is never a mere invention of humans, a product of pure human imagination. False religion is always true religion derailed, religion that has fallen off the rails, the track on which God's revelation has placed humanity. This

---
46. Ott (1972, 98).
47. Ouweneel (2019, chapters 1–4).

has been true since Adam and Noah. False religion is like a parasite living on and drawing strength from the true revelation of God.[48]

This is what I believe. These beliefs belong to the prolegomena to my doctrine of God. This is an important introductory subject, with which I deal in the next section.

1.4.2 Prolegomena to Theology Proper

The prolegomena to my theology proper (i.e., my doctrine of God) involve:

(a) My faith in the fact and the contents of the divine self-revelation, and thus also:

(b) My faith in the historical event of the human fall into sin,[49] which implied humanity's falling away from God's revelation.

(c) My faith in the necessity of regeneration and enlightenment by the Holy Spirit, in order to arrive at a true (though always finite) knowledge of God's revelation, which ultimately means: knowledge of God himself.

Therefore, I refer the reader to what I wrote in the first volume of this series about revelation in general, about the nature of false religion, about the hermeneutical circle, and about the internal testimony of the Holy Spirit (Lat. *testimonium Spiritus Sancti internum*)[50]. It is no use delving into theology proper if we are not clearly conscious of the fact that, for example, all our thinking about it is determined *a priori* by the transcendent-religious (existential) ground-motive that governs our hearts.

Now, these hearts are either believingly oriented toward the God of the Bible, or apostatically turned away from him. People must be conscious of this ground-motive before beginning to construct any doctrine of God. No meaningful *theolo-*

---

48. See especially Ouweneel (*EDR* 11:497–501; Vol. I/1, §3.10.2).
49. See extensively, Ouweneel (2018, especially chapters 8–10).
50. Ouweneel (2019, §1.9).

gia propria is possible without being aware that our thinking occurs *a priori* within a hermeneutical circle. Stated plainly: we basically believe about God what *we want* to believe about him. Our will is more significant here than our reason.

A theological doctrine of God constructed without making these prolegomena explicit will collapse even before the first block is laid, because it will convince only one's own followers, and it lacks all apologetic perspective. But what is worse, such a theological doctrine may easily create the very false impression that our true and most profound knowledge of God is *scientific* in nature, whereas in reality it is primarily pre-scientific and existential in nature.

(1) First, in order to distinguish between scientific and pre-scientific knowledge of God, we need a Christian philosophical view of the nature of science in general.

(2) Second, we need a Christian philosophical view of the scientific status of systematic theology.

(3) And third, we need a Christian philosophical view of the possibility of true knowledge of transcendent matters.

These ground-questions will be discussed in Volume V/1 of the present series, at the earliest.[51] However, two subjects must be dealt with at this earlier stage: (1) the distinction between faith knowledge of God and scientific knowledge of God, and (2) the precise nature of scientific knowledge of God (see the next sections).

1.5 Faith Knowledge of God
1.5.1 Knowledge Is Fellowship

In the Old Testament, the usual Hebrew verb for "to know" is *y-d-ᶜ*, which in the Greek Septuagint is commonly rendered as *oida* and *ginōskō*.[52] Here are a few details that may shed light on the biblical notion of the knowledge of God.

---

51. For those who cannot wait, and can read Dutch, see Ouweneel (*EDR* 12:chapters 6–14; for simpler surveys, see 2014a; 2014b).
52. *TDNT* 1:689–714; Brown (1992, 2:390–408).

The Hebrew verb can be used for sexual intercourse (Gen. 4:1, 17, 25), pertaining not only to the man but also to the woman (Num. 31:18, 35; Judg. 21:12). This use is adopted in the New Testament (Matt. 1:25, *ginōskō*). This meaning of "fellowship, intimacy" sheds light on the New Testament idea of "fellowship, intimacy" with God. Whereas John 17:3 says that eternal life involves "knowing" (*ginōskō*) God and Jesus Christ, 1 John 1:2–3 connects eternal life and "fellowship" with the Father and the Son. True knowledge of God in the divine and existential sense, not to be confused with purely intellectual knowledge, involves fellowship with divine persons: Father, Son, and Holy Spirit. The genitive—"fellowship *of* Jesus Christ" (1 Cor. 1:9) and "fellowship *of* the Holy Spirit" (2 Cor. 11:13; Phil. 2:1)—means either "fellowship *with* Jesus/the Spirit," or "fellowship [with each other] *in* [the power of] Jesus/the Spirit."

In various Old Testament passages, *y-d-ᶜ* is used in the sense of fellowship between God and his people, or for God's loving concern for them (Gen. 18:19 "known" = "chosen"; Exod. 2:25 "knew" = "concerned about" [NIV]; 33:12; Jer. 1:5; Hos. 13:5 "knew" = "cared for" [NIV]; Amos 3:2 "known" = "chosen" [NIV][53]). The complaint in Hosea 4:6, "My people are destroyed for lack of knowledge," points not to a lack of intellectual knowledge (as if God were complaining that there were too few theologians), but to a lack of existential knowledge, that is, of fellowship with the LORD. This is clarified in chapter 6:3, "Let us know; let us press on to know the LORD"; that is, let us deepen the practical fellowship with him. This is not a matter of *information* but of *relationship*.

In the Bible's wisdom literature, knowledge is more or less equivalent to wisdom, which itself is viewed as the true piety (godliness) (Prov. 1:4; 2:6; 5:2; Eccl. 1:18; cf. Wisdom 2:13;

---

53. Some take "knowing" in the latter two passages to mean "being married to" (cf. VOICE in Hos. 13:5, "I established the relationship with you"; EXB in Amos 3:2, "I have chosen [known; selected for a special relationship] only you").

8:2-4; 13:1; 14:22; 15:3; Sirach 39:7). This is the knowledge of discerning between good and evil, or between obedience and disobedience to God's commandments (1 Kings 3:9-12; Job 28:28; Eccl. 12:13-14; cf. Heb. 5:14). In Isaiah 11:2, there is a direct connection between "knowledge" and the "fear of the LORD." Here, "knowing" is especially knowing the "right way," the way that is according to God's mind: "Whoever is wise, let him understand these things; whoever is discerning, let him know them; for the ways of the LORD are right, and the upright walk in them, but transgressors stumble in them" (Hos. 14:9).

1.5.2 Care and Praise

God *makes* himself known by his power, both in blessing (salvation) and in punishment (judgment) (see the hiphil of y-d-^{c} in Ps. 77:14; 98:2; 106:8; Jer. 16:21). God does not simply furnish us with information about himself but he causes himself to be experienced, or felt, by us. He aims at an existential encounter with humans. The point is not so much knowledge of what he is (his being), or of his attributes, but rather knowledge of his claims, whether given in explicit commandments or implied in his government. Thus, knowledge of the LORD God (Heb. *dē^{c}ah et-JHWH, dacat Elohim*; cf. Ps. 19:2; Isa. 11:2, 9; Jer. 22:16; Hos. 4:1, 6; 6:6; Mal. 2:7) is never the mere ability of telling something about him—furnishing information about him—but the dedicated and obedient ac-knowledgement of his claims, of God's overwhelming commandments and government, rooted in a personal relationship with him. The knowledge of God is possessed only insofar as it is lived.

Therefore, both a theoretical doctrine of God and an uncommitted, mystical contemplation of God are foreign to both the Old and the New Testament. The great men of God often reasoned *with* God (think of Abraham [Gen. 18], Moses [Exod. 32-33], Job [throughout], Elijah [1 Kings 19], Jeremiah [Jer. 20], Habakkuk [Hab. 1]), but they never reasoned *about* God.

The active, responsive element in the knowledge of God is very important. Knowledge of God is true religion (cf. Hos. 4:1, 6; 6:6), is obedience (cf. 1 Sam. 2:12; Isa. 1:3; Jer. 2:8; 9:3–6), is reverently acknowledging his mighty or redemptive acts (Deut. 8:5; 11:2; 29:5–6; Isa. 41:20; Hos. 11:3; Micah 6:5), is sincerely searching for and honoring the LORD (Ps. 9:9–10; 36:10), and is loving and serving the neighbor (Jer. 22:16). I point especially to Isaiah 1:3, "The ox knows its owner, and the donkey its master's crib, but Israel does not know, my people do not understand." This significant verse refers not only to obedience, just as the ox obeys its master, but also to the affectionate relationship between an animal and its master, who cares for his ox and his donkey, and gives them food ("its master's crib"). Not only did Israel not obey the Lord, but it did not notice even his loving care.[54] And these matters were related: they did not obey the LORD because they did not know him as the *loving* LORD.

In addition to the ethical response (obedience), there is the doxological response. God is known to the extent to which he is worshiped. The Bible is full of such doxologies, which often seemingly have an objective form rather than a personal flavor: not "God, I glorify you," but "God is glorious." However, these doxologies are in fact thoroughly existential in the sense that believers, reluctant about their own needs and desires, present themselves primarily as a sacrifice of praise to God.[55] The longest book in the Bible, the book of Psalms, is a book of meditation, sometimes even laments, but it is first and foremost a book of praise. The Hebrew word *Hallelujah* is an encouragement among God's people to "praise the LORD," and the *bareki naphshi et-JHWH* (e.g., Ps. 103:1) is such an encouragement of one's own soul: never forget to praise the LORD. "Those who live in your house are truly happy; they praise you *constantly*" (Ps. 84:4 CEB). To know the LORD is to

---

54. Oswalt (1986, 85–86).
55. Schlink (1986b, 1736); in his dogmatics (1983), he begins his doctrine of God with a full chapter on the praise of God.

praise him; praising the LORD is knowing him.

1.5.3 The New Testament

Of the two Greek terms for "to know" in the New Testament, *oida* and *ginōskō*, the former word[56] (originally *woida*) comes from the Indo-European root *wid-*, "to see," which we encounter in Latin *videre*, "to see" (cf. video) but also in the English "to wit" (Dutch *weten*, German *wissen*, Swedish *veta*). The Greek *oida* is actually a perfect tense: "I have seen," and hence: "I know." This is significant. In the Bible, all true knowing is rooted in what people have seen of God and divine things with the enlightened eyes of their hearts (cf. Eph. 1:17). Thus, not knowing God does not mean not having information about him, but not having perceived anything of him in one's own heart and life, and even worse, not enjoying an existential relationship with him. We do not know God through theology—theology is only the *a posteriori* reflection upon this perceptive knowledge—but we know God through seeing him with the enlightened eyes of our hearts (cf. Eph. 1:17).

The Septuagint makes this very clear in the case of Israel: "[W]e acknowledge [or, know] only you" (Isa. 26:13 RSV). "I will give them a heart to know me" (Jer. 24:7 NKJV). The meaning of "knowing" becomes clear also in the negative sense of Israel's apostate religion (Isa. 5:13, they do not know the Lord), or in the case of the Gentiles (Job 18:21, "the place of him who know not God"; the wicked do not wish to know the Lord). The New Testament speaks in a similar way of the Gentiles: "Formerly, when you did not know God . . ." (Gal. 4:8); "the Gentiles who do not know God . . ." (1 Thess. 4:5; cf. 2 Thess. 1:8 as an echo of Ps. 79:6; Jer. 10:25; Heb. 8:11 as a quotation of Jer. 31:34), although sometimes the Gentiles do "profess to know God" (Titus 1:16).

The unregenerate, unenlightened person does not know God in the existential sense of the term. However, it is re-

---

56. Cf. *TDNT* 5:116–19.

markable that the demons do have a certain knowledge of Jesus (Gk. *oida* in Mark 1:24, 34; Luke 4:34, 41). That is, to a certain extent they have seen (perceived) his identity and the aim of his coming. In a certain sense they even believe, although with shuddering (James 2:19). But their ac-knowledge-ment (Mark 1:24, "I know who you are—the Holy One of God") is not a surrender of faith but grumbling rebellion.

In a similar way, Jesus recognized that the unbelieving Jewish leaders had some knowledge of him insofar as he had entered within their empirical horizon. But he did *add* that they had no knowledge of God the Father as he, Jesus himself, had this (John 7:28-29; 8:54-55; cf. 1:26). Nor did they know who he really was (8:14, 19; cf. 9:29, where they admit this themselves), not because of some intellectual disability but because of their moral degeneration (cf. 8:23). True knowledge of him comes through revelation only (1:31-34; cf. 4:10, 22), so that even the disciples know him insofar as they have received some form of revelation (14:7, where *ginōskō* is used). Thus, full knowledge is linked with the coming of the Holy Spirit and the latter's further revelations and enlightenment (14:16-17, where *ginōskō* is used; 16:7, 25-27).

Jesus' own knowledge of God is not abstract-theoretical but very practical; see 7:29 ("I know him, for I come from him, and he sent me") and 8:55b ("I do know him and I keep his word"; cf. also 13:3). As an example for the believers, such words can be applied to them as well: they know God insofar as they keep his word—and they (truly) keep his word insofar as they (truly) know him.

Although Paul rarely uses *oida* in reference to knowing Christ, the term is important in 1 Corinthians 2:2 ("I decided to know nothing among you except Jesus Christ and him crucified"), where Paul uses it as a demarcation against (pre-) Gnostic assertions concerning some mysterious, speculative, elitist knowledge of Christ (see below). In 2 Corinthians 5:16 ("Even though we have known Christ according to the flesh, yet now we know [Him thus] no longer," NKJV), Paul seems to be defending himself against Judaizers, who despised him because he had not known the earthly Christ.[57] Over against this, he states that what is needed now is the existential knowledge of the risen and glorified Lord.

Just as *oida* is etymologically related with the English "to wit" (Dutch *weten*), so *ginōskō* is related with "to know" and "to ken" (Dutch and German, *kennen*). The use of this verb in reference to the knowledge of God is rather extensive in the New Testament.[58] In the next sections, I will only mention a few elements in the use of *ginōskō* and *gnōsis* that shed light on the biblical notion of the knowledge of God. The use of the variant terms (intensified by means of prepositional prefixes) *epiginōskō* and *epignōsis* will be indicated by (*e*).

1.6 Cognitive, Theoretical, and Existential Knowledge of God

1.6.1 Theoretical and Practical

Just like in the Old Testament, knowledge of God is submissive knowledge of the will of God, or knowledge of God in terms of his command, government, blessing, and judgment. Several negative examples of this ("not knowing") could be mentioned (Luke 19:42, 44; Rom. 3:17 [= Isa. 59:8]; 2 Tim. 3:7 [e]; Heb. 3:10 [= Ps. 95:10]), as well as various positive examples (Matt. 13:11; Luke 1:77; John 10:38; Acts 22:14; 2 Cor. 8:9; Eph. 4:13 [e]; Col. 1:6 and 2:2 [e]; Heb. 8:11 (= Jer. 31:34); 1 John 4:6; 5:20; Rev. 2:23), and some examples of knowing where the meaning is not the existential sense (Luke 19:42,44; Rom. 3:17 [= Isa. 59:8]; 2 Tim. 3:7 (e); Heb. 3:10 [= Ps. 95:10]).

There is also distinction. The prophets of Israel did not need to tell the people about God as if they were a kind of evangelists. The people knew God, that is, knew about him, though not always in the true, existential sense. In the latter case, they did not know him in the sense that they did not

---

57. Cf. Hughes (1962, 198–201).
58. See note 50.

acknowledge him: they were disobedient and rebellious. This is not ignorance concerning, or denial of, God's existence, but a practical denial of his claims and his rule. However, the apostles' preaching was to the Gentiles, who did not know God in the sense that they were ignorant with respect to his self-revelation in Scripture and in the person of Jesus Christ. The "knowledge of God" is spread among them in order that they may receive this knowledge in their hearts (2 Cor. 2:14; 4:6; 1 Tim. 2:4 [e]).

Matters are complicated here, though, for in a basic sense the Gentiles also know God (are aware of God): in the objective sense, they have God's revelation in creation at their disposal, and in the subjective sense, they have what has been called the "seed of religion" (Lat. *semen religionis*) or the "sense of divinity" (Lat. *sensus divinitatis*).[59] Therefore, Romans 1:8 says that they suppress the truth, not that they do not know the truth. Verse 19 says that "what can be known about God is plain to them, because God has shown it to them." Verse 21 even says that they "knew" God, but verse 28 adds that "they did not see fit to acknowledge [e] God." However, apart from this basic knowledge of God's general revelation, Paul says that "the world did not know God through wisdom" (1 Cor. 1:21), and to the converted Gentiles he writes: "You did not know God," and, "now that you have come to know God" (Gal. 4:8–9). And the apostle John says, "The world did not know him" (John 1:10).

There is no room for any speculative, theoretical knowledge of God, as we learn from Romans 11:34 and 1 Corinthians 2:16 (cf. Isa. 40:13): "Who has known the mind of the Lord?" There is some room for knowledge about God (cf. 1 Cor. 8:4), but this can hardly be severed from the existential knowledge of him (cf. v. 6). German theologian Rudolf Bultmann (d. 1976) claimed that some theoretical elements in the knowledge of God can be found in certain Bible passag-

---

59. See Ouweneel (2019, §4.1.3).

es (examples: Luke 11:52, "key of knowledge"; 1 Cor. 8:4–6; 1 Tim. 4:3, "know the truth"; 2 Pet. 2:21, "known the way of righteousness"; and knowledge received through studying Scripture, e.g., Gal. 3:7; James 2:20).[60] However, this claim is based upon confusing the theoretical (which is always rational) and the practical-rational or cognitive (which is often not theoretical at all) as well as the supra-rational (not *ir*-rational!).[61]

1.6.2 Fellowship with God

True (existential) knowledge of God entails intimate fellowship, a correlation that arises from the reciprocal character of this knowledge. That is to say, such a knowledge of God is interwoven with God's knowledge of *us* in a bond of communion (see 1 Cor. 8:3; 13:12; Gal. 4:9; 2 Tim. 2:19 [= Num. 16:5]; cf. the opposite in Matt. 7:23). A beautiful example is the bond of knowledge between the good Shepherd and his sheep: "I am the good shepherd. I know my own and my own know me. . . . My sheep hear my voice, and I know them, and they follow me" (John 10:14, 27). This bond is strengthened by the ministry of the Word in the meetings of the local church (1 Cor. 12:8; 14:6) and by prayer (Eph. 1:17; Phil. 1:9–10; Col. 1:9–10; Phlm. 6 [all (e)]; Eph. 3:19), leading to continual spiritual growth (Phil. 3:8, 10, 12–14; Col. 3:10 (e); 2 Pet. 1:5–6; 3:18).

This fellowship must not be confused with some mystical relationship, for it is manifested in very practical behavior, such as brotherly love (1 Cor. 8, especially vv. 10–11; 1 John 2:3–5; 3:6; 4:7–8). The New Testament writers had to fight against, among other things, the rising mysticism of (proto-)Gnosticism (from Gk. *gnōsis* = knowledge). According to many expositors, various Bible passages can be understood only against this background, such as several in 1 Corinthians (the battle against speculative wisdom and knowledge;

---

60. *TDNT* 1:705–708.
61. See extensively, Vol. IV/1 of this series, and Ouweneel (2014b).

1:17–31; 6:12–20; 8:1–6; 13:8[62]); Colossians 1:26–27 (possibly written against the Essenes,[63] who claimed to know mysteries that they possessed alone, and into which those who joined them were allowed to enter, cf. 2:18b; thus, the true knowledge was possessed only by some, cf. 1:23b, 28; 2:3); 1 Timothy 6:20 ("what is falsely called 'knowledge'").

Revelation 2:24 seems to point to those who allegedly have known "the deep things of Satan."[64] Presumably, the false prophetess ("Jezebel") in the church of Thyatira argued that, by taking part in pagan (demonic) idolatry and sexual immorality, believers could show how limited the power of Satan was, and how large their own spiritual strength was (a typically Gnostic idea). Others read the text to mean that the unfaithful in Thyatira claimed that they had come to know the depths *of God* (cf. 1 Cor. 2:10), whereas Jesus explained that what they had in fact known had been the depths of Satan.

Rudolf Bultmann believed that in the apostle John's writings, John's view "is paradoxically building on the *ginōskein* of Hellenistic Gnosticism."[65] This claim has been effectively rebutted by Australian theologian Leon Morris (d. 2006).[66] Matthew 11:27 occupies a special position here: "No one knows [*e*] the Son except the Father, and no one knows [*e*] the Father except the Son and anyone to whom the Son chooses to reveal him" (and its parallel in Luke 10:22), which Bultmann viewed as employing Gnostic terminology as well.[67] The latter part of Matthew 11:27 is less troublesome because not knowing the Father is true in a limited sense only: to believers, the Son does reveal the Father. However, the first part of the verse seems rather absolute: "No one knows the Son except the

---

62. See extensively, Fee (1987, 7–15 passim).
63. Thus Lightfoot (1880).
64. Cf. Ouweneel (1988a, 184).
65. *TDNT* 1:712.
66. Morris (1971, 17–18, 20, 22–25, 36, 62–63, 80, especially 223, with reference to other publications by Bultmann).
67. *TDNT* 1:713; but see, e.g., Carson (1984, 276–77).

Father," without any exception. Such an exception *is* mentioned in Matthew 16:16–17, though, where Jesus replies to Peter's confession of him as the Christ, the Son of the living God, as follows: "Blessed are you, Simon Bar-Jonah! For flesh and blood has not revealed this to you, but my Father who is in heaven."

Such passages illustrate in a remarkable way the broad semantic range of *ginōskō*: in one sense, even the most corrupt pagans possess a certain knowledge of God (Rom. 1:18–19, 21, 28); in another sense it can be said in the most absolute way that no one knows the Son except the Father, not even believers; that is, no one fathoms the depths of the Son's being except the Father.

1.6.3 In Summary

Let us now briefly summarize what we have found, and reformulate it in anthropological terminology.

(a) "Knowledge of God" or "of Christ" in its loftiest and most intimate form is existential faith knowledge of the human transcendent heart. This involves: eternal life,[68] the divine *agapē* (e.g., Rom. 5:5), intimate fellowship with divine persons (1 John 1:1–4).

(b) This knowledge comes to expression within the immanent-spiritive life in its cognitive dimension (knowing about God, as governed by the heart's faith knowledge), its creative-imaginative dimension (creatively shaping Christian life in agreement with this faith knowledge), and its conative dimension (the will to put this knowledge into practice through obedience to God's commandments). [69]

(c) This knowledge comes to expression in specific immanent-spiritive knowing-acts, especially qualified by the pistical modality, but often intertwined with, for instance, sensitive acts (emotion, affection), logical-analytical acts (meaningful

---

68. See Vol. III/4 in this series.
69. For these terms, see Ouweneel (2015, chapter 7).

distinctions), lingual acts (faith responses in prayer and worship), social acts (collective worship in church services), economic acts (thankfully offering), juridical acts (practicing justice), moral acts (practical brotherly love), and so on.

(d) To a limited extent, there is knowledge of God in the sense of a certain rational awareness due to God's revelation, but without faith surrender (dedication, obedience, worship), due to an apostate heart.

(e) Finally, there is such a thing as scientific (theological, philosophical) knowledge of God, as emphatically distinguished from practical faith knowledge. This is the subject of the next sections.

1.7 Protestant Scholasticism
1.7.1 Abraham Kuyper

After having briefly investigated the nature of faith knowledge of God, we now come to the question concerning the nature of scientific knowledge of God, and the possibility of obtaining such knowledge. In Volume IV/1 of this series, I will explain how theologians traditionally viewed theology as the scientific study of God without providing any accounting at all for the problems that are attached to such an approach from the outset. Here in this volume, I will mention a few of these aspects.[70] Some of the special subjects that I will summarize in this and the next sections (knowledge of God's being versus knowledge of his attributes, negative theology, the scholastic doctrine of the *analogia entis*) will be dealt with more extensively in chapters 3 and 4 in this volume.

Dutch theologian Abraham Kuyper (d. 1920) believed that God is the object of study in theology—not religion, because in that case theology would be nothing but the science of religion (Ger. *Religionswissenschaft*).[71] Theology entails the knowledge of God, just as natural science entails the knowledge of

---
70. Cf. also Ouweneel (2014b, especially chapters 2–3).
71. Kuyper (1898, *EHG* 2:45, 163, 173).

nature[72]. Kuyper overlooked the fact that knowledge of nature is empirical, but knowledge of God is based on Scripture; the proper analogy would therefore be: theology is scientific knowledge of Scripture, just as natural science is scientific knowledge of nature.

Kuyper did discern, though, the difference between faith knowledge and theological knowledge. When he called theology "knowledge of God," he was aware that God as such cannot be the object of scientific investigation. Thus, Kuyper identified the object of study in theology as *ectypal* knowledge of God, that is, such knowledge as has been revealed to humanity.[73] He seemed to maintain the ancient scholastic distinction between archetypal knowledge of God (Lat. *cognitio Dei archetypa*, the knowledge that God alone has of himself) and ectypal knowledge of God (Lat. *cognitio Dei ectypa*, the knowledge of God in a form that humans can apprehend).[74] In such a representation of things, a theologian, or humans in general, can have no knowledge of God's *being*.[75] The object of study in *all* science and scholarship is the cosmos, which is true for theology as well, because revealed ectypal knowledge of God (Lat. *cognitio Dei ectypa revelata*) lies within the cosmos.[76]

1.7.2 Herman Bavinck

Dutch theologian Herman Bavinck (d. 1921) had a similar view. He said that dogmatics is a scholarly system of the knowledge of God insofar as the latter has been revealed in God's Word. The knowledge of God (Lat. *cognitio Dei*) is objectively contained in this revelation, and as such it is the object of study in theology, especially in dogmatics.[77] The knowledge of God being pursued in dogmatics is a transcript

---

72. Ibid., 140.
73. Ibid., 166.
74. Regarding the difference, see ibid., 175–81.
75. Ibid., 168.
76. Ibid., 170.
77. Bavinck (*RD* 1:38).

of the knowledge that God has revealed in his Word concerning himself.[78] This knowledge is reconstructed in a scholarly manner in the mind, and summarized in a system (hence the term "systematic theology"). The dogmatician can do nothing more than thinkingly reproduce God-given truth.[79] Dogmatics pursues knowing God "in the face of Jesus Christ" (cf. 2 Cor. 4:6).[80] Bavinck spoke of dogmatics as a science about God (Lat. *scientia de Deo*).[81] Similar to Kuyper, Bavinck distinguished between archetypal theology (Lat. *theologia archetypa*) in the divine consciousness, external ectypal theology (Lat. *theologia ectypa externa*) that has been objectively given in God's revelation and set forth in Scripture, and internal ectypal theology (Lat. *theologia ectypa interna*) or theology within the (knowing)–subject (Lat. *theologia in subjecto*), the subjective knowledge of God within the believer.[82]

1.7.3 Divergent Views

Within Reformational theology, the views of Kuyper and Bavinck have not remained without criticisms. South African theologian Adrio König rightly remarked that God is not just a given object that, so to speak, is surrendered to our investigation, just like, for instance, a rock, a plant, or a painting.[83] God is not available to us immediately, and at any time, like empirical objects are, but is knowable only insofar as he has revealed himself. Yet, König maintained that the aspect of reality that is studied by theology is God and his creation.[84]

Another South African theologian, Johan A. Heyns (d. 1994) noted that, from early scholasticism to Protestant post-Reformational scholasticism, the object of study in the-

---

78. Ibid., 42.
79. Ibid., 39.
80. Ibid., 53.
81. Ibid., 43, 209.
82. Ibid., 213–14.
83. König (1982, 25).
84. Ibid., 25, 27–28.

ology has always been sought in God.[85] He pointed out that Dutch theologian Hendrikus Berkhof (d. 1995) still maintained that God can be an object of scientific investigation, a unique object of a very special science.[86] But, as Heyns rightly added, all science is necessarily knowledge of cosmic reality, and therefore the object of study in theology, too, must be sought within the cosmos. What is empirically available to us as the source of theology is *Scripture*, which is believingly accepted as God's Word, including God's self-revelation.

German theologian Otto Weber (d. 1966) rightly remarked that God cannot be supposed to be generally known, such as, for instance, the object of study in the natural sciences.[87] As the "object" of dogmatics, one cannot assign a "place" (*Ort*) to him within the totality of knowable things. In Weber's view, such a God, as a component of what is knowable, is not the God of whom the church bears witness and in whom the Christian believes. In my own words, the "God" who is the object of study in any scholarly enterprise is in danger of coming to resemble the God of the philosophers more than the God of Abraham, Isaac, and Jacob (see §1.1.2).

1.8 Theoretical and Practical Knowledge of God
1.8.1 Distinctions

The claim that theology is about God presupposes a certain view of reality. One component of this view involves the transcendental conditions of true knowledge, in this case the conviction that a scientific investigation of God is even *possible*; otherwise, theology would not be possible. However, is it self-evident that a science of God is possible? And if so, in what ways is it possible? In other words, in what way can we speak scientifically about God?[88] Such questions can be answered only through a philosophical analysis of the nature

---

85. Heyns (1977, 150).
86. Berkhof (1960, 13–14).
87. Weber (1981, 8).
88. Cf. Strauss (1991).

of scientific knowledge in general, and scientific knowledge about God in particular. The replies to these questions traditionally given by theology usually presupposed a view of reality that is foreign to Scripture, expressing itself either in a negative theology (Plotinus [d. 270] and his Christian adherents), or in the scholastic doctrine of the *analogia entis* (Thomas Aquinas) (see §4.8.2).

The first difficulty of the traditional view lies in the fact that it does not (sufficiently) distinguish between practical faith knowledge of God and the scientific knowledge of theology. Elsewhere, I have extensively argued that the practical knowing-attitude with regard to Scripture is of an *integral* nature as far as the Bible reader is concerned.[89] The Bible reader may not and will not ever dispense with their thinking function. However, reason is only one of many functions that proceed from, and are concentrated in, one's heart, through which one reads the Bible. Many of these modal functions (physical, sensitive, formative-historical, lingual, social, moral, pistical, etc.) are active throughout the process of reading; but never is one of these modalities abstracted from the others within the Bible reader. However, this is precisely what does occur in theoretical thought: the theologian is not active as a psychologist or an economist; in addition, for instance, the theologian's juridical or economic function are present only in the background. The theologian is concentrated primarily on the contents of Scripture according to its (Scripture's) *pistical* aspect, and as a scientist the theologian focuses on the *logical distinctions* that are present in the Bible's faith contents.

Moreover, the practical knowing-attitude with regard to Scripture is of an *immediate* nature, in the sense of a direct relationship with God's Word, without the *distance* that is characteristic of the theoretical knowing-attitude. In practical thought, the Word is directly received from the Lord, and not approximated, for every approximation presupposes the

---

89. Ouweneel (2014b); see Vol. IV/1 in the present series.

theoretical distance. In theoretical thought, too, the theologian never stops being a believer, even when thinking in an apostate manner. But the theologian's scholarly interaction with the Word relates to the practical faith attitude, just as the chemical analysis of bread relates to the eating of bread.

1.8.2 Theoreticalizing Everyday Thought

In my view, one of the most profound misunderstandings of modern epistemology is to stamp everyday thinking and speaking with some theoretical truth concept.[90] In this case, this means imposing some theological concept of God upon our practical faith knowledge of God. This implies imposing the theoretical *distancing* upon the *direct, immediate* relationship between the believer and their God, that is, theories are pressed between the believer and their God. In my view, this is exactly the same as claiming that a person's understanding of his wife (or her husband) depends on sufficient *scientific* understanding of women (or men) in general.[91]

The basic misunderstanding is this. Our practical faith knowledge of God does not presuppose a certain epistemological *theory* about God, just like marriage does not require a certain epistemological *theory* about people of the other sex. Believers may have different images of God, just like children of the same parents may have different images of these parents. However, these images do not have the character of the theological concept of God (or a scientific concept of parents or partners, for that matter). The truth of faith is based upon the simplicity and perspicuity of the Scripture,[92] and is accepted and confessed in sincerity of heart (cf. Acts 2:46; Eph. 6:5; Col. 3:22; also see 2 Cor. 1:12; 11:3), and in *a priori* submission

---

90. E.g., Stone and Duke (2006, 1) called it a simple fact of life for Christians that their faith makes them theologians: purposely or not, Christians think and act from a theological understanding of existence, and their faith calls upon them to be the best theologians they could possibly be.
91. Cf. the profound study by Buytendijk (2008) about the phenomenon of "woman," which tells us nothing about his own marriage.
92. See Ouweneel (2019; cf. *EDR* 11:25, 218–19).

to Scripture. No theology may ever interfere in this relationship.

Of course, theology does have the God-given task of *accounting* for the pistical structures of empirical reality as *given* by the Creator to pre-theoretical faith experience. However, we should never overestimate its results with regard to practical faith experiences. Theological theories are only human artifacts, as I plan to show extensively in Volume IV/1 of the present series. Thus, there is an enormous distance between, on the one hand, the *human* scientific theories concerning God and, on the other hand, the true, immediate, supra-rational knowledge of God that the believer possesses in their heart; in other words, between, on the one hand, the fallible trial-and-error development of theological theories and, on the other hand, God's revealed thoughts.

1.8.3 A Basic Error

Still more important is that in principle it is conceivable that certain theological theories are excellent approximations of God. But even in such a case, it is not in the theoretical (abstract, distanced, unilateral) thinking, but in the practical (concrete, immediate, integral) thought attitude that God is truly known in the existential sense. Basically, it is the same with regard to the relationship between husband and wife, or the relationship between parents and children.

It is a fundamental error of scientism to view theological knowledge as more scientific (in the sense of more methodical and systematic), and *therefore* as superior with respect to practical (existential) faith knowledge. It is the very same error as the one involved in saying that scientific knowledge of women in general is superior to the practical (existential) knowledge of a person's own wife. The ultimate consequence of such an idea is that systematic theology is thought to be more systematic, and therefore more reliable, than Scripture itself.

It is true that theological theories may contain elements of truth, and no doubt often do so. But their truth character is disclosed only in practical faith experience, which is oriented toward the full Truth in Christ. The practical attitude of thought and experience is definitely not naïve in the sense of simplistic or limited (again, the same can be said with regard to a person's attitude toward his wife, or her husband). On the contrary, in this practical attitude the transcendent, existential dimension of empirical reality is disclosed.[93] Or, to put it another way: the theoretical knowledge of God is marked by *reason*, whereas the practical faith knowledge is marked by *love*, in such a way that it does not contravene reason but surpasses it. (Compare again a person's relationship with loved ones.)

1.9 Concepts and Ideas
1.9.1 Theoretical and Practical

The modal-abstract character of systematic theology comes to light in a remarkable way in the status of systematic-theological concepts. Such concepts belong to theoretical-abstract thinking within immanent reality. In contrast with them, biblical concepts form the expression, *within* immanent reality, of the *transcendent* Word of God, and do so in the richly checkered language of everyday experience, not in the strictly delineated language of theoretical thought.[94] Scripture does not expound "concepts" such as God, creation, sin, redemption, and so on; even less does it do so in the abstract-theoretical manner of theology. God's revelation in Scripture with regard to such subjects even *surpasses* all human conceptualization because it is of a supra-rational nature.[95]

When in everyday life we speak of God, creation, the Fall, or redemption, we necessarily use concepts. The Bible language, too, contains certain practical concepts with regard to such subjects. If we did not conceive of redemption more or

---
93. Cf. Dooyeweerd (*NC* 3:28–36).
94. Cf. Brunner (1946, 72).
95. Cf. Dooyeweerd (1971, 84–85).

The God Question

less the way the Bible conceives of it, it would be impossible to understand the biblical message concerning redemption. However, in this respect we might commit four errors:

(a) A *rationalist* error, namely, *reducing* the biblical language, or any language for that matter, to nothing but a totality of logical concepts.[96]

(b) A *scientistic* error, namely, an *overestimation* of theology, that is, by considering these biblical concepts (see [a]) as *theoretical concepts*, which would be of the same nature as those of systematic theology. (Biblical concepts usually have many meanings, whereas theological concepts ideally have only one meaning.)

(c) The previous points *affirm* that, in general, biblical terms do refer not at all to (logical, rational) concepts but rather to (supra-logical, supra-rational) border-concepts or *ideas*.[97]

(d) In particular, points [a] and [b] *deny* that the primarily revelational, transcendent meaning of biblical ideas refer to God and his transcendent relationship to humanity.

1.9.2 What Are Ideas?

One particular aspect of conceptualization is the distinction just mentioned between (common) concepts and ideas (or border-concepts, supra-concepts). Only matters that belong to our immanent, modal, functional reality, things toward which the logical thinking-act is oriented and which in principle can be conceived of in a logical-analytical way, can be contained in a concept. And even within our immanent world there are exceptions: the kernels of the modal aspects as well as the individual entities cannot be defined.[98] If the modal kernels could be defined in the ancient Aristotelian way, that is, by reducing them to a a higher category (Lat. *ge-*

---

96. Cf. Ouweneel (2019, chapter 9, on the allegedly propositional character of God's Word).
97. See extensively, Ouweneel (*EDR* 3:24–32; 2014b, chapter 6).
98. See more extensively, Ouweneel (2014a, chapters 3–5).

nus proximum),[99] it would turn out that no modal kernels are involved at all because by definition they are *ground*-concepts that cannot be reduced to broader, higher concepts.

Individual entities (this or that thing, plant, animal, human, state of affairs) can at best be described; they cannot be defined in the proper sense because definitions always refer to classes of entities. We can say, "a human is a creature that . . .," but we cannot define *this* or *that* particular human. Modal kernels and individual entities can only be rationally contained in an idea (Gk. *idea*, here, mental representation), that is, in terms that do not refer to concepts but surpass the strictly conceptual; I will give several examples below.[100] Also, when human thought directs itself to the transcendent, supra-modal, supra-functional reality, it can form only an idea of it.

Knowledge in the form of ideas is certainly knowledge, even rational knowledge; but it is a form of knowledge that surpasses conceptual knowledge. Without this distinction, it is easily possible to construe paradoxes, that is, contradictions between certain biblical truths. However, the Bible is never interested in possible *conceptual* similarities or contradictions between such truths. It freely reveals both God's unity and his multiplicity; both his omnipresence and his sometimes being far away; both his transcendence and his immanence; both his immutability and his changing his mind; both his being spiritual and his being corporeal; both his peace and his unrest; both his retribution and his mercy; both his love and his hate (see extensively chapters 4 and 5). And to widen the circle: both God's sovereignty and human responsibility (freedom of choice);[101] and so on.

It is only theologians who construe contradictions between such notions, and they do so by understanding them in a con-

---

99. In the phrase, "A is a B that (distinguishes itself from other Bs by) . . .," B is the genus proximum (cf. the phrase "carnivores are mammals that . . .").
100. See, e.g., Troost (2004, 96, 174–75; 2005, 247–48); Ouweneel (*EDR* 3:28–32; 2014b, chapter 6).
101. Cf. extensively, Ouweneel (*EDR* 4; and Vol. III/1 in the present series).

ceptual way. Two *conceptual* systems P and Q are contradictory if a feature of system P can be predicated as A, and a feature of system Q as non-A. However, two systems of *ideas* cannot be contradictory in this way because the question whether the one or the other feature can be predicated as A or non-A surpasses our knowledge. Here is a simple example: God is non-human, and thus surpasses the distinction between the sexes. Yet, he is called Father. In the *conceptual definition* of a father, this is a male person who has begotten one or more children through sexual intercourse with a woman. But in the *idea* of a father, some features are indeed present (having one or more children) but others are not necessarily present, such as being a male or having had sexual intercourse with one or more women.

1.9.3 Consequences of Misunderstanding

The Westminster Confession of Faith (I.6) speaks of truths "either expressly set down in Scripture, or by good and necessary consequence [inference] may be deduced from Scripture."[102] However, the latter holds for *concepts* only (the concept of a father necessarily implies, e.g., his masculinity), not for *ideas*: from the *idea* of God's Fatherhood we cannot "by good and necessary inference" deduce that God is male and has had intercourse with the female sex. This is an obvious example; but the error has been committed over and over in less obvious cases. For instance, from God's eternal decree of election, people have deduced "by good and necessary inference" a parallel eternal decree of reprobation. There is not the slightest biblical foundation for such an idea; it is derived only from the notion of eternal election. However, we are dealing here with an *idea*, not a concept. That is, only those inferences may be made from such an idea that are fully covered by direct biblical evidence.

Not (properly) distinguishing these things has often led theologians to claim that the Bible *says* A but really *means*

---

102. Dennison (2008, 4:235).

non-A. For instance, it *seems* as though God gave in to Moses (Exod. 32), or to the people of Nineveh (Jonah 3), since in both cases God relented, but God *really* knew all along what he was going to do. Such an argument is based on the false idea that A cannot be correct on the basis of the conceptual framework construed by these theologians; we will find more examples of this. However, the problem lies not with a Bible that *really* means the opposite of what it says, but with the theologians' conceptual framework. As soon as they would surrender this framework, and would approximate divine truth with the help of creaturely terms referring to ideas, they could maintain all the attributes of God without any alleged *conceptual* contradictions. In fact, it is mere hybris—though often unintentional and unconscious—to assert that we could treat biblical truths like conceptual systems, of which each feature could be predicated.

For every systematic theology, it is of the greatest importance to realize that there are logical objects in theology of which no theoretical concepts can be formed. A few examples of such logical objects are:

(a) (the being of) God (even apart from the question of the Trinity);

(b) the unity of the divine and the human nature in the one person of the Christ;

(c) the transcendent-religious meaning of Scripture as the eternal Word of God;[103]

(d) the transcendent heart of each human being in its most emphatic sense, as well as all its immanent utterances and movements;

(e) the religious relationship between this heart and God (or, idols, for that matter);

(f) the church of God in its transcendent fullness and unity;

---
103. See Ouweneel (2019, especially chapter 5).

(g) faith in the sense of the modal kernel of the pistical modality.

Of such *transcendent* matters we can speak only in terms that have been derived from our *immanent* reality, simply because we do not know any other terms. In such cases, these terms do not refer to concepts but to supra-concepts or ideas in the sense that they refer to matters that surpass the boundaries of strict conceptualization and, in this case, even surpass our immanent reality.

The obvious exception is the very term "God," which does *not* refer primarily to something immanent-rational. Thus, there is no cosmic term that, used as an idea, refers to God "as such." The term "heart" refers, as a concept, to the biotic heart but, as an idea, to a person's deepest self. The term "word" refers, as a concept, to lingual (spoken or written) words but, as an idea, to God's Word, for instance. However, the term "God" in any conceptual sense does not refer to anything within our immanent reality but only to a transcendent reality. Thus, when it is a matter of speaking scientifically of God, theology is in a difficult position. It can approximate the truth of God only through ideas, namely, ideas referring to

(a) his attributes, such as his holiness, his righteousness, his mercy;

(b) his actions, such as his descending, his judgment, his redemption;

(c) his being (see below and chapter 3).[104]

1.10 Ideas and Metaphors Concerning God
1.10.1 Again, Concepts and Ideas

Let us first take a closer look at the distinction between concepts and ideas. A concept is a certain analytical figure at the subject side of reality, determined by logical norms at the law

---

104. Cf. Pailin (1986, chapter 7); Brümmer (1988, chapter 2); Peterson et al. (1991, chapter 8).

side of reality.[105] In such a concept, certain modal features are contained within the modalities concerned; that is, data that (a) function within the boundaries of the modalities concerned, and (b) have been logically objectified, that is, made into a logical object through identification and distinction, and (c) can be taken (predicated) separately in logical judgments.

For instance, in the concept "house" we are dealing with features that (a) are of a physical nature (the foundational function of the house), but also of a social nature (the destination-function of the house as a habitation), (b) are identified as essentially belonging to the house as a habitation, and are distinct from features that are not essential (size, building materials, colors), and (c) can be expressed in logical judgments, both essential features ("a house is a habitation") and non-essential features ("*this* house is small, opulent, wooden, brown"). It is not essential whether a house is green or white, with angular or circular forms, made of wood or of stone, a row house or a single house. However, *each* house in the conceptual sense does have a color, a form, was made of certain materials, has a certain location, and a certain function (viz., to be a habitation).

Now, the same modal terms that refer to concepts can also refer to ideas, namely, when referring to matters that can be known only in terms that are logically objectifiable but that themselves surpass logical objectification. This concerns data that can be *approximated* only through an act of objectification leading to an idea that is of an indicative (regulative) nature. This occurs when we speak of the Father's house with the many rooms (John 14:1–3), or of the church as the house or the temple of God (1 Cor. 3:16; 2 Cor. 6:16; Eph. 2:20–22; 1 Tim. 3:15; 1 Pet. 2:5; Heb. 3:6). Indeed, this house or temple is a "habitation" (viz., of the Holy Spirit), it is even said of the Father's house that it contains "many rooms," and apparently the church is a "big" house because millions of believers are

---

105. Again, for many of the specific terms being used in the text, I refer to my concise introductions: Ouweneel (2014a; 2014b).

part of it. However, other features, which in conceptual houses are quite common, and even indispensable (address, shape, building materials, colors) are irrelevant when it comes to the Father's house or to the church. Insofar as the texts do suggest an address (the Father's house is in heaven, the church is global), or building materials (the church consists of "living stones," 1 Pet. 2:5, that is, believers), we can speak of such things only in the form of ideas.

1.10.2 Metaphors

We may sense the temptation here to assert that ideas are simply the same as metaphors. I believe this to be incorrect. This is because the term "idea" is strictly logical in nature, and the term "metaphor" is strictly lingual in nature. In other words, ideas belong, as do concepts, to the science of logics, whereas metaphors belong to linguistics and the science of literature. Metaphors are always more or less arbitrary; they can easily be replaced by other metaphors. They are characterized by the fluidity and flexibility that is proper to all language. However, ideas, because they are logical in nature, do not fully possess this feature. The Father's house *is* the house where the Father dwells, and it is hardly possible to replaces the terms "house" and "dwelling" by other terms that, through a very different imagery, express the same thing. However, if we say that the Word of God is like a fire and a hammer (Jer. 23:29), like milk or seed (1 Pet. 1:23; 2:2), like a sword (Eph. 6:17; Heb. 4:12), or bread (Matt. 4:4), we feel that the same things referred to by these metaphors could be described by different metaphors as well.

I do not wish to stress the difference between ideas and metaphors too strongly, though, because I do not need this for my argument. It is much more important to properly grasp the difference between concepts and ideas because it plays a considerable role in the present volume. Rational knowledge is not limited to conceptual knowledge, as rationalism—also within theology!—has often implied. Rather, it also contains knowledge that we possess in the form of ideas. Our supra-rational faith knowledge of God and his Word can be made explicit in beliefs that are rational but not conceptual. If this is not grasped, people usually seek refuge in one of two possible ways. Either people claim that knowledge of transcendent matters, including knowledge of God, is not rational, and is therefore irrational, and thereby land in mysticism and bigotry. Or people claim that knowledge of the transcendent is possible only if, or because, the transcendent falls under the rational order that obtains for the entire cosmos. This would imply that, for instance, the transcendent God would be subjected to the laws of logic that he himself, as the Creator, has instituted.

Dutch-American philosopher Cornelius Van Til (d. 1987) was a striking example of this type of reasoning.[106] He continually spoke of our conception of God, and told us that our knowledge must be analogous, that is, based on the knowledge that God has of himself and of the world.[107] He said in an explanatory way that humans cannot, except to their own detriment, look at the facts without looking at God's interpretation of the facts. That is, human knowledge of the facts is a reinterpretation of God's interpretation. That was Van Til's prominent claim.[108] But the counter-questions are immediately obvious: (a) Why reinterpret what God has already interpreted? (b) What do we actually *know* about God's knowledge? (c) By what criteria do we assess his knowledge without subjecting his knowledge to the rational order that is true for *our* knowledge? (d) Why do we not simply stick to the things that God has revealed to us in order that *we* would know them, without bothering about the question what knowledge God *possesses*?

Another consequence of the wrong way of thinking just described was that, already in medieval times, people began

---

106. Van Til (1969, 200–209; cf. 1955, 52–63).
107. Ibid., 200.
108. Ibid., 204.

making a distinction between God's (alleged) incommunicable or absolute attributes (Lat. *attributa incommunicabilia vel absoluta*, which are proper to God, not communicated to humanity, and independent of his creation) and his communicable or relative attributes (Lat. *attributa communicabilia vel relativa*, which are communicated to humanity as referring to his relationship with his creation).[109] One effect of this distinction was that a negative theology was formulated, which enumerated only what God was *not* (infinite, inaccessible, immaterial, etc.). Another conclusion was that we know God only in terms of the created relationships in which he chose to reveal himself. This implies that God revealed only his relationships, not his being, that is, not *himself*. In this case, we would not possess any revelation of *God* at all — an idea that would affect the foundations of Christianity as such. In this case, Christians would not know *God* at all, but only the forms in which he wished to present himself to us.

1.10.3 A New Way

We no longer need to seek refuge in the ways just described, as soon as we recognize that indeed there is *rational* knowledge in the form of *ideas* or supra-concepts, or knowledge that is rational but surpasses the boundaries of conceptualization. In this case, it is no longer a problem that God used creational terms in order to truly reveal his *being*, that is, *himself*. Of course, this does not at all mean that God is entirely *contained* within our rational knowledge. On the contrary, knowledge of the transcendent ultimately surpasses all rational knowledge. In the truest sense, knowledge of God is itself *transcendent* (i.e., supra-rational) knowledge in that it is the existential possession of the supra-rational heart. However, this supra-rational heart is not irrational, as mysticism suggests. Rational knowledge of God in the form of ideas nourishes and enriches the heart's supra-rational knowledge. Even if there

---

109. Cf. Bavinck (*RD* 2:148–255); Strauss (1983, 53–54; 2009, 202–203; 2010).

is no rational-*conceptual* knowledge of the transcendent, there is rational knowledge of it in the form of *ideas*, as in theology. This knowledge does not encompass the transcendent but certainly does approximate it. Moreover, there is *supra*-rational knowledge of the transcendent in the sense of knowledge in the full, transcendent, existential sense.

Let me say something here about what is called root or key metaphors. Usually these do not involve logical concepts but logical ideas; that is, usually they are rational metaphors that *refer* to the supra-conceptual as well as supra-rational. Such root or key metaphors play a great role in the Bible, especially with regard to God.[110] One of these root metaphors concerning God is found in the expression that God is Father. Here, we discover again that misunderstanding the nature of concepts and ideas has led to various unfortunate theological models.[111] God's Fatherhood is often considered to be just a metaphor, telling us nothing about what God *really* is in his *being* (negative theology). We are dealing with a metaphor here because, unlike human fatherhood, God's Fatherhood does not imply that God is masculine or begets children through a feminine being.[112] In the same way, another metaphor such as the hands of God does not necessarily imply that God has fingernails or fingers.

However, by not grasping the distinction between metaphors that are concepts and metaphors that are ideas, theologians began to approach this matter either from the mystical viewpoint of some negative theology, or from a rationalist viewpoint. It was claimed that God's Fatherhood is of a different order than earthly fatherhood, such that our experience of what fatherhood is involves only a vague and imperfect image of the original and perfect way God himself is Father. In this way, such metaphors concerning God are severed from

---

110. Cf. the studies by Jüngel (1983; 2003); McFague (1983; 1987); Van Herck (1999); and Muis (2010).
111. See Strauss (1983, 54–55; 1988, 135, 150).
112. Cf. Hart (1983, 229–30).

creation and transferred to God, in whom they are supposed to have their origin. In God, we supposedly find the so-called *archetype* of Fatherhood, and in humanity we find the *ectype*, which relates to the archetype as an imprint relates to a stamp.

We encounter this scholastic dualism with Abraham Kuyper and Herman Bavinck.[113] Since antiquity, it is stamped by Neo-Platonism, which elevated the universal order instituted for immanent reality to the realm of the ideas (not to be confused with "ideas" the way we are speaking of them in the present chapter). Later, Christianity equated these ideas to the ideas in the mind of God. Humans were supposed to participate in these ideas in a derived, weak, and imperfect manner. Here, the fundamental boundary between Creator and creature is in danger of being erased because God and humanity are united in one ontological framework. In this way, Thomism could develop the doctrine of the analogy of being (Lat. *analogia entis*) on the basis of the alleged ontic continuity between Creator and creature. However, it is a fundamental mistake to bring God into one ontological framework with humanity. The Bible does not speak of God's Fatherhood because of some ontic analogy between God and humanity, but in the sense of a metaphoric idea. That is, it uses an image derived from immanent reality, one that refers to what surpasses this empirical reality and yet brings to expression something of the being of God.

---

113. Bavinck (*RD* 2:107–10).

Chapter 2
The Science of Religion

Behold, God is exalted in his power;
who is a teacher like him

Job 36:22

2.1 Religious Studies, Elenctics, Theology
2.1.1 Boundaries

AS A PART OF SYSTEMATIC THEOLOGY, theology proper (Lat. *theologia propria*, i.e., in the narrower sense: the doctrine of God) is usually carefully distinguished from the science of religion (Ger. *Religionswissenschaft*, religious studies) and from what the Germans call "fundamental theology" (Ger. *Fundamentaltheologie*), which, among other things, deals with the so-called theistic proofs (*Gottesbeweise*). Usually, as the doctrine of God, *theologia propria* has simply presupposed the existence of God and his relationship to humanity. It accepts the knowledge of God, received through faith by the power of the Holy Spirit, as self-evident, and thus also the possibility to elaborate this knowledge in a scientific manner. However, since more than a century ago, the science of religion came to development, which attempted to stay away from religious axioms as much as possible, and to limit itself to the questions concerning the nature and significance of religiosity, and the relevant factors in this religiosity. It explicitly wished to do so without entering into the (possible) *truth* of religious claims, that is, into the possible transcendent backdrop of the empirical phenomena that were being investigated.

The science of religion is an agglomerate of various sciences, among which German theologian Heinrich Frick (d. 1952) distinguished: (a) the history of religion (i.e., of religious phenomena), (b) the psychology of religion (the study of the mental aspects of religious phenomena), (c) the typology of religion (usually called phenomenology of religion: systematics of religious phenomena), and (d) the philosophy of religion (dealing with the ground-questions and the normative aspects of religious phenomena).[1] According to Frick, the first two deal mainly with the reality of religion, and the last two with the essence of religion. This viewpoint cannot be correct because the essence of (true and false) religion is the very thing that is *not* dealt with in any science of religion but rather in theology (see below). And even in theology, religion can never be conceptualized (captured in concepts); we can form only a theological or philosophical idea of it (see chapter 1).

Dutch missiologist and theologian Johan Herman Bavinck (d. 1964; nephew of Herman Bavinck) distinguished between the science of religion and *elenctics*, the latter being the science of persuasion and refutation (from Gk. *elengchō*, "to bring to light," "to persuade," "to refute," "to expose"). This is the science that endeavors to persuade other religions of the truth of the Christian religion.[2] It is a science whose nature is to go on the offensive, distinct from apologetics, which is more defensive in nature: Gk. *apologia* refers to a "defense," namely, of the Christian religion against its attackers.

Both the science of religion and elenctics investigate mainly non-Christian religions, but the latter is part of theology, whereas the former is not. Elenctics attempts to understand non-Christian religions in their deepest ground-motives, and to appeal to these religions to account for these ground-mo-

---
1. Frick (1928).
2. Bavinck (1957; 1958).

tives in the light of the divine revelation in Jesus Christ. Therefore, Bavinck viewed the Holy Spirit as the actual subject of elenctics in the sense of John 16:8, the Spirit "will convict the world concerning sin and righteousness and judgment."[3] Over against this, Bavinck viewed the science of religion as belonging to the literary faculty.[4] First, the science of religion investigates a certain non-Christian religion according to the methods of supposedly neutral science, that is, in as objective and unbiased a way possible. The scholar earnestly and attentively listens to what that religion has to say about God (or the gods), about humanity, and about redemption. However, in the end we cannot escape the question how we must view that religion in the light of the divine revelation. But answering this question is no longer the task of the science of religion but of elenctics as part of theology. That was the view of J. H. Bavinck.

2.1.2 No Basic Differences

Although Bavinck acknowledged that the practitioner of the science of religion cannot eliminate their own religious views, and though he admitted that absolute objectivity is impossible, he nonetheless saw this as something to be seriously pursued. I agree with this, but I do not see here any basic difference with theology. Religious presuppositions *always* play a role, and objectivity must *always* be pursued, whether in the science of religion or in theology. As I see it, Bavinck's view is dominated by the scholastic nature–grace dualism. In this view, the science of religion belongs to the rational-objective "lower story" of nature, and thus investigates natural phenomena. Elenctics, and theology in general, belong to the "upper story" of grace, and thus investigates supernatural phenomena, such as divine revelation, and so on.

I fundamentally reject this distinction. *Both* theology and the science of religion, each with their various ramifications,

---

3. Bavinck (1957).
4. Bavinck (1958).

investigate *exclusively* empirical phenomena, because this is the only matter that is at the disposal of each science. But in the end, both theology and the science of religion do so on the basis of a transcendent-religious—biblical or non-biblical, God-oriented or idol-oriented—ground-motive. That is, they both do so by the light of divine revelation *or* by the light of natural reason, or whatever one likes to call the latter. Moreover, who would be genuinely interested in some supposedly neutral science of religion? That is, who would really be rationally interested in the phenomenon of religion, and at the same time completely exclude the religious (God-oriented or idol-oriented) attitude of one's own heart? At a later stage, we will define religion as the existential orientation toward, and surrender to, what a person views as the Ultimate Ground of their existence, the ultimate reality, in which their heart finds rest and support. In *this* basic sense, all people, even if they call themselves atheists or do not engage in any religious activities whatsoever, are definitely religious.[5] At the deepest level, the heart's ground-motives are *religious* ground-motives.[6] No person could ever investigate religion apart from the religious ground-attitude of their own heart.

So what *is* the difference between theology and the science of religion? In contrast with other special disciplines, *both* theology and the science of religion investigate *pistically qualified* phenomena within empirical reality. The difference between them is this:

(a) *Theology* investigates the *pistical aspect* of these phenomena, that is, the aspect by which these phenomena are qualified.

(b) The *science of the history of religion* investigates the *cultural-historical* aspect of these pistical phenomena (often in relation to Christianity; this is called "comparative religion," more correctly: "the comparative study of religiosity"; see

---
5. Cf. Vander Goot (1981, book title: *Life Is Religion*).
6. Dooyeweerd (NC 1:61).

below).

(c) The *psychology of religion* investigates the *perceptive* and *sensitive* aspects of these pistical phenomena.

(d) The *sociology of religion* investigates the *social* aspect of these pistical phenomena. And so on.[7]

Each of these disciplines performs its task on the basis of a certain transcendent-religious ground-motive, which can be either positively Christian (biblical, God-oriented) or apostate (pagan, humanistic, idol-oriented), or a mixture of both.

Let me *add* here these further specifications:

(1) Christian theology investigates mainly (Jewish-)Christian phenomena, whereas the various branches of the science of religion investigate also, or mainly, other religions.

(2) A separate position is occupied by the *phenomenology of religion*, which is strongly linked with phenomenology as a philosophical school.[8] This science usually investigates non-Christian religions, often in comparison with Christianity ("comparative religion," see above).

(3) The *philosophy of religion* occupies a special position as well; strictly speaking, in practice it is, and ought to be, nothing but the special philosophy (Ger. *Fachphilosophy*; Dutch *vakfilosofie*) of the special discipline (*Fachwissenschaft, vakwetenschap*) of theology.

2.2 Religiosity and Religion
2.2.1 Immanent and Transcendent

The terms "psychology of religion, sociology of religion, and phenomenology of religion," and so on, can be used only with great prudence. This is because, strictly speaking, there is no such thing as a phenomenon of religion that can be analyzed by some science of religion. Religion is the transcendent, existential relationship between humans and God (or, in apostate

---
7. Cf. Troost (2004, 153–54).
8. See the standard work by Van der Leeuw (1956).

religion, between some god, or gods). In this sense, religion is not at all an empirical phenomenon, and thus cannot be enclosed in scientific concepts.[9] However, this transcendent, existential, supra-temporal relationship *manifests* itself in religiosity, that is, in immanent, empirical, temporal-religious phenomena. It is only this religiosity that is open to scientific investigation—necessarily always in the light of a certain transcendent-religious ground-motive—so that the science of religion is in fact only the science of religiosity. As Dutch philosopher Andree Troost (d. 2008) put it, *religiosity* can, and *religion* cannot, be the object of study of any science.[10] Only insofar as this is grasped we can still use traditional terms such as "comparative religion," which more correctly is the comparative study of religiosity.[11]

Let me refer here to a statement by the Swedish practitioner of the science of religion, Nathan Söderblom (d. 1931).[12] He stated that the general history of religion leaves open the question about revelation. The practitioner of this discipline may be inspired by the conviction that behind religious phenomena there exists a supra-natural reality. Or he can deny every belief in the spiritual that underlies religion. Or he can keep asking and be unsure about revelation, perhaps sure only about the impossibility of knowing anything about it. Or he may lose any interest in the question concerning the truth of religion. In my terminology, the scholar may be occupied with *religiosity* without being very concerned with a possible underlying *transcendent-religious relationship*.

In this context another distinction is important, one made by German-American theologian Paul Tillich (d. 1965), namely, between religion in the narrower sense and religion in the broader sense.[13] If I understand him correctly, in the former

---

9. This thought was expressed already in ibid., 3.
10. Troost (2004, 153).
11. Pannenberg (1971, 277–95; 1988, chapter 3, especially 167–88).
12. Söderblom (1942, 372), quoted in Pannenberg (1971, 277).
13. Tillich (1964, 7–9); cf. Troost (2004, 162).

sense, we are dealing with what I call religiosity. The latter sense involves the depth dimension of all religiosity, that is, in all functions and sectors of human life. In my terminology, it is the immanent-empirical versus the transcendent.

Not all religion or religiosity is about (belief in) God (or gods). The Dutch and Afrikaans languages distinguish between religiosity and *godsdienstigheid*, literally, "service of God."[14] As the term indicates, *godsdienst(igheid)* implies belief in God, or god, or gods, whereas religiosity, being a much broader term, does not necessarily imply this. Religiosity also includes every form of mysticism, and even the vaguest awe or respect for "the numinous," or the *tremendum* (that which makes people tremble), or the *fascinosum* (that which fascinates people) in the broadest sense,[15] that which makes us wonder.[16] Or take this example: British scholar Julian S. Huxley (d. 1975), one of the fathers of religious humanism, defined religion as "essentially an attitude to the world as a whole. Thus evolution, for example, may prove as powerful a principle to co-ordinate men's beliefs and hopes as God was in the past. Such ideas underlie the various forms of Rationalism, the Ethical movement and scientific Humanism."[17]

2.2.2 Forms of Religiosity

In the broad sense just described, it has become clear that all known nations are, and have been, religious. All these forms of religiosity must have certain characteristics in common, otherwise we could never have arranged them under the same denominator of "religion/religiosity." Missiologist Johan H. Bavinck (see above) found the following five characteristics, which I describe in my own terminology:

(a) *Totality*: the "experience of totality," which is expressed in the ideas of the macro- and the microcosmos, which corre-

---

14. Not to be confused with the German word Gottesdienst, which means "church service."
15. Cf. the standard work by Otto (1958).
16. Lewis (1959).
17. Huxley et al. (1965, 99).

spond with each other and in fact are one.

(b) *Normativity*: the normative consciousness, which is expressed, for instance, in ideas such as the *Tao* in the Chinese religions and *Rta* in India (i.e., the natural order, and thus the right way).

(c) *God or divinity*: the reference to a higher power (God or gods, transcendent or immanent, e.g., one or more deified natural forces).

(d) *Perfection*: the longing for redemption or salvation (renewal, consummation, the perfect that one day will break through).

(e) *Providence*: the awareness of life being directed and governed (by God, by deified natural forces, by fate, by destiny).[18]

As we see, this description does not make any distinction between true and false religion. Both exhibit certain common features, so that what we call false religion is still religion. It is the task not of the science of religion but rather of theology to enter into the matter of true versus false religion. Early Protestant theology had no difficulty describing the notion of true religion.[19] Thus, German theologian David Hollaz (d. 1713) wrote in 1707, *Vera Religio est, quae verbo divini est conformis* ("True Religion is that which conforms to the Word of God").[20] This is still the viewpoint of all orthodox theologians, at least if the description is not taken in an excessively dogmatic way. This would happen were it thought to imply the notion of mechanical inspiration,[21] or of a specific confession, or of specific forms of religiosity.

Over against Hollaz's objective definition, I would rather begin with a subjective one: true religion is a transcendent, existential matter of a heart that is regenerated by the Holy

---

18. Bavinck (1989); for a modern survey, see Harrison (2007, especially chapter 2).
19. See extensively, Pannenberg (1988, chapter 3).
20. Examen theol. acr. 39.
21. See *EDR* 11:254–58, 285–88.

Spirit in submission to the Word of God in its transcendent meaning. Hollaz was consistent with this when he defined false religion as, first, the worship of false gods, as in paganism, and second, the false worship of the true God.[22]

2.2.3 More Recent Views

In the nineteenth century, the lectures by German theologian Friedrich Schleiermacher (d. 1834), *On Religion: Speeches to its Cultured Despisers*, as well as his "doctrine of faith," (Ger. *Kurze Darstellung des theologischen Studiums zum Behuf einleitender Vorlesungen*)[23] exerted great influence. In his view, true religion is no longer primarily a matter of God's Word but of religiosity— piety, godliness (Ger. *Frömmigkeit*), as Schleiermacher called it. Here, religiosity is the feeling of pure/absolute dependence (Ger. *das Gefühl schlechthinniger Abhängigkeit*), which must be distinguished from the idea of God. The latter expresses that on which the religious depends. Yet, Schleiermacher did not consider piety to be a consequence of the knowledge of God, but conversely: the awareness of God is the expression of piety.[24] In this way, it remains unclear whether the idea of God is the independent (objective) starting-point for our understanding of religion, or whether the idea of God can be entirely explained (away) from people's religious consciousness. During the nineteenth century, many German theologians, who were inspired in part by the German philosopher Georg W. F. Hegel (d. 1831), gave the primacy to the idea of God (Alois E. Biedermann, Isaak A. Dorner, Ernst Troeltsch), although based no longer on Scripture but on anthropological arguments: religion is proper to the nature of humanity. In this way, the idea of God is legitimized by human nature; theology is legitimized by anthropology.

In the twentieth century, this view was combated by the

---

22. Examen theol. acr. 83.
23. Schleiermacher (1996 and 1977, respectively).
24. Cf. Pannenberg (1988, 140).

German theologian Rudolf Otto (d. 1937).[25] He pointed out that Schleiermacher's feeling of dependence—at least in his later view[26]—is a mere self-feeling, which relates to the idea of God only indirectly. In Otto's view, genuine religious consciousness is primarily and directly oriented toward an object outside itself. The numinous is first; only secondarily is a feeling of dependence coupled with an experience of the numinous. This view was certainly a step in the right direction. However, is the numinous related in any way to the God of the Bible, who reveals himself in Jesus Christ? This was the profound question asked particularly by Swiss theologian Karl Barth (d. 1968), who thereby became the twentieth-century counterpart of the nineteenth-century Schleiermacher.

Barth protested against the view of Schleiermacher and his school because they reversed the relationship between revelation and religion.[27] He emphasized again that knowledge of revelation is due not to religion, that is, to human nature. Rather, we know of (true) religion due to God's revelation of himself in Jesus Christ, and we know about Christ through Holy Scripture. Revelation precedes religion, not only chronologically but also logically. I agree with this. Yet, German theologian Wolfhart Pannenberg was right when he remarked that dogmatics does have the duty of identifying elements of truth in the preceding views, especially those of Schleiermacher. Faith may appeal to a statement in dogmatics about the primacy of God's revelation; but theology must not simply limit itself to this. The primacy of God's revelation, as postulated by orthodox Christianity, must be theologically *accounted for*, against the backdrop of what the modern science of religion has to say about human functioning as a religious being. Theology does demand anthropological considerations here. This subject will be dealt with in the next sections.

---

25. Otto (1958).
26. Pannenberg (1988, 153–54).
27. See especially Barth (*CD* I,2, 304–24: "The Problem of Religion in Theology").

2.3 Some Views from the Psychology of Religion[28]
2.3.1 William James

The psychology of religion is the science of the psychological study of religiosity, which arose immediately after the Enlightenment. The description indicates that it was no longer self-evident that theology would proceed from divine revelation, and that religiosity had become more important, or interesting, than God. Schleiermacher, who considered religiosity to be mainly an experience and a feeling, proper to all people, has often been referred to as the founder of the psychology of religion, or in the broader sense of what today is called the phenomenology of religion. However, the actual development of the psychology of religion occurred in the United States. Throughout its history, America has seen religious awakenings and revivals, which so often exhibited remarkable religious phenomena, which in turn aroused the interest of the psychologists.

The great pioneer of the psychology of religion was the philosopher of pragmatism and psychologist William James (d. 1910). In his famous Gifford Lectures, he dealt with the so-called "relevant factors" in religiosity.[29] James rejected both rationalist reductionism, which shoved religion aside as an evolutionary atavism, and the official, institutionalized denominational religion, which allegedly had reduced religion to hollow, rigid, external forms. He made a fundamental distinction between, on the one hand, personal religion, linked with the inner condition of people themselves, their consciences, their helplessness, their imperfections, and, on the other hand, conventional religiosity, linked with a theology of dogmatism, church organization, and the maintenance of creeds and religious ceremonies. In other words, James dis-

---

28. Cf. Ouweneel (1984, §5.2.3 [De religieuze ervaring]) and idem (1989a); also cf. Brillenburg Wurth (1958). For more recent surveys, see Loewenthal (2000); Fontana (2003); Wainwright (2004); Paloutzian and Park (2005); Hood et al. (2009); Saroglou (2013); and Benton et al. (2018).
29. James (1902).

tinguished between religiosity as an inner matter of the heart, and religiosity as an external behavioral form. In the course of this chapter, it may become clear why I myself would prefer to speak of:

(a) Religiosity in which the external behavior is rooted in a pious heart (pious in the sense of devoted to the divine; in the Jewish-Christian sense: a God-fearing heart).

(b) Religiosity that is entirely confined to external actions and (possibly) inner acts; or, more precisely, that is rooted in a cold, or even hypocritical heart, devoted only to itself and its own idols (cf. Matt. 15:1–20; Rom. 2:17–29).

Later, I will try to formulate this distinction in more philosophical terms.

It must be stated *a priori* that this difference between heart and life must be sharply distinguished from the difference between true and false religion (or derailed religion, i.e., religion that has deviated from the track on which God's revelation has placed humanity; see §1.4.1). The latter difference involves a good versus a broken relationship with God, a believing or an apostate relationship. In *both* types of relationship, there is an internal (transcendent, existential) side, and an external side that often expresses itself in the smallest details of immanent human life. In both true religion and false religion, the discrepancy signaled by James occurs: between religiosity as an internal matter of the heart and religiosity as a mainly external form of behavior.

2.3.2 Sigmund Freud[30]

The man who, during the twentieth century, perhaps more than any other person, influenced people's views concerning religion, was the Austrian psychoanalytic Sigmund Freud. In Freud's thinking,[31] there was never any distinct room for the

---
30. See Plantinga (2000, 135–63) on what he called the "Freud-and-Marx" complaint against religion.
31. Among his works (Freud [2011]), see especially his *Totem and Taboo*

specific-modal nature of human analytical thought, the will, creativity, morality, and faith, in short: for the unique human spiritive life, as I have called it.[32] Of course, Freud recognized these phenomena, but viewed them as purely psychically qualified; concretely, they are sublimations of the suppressed libido. He did not assign them any independence, as distinct from the psychic, but reduced them to sensitive, especially unconscious, drives. Thus, we could call his view a form of psychologism or sensitivism.[33]

According to Freud, the religious need sprouts from the desire to overcome the frustrations of life. To this end, a person regresses to a life stage when they were still dependent on their father, thus designing a substitute father figure called "God." In a person's speaking about religious matters, Freud did not hear the echo of the voice of God, or a god, but only the voice of the parent, who has become part of the Super-Ego (Ger. *Über-Ich*) of that person. This process unfolds when the person's Oedipus complex is resolved, a process that is necessary to remove sexual frustration. Freud considered all religion to be an anxiety neurosis or a compulsion, as an illusion rooted in human desires.[34] In his view, a religious system can address the needs of certain people for a given period of time, yet it forms a social neurosis, from which people must free themselves.

In his *Moses and Monotheism* (1937–1939),[35] the Jew Freud applied the idea of the Oedipus complex to the history of

---

(1913), *The Ego and the Id* (1923), *The Future of an Illusion* (1927), and *Civilization and Its Discontents* (1930).
32. Ouweneel (1986; 2015).
33. Because, within Dooyeweerd's "psychical" modality, I believe to discern in fact two modalities, the perceptive and the sensitive one (Ouweneel, 1986; 2015), I call psychoanalysis a form of sensitivism, and, for instance, behaviorism a form of perceptivism (viewing the stimulus–response model as perceptively qualified).
34. The basis for this view can be found in Freud's brief treatise, *Formulations on the Two Principles of Mental Functioning* (in Freud [2011]).
35. Found in Freud (2011).

Israel, beginning with the supposition that Moses was an Egyptian, and that Israel had killed him. He also believed that Israel had suppressed its sexuality by disconnecting God entirely from sexuality. This was done in opposition to the Canaanite Baals, who were real fertility gods, with all kinds of lascivious ceremonies connected with them.

The reason for referring to this example of Freud is that it has become clear since Freud's day how extensively his views of religion were themselves religiously determined. To begin with, it is remarkable that the theories of a man who emphasized so strongly the suppressed youthful conflicts between a father and son can be largely explained from his own youthful conflicts. Psychotherapist Adam Crabtree has described how, during his own early youth, Freud was dominated by a strict and elderly father in contrast to his attractive and intelligent mother, who was twenty years younger.[36] If one considers that, among the seven children, Sigmund was his mother's favorite, can Freud's theory of the Oedipus complex (about the conflict between father and son, both competing for the mother's favor) be disconnected from this? Freud's theories were formed not only by his intellect but also by his own suppressed youthful conflicts, that is, his own feelings. In other words, his theories were governed by his sensitivistic internal experiences at least as much as by his rational theorizing.

His view of religion was governed especially by his own *religious* condition. He called himself a "fully god-less Jew" and a "hopeless pagan." After an episode of the humiliation of his Jewish father by anti-Semites, he was forever filled with revenge against "the Christians."[37] More concretely, we can say that Freud's religious-philosophical prejudices were materialism and evolutionism. As a student he had worked under the German physiologist Ernst Wilhelm von Brücke (Ernst Brücke, d. 1892), whom he called "the greatest authority, who more than anyone else has influenced my entire life."

---

36. Crabtree (1984).
37. Jones (1953, 25); cf. Rushdoony (1965, 34), and references there.

It was this very Brücke of whom his friend, the German physiologist Emil du Bois-Reymond (d. 1896), once said, "Brücke and I swore a solemn oath that we would practice this truth: 'No other forces than the common physical and chemical ones are operative in the organism'."[38] On the basis of this absolutization of matter, Freud, too, worked out a psychology on a foundation that was as materialistic as possible. For instance, he explained a typically psychological phenomenon like the Oedipus complex entirely from humanity's alleged evolutionary development, which itself, in his view, must be explained entirely materialistically in the spirit of Darwin.

Freud's transcendent-existential orientation becomes still more clear in his deep rootedness in Jewish-heretical thought.[39] These heresies involve cabbalistic-mystical attempts to break the yoke of the Torah. Freud's idea of the Oedipus complex goes back to hints in the *Zohar* (the medieval main work of the Cabbala) that "the depths of sexual satisfaction lie in having sexual intercourse with the Mother."[40] American psychologist David Bakan (d. 2004) offered evidence that psychoanalysis is a secularized form of Jewish-heretical mysticism in the line of Sabbatai Zvi, the false Jewish Messiah (d. 1676);[41] that Freud viewed himself as both the enemy of Moses and another Moses[???];[42] that, in contrast with Moses, he wished to lead people to the fertility cult of the golden calf and the Baals.[43] In his rooms, Freud surrounded himself with every pagan god that he could find.[44] He called himself the Devil in the sense that, he too, wished to seduce people to apostasy by freeing themselves from the Torah.[45] Freud's own transcendent-religious orientation is the most outspoken form of

---

38. Jones (1953, 31, 45).
39. See extensively, Bakan (1958); cf. Rushdoony (1965, 35–38).
40. Bakan (1958, 288).
41. Ibid., viii, 25, 132.
42. Cf. Jones (1955, 33, 96, 363 and further).
43. Bakan (1958, 127, 159–60, 177, 181, 227).
44. Ibid., 134.
45. Ibid., 169–71, 181, 229.

apostasy that one could imagine.

2.4 Carl G. Jung
2.4.1 Archetypes

Let me briefly refer here to another psychologist, the Swiss psychiatrist Carl G. Jung (d. 1961), who associated religion with the ground-concept of the archetype. Jung was of the opinion that the supposed human evolution involved a gradual broadening of human consciousness. He spoke of the personal unconscious, proper to the individual, as well as of the collective unconscious. The latter constitutes a deeper layer of mental life, and is proper to all humanity collectively. Further, he spoke of archetypes within this collective unconscious in the sense of collectively present dynamic patterns. These patterns are formed by the experiences of humanity in its (alleged) remote evolutionary past. They come to light in our dreams, and also in the archetypical symbols encountered in legends and myths all over the world. The collective unconscious is a storeroom of common symbols, the memory of humanity, the total knowledge of the human race. Of course, from a strictly Darwinistic viewpoint, archetypes must have a physiological basis, which was formed during the evolutionary process.

According to Jung, "God" is one of these archetypes, not in the sense that God would be only a mental product of humanity, but that the idea of "God" goes back to a (transcendent) primordial experience of primitive humanity, of whatever nature this may have been. This is because archetypes are viewed as a kind of imprints, and these presuppose an imprinter. The psychologist investigates the imprints, but theology and philosophy, and especially the religious person as such, inquires about the imprinter.

Like Freud's view, Jung's theory was strongly colored by his philosophical views and was equally hard to verify with the help of empirical-scientific methods. I believe the cause for this is that such views concerning religion arise not primarily from scientific investigation but from the worldview of Freud and Jung, respectively. This worldview itself was rooted in their respective transcendent-religious ground-motives. As to Jung, the study of his life and thought has shown not only that his thought was governed by the humanistic ground-motive but also that he exhibited a strong existential inclination toward the purely pagan.[46] He was exceptionally interested in the occult—it was already the subject of his dissertation—in the sense of the secret science (Ger. *Geheimwissenschaft*) of magic and mantics that characterizes all pagan religions, and also Christianity insofar as it is open to heathen influences. Moreover, Jung's autobiography shows that he himself had several psychic talents, regularly had visions, and had paranormal experiences.[47]

2.4.2 Conjunction

Since Jung had broken with Freud, he began interpreting his own mental life by means of Indian, magical, and Gnostic symbols, together with his in-depth studies concerning religious feeling, Eastern religions, ancient mysteries, gnostic brotherhood, and his discovery of certain similarities between the symbols of the ancient alchemists and mystics and certain symptoms of psychopaths. His last great work in particular was devoted to this.[48] Paul J. Stern said about this work that the quest for the great synthesis that would make the two halves one was not only the leitmotiv of Jung's work but also of his life. From the moment he first became aware of his internal bifurcation, Jung felt urged to search for the panacea that would heal his psychic wound. He viewed this internal division as an expression not so much of a personal condition but rather of a fundamental disorder in the universe. Thus, he was haunted by the thought of the terrible double-aspect of God, in whom a sea of grace collides with a boiling pool of

---

46. For this part, see Stern (1976).
47. See Jaffé (1962).
48. Jung (1976).

fire. From the sensitive irritability with which *YHWH* treated his chosen people Israel, Jung concluded that the Almighty himself was tortured by dissociation. Jung's great healing was to encompass not only suffering humanity but God himself. That was the claim of Stern.[49]

For Jung, healing neuroses implied a renewed confrontation with the "suppressed God" in the mind of people—a god created after Jung's image, a god who, according to Jung, himself needed redemption. Stern again: Jung discovered God literally underground, in the subterranean vaults of dream images, in the catacombs of the psyche, which are known as the domain of the unconscious. This unconscious became the main focus and reference point for Jung's spiritual science. It became the refuge of the divine.[50]

For Jung, the mystical and occult, which form the bridge to the transcendent, formed the indispensable context of the healthy person. Only if the conscious would direct itself toward the unconscious, which in fact cannot be distinguished from the deity, it can function as "the light that comprehends the darkness" (cf. John 1:5 *KJV*). Where the unconscious takes the lead, God's incarnation in the person becomes visible. The "myth of the ruse of the God-man" from the unconscious[51] as that which overcomes the cosmic disharmony, as the completer of the Messianic *conjunction* between the Ego and the unconscious, *this* was Jung's (purely religious!) ground-idea—an idea that frightened the mentally unstable Jung himself, so that he shrank from the consequences of it. Jung's tragedy is that the failure of his great experiment of self-healing gradually became manifest. He who himself was his greatest and most important patient did not manage to prevent or heal the schizophrenic deformity of his personality—at least, this is the conclusion of his biographer Stern.

---

49. Stern (1976, 251–52).
50. Ibid., 253.
51. Ibid., 256.

2.4.3 Buber's Comments

In his remarkable book, *Eclipse of God*, Austrian-Israeli philosopher Martin Buber gave us an implicit and penetrating analysis of Jung's transcendent-religious orientation.[52] On the one hand, Jung rightly remarked that psychology as such cannot tell us anything about the possible existence of the transcendent, apart from human consciousness. On the other hand, Jung trespassed this boundary time and again by reducing religion to purely psychic phenomena, which do not refer to a transcendent reality. In this manner, Jung made statements that were no longer purely psychological but were metaphysical. In my terminology, Jung's own transcendent-religious (apostate) orientation lay at the basis of his scientific views. This is the only explanation for such un-psychological remarks as this one by Jung: "Modern consciousness abhors faith, and as a result, also all religions based upon it."[53] As Buber put it, "Although the new psychology protests that it is 'not a worldview but a science,' it is no longer satisfied with the role of interpreter of religion. It announces the new religion, the only one that can still be true, the religion of the pure psychical immanence."[54]

Buber showed that Jung's transcendent-religious orientation was fundamentally Gnostic, as Jung himself sometimes admitted. Jung abhorred the Christian faith but not the Gnostic god, in whom good and evil are linked together; thus, the soul or the Ego is the "bridal conjunction of opposite halves."[55] Buber said in this context that, according to Jung, self-realization must be described as "the incarnation of God." This god, who unites good and evil in himself, whose contrasting nature expresses itself also in his androgyny (his being masculine and feminine in one), is a Gnostic figure. This figure probably goes back to the ancient Iranian deity Zurvan,

---

52. Buber (1989, 78–92, 133–37).
53. Jung (1931, 417).
54. Buber (1989, 83–84).
55. Jung (1948, 315; cf. 1944, 61).

source of the god of light as well as of his dark counterpart. That was Buber's analysis.[56]

Some of the most prominent twentieth-century thinkers (as well as some nineteenth century thinkers, like Ludwig Feuerbach and Karl Marx) offer us what amounts to no proof, but at least a provocative illustration, of a fundamental-Christian conviction. This is the conviction that all human thought, about religion in particular, springs from and is governed by the transcendent-religious condition of a person's own heart. Without any further arguments, I claim that, in the case of Freud and Jung, this means that their hearts were dominated by the transcendent-religious ground-motive of humanism, namely, the nature–freedom motive. For instance, in the case of Freud, this implies, on the one hand, a materialistic ideal of science (the nature motive), and on the other hand, a sensitivistic personality ideal (the freedom move). Later, I will return often to this important matter of the religious determination of human thought. Let us first deal with the view of religion as we find it in Reformational philosophy, more specifically in that of Dutch philosopher Herman Dooyeweerd. Subsequently, we will deal with some more recent views in the field of the science of religion.

2.5   Transcendental Critique
2.5.1   True Self-Knowledge

In many different manners, Dooyeweerd entered into the philosophical aspects of religion, but in particular in his transcendental critique of theoretical thought. He argued that only through human self-reflection, that is, through self-knowledge, does theoretical thought acquire insight into the Archimedic point, the absolute point of unity and concentration of theoretical thought that surpasses all modalities of the immanent-empirical reality. It is only in his own Ego that a person seems to have knowledge of such a point. Dooyeweerd links this consideration with the following question (the so-called

---

56. Buber (1989, 90).

third problem of his transcendental thought critique): "How is this critical self-reflection, this concentric direction of theoretical thought to the I-ness, possible, and what is its true character?"[57]

In short, this question primarily involves another one: How does a person arrive at true self-knowledge? One might propose three different answers:

(a) Can relationships with the *Umwelt* (the "environment": the world of the lifeless things, plants, and animals) supply us with any insight in our I-ness? The answer is negative: if our I-ness were determined by its many *Umwelt* relationships, it would be dispersed in them, and no root unity could be found in empirical reality.

(b) Can relationships with the *Mitwelt* (the world of our fellow-humans) supply us with this insight? This is not possible either. Relationships with other I-nesses, which place us before the same mystery as our own I-ness, cannot shed light on the nature of our I-ness as such.

(c) Therefore, we must search for a third possibility, which surpasses both our *Umwelt* and our *Mitwelt*. This possibility involves the human I-ness to be essentially determined by the vertical relationship with the (true or pretended) divine origin of our immanent reality. (We might speak here of *Überwelt*: the realm beyond us).

As Dooyeweerd put it: "The selfhood cannot give this central direction to its theoretical thought without concentrating itself upon the true, or upon a pretended absolute origin of all meaning. That is to say, that self-knowledge in the last analysis appears to be dependent upon knowledge of God, ..."[58] In brief: acquiring any true self-knowledge is possible only through knowledge of God. Dooyeweerd is referring here to the religious, human search for the ultimate ground (certain-

---

57. Dooyeweerd (*NC* 1:52).
58. Ibid., 54–55.

ty) *ex-istentially*[59] or *excentrically*, that is, outside oneself, in one's (true or pretended) divine origin.

The way Dooyeweerd spoke of God as origin has sometimes been criticized because he used terms that have non-Christian overtones. For instance, regarding his statement that "the true *Origin . . . is absolute* and *self-sufficient*,"[60] Dutch philosopher Theo de Boer commented that this is not Calvinistic but Aristotelian.[61] He praised Dooyeweerd, as well as his ally Dirk H. Th. Vollenhoven, for their courage and clear vision with which they identified and combated Greek and scholastic views in theology. But he objected that the idea of God as the absolute Origin of everything, and of the relativity of everything that is non-divine, was an ancient metaphysical inheritance, in which there was nothing specifically Christian. Yet, it is not fair to accuse Dooyeweerd of presenting the "God of the philosophers" rather than the "God of Abraham, Isaac and Jacob." Another Dutch philosopher, René van Woudenberg, rightly remarked that, today, we have certainly become more sensitive to descriptions of God with Greek terms such as "Origin" and "Absolute." Yet, Dooyeweerd's philosophy made clear that what was echoing in his way of speaking about God were not Greek notions but a biblical, non-philosophical awareness of Supremacy and Power.[62]

2.5.2 Knowledge of Self and of God

The primary insight that the ground of human existence is *ex-istential*, that is, lies outside humanity, is of eminent importance for the science of religion. Ultimately, every science that deals with religion can do so only from the transcendent-existential-religious attitude of the scientist's own heart. *Good*

---

59. Literally "standing outside itself," to use a technical term of Martin Heidegger (1927), but used here in the sense of the I-ness being directed "outside itself" toward its Ground or Origin.
60. Dooyeweerd (*NC* 1:10).
61. De Boer (1984, 250; cf. 260).
62. Van Woudenberg (1992, 212–13); cf. Van der Hoeven (1986, 17–20; 1991, 29).

The Science of Religion

science of religion is practiced, with regard to its (horizontal) structure, according to strict scientific criteria, and with regard to its (vertical) direction,[63] from a heart that is in the grip of *good* religion, that is, on the basis of the transcendent-existential insight in what is *true* religion. There can be horizontally good science of religion that vertically speaking is bad, and *vice versa*. Where the transcendent-existential insight in *true* religion is lacking, or where this is not consciously applied from the beginning of the research, the science of religion cannot offer us true insight in the perceptive, sensitive, cultural-historical, social, juridical, ethical (etc.) aspects of religious (i.e., pistical) phenomena. This is the case, for instance, in several treatises (in the Dutch language) in the field of the psychology of religion that come from Roman Catholic faculties.[64] In spite of the useful material that is offered in such studies, we must reject their starting-points. As Dooyeweerd rightly said in his sixth anthropological thesis: "Knowledge about the human soul is *religious self-knowledge*, and *true self-knowledge* is only possible by way of *true knowledge of God* from divine Word Revelation."[65]

Thus, self-knowledge is *religious* knowledge, that is, self-knowledge depends on the person's knowledge of God. It is remarkable that this is precisely the insight with which John Calvin opened his *Institutes of the Christian Religion*: "In the first place, no man can survey himself without forthwith turning his thoughts towards the God in whom he lives and moves [Acts 17:28]"; "it is evident that man never attains to a true self-knowledge until he has previously contemplated the face of God, and come down after such contemplation

---

63. For this relationship between structure and direction see extensively, *EDR* 3:246–50; Vol. I/1, §§3.5.1, 3.10.2, 4.4.2, 4.5.3 in this series; 2014a; 2014b; 2015; 2017, 66–69 passim).
64. See, e.g., Vergote (1967) of Leuven; Van der Lans (1978), Janssen et al. (2001), and Van Uden and Pieper (2009) of Nijmegen; Weima (1981), and Janssen (2007) of Tilburg.
65. Dooyeweerd (1942, 6).

to look into himself."⁶⁶

The scientific insight into the coherence between self-knowledge and knowledge of God is not merely a theological matter. This insight has important philosophical aspects as well. In more general terms, the close relationship between a person's self-understanding and their awareness of God (or god[s]) is an empirical given, investigated by several disciplines. As Dooyeweerd notes, it has been thoroughly documented by the Jewish-German-American neo-Kantian philosopher Ernst Cassirer (d. 1945) on the basis of extensive cultural-anthropological material.[67]

2.5.3 The Religious Root of All Human Thought

The cultural-anthropological and theological considerations involved are supported by the biblical testimony. The Bible expresses a person's religious relationship of dependence with regard to their divine origin, among other things, in the term "image of God" (Gen. 1:26–27 [cf. 5:3]; 9:6; 1 Cor. 11:7; Col. 3:10; cf. 2 Cor. 4:4; Col. 1:15).[68] Dooyeweerd said of this image of God:

> Humans have been created according to God's image and likeness, and this image finds its central seat precisely in the human Ego, as the radix or the 'heart' of human existence. The likeness of this imago Dei [= image of God] is nothing but the central urge of love toward its divine Origin, in which the overwhelming love of God toward humanity and toward the entire temporal world concentrated in humanity ought to find its creaturely echo, and without which no fellowship with God and the fellow-humans in the Holy Spirit is possible.[69]

---

66. Calvin, *Institutes* 1.1.1, 2); available at http://www.ccel.org/ccel/calvin/institutes.iii.ii.html.
67. Dooyeweerd (*NC* 1:55; 2:319–30); Cassirer (1954).
68. See Ouweneel, *EDR* 3: §§5.1 and 5.2; 2019, chapter 6; cf. Dooyeweerd (NC 1:4, 55, 60, 174; 2:30, 248, 307, 549; 3:6, 69, 71, 88; 1942, 765; 1944, 32–33; 1960, 31–32).
69. Dooyeweerd (1966, 203).

We may wonder whether, exegetically, Dooyeweerd is entirely correct here. "Image" (Heb. *tsēlem*) and "likeness" (Heb. *d'mut*) must be distinguished; we cannot speak of the "likeness" of the "image." Moreover, Dooyeweerd read too much philosophical anthropology into these terms. But this does not alter his central thesis: humans have transcendent hearts, which — at least before the Fall — were filled with love toward God and toward fellow-humans, and in some way this fact is expressed in the biblical terms "image" and "likeness." By nature — apart from sin — humans are "like" God, who is the loving God (1 John 4:8, 16).

Without discussing this any further, I want to identify an important element in Dooyeweerd's view[70]. The transcendental critique of theoretical thought *itself* shows that the concentric direction of this thought does not find its origin in this thought itself but, beyond this, refers to the Ego as the supra-theoretical, religious center of human existence. If this is correct — and I believe it is — then it is not reason, which is usually presented as autonomous, but religion (as defined above) that ultimately governs all human thought, and all human existence. In that case, religion also governs the totality of the transcendental thought critique *itself*.[71] Viewed this way, there can be no autonomous, neutral, objective, unprejudiced philosophy or special disciplines, including theology. On the contrary, religion governs every philosophical or theological (or psychological, or sociological, etc.) speaking about religion (or rather, about religiosity). We can speak about religion and religiosity only from the religious direction of our own heart.

This was totally misunderstood by Dutch theologian Gijsbert van den Brink, who made the fundamental error

---

70. See Dooyeweerd (1960, 53).
71. Cf., e.g., these claims: "[I]t is only in its central religious relation to its divine origin that the thinking ego can direct itself and the modal diversity of its temporal world upon the absolute. The inner tendency to do so is an innate religious impulsion of the ego" (ibid., 32).

of claiming that Dooyeweerd's arguments "try to show in a neutral-philosophical way that no neutral philosophy is possible!"[72] This suggests that Dooyeweerd was unaware that his own thinking, too, was governed by his religious starting-points. The truth of the matter is this: Dooyeweerd was the first to point out that the view that all thinking is *a priori* religiously determined is itself necessarily *a priori* religiously determined.

2.6   What Is Religion?
2.6.1   Various Descriptions

At his point we must say a bit more about the meaning of the term "religion." The etymology of the Latin term *religio* is unclear: must we follow the Roman philosopher Cicero (d. 43 BC), who reduced it to *relegere*, "to take heed, to observe carefully,"[73] or should we follow traditional Christian thinkers (Lactantius, d. 320; Augustine, d. 430), who derived it from *religare*, "to connect again" (viz., God and humanity, after the Fall)? In the most compact form, Dooyeweerd gave the following description of the term "religion": "To the question, what is understood here by religion? I reply: the innate impulse of human selfhood to direct itself toward the *true* or toward a *pretended* absolute Origin of all temporal diversity of meaning, which it finds focused concentrically in itself."[74] This ties in closely with both meanings of *religio*. Stated more simply and concisely: *religion is the drive of the heart to Something (or Someone) beyond it and beyond all of empirical reality.*

Dooyeweerd empasized the importance of this as a philosophical description. Thus, it is not a biblical description, like this one: "Religion [Gk. *thrēskeia*] that is pure and undefiled before God the Father is this: to visit orphans and widows in their affliction, and to keep oneself unstained from the world"

---

72. Van den Brink (2000, 335).
73. So, e.g., Broekhuis (1994, 26), who calls it the antonym of neglegere, "to neglect."
74. Dooyeweerd (*NC* 1:57).

(James 1:27; also cf. Rom. 12:1 KJV, "reasonable service," Gk. *latreia* [Dutch: *godsdienst*]). Nor is it a theological description, though it is, I venture to say, in the spirit of Scripture. This does not mean that Dooyeweerd's description of religion is the result of philosophical analysis, for such an analysis could never go beyond claiming that religion is one *possible* relationship between God (or god[s]) and humanity. No, this description of religion is nothing other than a confession of faith, though one supported by philosophical arguments; and it is a view of the essence of humanity, stated in an anthropological-philosophical form.

Compare here the description of religion by German Roman Catholic theologian Karl Rahner (d. 1984):

> Whether a person is consciously aware of it or not, whether he is open to this truth or suppresses it, his entire spiritual and intellectual existence is directed toward a holy mystery, which is the basis of his being. This mystery . . . is our most fundamental, most natural condition, but for this very reason it is also the most concealed and least considered reality, which speaks to us through its silence, and even when it seems absent, reveals its presence by bringing us to the awareness of our limitations. We call it God.[75]

In his twenty-four theses on the question of God, Swiss Roman Catholic theologian Hans Küng reasoned as follows (in summary): humans are beings of desire and hope but, at the level of just the horizontal and purely human, no true transcending to a truly other dimension seems possible: without the truly transcendent out there, there is no true transcending toward it. Thus, faith in God, though it cannot be proven (nor refuted, for that matter), can be verified in a supra-rational, existential way, in that it supplies answers to the riddles of things like cosmic reality and human origin and destiny, which otherwise would be unsolved. Our basic confidence in reality merges with our confidence in God.

---

75. Rahner (1972, 122).

German Lutheran theologian Wolfhart Pannenberg argued that the cosmological argument (see §3.3.3), even though it proves nothing, at least points to reason's need of meaning—I would rather say, the *heart's* need of meaning, reason being just one of the heart's functions—in the light of the world's dependence. In this way, it contributes to the comprehensibility of our speaking about God.[76]

2.6.2 Again, Concept and Idea

In his transcendental critique of theoretical thought, Dooyeweerd wanted a philosophical description of religion that encompassed both the central I-ness and the concentric directedness toward the transcendent divine Origin. This explains the formal nature of his description of religion. It necessarily sounds very different from a creed, which speaks of the concrete, intimate fellowship of the believer with their heavenly Father. Philosophical speaking about religion inevitably develops its own specific terminology, which must link with the entire terminology of theoretical thought. Biblical parlance, excellently appropriate as the faith language of the believer, is not philosophical in nature—fortunately, I would say—and therefore is hardly fit to solve philosophical problems.

At the same time, we must keep in mind that we cannot form a philosophical *concept* of religion as described, but only a philosophical *idea* (see §1.9). Only what belongs to immanent reality, that toward which the logical thinking-act can direct itself, that which in principle, through logical-analytical objectification can be conceived, can be contained in a concept. However, when, in a transcendental critique, our thinking directs itself toward the possibilities and boundaries of knowledge and the analyzable, it can form an idea (Gk. *idea*, here: "image," or "mental representation") of it. As mentioned earlier, knowledge in the form of ideas is also rational knowledge, but the kinds that surpasses conceptual knowledge. We cannot form a theoretical concept of the hu-

---

76. Pannenberg (1988, 106).

The Science of Religion

man heart and of its religious direction toward God, not even a pre- or supra-theoretical concept. We have only an idea of it. As Dooyeweerd expressed this in his seventh anthropological thesis:

> Actual *scientific* knowledge about man remains limited in principle to the structure of the human body, in its broad sense of the *temporal form of existence of human life*. However, because philosophical inquiry is religious determined, any such inquiry concerning man's temporal existence should, from a scriptural standpoint, be *directed* by an *Idea* of the *human soul* . . ., in which God's revelation concerning the root of human existence — as religious presupposition — is focused on the basic problem of anthropology.
>
> This fundamental theoretical problem [of anthropology] can be formulated as follows: How can man's temporal existence, which we theoretically split apart into its different aspects and individuality structures, nevertheless be grasped as a *deeper whole* and as a *deeper unity*?[77]

Thus, we are certainly able to provide philosophical descriptions of religion, or of the heart (or the soul or spirit in their transcendent meanings), as long as we keep in mind that religion as such surpasses our theoretical concepts. This is the case because the (transcendent-religious) heart surpasses all modal aspects of the immanent reality. Religion is *not* a purely immanent phenomenon, which is manifested absolutely and exclusively within the immanent structure of our human mental life. We can have knowledge of it only in the transcendent direction of our hearts, not in the immanent direction, and even less as a theoretical object of study. This is why I said above that we can speak of the psychology (history, sociology, phenomenology) of religion only if we conceive of it as *religiosity*, not as religion in its transcendent-existen-

---

77. Dooyeweerd (1942, 7).

tial sense.[78] This remains true, even though so many historians, ethnologists, sociologists, psychologists, theologians, and philosophers have attempted to get the phenomenon of religion in their theoretical grip.[79] All theoretical thought is rooted in the religious condition of the heart,[80] and therefore it is in principle also the religious condition of the investigator's heart that, from beginning to end, stamps their thinking about religion, and indicates in what direction their investigation will move. We can even say that the investigator is never more in the grip of their religious ground-motive than when they try to turn religion itself into their object of study.

2.6.3 Again, the Immanent and the Transcendent

There have been several other, more liberal thinkers, such as the Scottish-American existentialist and theologian Geddes MacGregor (d. 1998),[81] who were of the opinion that the study of religion ought to be not objective at all. According to him, the investigator must learn to think existentially about their object of study, that is, from a profound (religious) engagement with it. MacGregor believed that someone who is personally involved in (a certain) religion is able to notice various factors that an outsider would easily overlook. This is because this noticing is not strictly empirical in nature but a matter of the heart itself, and of the investigator's personal religious commitment. In this way, they know of (God-oriented or idolatrous) religious relationships about which empirical science as such has nothing meaningful to say.

Those who practice the science (psychology, sociology, history, etc.) of religion may be occupied with beliefs, religious behavior, rituals, feelings, and experiences. But these are all immanent phenomena within empirical reality. However, such practitioners have no theoretical knowledge con-

---

78. Dooyeweerd (*NC* 1:57–58).
79. See the survey by Scobie (1975, 13–24).
80. Dooyeweerd (*NC* 1:22–68).
81. MacGregor (1960).

cerning the extent to which these phenomena go back to a transcendent-existential religious reality. It is only on the basis of their own (God-oriented or idolatrous) faith idea of religion that they may arrive at the conviction that religion is either entirely *confined to* the empirical results of their investigations, *or* that it surpasses these.

I believe the latter. The religious person—in the transcendent-existential sense, *every* human being, even the staunchest atheist—not only *believes* (sometimes) that they experience the transcendent (although they may call it very differently, such as "the numinous"), and stand in a relationship with it, but they *do* experience it, and *do* stand in a relationship with it. This fact is totally independent of what this transcendent experience may involve: God or the idols, being demons, or ideologies[82] that basically are of a demonic origin. The heart has its own reasons to believe this, reasons that reason does not know, to echo Blaise Pascal.[83]

Andree Troost rightly pointed out that the so-called "problem of the 'existence' of God" is a typically rationalistic camouflage of a lack of true faith.[84] An existential problem is hiding here behind an intellectual problem; in other words, the intellectual doubt follows upon the existential doubt, not the other way around. Since ancient Greek philosophy, especially Xenophanes (d. about 478 BC), the existence of God has been an acknowledged philosophical or theological problem, in which, in fact, the transcendent-religious aspect remained untouched. Only in the last centuries has it become, for large parts of the secularized world, also a practical, vital, existential problem.

Empirical science has a grip only on one *relatum* of the

---

82. Notice the etymological connection between "idolatry" and "ideology," both terms coming from Gk. *idein*, "to see," hence the notion of "form, representation."
83. *Pensées* 423–277 (Le cœur a ses raisons que la raison ne connaît point); cf. Turnell (1962, 163).
84. Troost (1992a, [2]).

religious relationship, and this only to a limited extent, namely, only insofar as it concerns the modal-functional expressions such as religious feelings (sensitive) as well as religious considerations and decisions (spiritive). The heart as such, as the *transcendent*-religious center of a *total*-religious existence, is not accessible to empirical-theoretical conceptualization. This is even less the case with the religious relationship itself, and even less with the other *relatum*: the transcendent. These are four levels (modal diversity – the heart – the relationship – the transcendent) of which *only the first one* is open to scientific investigation. A simple comparison: when it comes to love among fellow-humans, we find three of the four levels: modal diversity – the heart – the relationship. Even here, only the first, involving feelings (rooted in bio-physical processes), considerations, choices, and behavioral patterns of loving, is accessible to research. These things may become clearer as we now look briefly at some results of the science of religion.

2.7 Questions in the Field of the Science of Religion
2.7.1 The Religious Variable

By the end of the sixties, the American psychologist of religion, James E. Dittes (d. 2009), concluded in a large survey about the psychology of religion that this science still found itself at a primitive level.[85] And in 1971, Merton P. Strommen gave as his opinion that the largest part of the research could be best described as sporadic, piecemeal, and unsystematic.[86] Apart from poor methodology and badly formulated presuppositions, Dittes saw the main problems studied by the science of religion to be (a) the extent of differentiation between religion and related phenomena, such as mysticism and art, and (b) the extent of differentiation within religion, that is, genuine and non-genuine religion.[87] That is—to use a current scientific term—how must the religious variable be defined?

---

85. Dittes (1969).
86. Strommen (1971, xviii).
87. Not to be confused with true (biblical) and false (idolatrous) religion! E.g., Hinduism is a genuine religion, but a false one.

And is this variable uni- or multidimensional, that is, do both religious experiences and religious behaviors and attitudes belong to the essence of religion, or does only one of these factors?

Already in the way the problem is stated, we encounter a number of religious and philosophical presuppositions. First, religion is not one among a number of different phenomena, as Dittes apparently supposed. In fact, he referred to religiosity only; in Dooyeweerdian terminology this is *pistical life*, that is, those immanent phenomena in human life that are pistically qualified. Therefore, I believe that the problem, at least in the philosophy of religion—which remains the theoretical basis for all sciences of religion, including theology—must instead be formulated as follows: In what way does the pistical aspect of human life differ from, for instance, the sensitive, social, aesthetic, or ethical aspects of it? In asking this, we constantly keep in mind that, in *all* these modal aspects, humans function as *religious* beings ("religious" in its transcendent-existential meaning). In other words, the immanent-pistical modality and the transcendent-religious human heart differ essentially from each other.[88] Also our religious (more correctly, pistical) experiences, actions, attitudes, beliefs, ceremonies, and so on, are all transcendent-religiously determined, even though these, in themselves, are all actions and mental acts that may be qualified by various immanent modalities, especially, but not necessarily always, the pistical modality.

By reducing religion *a priori* to one or more pistical (therefore immanent-modal) variables, people have often made the mistake in the past of measuring the religious variable by means of religious membership, denominational preference, frequency of attending church services, religious beliefs, or through questions such as, "Do you believe in God?," "Do you believe in some kind of life after death?" Gradually, however, people discovered that such investigations say little

---

88. See, e.g., Dooyeweerd (*NC* 2:298–330); Ouweneel (1986, chapter 5; 2014a; 2014b; 2015; see also 2018, chapter 6).

or nothing about the full and real functioning of religion in all modal aspects of human life.[89] To mention some typical examples: earlier research pointed to either a positive or a negative correlation between religion and mental health, or between religion and ethnocentrism. Gradually, however, people saw more clearly that—in the case of conflicting findings—mental health or ethnocentrism had been compared with very different religious (i.e., pistical) factors, or even with non-pistical factors, especially sensitive and social ones.[90]

More and more the insight grew that what must be investigated are not the pistical beliefs and actions themselves, but the extent to which the religion confessed was a matter of inner conviction, which pervaded a person's entire inner life, and hence also their entire external existence. Again, we must notice immediately that religion is *always* a matter of the entire internal life and the entire external existence. The point can be better formulated as follows: in the case of a person with Christian (or Hindu, or humanist) beliefs and practices, to what extent does the *heart* really stand under the influence of the corresponding Christian (or Hindu, or humanist) *ground-motive*? Or do we find in that person all kinds of non-Christian (or non-Hindu, or non-humanist) beliefs and practices because that person is dominated, largely or entirely, consciously or unconsciously, by one or more ground-motives that are much less lofty than the Christian (or Hindu, or humanist) ground-motive?

Again, we must strongly emphasize that these questions must be sharply distinguished from the questions concerning true and false religion. These latter are questions that will be discussed below, in a Christian-philosophical context. However, they can never arise within the limited horizon of the empirical disciplines as such, no matter how the latter themselves are rooted in a transcendent-religious ground-motive. In anticipation, I give this example of what I am trying to say:

---

89. Allen and Spilka (1973).
90. See extensively, Levin (2001).

a person confessing the true, Christian religion may do so being driven by quite a false ground-motive (e.g., that of hedonism, or populism, or egotism). Conversely, a person confessing a false religion may do so with a basically upright and honest and devoted attitude.

2.7.2 Various Types of Religiosity

We have now arrived at a point where we can clearly distinguish between two forms of religiosity: (a) a form in which pistical beliefs and practices sprout (mainly) from a transcendent-religious ground-attitude (or, as Andree Troost liked to call it, *ethos*[91]) that corresponds to it, and (b) a form in which the heart is governed (to a large extent) by other transcendent-religious influences that do *not* correspond with the beliefs and practices mentioned.

The initial investigators who, each in their own way, were aware of these two different forms of religiosity—here formulated as a sharp contrast—were the German Neo-Marxist philosopher Theodor W. Adorno (d. 1969) and his collaborators in their sensational book *The Authoritarian Personality*.[92] We must also mention here the pioneering work by the American psychologist Gordon W. Allport (d. 1967), who at the same time tried to make a distinction between intrinsic and extrinsic religiosity, to which I will return in a moment. These and other authors[93] showed that, for some people, religion implies prejudice, intolerance, revenge, safety, and status; for others, it involves love, brotherhood, care for fellow-humans, fellowship with God (or the god/gods), and so on. I would express the matter as follows: this involves, first, the actual condition of the religious person's heart, that is, their *ethos*, and second, the extent to which, and the manner in which, this ethos comes to expression in the religion confessed, and the latter in turn in the religion practiced.

---

91. See Troost (1983).
92. Adorno et al. (1950).
93. Dittes (1969); Rokeach (1969); Allen and Spilka (1973).

An early attempt to discern between the various modern sociological views of religion was made by American psychologist of religion, Walter H. Clark (d. 1994).[94] By means of an inquiry among social scientists, he arrived at the following main distinctions within the views of religion.

(1) Religion is (a) an experience of the transcendent ("religious perception"), (b) the cognitive awareness of standing in relationship with the transcendent, and (c) a change of life, that is, of personality and behavior, brought about by (a) and (b).

(2) Religion is being directed toward the ultimate value of life, that which gives meaning to our entire existence. This, too, involves an experience of the transcendent, but emphasizes at the same time an ideological-theological elaboration of this experience of the transcendent.

(3) Religion is a totality of ethical values, which determine our behavior toward other people. This horizontalism, that is, the identification of religion and morality, must be distinguished from (1[c]) above: the moral change of life *caused* by religion.

From a Christian-philosophical standpoint, view (1) approximates most closely what I prefer to call religiosity, though with some nuance, explained below. There is also room for view (2), as long as the cognitive dimension of immanent-spiritive life[95] is viewed as remaining subordinate to the supratemporal-supramodal element of the relationship with, and experience of, the transcendent.

A well-known psychological distinction within religiosity is the one made by Gordon W. Allport, mentioned earlier.[96] It goes back to the difference between, on the one hand, a personally experience faith and, on the other hand, a religious (pistical) conventionalism, which is strongly authoritarian,

---

94. Clark (1958).
95. Cf. Ouweneel (1986, 232–39).
96. Allport (1950; 1954; 1963; 1966); Allport and Ross (1967).

heavily burdened with prejudices, and strongly ethnocentric. Allport spoke here of *intrinsic* and *extrinsic religiosity*, respectively. In this view, the latter is a religiosity on the outside, a matter of social status and self-interest, presumably just like the authoritarian-ethnocentric attitude is actually rooted in people's sensitively qualified needs for certainty and safety.[97] In the intrinsically religious person, it is not their own (sensitive, unarticulated) needs that are central, but certain ethical-religious values. This person is governed far less by (the values of) the group, and much more by the personal religious values of their own heart. One could say that the God (or god!) whom a person serves in their actions is also the true God (or god!) of their heart. (Notice: God or god; we are not distinguishing between true and false religion.)

Both the extrinsically religious person and the intrinsically religious person are ultimately dominated by the religious ground-attitude of their heart, that is, by their ethos. However, were we to use the Christian as an example, the intrinsically religious Christian is governed by a Christian-religious ethos, at least to some extent, for the influence of sin in the believer must never be disregarded. The extrinsically religious Christian, however, is largely or entirely in the grip of some idolatrous-religious ethos. In biblical terms, this means that the latter either has an unregenerated heart (and is thus a pseudo- or nominal Christian), or a regenerated heart that is strongly dominated by his sinful nature (cf., e.g., John 6:63; Rom. 8:4–14; Gal. 5:16–22; 1 Pet. 1:22–2:1).

2.7.3 Intrinsic and Extrinsic

The psychological differences between the extrinsically and the intrinsically religious person are highly interesting.[98] The former seems to be characterized by a certain self-importance, feelings of safety and certainty within the group (church, denomination, faith movement, sect, monastery, etc.), a rather

---
97. See extensively, Maslow (1954); Ouweneel (1986, §3.1.6).
98. See Tisdale (1966; 1967).

uncritical acceptance of certain beliefs, and a kind of timidity and inner uncertainty. This is precisely what Theodor Adorno and others have called the "authoritarian personality."[99] This is the person who strengthens their feeling of safety by looking down upon others not belonging to their group (ethnocentrism).

The interesting thing, however, is that it is far more difficult, if not impossible, to supply a personality description of the intrinsically religious person. This is because this person experiences their religion *with their heart*, and subordinates all needs and values in life to this. Think of the reasons why people come to church. Some come to praise and glorify God, and to seek his blessing. Others are focused on what they can "get out of it," as the saying goes—they attempt to exert authority over religion, to profit from it, instead of serving it.[100]

I would formulate the distinctions found so far in the following (Dooyeweerdian) way: the religious *actions* of the extrinsically religious Christian are indeed pistically qualified but intertwined with *actions* that, in contrast with those of the intrinsically religious person, are pistical only to a small extent; for the rest they are particularly sensitively, logically, socially, aesthetically, or morally qualified. This is so because one or more idolatrously absolutized aspects of immanent reality have obtained a religious grip on the heart. Intrinsically religious people have the greatest esteem for values such as redemption, forgiveness, equality, love, and compassion, and extrinsically religious people for values such as a comfortable life, pleasure, ambition, achievement, inner harmony, social recognition, ability, and independence.[101] Intrinsic religiosity is linked more with the experiential dimension in religiosity, and extrinsic religiosity more with the dimensions in religiosity of ideology, ritual, and self-interest.[102]

---

99. Adorno et al. (1950).
100. Cf. Allport and Ross (1967, 434).
101. Cf. Tate and Miller (1971).
102. Cf. Glock (1965).

The Science of Religion

Summarizing, we may conclude that the intrinsically religious person is characterized by pistical values in the sense that htheiris life and ethos are governed by the relationship with the *transcendent* (whether the God of the Bible, or idolatrous powers). In contrast with this, the pistical orientation of the extrinsically religious person is especially *immanent* in nature: that person is governed by logical (intellectual), social, aesthetic, ethical, and other interests. Please note again that there are intrinsically *and* extrinsically religious Christians, and there are extrinsically *and* intrinsically religious Muslims, Hindus, and Buddhists.

2.8 Elements of Religiosity
2.8.1 Intrinsic Religiosity

As we saw, in religiosity we first discern a transcendent dimension: the inner drive of the human I-ness as the (positive or negative) response to God's self-revelation. These last words are vital, though lacking in almost all publications in the field of the science of religion because of a mistaken idea of neutrality and objectivity. The transcendent I-ness directs itself to the true *or* pretended Origin of all immanent reality. The true Origin is known only through God's self-revelation, and each idea concerning the pretended Origin is only living parasitically on this divine self-revelation. To me, excluding the notion of revelation is like studying the visual arts while excluding visibility.

Secondly, we discern many immanent elements, of which, in the light of the current psychology of religion, I believe the following to be the most relevant. First of all,

1. *Intrinsic religiosity*, that is, *piety*: in the intertwining of pistical actions with many kinds of spiritive acts,[103] pistical acts are first and foremost. All other acts, all dispositions, all sectors of life, are subordinate to this pistical ground-attitude (the *ethos*), and have been brought into harmony with it.

---
103. Notice the difference between "actions" (deeds, activities) and "acts" (spiritive considerations, inventions, decisions, etc.).

Special features:

1.1   *Pistical acts:*

1.1.1 A *perceptive* awareness of God or the divine, rooted in the heart and the (true or pretended) divine revelation. [104]

1.1.2 An affectively "charging" of this pistical awareness, be it in the sense of euphoria, joy, elevation, harmony, peace, emotion, or of respect, fear, awe, or a mixture, depending on how one knows God (or god) and of the momentaneous attitude of the heart. Here, the pistical experience is intertwined with *sensitive* emotions.

1.1.3 A *cognitive* recognition and knowledge of what one has experienced of God (or god). Here, the pistical experience is intertwined with *spiritive* considerations. Part of the latter is the creative way of dealing with what one has experienced of God (or god), and the decisions that may be the effect of this, both in practical life and in theology.

Generally speaking, we might argue that perception plus affection, but without much cognition, may lead to mysticism; and cognition without much perception and affection may lead to dogmatism.[105]

1.2   *Pistical dispositions:*

1.2.1 Somewhat authoritarian ("authoritarian" here in the sense of an inclination to submission, to a rigid conventionality, a law-and-order mentality, legalism, dogmatism).

1.2.2 Somewhat ethnocentric ("ethnocentrism" here in the sense of a superiority feeling with respect to other groups, which allegedly are not inspired by a true religious conviction; strongly related to the concept of sectarianism[106]).

1.2.3 Deeply convinced of one's own beliefs, but flexible

---

104. More precisely (in Dooyeweerdian terminology): we are dealing here with perceptive retrocipations within the pistical modality; cf. Ouweneel (1986) for this terminology.
105. Cf. Peterson et al. (1991, chapter 2).
106. Cf. *EDR* 7:chapters 13–14.

and tolerant toward those of others.

1.2.4 A mentally healthy attitude of life.

2.8.2 Other Features

2. *Committed religious cognition.* This type of committed religiosity has been contrasted by American scholars Russell O. Allen and Bernard Spilka with the consensual (conformist) type of religious cognition.[107] In the committed type, faith conviction plays the central role in all aspects of daily life. It is freely confessed to people of other convictions, but not in a rigid, dogmatic way. The believer (whether in the true or the false religion) is open to correction in all kinds of details in his conviction. They are not afraid of confrontation and of critical self-evaluation. Their beliefs are clearly coherent, carefully thought through, thoroughly differentiated, not limited to some practical notions but founded upon broader ground-convictions.

3. The pious person scores high in *vertical religiosity*, distinguished by American scholar James D. Davidson from *horizontal religiosity* (see 4. below).[108] For Christians, this means that they have a profound faith in the God of the Bible, a living fellowship with him in Bible reading, prayer, and worship, a devotedness to doing his will, and the certain hope of the eternal bliss with him. With somewhat different words, we can say the same of the pious person in other religions, for again, all these distinctions do not discriminate between true and false religion but are genuine features of religiosity in general.

4. The pious person scores high in *horizontal religiosity*. This involves a deep desire to seek what is good for one's fellow-humans, to show them all love and compassion, and to express this in honesty, sincerity, respect, compassion, meekness, humility, support, comfort, encouragement, and so on (of course, with all the weaknesses and failures that charac-

---

107. Allen and Spilka (1973).
108. Davidson (1972a–c)

terize *all* people).

2.8.3 Three Dimensions

According to a classification by Laurence B. Brown and Joseph P. Forgas,[109] the pious person possesses

(a) more *individual* orientations (linked with notions such as inner peace, faith, personal goodness, a purpose of life, experiences with God (or god[s]) than *institutional* ones (linked with notions such as church, synagogue, mosque, temple, authority, spiritual leaders, dogmas, rituals, and holy books);

(b) more *positive* evaluations (linked with notions such as a purpose of life, brotherhood, the personal and the immediate) than *negative* ones (linked with notions such as revenge, paganism, myth, ritual, the legalistic, and the dogmatic);

(c) more directed toward the *religiously* intangible (such as life after death, mystery, God/god as a person, miracles, the upper-worldly, the transcendent, and the mystical) than toward the *religiously* [read, pistically] *tangible* (such as institutions, official authorities, attendance of church, synagogue, mosque, or temple, the inner-worldly).

We can imagine these three dimensions as perpendicular in relation to each other, so that they form a cube, and the categories are divided over eight sectors, which explains the partial overlap. In a similar way, Marie Cornwall and others discerned six dimensions of religiosity, based on three general components—a cognitive (religious faith), an affective (commitment), and a behavioral—and two modes of religiosity: personal and institutional.[110]

These are just a few of the many ways of characterizing religiosity in terms of its very complex manner of functioning. The two most important points to keep in mind are the following:

(1) All of these characterizations describe various forms of

---

109. Brown and Forgas (1980).
110. Cornwall et al. (1980).

immanent religiosity, not of *transcendent religion*: the existential relationship between God (or gods) and a person's heart.

(2) They describe immanent religiosity in general, without being able to distinguish between true and false religion, or the service of the true God and of the gods (idols, ideologies).

In order to understand these two points, investigations in the field of the psychology of religion will not help us any further. What we need is a philosophical idea of the human heart (or, the soul/spirit, or the I-ness),[111] as well as of its transcendent-religious relationship of dependence with its divine Origin. Such an idea can be formed only pre-theoretically, in the light of God's self-revelation.

---

111. See *EDR* 3:§6.4; Ouweneel (2014a; 2014b; 2015).

Chapter 3
Apologetics and the Theistic Proofs

> *[I]n your hearts honor Christ the Lord as holy,*
> *always being prepared to make a defense*
> *to anyone who asks you for a reason*
> *for the hope that is in you;*
> *yet do it with gentleness and respect.*
>
> 1 Peter 3:15

3.1 Theology Proper and Apologetics
3.1.1 Types of Apologetics

THEOLOGY HAS BEEN NEATLY DIVIDED into compartments, so that, for instance, systematic theology is a discipline different from the science of religion and from apologetics. As a consequence, theology proper deals with the biblical doctrine of God, but not with the prior question of God's existence.[1] This matter is left to the science of religion, or to apologetics. However, in a broader presentation of the doctrine of God like we are offering, some remarks concerning this matter are desirable: How can we make the existence of God acceptable to modern humanity?[2]

As with all sciences, apologetics is a logical-analytically qualified human enterprise. It involves designing rational

---
1. Cf. Ott (1972, 93).
2. Cf. Ouweneel (1991a; 2005).

arguments for the various elements of Christian faith over against those who are of a different opinion, and refuting arguments that have been adduced against it. As with all science, including the other disciplines within theology, apologetics by nature (whether this is realized or not) is rooted in a philosophical view of reality and knowledge (ontology or cosmology and epistemology, respectively). As with other theological sciences, apologetics is not always rooted in a philosophical cosmology and epistemology that are congenial with it, that is, that are rooted in Scriptural thinking to the same extent that apologetics itself wishes to be, and pretends to be. Unconsciously and unintentionally, many apologists have worked within a philosophical framework that is plagued by three dangers: biblicism, scholasticism, and/or humanism. This can be clearly seen in the various types of apologetics that may be discerned in the history of Christian thought.

(1) The *rational* types, such as (a) scholasticism's *natural theology* with its proofs for the existence of God (see next section), and (b) so-called *apriorism* or *presuppositionalism*, which ties in with the rational presuppositions that every human is supposed to maintain.[3] This is the apologetic approach of, for instance, American thinkers Francis A. Schaeffer (d. 1984),[4] Gordon H. Clark (d. 1985), and Cornelius Van Til (d. 1987).[5] All these types of rational — if not rationalistic — apologetics make use of intelligent, powerful arguments that appeal to the listener's common sense in order to make the truth of Christian faith acceptable.

(2) The *rational-empirical* types, that is, a defense of the Christian faith through an appeal to empirical facts, such as the biblical miracles that people experienced, biblical proph-

---

3. On this see, e.g., Van Huyssteen (1997); Shults (1999); Thiel (2000); Grenz and Franke (2001).
4. See the critical analysis of Schaeffer's apologetics by Thomas V. Morris (1976); also cf. Ouweneel (1987a).
5. Cf. the refutation by Dooyeweerd (1971).

ecies literally and accurately fulfilled, the historical trustworthiness of the Bible, and so on. This kind of apologetics is called rational-empirical because it appeals to reason, too. No modern people ever saw the biblical miracles or the fulfillment of certain biblical prophecies. Therefore, as with the historical trustworthiness of the Bible, these matters must first be made logically acceptable, and thus they are in fact primarily logical arguments. Even where biblical miracles are experienced today, especially in miraculous healings, it still must be made logically acceptable *that* (a) we are dealing with genuine (i.e., not naturally explicable) miracles, and (b) they are same in nature and origin as the biblical miracles. And where today the fulfillment of a biblical prophecy is observed — many Jews and Christians view the foundation of the state of Israel in 1948 as such a fulfillment (or at least the beginning of it)[6] — the claim must still be logically supported that the events involved are indeed related to prophecies being adduced for them.

(3) The *irrational-empirical* types, such as the typically irrationalist approach of German theologian Friedrich Schleiermacher or Danish philosopher Søren Kierkegaard (d. 1855), and of twentieth-century Christian existentialism, as well as the approach of the pietistic Methodist and hyper-Calvinist appeal to conversion stories. They attempt to make the Christian faith plausible by appealing to (irrational) emotions and sentiments of people through a highly emotion-filled description of religious phenomena such as (alleged) conversions, faith experiences, mystical ecstasies, and so on. Here, too, the logical element is present (notice the term "plausible"), for it must be logically argued that such religious phenomena indeed have transcendent content, and cannot be explained (away) in a simple psychological manner.

Again, on the basis of the evidence being supplied, the listener is challenged here to reach the logical conclusion

---

6. See *EDR* 10:chapters 5 and 7.

that Christianity is true. Ultimately, therefore, all apologetic arguments are *logical-rational* arguments; even an irrational apologetics remains apo-*logetics* (cf. the Gk. root *logos*). In principle, nothing is wrong with this; compare 1 Peter 3:15, "In your hearts honor Christ the Lord as holy, always being prepared to make a defense [Gk. *apologia*] to anyone who asks you for a reason [Gk. *logos*] for the hope that is in you." At the same time, we always keep in mind that true faith is rooted in the (supra-logical!) *heart* being touched by the Holy Spirit—although it is sure that logical arguments can be used in this process: "Now when they heard this they were cut to the *heart*, and said to Peter and the rest of the apostles, 'Brothers, what shall we do?'" (Acts 2:37). "The Lord opened her *heart* to pay attention to what was said by Paul" (16:14). "If you confess with your mouth that Jesus is Lord and believe in your heart that God raised him from the dead, you will be saved. For with the heart one believes and is justified, and with the mouth one confesses and is saved" (Rom. 10:9–10).

3.1.2 Problems in Apologetics

Before we consider apologetic arguments, let us notice that many apologetic theologians were first of all preachers and evangelists, often with an enormous impact, a strong prophetic radiance, a biblical charisma, which apparently was used by God to lead many to accept the Christian faith. However, as soon as they wished to practice apologetics in the sense of a scientific enterprise, they were often on shaky footing. And thus they must be scientifically evaluated, no matter how successful they may seem to have been in preaching the gospel. A good evangelist may be a bad apologist (and *vice versa*).

Let me briefly mention some of the usual misunderstandings.

(a) We witness the failure to discern between a *contradictory* pair of judgments (in which there is always one that is true and one that is false; A and non-A) and a *contrary* pair of judgments (in which both judgments cannot be true, but both can certainly be false: in addition to A and B, C or D is possible). Thus, in the arena of apologetics, Christian presuppositions and similar non-Christian presuppositions are usually contrary, not contradictory, pairs of judgments. That is, arguments against certain non-Christian presuppositions may be very correct and efficient, but by itself this does not prove that the parallel Christian presuppositions are true. Perhaps it can be made plausible that the latter are better (more plausible), but this is very different from true. The truth of Christianity is often powerfully defended; but this power often lies more in the *believing heart* of the apologist than in the power of their *logical arguments*. Strictly logically speaking, many apologetic arguments show only that Christianity is a possible, or even excellent, or even the best alternative, without thereby proving that it is the only, or the correct, alternative.

(b) The presuppositions of the opponent who must be convinced of the Christian faith are often taken too much in the logical-rational sense, as arguments that can and must be refuted. In this way, people neglect the sensitive, cultural-historical, social, aesthetic, moral, and pistical elements that are of equal or surpassing importance for the opponent. Worse still is that these presuppositions are also heavily theoreticalized. Thus, Francis A. Schaeffer described a presupposition as a belief or theory that is accepted before the next step in logic is developed, and as a preceding postulate that influences, consciously or unconsciously, the way a person argues.[7] Such use of terms like "theory," "logic," "postulate," and "arguing" is purely rationalistic in the sense that they reduce a person's most profound beliefs to a logical-analytical system, which could and should be tested in the same way a scientific hypothesis is verified or falsified. In other words, the *heart's* faith conviction is tested regarding its logical capacity to explain all the data of human reason and experience in an adequate and coherent way.

---

7. Schaeffer (1968, 179).

Presuppositionalists seem to forget—*not* in their practical evangelizing but certainly in their own rationalistic analysis of their evangelizing—that what keeps a person from accepting the Christian faith is not only having wrong presuppositions but also having all kinds of non-logical predispositions. Along with presuppositions, these are governed by the sinful, apostate human heart, which by nature hates God's truth, and can see the truth only if this heart is enlightened by the Holy Spirit. As Andree Troost put it, traditional apologetics seems to consist in a concession to outsiders who, with respect to the deep, existential *certainty* that people desire in their lives, prefer to seek it in a logical and scientific certainty rather than in the unique, specific certainty of *faith*.[8]

(c) There is also the danger that both the Bible and Christianity themselves are reduced to a logical-rational system. It is purely rationalistic to view Scripture as a system of verbal propositions, of intellectual answers to logical questions, and thereby reducing it to its logical-analytical modality. The logical aspect of Scripture is only one of many aspects, all of which converge into the *supra*-logical Word of God.[9] I recall how, on one occasion (years ago), after Francis Schaeffer and I (and a third person) had prayed together, he told me, "We have the better system." In my youthful pedantry, I could not help responding, "We have the better Person." To me, this was not hair-splitting but essential, as it still is today.

3.1.3 The Central Problem

The central problem of all apologetics, evident in the frequent misunderstandings just mentioned, can be described as follows. Through strictly logical arguments, no matter how brilliant, no person will ever be led to accept the Christian faith in their heart. Nobody becomes a Christian purely on the basis of (a) their common sense, (b) their observation of solid facts, or (c) the faith experiences of others. What must be touched is

---

8. Troost (2005, 57 note 22).
9. See *EDR* 11:187–191 passim; see Vol. I/1, chapter 5 in this series.

not (only) their *intellect* but (primarily) their *heart* (which does not exclude reason as one of its immanent functions). And this can be the fruit only of the operation of God's Word under the guidance of the Holy Spirit. This work does not occur primarily in the arena of reason, perception, or feeling, but in the regenerate heart, and as it proceeds only from there, the Word and Spirit enlighten all immanent functions, such as reason, perception, and feeling (the logical, perceptive, and sensitive modalities, respectively). Yet, the entire idea of an apologetics is precisely rooted in supplying logical arguments, which appeal to the human logical-analytical ability of meaningful distinction.

Here lies the internal conflict of apologetics, which can be scientifically solved only through a thorough philosophical-anthropological analysis of the relationship between the heart—to which the gospel is directed, and in which, through the Spirit, faith is brought about—and logical reason.[10] This is hardly an easy task, because Western thinkers are working from a (thinking!) tradition that has always placed enormous emphasis on the significance of logical reason (viewing persons largely as rational beings), and has reduced the human heart (in the metaphorical sense) merely to the seat of feeling. This tradition is rooted in medieval scholasticism; or perhaps we should say, in the strongly Greek-oriented thought of the early Christian Apologists. As a consequence of this tradition, apologists such as the British C. S. Lewis and the American Francis Schaeffer—to mention two of the best known from the twentieth century—believed they could design a Christian apologetic in which each Christian truth could be logically deduced from the facts, or at least could be defended in a rational and convincing way. Here, the Christian faith is made to depend largely upon the logical reliability of the underlying arguments.

We must *add* here, though, that we do not make any

---

10. Cf. *EDR* 3:chapter 6.

progress, in rejecting this approach, if we follow the equally mistaken method opposed to it, viz., irrationally making the Christian faith to depend upon pious sentiments (hyper-Calvinism), mystical experiences, and so on. The pendulum that swings between feeling and reason can never produce any solution as long as feeling and reason are not *equally* understood to be immanent-modal functions of the existential-supramodal human heart in its full transcendent-religious meaning. To put it another way: the maxim of Augustine, *crede ut intelligas* ("believe so that you may understand"),[11] should be restored to prominence. This should be done in such a way that the *credo* is understood as a matter of the transcendent heart, and the *intelligas* as a matter of one of the immanent-modal functions of this heart, namely, reason.

3.1.4 Dooyeweerdian Anthropology

It has been the merit of Herman Dooyeweerd that he has clearly brought these things to light, and in this way has theoretically shown the religious meaning of all rational and all theoretical thought.[12] Reason, feeling, and perception must not be absolutized, nor can they be reduced to each other. They are only functions, ways of functioning, expressions of the human heart in its biblical sense. This is the heart as the ultimate, transcendent-religious concentration point of human existence, directed toward the (true or pretended) divine Origin of humanity, in which all functions of human immanent existence converge, and from which they issue (cf. the same in biblical language: "Keep thy heart with all diligence; for out of it are the issues of life," Prov. 4:23 KJV).

It is difficult to explain to (post)modern people the significance of such essential matters. Massive numbers of (post)modern people—orthodox, liberal, humanistic—are paying homage to the idol of the alleged separation between reason

---

11. Tract. Evang. Joh. 29.6; Anselm of Canterbury rendered it as *credo ut intelligam* ("I believe so that I may understand"; Proslogion 1)
12. See especially his standard work: Dooyeweerd, *NC*.

(science) and faith. They no longer grasp that a person's faith, religion, or (ultimately religious) worldview encompasses their entire life, including their scientific (or political, or economical or artistic, etc.) activities. Not for one moment does a person, even an atheist, cease being a religious being (i.e., directed toward the ultimate [true or pretended] ground of his/her existence), whether he/she functions as a husband/wife, a parent, a church member, a citizen, a consumer, a road user, a politician, an artist, a business person, or a scientist. Applied to apologetics, this means that the defense of the faith is not just a matter of logic but first and foremost an existential matter, a matter of the *ultimate commitment* of a person's heart.[13]

This does not imply that this heart could ever be severed from reason. On the contrary, each conviction of the heart can be expressed to a certain extent in pistical beliefs, which are always intertwined with logical-analytical acts. In this way, a believer can *logically* account to a certain extent for the *supra*-logical convictions of his heart. This is a partial vindication of apologetics, which can be viewed as the study and elaboration of these logical acts. But in doing so, we must maintain that the heart logically precedes reason. Thus, all apologetics is rooted in a certain religious ground-conviction, which comes to expression in feelings and considerations, in sentiment and reason, both in our everyday practical reason and in our theoretical-scientific reason.

3.2 Natural Theology and Its Problems
3.2.1 Thomism

When speaking of the relationships between the doctrine of God and the other disciplines within theology, we cannot ignore so-called "natural theology." On the contrary, medieval natural theology claimed to be able to prove the existence of God, thus supplying us with a solid foundation for theology proper. In Volume I/1 of this series, I discussed the nature of natural theology and its false claims, especially those based in

---

13. Cf. Heyns (1988, 39).

Romans 1.[14] Here is a brief summary of the arguments.

Natural theology is a theology that ostensibly can be scientifically proven to each thinking person. It thus appeals to nature, which refers here to autonomous human reason, without presupposing (supernatural) faith.[15] This theology believes in particular that it can prove the existence of God by purely rational arguments. According to the Thomists, human reason was not entirely corrupted by the Fall. Thus, it would still possess a relative autonomy in the domain of nature, to be able to deduce by its own light natural truths from the created reality. However, reason supposedly is not able to prove *super*natural truths, such as the nature of God, the Trinity, the incarnation, the resurrection, redemption, or the Last Judgment.

The nature–grace dualism can be observed especially in Roman Catholicism, where the First Vatican Council in 1870 accepted the dual order of knowledge in the Thomistic sense: knowledge through reason and knowledge through faith. It pronounced an *anathema* ("be cursed!") upon all those who deny that the one true God can be known with certainty from creation by the natural light of human reason. In the oath against the errors of modernism, instituted in 1910, the pope declared that this means that God's existence can be proven with certainty from the visible things, namely, as a cause can be demonstrated from its consequences.[16] German cardinal Walter Kasper mentioned this oath,[17] which clearly seems to reflect the Council's intentions. Yet, he suggested that the Council did not mean to say that "one can prove God by the light of natural reason" (italics added), or "whether such a natural knowledge actually exists."[18] This is not very convincing; it cannot be reasonably denied that the Council fully

---

14. Vol. I/1, chapter 2 in this series; also see *EDR* 12:§ 9.5.
15. See extensively, Berkouwer (1951, 47–68).
16. See extensively, Wentsel (1970).
17. Kasper (1983, 339).
18. Ibid., 69.

maintained natural theology. Thus, recently several theistic proofs have been extensively defended again by the Jesuit philosopher Walter Brugger (d. 1990), though with many nuances.[19]

3.2.2 Reformational Thought

This nature–grace dualism can also be encountered at many places in traditional Reformational theology. Traces of natural theology are found with Martin Luther, Philip Melanchthon, and John Calvin.[20] In early Protestant orthodoxy, natural theology was generally accepted; Reformed examples were German theologian Johann Heinrich Alsted (d. 1638), German-Dutch theologian Nicolaus Arnoldi (d. 1680), and Dutch theologian Johannes à Marck (d. 1731).[21] In Enlightenment theology, natural theology was popular because it attributed a high position to natural reason. However, this lasted only until German philosopher Immanuel Kant (d. 1804), who extensively and efficiently rebutted the so-called proofs for God's existence.[22]

Dutch theologian of Reformed conviction, Abraham Kuyper (d. 1920), fully accepted the notion of a natural theology,[23] and congenial thinker Herman Bavinck (d. 1921) clearly left some room for it.[24] However, Reformational philosophers Herman Dooyeweerd and Dirk H. Th. Vollenhoven (d. 1978), though theologically congenial with Kuyper and Bavinck, fully rejected this separation between nature and grace, and thus also between a natural and a supernatural theology, as being entirely against the spirit of Scripture. Reformational philosophy supplied a brilliant answer to the following question: If the Fall *totally* corrupted humanity, including human reason, how can this reason still work so excellently in brilliant,

---

19. Brugger (1979, 43–203).
20. Weber (1981, 221); P. Barth (1935).
21. Van Genderen (2008, 126–29).
22. See Bavinck (*RD* 2:79).
23. Kuyper (*EHG* 2:253–59).
24. Bavinck (*RD* 2:81–91).

though unregenerate thinkers? The answer is this: as to its (creational) *structure*, human reason may still be brilliant, yet it is not autonomous but depends on the spiritual (apostate *or* biblical) attitude of the heart, from where all immanent functions issue, including the logical thinking function. As to its *direction*,[25] reason in unregenerate humans is totally corrupt because of their corrupted hearts. Human reason darkened by sin is not at all able to prove the existence of God from creational reality through purely rational arguments.

Here lies the answer as to whether reason was affected by the Fall, totally or only partially. As to its *structure*, reason was not necessarily affected; through the Fall, humans did not necessarily become less intelligent (although in itself this is quite possible). However, the Fall did fundamentally and radically corrupt the *direction* of the human heart.

Interestingly, natural theology can be defended equally well in both a traditionally orthodox and a liberal modernist theology. Thus, Harry Kuitert (d. 2017), a Dutch theologian with Reformed roots, extensively developed the idea of religion as *the* presupposition of theology, and accounted for his idea of religion in a purely phenomenal and rational way.[26] Humans are described as beings that form for themselves an image (representation) of reality in which they attribute meaning to their environment. This attribution necessarily implies an ultimate "meaning-assigning totality," without which human life is impossible, and which is viewed as being the consequence of that power that we call God. Kuitert himself explicitly referred to this interpretation as natural theology, and did not see anything wrong in it.[27] This interpretation is a striking example of how people, in a scholastic or a humanistic manner, can deduce the notion of God without any reference to the Fall (through which the human awareness of God is darkened, Rom. 1:21), or to regeneration and

---

25. Regarding the relationship between structure and direction, see note 62.
26. Kuitert (1993, 42–65).
27. Ibid., 79.

enlightenment by the Spirit (through which people can solely have true knowledge of God) — to say nothing of any reference to *revelation*. Kuitert's friend, Roman Catholic theologian Edward Schillebeeckx (d. 2009), wondered in what respect theology as Kuitert saw it was anything other than philosophy of religion, and what room Kuitert still had for any "revelational offer" on behalf of God.[28]

3.2.3   Romans 1

Bible passages that often have been used as proof texts, not only for a natural or creational revelation[29] but also for a natural theology, are Acts 14:15-17; 17:26-28 and Romans 1:19-21; 2:14-16.[30] Especially Romans 1:19-21 has often been viewed as an undeniable proof for the existence of natural theology.[31] However, the passage does not at all teach that humans are able to deduce through natural reason the existence of God from his creational works. On the contrary, the chapter speaks of human corruption and God's wrath with regard to this (cf. vv. 18-19) in such a clear and radical manner that no basis at all can be found here for the assumption of autonomous, non-sinful reason. Humans indeed do know God here (v. 21) but not through the natural light of reason; nevertheless they possess this knowledge in the greatest *foolishness* (v. 22). The images that the pagan has here of God are not those of the scholastic *prima causa* ("first cause"), or the *primum movens* ("first mover"), but "images resembling mortal man and birds and animals and creeping things" (v. 23). The text does speak of a "clear perceiving" (v. 20, Gk. *nooumena kathoratai*; Darby: "perceived, being apprehended by the mind [Gk. *nous*]"), but the entire context makes very obvious how *corrupted* this mind is. To be sure, God's revelation in his works has become too overwhelming for unregenerated

---

28. Schillebeeckx (1989, 222, 229).
29. For a discussion of these phrases, see Vol. I/1, chapter 2 in this series.
30. Cf. Weber (1981, 231–35); Buri (1956, 226–29).
31. Cf. Berkouwer (1951, chapter 4); Henry (1976a, 83–90, 104–23); Pannenberg (1988, 121).

human beings to miss; they cannot escape God's "eternal power and divine nature" (v. 20). However, through the corruption of their hearts, which is manifested in all the immanent functions of their heart, including the logical and the pistical functions, people's sole response is apostasy. They use this knowledge of God of theirs to construct idols.

Actually, Romans 1:20 says that what is perceived from God's works is not his *existence* but rather his "eternal power and divine nature." These perceived qualities of the divine presuppose his existence. People have a "natural knowledge of God," or, as John Calvin called it, a "sense/awareness of the divine" (Lat. *sensus divinitatis*) or "the seed of religion"(Lat. *semen religionis*).[32] It seems justified to speak here of a "knowledge" of God since the term "conscience" (Gk. *syneidēsis*, from *syn-oida*), mentioned in Romans 2:15, does entail a knowing (Gk. *oida*), and 1:21–23 implies that real knowledge of God was changed into idolatry. That is, in their hearts humans know of God's existence, and because of this awareness they recognize in God's works his eternal power and divine nature. However, this knowledge is subsequently manifested in all the degeneration of paganism with its manifold idolatry. Here, there is no autonomous-rational organ for knowing God that is unaffected by sin, but only an inescapable impression, evoked by the intrusion of the natural revelation into people's hearts. In Romans 1, it is not the argumentation of some natural theology but the idolatry existing in this world that constitutes the proof for a certain *sensus divinitatis*.

Andree Troost pointed to the remarkable word "yet" (Gk. *kai ge*; KJV: "though") in Acts 17:27, ". . . that they should seek God, and perhaps feel their way toward him and find him. Yet he is actually not far from each one of us."[33] Why seek God, if he is not far from each of us, and if "in him we live" (v. 28)? Why this endless groping by all the nations throughout the ages? Why always yearning, and especially al-

---
32. *Institutes* 1.3.1; cf. 1.3.3 and 1.4.1; cf. Heyns (1988, 52–54).
33. Troost (1978, 112).

ways missing and muffing? The answer lies in the Fall, which elicited both the wrath of God and the darkness of the human heart (Rom. 1:18, 21). Instead of people finding God, and in that way re-finding themselves, as befits them *by nature*, their groping becomes missing, their seeking a not finding, their autonomy as equally tragic as ridiculous losing themselves. Their nature has become unnatural because their thoughts — the greatness of autonomous humanity! — have become futile, and their foolish hearts became darkened (Rom. 1:21).

3.3 An Evangelical Approach
3.3.1 Norman L. Geisler

Another example of modern natural theology, this time in Evangelical circles, is the work by American theologian Norman L. Geisler in the philosophy of religion, which largely overlaps with apologetics.[34] If I am not mistaken, Geisler himself does not use the term "natural theology." However, his work certainly belongs to this category because of his overestimation of the power of logical arguments, and his underestimation of the significance of the Fall and of the need for the Spirit's enlightenment. I hasten to add that these truths are definitely at the forefront of Geisler's Evangelical thinking. However, this does not change the fact that, to a large extent, his theology is in the grip of rationalism and scientism; elsewhere, I have pointed this out several times.[35] It is evident, for instance, from the extensive attention that he gives to rational arguments for the existence of God.[36]

In the introduction to Part II of his book,[37] Geisler tried to refute modern objections to the theistic proofs, namely, the objections that these alleged proofs are (a) not psychologically convincing, (b) logically invalid, (c) epistemologically defective, (d) ontologically inadequate, and (e) axiologically

---
34. Geisler (1974).
35. See *EDR* 11:325–29; 2014b.
36. Geisler (1974, 87–226, which amounts to one third of his book).
37. Ibid., 87–103.

mistaken. Geisler acknowledged some value in these objections, yet completely rejected them as a retreat into fideism,[38] which he seems to think is a form of irrationalism. Clearly, rationalists often defend themselves by accusing their opponents of irrationalism. My calling Geisler a rationalist might be enough for him to call me an *irr*ationalist. This objection does not hold water because it is the very aim of my arguments to *overcome* the age-old dilemma of choosing between feeling (the irrational) and intellect (the rational). I try to do this through an anthropological reflection (in the spirit of Reformational philosophy) upon humans in their basic-religious transcendence, in which feeling and intellect converge, and at the same time surpass all immanent functioning.

As long as Geisler does not supply an anthropological foundation for his epistemology, I must call his system rationalistic. As long as he claims that philosophical underpinning of beliefs is essential for modern humanity,[39] I call his system scientistic rationalistic. Philosophy, or theoretical thought in general, may be helpful, but they cannot be essential for modern people; only regeneration and the enlightenment by the Holy Spirit can be termed essential.

Yet, Geisler is certainly not a full-fledged adherent of natural theology. Nowhere does he claim that theistic proofs inevitably and undeniably demonstrate that God exists. He does claim that religious experience reveals the human need for God, and if reason can help to assure people that there is a God to fill this need, all the better. He adds that, if the theistic arguments turn out to be unreasonable, it is still possible that there is a God, but so far no good reasons to believe in God's existence have been supplied.[40]

To a certain extent I can agree with this. That is to say — in my terms — belief in God's existence is in itself necessarily of a supra-logical, namely, transcendent-religious character;

---
38. Ibid., 93.
39. Ibid., 93.
40. Ibid., 102.

in simple words, it is a matter of the heart. However, *if enlightened by the Holy Spirit*, reason can rationally account for this faith *a posteriori*. It can rationally formulate the beliefs of the person involved, and can even formulate the plausibility of these beliefs, but only within the religious context just described. Logical arguments, whether by theists or by their opponents, never function outside this religious context, or this hermeneutical circle.[41] I do appreciate that Geisler speaks carefully of a rational help merely to "assure" to people that their faith is plausible. However, it is basically incorrect to say that, if the theistic arguments turn out to be unreasonable, no good reasons to believe in God's existence would have been supplied. This would imply that only theistic arguments supply good reasons to believe in God's existence. If I may quote Blaise Pascal here again (§2.6.3): the heart can have many other, and many more, good reasons to believe in God than just reason alone.

In my view, Geisler expressed himself in a more satisfactory way when he said that even without rational proofs belief in the "God of theism" can be credible and plausible,[42] even though I myself would never use a scientistic term such as "theism" in this context. There is no such thing as the "God of theism"; we are instead dealing with the God of the Bible, who far surpasses as human "-isms," including theism. This is not hair-splitting or nit-picking; this claim is essential in the face of the comprehensive plague infecting Western thought, namely, rationalistic scientism, which is clearly present in an expression like the "God of theism."

3.3.2 Teleology, Ethics, Ontology

In accordance with tradition, Geisler distinguished between teleological, moral, ontological, and cosmological arguments for the existence of God.[43] Let us look at them briefly.

---

41. See *EDR* 11:41–44; 2014b.
42. Geisler (1974, 163).
43. Ibid., 104–226. Pailin (1986, chapter 8) distinguished eight theistic proofs:

(a) *Teleological arguments.* The term "teleology" comes from the Greek word *telos*, "goal, purpose." These arguments are based on the apparent design that can be found in the world, and imply that this design furnishes evidence for an intelligent Builder of the universe. Geisler discussed a number of writers, especially Scottish philosopher David Hume (d. 1776), and concluded that the teleological argument as such fails as a demonstrable proof for an absolutely perfect God.[44] One reason for this is that no teleological argument can ever exclude with any certainty the possibility of coincidence. However, the main reason for this failure is that the teleological argument is rooted in the cosmological argument, which claims that there must be a *cause* for the design in the world.[45] If, on the contrary, there is not necessarily a cause of, or a reason for, the order in the world, the alleged design could simply be imaginary or coincidental. Thus, this argument depends on the cosmological argument (see §3.3.3).[46]

(b) *Moral arguments.* These arguments are based upon the apparent moral law that obtains in this world, and involve the claim that this moral law points to a moral Law-Giver. Again, Geisler, discussed a number of writers, especially German philosopher Immanuel Kant (d. 1804) and British apologist C. S. Lewis (d. 1963), and concluded that these moral arguments for the existence of God are not decisive either. This is because the moral law could be merely a psychological projection or a social convention; or there might be a moral law but without a Moral Law-Giver behind it. That is, our universe could possess an objective moral standard (apart from God) to which, if there were a God, the latter does not

---

the cosmological, the teleological, the theological, the moral, the experiential, the existential, the ontological, and the cumulative argument. See also Peterson et al. (1991, chapter 5).
44. Geisler (1974, 116).
45. Ibid., 116–17).
46. See more extensively, Ouweneel (2005, chapters 5 and 6) on theistic proofs in general.

answer.[47] The moral arguments are weak in particular because they, too, depend on a presupposition derived from the cosmological argument, namely, that laws demand causes or explanations.[48] Thus, this argument depends on the cosmological argument as well (see §3.3.3). Geisler did emphasize, though, that a definitive moral *refutation* of the existence of God has not been furnished either.

(c) *Ontological arguments.* These arguments are not based upon empirical experience, as are the previous ones, but on pure reason. The essence of them is that the existence of God is viewed as a necessity on the basis of certain features of a concept, here the concept of God. Here too, Geisler, discussed a number of writers, especially Italian-British theologian Anselm of Canterbury (d. 1109), French philosopher René Descartes (d. 1650), Dutch philosopher Baruch Spinoza (d. 1677), and German philosopher Gottfried W. Leibniz (d. 1716), as well as the objections by David Hume and Immanuel Kant. Geisler concluded that the arguments of the former group are not decisive either; no valid ontological evidence was supplied that makes it rationally inescapable to conclude that a necessary Being exists.[49] Geisler added some important points: (1) Nor has anyone ever supplied a successful ontological refutation of God, which makes it logically impossible that there is a God. (2) Some so-called *a priori* ontological arguments ("something exists, therefore God exists") are in fact *a posteriori* cosmological arguments (see §3.3.3). (3) Even if a certain theistic argument could be supported, one would still need to travel a long logical distance to reach the one, absolutely perfect God of the Bible. The latter point is evident from the fact that all kinds of "Gods" have been deduced from the same kind of ontological argumentation: theistic (Descartes, Leibniz), pantheistic (Spinoza), panentheistic (American philosopher Charles Hartshorne, d. 2000), and polytheistic (Ameri-

---

47. Geisler (1974, 130).
48. Ibid., 131.
49. Ibid., 161.

can Robert J. Henle, d. 2001).

3.3.3 The Cosmological Proof of God

(d) *Cosmological arguments*. These are the ultimate hope for the theistic proofs, since both teleological and moral arguments depend on them, while the ontological argument can be defended only by reconstructing it as a cosmological type of argument. This latter type is also called "etiological" (from Gk. *aitia*, "cause"; *aitios*, "causer") because all cosmological arguments reason from the cosmos to a necessary cause or causer of the cosmos. Again, Geisler, discussed a number of writers, especially Greek philosophers Plato (d. 347 BC) and Aristotle (d. 322 BC), Anselm of Canterbury, Italian thinker Thomas Aquinas (d. 1274), Descartes and Leibniz, together with the objections by British thinker William of Ockham (d. 1347), David Hume, and Immanuel Kant. Geisler concluded that the cosmological argument, too, encountered various problems.[50]

(1) It is not necessarily true that all things have sufficient reasons to explain their existence.

(2) The argument does not seem to escape from Kant's objection that, in order to demonstrate its case, the argument always makes a step into the purely conceptual domain by appealing to the conceivability of the world's non-existence, or the inconceivability of God's existence on the basis of certain arguments.

To these problems I add the following.

(3) What a colorless being is this God. Why should he be God, or a god, at all? Why not some impersonal quantity of matter or energy? What Christian could be interested in this cosmological god? What does this being or entity have in common with the God of the Bible, apart from existing?

(4) Cosmological arguments may have made some impression on Enlightenment thinkers when nature was still a pristine garden. But even then, there were devouring mon-

---
50. Ibid., 187.

sters in nature, earthquakes, fires, volcanic eruptions, and catastrophic inundations. No wonder: natural theology as such contain no doctrine of sin. It does not determine whether only the good things of nature point to God, or also the evil things. Does cosmology not necessarily produce a Janus figure with a good and an evil side? And if so, who could, purely on the basis of a natural theology, tell the difference between the two?

(5) Even if natural theology would contain criteria for good and evil, where in the cosmos would we find a testimony of God's love and mercy? It is only because we have a theology based upon God's Word revelation that we, in hindsight, find God's goodness in his works. But if we consider these works in themselves, what a meager godhead they supply. I repeat, who would be interested in such a god?[51]

(6) The actual ineffectiveness of the theistic proofs can perhaps be best illustrated by the fact that some theists reject their validity and nevertheless believe in God.[52] Dutch philosopher Theo de Boer referred to a philosopher who said,[53] "Actually I am an atheist who believes in God"[54] — perhaps Dutch theologian Klaas Hendrikse (d. 2018) was an example of this — just as, conversely, there are many theists for whom, in practical life, God hardly seems to mean anything. What illustrates the modern confusion surrounding the God-question more clearly than the phenomenon of these "atheistic theists," and these "theistic atheists"?

(7) The cosmological proof has also been called the proof from the contingency of the world. This contingency is viewed as pointing to a being that itself is not contingent but necessary in the sense that its existence follows from its own being. Contingency is viewed here as a problem that must be solved by resorting to a Necessary Being, which is viewed as the ground of all contingent being. However, the

---

51. Cf. De Boer (1989, 35–42, 49–52).
52. Cf. Hubbeling (1983/4, 158, 165).
53. De Boer (1989, 79).
54. Cf. Altizer (1966, book title: ". . . *Christian Atheism*").

objection lies in viewing contingency as a *problem* at all. More modern thinkers such as French existentialist Jean-Paul Sartre (d. 1980) would ask: Why do we not simply accept contingency as what it is: the ultimate meaninglessness? In what sense does some Necessary Being take away this meaninglessness? Why would this Being itself not rather be the climax of meaninglessness?[55] Please note, Christians may have very good reasons to reject the idea of cosmic meaninglessness; but we must admit at least that cosmic meaningfulness cannot be demonstrated from the notion of contingency. To the (post)modern mind, contingency demonstrates the opposite instead; in addition to Sartre, others who could be mentioned here include French existentialists Maurice Merleau-Ponty (d. 1961) and Emmanuel Levinas (d. 1995), and German existentialist Martin Heidegger (d. 1976). In a sense, the entire death of God movement[56] has been nothing but the expression of the total failure of all the alleged proofs for the existence of God.

3.4 The Theistic Proofs and the Supra-Rational
3.4.1 A False Dilemma

After having described the failure of the cosmological arguments, Geisler added a chapter in which he tried to circumvent the problems just mentioned.[57] He explained the mistake made by the advocates of this kind of argument, especially Leibniz. In contrast with them, Geisler tried to reformulate the argument, beginning with limited existence, and, through the principle of existential causality, arriving ultimately at an unlimited cause of all existence. He admitted that the conclusion was not rationally inescapable, but argued that it *was* existentially undeniable. In short, if there is any finite being, then there exists an infinite Being as an actual and necessary

---

55. Sartre (1943, 33–34); cf. De Boer (1989, 55–57, 69–73).
56. See especially Altizer and Hamilton (1966); 1966/67 was a vital year in the debate; see treatises by Montgomery (1966), Ogletree (1966), Ice and Carey (1967), and Murchland (1967).
57. Geisler (1974, 190–226).

ground for finite existence.[58]

I will not discuss Geisler's argument in detail here; others have done so.[59] No matter how clever this argument may be, Geisler did not see, or did not sufficiently see, that he has produced simply one more philosophical theory. And theories are human constructs that have always been falsified, sooner or later, and thus have been corrected, rejected, or replaced. Therefore, I am not quite reassured when Geisler continues by saying that the existence of God does not result from the cosmological argument (which, of course, is stating the obvious). What does result, in his view, is a *truth*, namely, a statement concerning God's existence. I appreciate Geisler's good intentions. But do philosophical (or scientific, or theological) arguments ever produce *truths* in any true sense of this term?[60] *Theories* may contain kernels of truth, but basically they are only models awaiting correction or rejection.

How do we know whether Geisler's cosmological argument produces a truth? That is, we may know the conclusion to be true — because of God's revelation — but does this conclusion really *follow* from the argument? The biblical testimony does not produce cosmological theories; rather, the Bible seems uninterested in them. Is the real truth not this, that Geisler's judgment concerning the value of his cosmological argument, and the truth of its conclusion, was determined *a priori* by his faith knowledge of Divine Truth? That is, from the outset his argument was governed by what he already knew in his believing heart, namely, that God exists. Is there any believer who, through examining Geisler's book, or cosmological arguments in general, became more certain about God's existence? Did Geisler convince any philosopher? It is quite difficult to follow Geisler's argument, even for professional philosophers. How many were converted through it? How many believers felt their hearts begin to warm when

---
58. Ibid., 224.
59. See Macquarrie (1975, 132–34).
60. See extensively, *EDR* 12:chapter 14; Vol. V/1 in this series.

studying such arguments?

I presume what Geisler's response would be: Fideism. Irrationalism. Existentialism. This is because many thinkers, including Christians, are aware of only these two options: rationalism and irrationalism. If A accuses B of rationalism, B knows immediately what A's problem is: irrationalism. For ages, Western thinking has been caught in this dilemma. But for almost a century now, we should have known better. Proper Christian thinking is neither rationalistic, nor irrationalistic, although rational and non-rational arguments do play a role in it. At a minimum, biblical thinking does not believe in the autonomy of human reason, just as it does not believe in some autonomous feeling, or autonomous existential experiences. Reason, feeling, perception, and so on, are just—what we call—immanent functions of the transcendent-religious human heart. The latter is neither rational, nor irrational, but could be called supra-rational, just as the transcendent is beyond (supra) the immanent. Actually, Christian thinkers do not believe in the autonomy of the human heart; they do believe in the autonomy of God's Word, which, through God's Spirit, works in people's hearts the conviction that God exists, an existence evident through his speaking to them, his refreshing and restoring them, his forgiving their sins, his cheering them through his precious Word and his Holy Spirit.

3.4.2 Again, the Ontological Argument

Only in the way just described does Karl Barth leave some room, if I understand him correctly, for the famous ontological theistic proof of Anselm of Canterbury.[61] Anselm's well-known expression that God is "something beyond which nothing greater could be thought of" (Lat. *aliquid quo nihil maius cogitare possit*)[62] is not dealt with by Barth in the traditional rationalistic-scholastic manner, but in an existential way: the person who knows what the term "God" entails cannot avoid

---

61. Barth (1960).
62. Anselm (Proslogion 2).

taking into account the reality of God. However, this knowledge of God is not the knowledge of natural reason. It is the knowledge of faith on the part of the person to whom the Holy Spirit has made known the revelation of God. They who know in their heart what God is—that reality beyond which we cannot think of anything greater—and are overwhelmed by this knowledge: they can do nothing other than believe in this God, that is, surrender in faith to him.[63]

This is the proof that God exists. It is evidence far beyond the entire domain of the traditional theistic proofs. At best, the cosmological argument can bring a person to Aristotle's "first cause" (Lat. *prima causa*) but it never brings them to the arms of God, the Father of our Lord Jesus Christ. Let me quote here Pascal's *Pensées* again:

> The metaphysical proofs of God are so remote from the reasoning of men, and so complicated, that they make little impression; and if they should be of service to some, it would be only during the moment that they see such demonstration; but an hour afterwards they fear they have been mistaken.
>
> *Quod curiositate cognoverunt superbia amiserunt.*[64] ["What they have found by their curiosity, they have lost by their pride."]
>
> This is the result of the knowledge of God obtained without Jesus Christ; it is communion without a mediator with the God whom they have known without a mediator. Whereas those who have known God by a mediator know their own wretchedness.[65]

In other words, true knowledge of God is not primarily about *his* existence but about *our* sins.

American theologian Colin Brown wrote about Pascal's famous wager (Fr. *pari*), in which he challenged people to put their lives at stake for the possibility that Christianity could

---

63. Cf. Ott (1972, 94).
64. Augustine (Serm. CXLI).
65. Pascal (n.d., 103).

be true. We cannot see God, that is, perceive him in any direct way. We cannot demonstrate the truth of the gospel beyond any possible doubt. We can discover the truth of Christianity only by venturing our entire lives for it.[66]

3.4.3 Supra-Rationality

The true meaning of the theistic proofs has been sensed by some modern theologians in a manner that is more convincing than Geisler's concealed rationalism. For example, Karl Barth gave a new interpretation of Anselm's ontological argument by divesting it of its rationalistic context.[67] In this way, Anselm's argument is no longer a real proof in the sense of an attempt to rationally convince the non-believer, but rather it is "faith's own description that it gives of itself, a reflective presentation of what occurs in faith."[68] Faith is the right knowledge of God, and it is because of this faith that we are urged to confess that God is.

In this representation of Anselm's proof, one can sense the implication that faith is not rational, nor irrational, but supra-rational. In our innermost being, which surpasses reason, a compelling proof for God's existence would draw us down to "something inner-worldly, something that we can encompass with our human reason," and that therefore "no longer would be God," and thus something that no longer matters.[69] In other words, the knowledge of God's existence is relevant for us precisely because it is *supra*-rational, and moves us in our deepest feelings, our will, our sense of responsibility, and above all, our heart, our ultimate Ego. In a certain sense, God is relevant for us precisely because he is *beyond* rational proofs, no matter how fideistic they may sound in the ears of those who accustomed to rationalist fundamentalism.

Interestingly, this also resembles the approach of some

---

66. Brown (1971, 59).
67. Barth (1960).
68. Ott (1974, 31); cf. De Boer (1989, 42–49).
69. Ott (1974, 33–34; cf. 106).

twentieth-century Roman Catholic theologians. Karl Rahner formally agreed with the First Vatican Council of 1870, but no longer understood the Thomistic theistic proofs as intellectually closed arguments but "rather as different expressions of a basic experience that in principle everyone can have. It is the metaphysical experience that one is enclosed and carried by an infinite and unspeakable mystery of 'being' itself," as Heinrich Ott summarized it.[70]

The approach of Hans Küng strongly agreed with this.[71] He rejected the theistic proofs as deductive derivations of God from the empirical world, and, over against this, stated that God can be "made true" (Ger. *bewahrheitet*) beyond pure reason, namely, from the existentially experienced reality of humanity and the world. This demands the entire person, including their rationality, while at the same time surpassing it. Küng's twelfth thesis states, "Faith in God can be rationally accounted for: the rationality of it demonstrates itself in the practice of daring trust in God. Fundamental trust and trust in God are mutually related."[72] This "fundamental trust" is nothing other than what I have described as people's ultimate commitment (surrender, entrusting oneself to God) in the transcendent-religious sense. Other theologians have argued along the same lines, including three Germans: Protestants Wolfhart Pannenberg and Eberhard Jüngel, and Roman Catholic Walter Kasper.[73]

---

70. Ibid., 36; cf. 37 and further.
71. Küng (1978, 529–51; 1979, 51–52, 65).
72. Küng (1979, 65; cf. 1978, 573–75).
73. Jüngel (1983, 241–44, 258–60; Kasper (1983, Part. 1, chapter 4); Pannenberg (1988, 105–08).

Chapter 4
The Being of God

Who is like you, O LORD, among the gods?
Who is like you, majestic in holiness,
awesome in glorious deeds, doing wonders?

Exodus 15:11

4.1 Introduction
4.1.1 Image-Building

IN THIS AND THE NEXT TWO CHAPTERS, we will deal with one of the most dangerous subjects in theology: designing an image of God. From the outset, this seems to conflict with the second of the Ten Commandments (Exod. 20:4): "You shall not make for yourself a carved image" of any deity, but especially images of the God of Israel. "You shall not bow down before them" (v. 5) to worship them, for in this way the image of God would replace God himself. At the same time, designing images of God—not of wood or stone, silver or gold, but mental representations—is inevitable. No person could ever think about God without forming a certain image of God. It is the task of theology to critically examine these images. Images of God are inherent to our human nature—the only caution is that we should not worship them. C. S. Lewis wrote that the deepest place in hell is reserved for theologians who find their representations of God more important than God himself.¹

Jewish thinker Martin Buber described a related danger: remaining locked in the images of God. He argued that the idea of God, this masterpiece of human construction, is only the image of images, the loftiest of all images with which people imagine the imageless God. When people learn to love God, they feel an actuality that surpasses the idea. Even if the image results from the philosopher's monumental attempt to preserve the object of their love as an object of their philosophical thought, this love itself witnesses to the existence of the Beloved One.² In other words, those who really learn to know the God of the philosophers (and, I may add, the God of the theologians) want more: they reach out for the God of the loving intimacy of faith.

German theologian Eberhard Jüngel called the being of God the hermeneutical problem of theology; more accurately (as he said), the fact that the being of God *coming forth* is the essential hermeneutical problem. For only because this being of God is coming forth is there an encounter between God and humans. And the hermeneutical problem is rooted in this very encounter between God and humans, which finds its origin in the movement of God's being.³ God took the initiative. God comes forth to meet humanity. The core question for humanity is then: What is it that has met me here? Or more importantly, *who* is the One who has met me? This "who" refers to God's personality. Just as we should not ask "what" are humans, but "who" are humans (see §4.2.1), the Christian believes that, where God meets a human being, one "who?" meets the other "who?" There may be many differences between the divine personality and a human personality, yet there is the deep conviction that it is a *person* who meets me who himself is a person. Only in this way we can speak of a genuine *encounter*.

---

1. Lewis (1944).
2. Buber (1989, 62).
3. Jüngel (1976, XXX–XXI).

4.1.2 The Term "God"

In chapter 1, we briefly investigated in what ways we can speak of God in a scientific way. We saw that theology proper (the doctrine of God) is an exceptional doctrine because the term "God," or whatever related term, does not refer to an immanent-rational concept. Thus, there is nothing like an *idea* (adopted from our creaturely world) that refers to "God as such." The immanent-rational concept of "heart" can be used as an idea to refer to the transcendent human heart; the immanent-rational concept of "word" can be used as an idea to refer to the transcendent Word of God, and so on. But with regard to God, such terms are not available. Therefore, when it comes to speaking scientifically about God, theology proper is in a precarious position. It can approximate the truth of God only through creational terms that are used as (a) modal ideas referring to God's so-called attributes, such as his immutability, his wisdom, his holiness, his righteousness, his mercy, and the like; (b) modal ideas referring to his works, such as his condescension, his judgment, his redemptive work, etc.; and (c) entitary-analogous metaphors referring to his being, such as Father, Shepherd, King, and the like.

In theological tradition, divine names based on God's attributes, such as the Almighty One, the Holy One, and the Most High, are identified as essential or attributive names. In addition to this, theology proper can analyze the non-metaphoric appellative names of God, such as Hebrew *Elohim*, *YHWH*, and Greek *theos*. All of this supplies us with a program for this and the next two chapters. First, we will deal with the personality of God (this chapter), and then with the attributive and appellative names of God (chapters 4 and 5). After that, we will deal with the so-called personal names of God: Father, Son, and Holy Spirit (chapters 6–8).

Theology proper has often wrestled with the question whether the doctrine of God's attributes must precede the doctrine of the Trinity, as is the case in traditional dogmatics, or the reverse, as some more recent authors prefer.[4] Both orders have been defended.[5] However, it is obvious that true knowledge of the divine attributes presupposes knowledge of Trinitarian doctrine, just as the latter presupposes the former. Thus, the order in which these subjects are dealt with is basically irrelevant. In a similar way, one could argue that theology proper cannot be understood without soteriology (the doctrine of salvation), while the opposite is equally true. Systematic theology must necessarily begin somewhere.

4.2 The Personal God
4.2.1 The Who-ness of God and Human Beings

Already the question "Who is God?" instead of "What is God?" is, as we saw, implicitly a question about a person. There is a certain analogy with human beings here; as Polish-American rabbi Abraham J. Heschel (d. 1972) put it, we ask, "What is Man?" whereas the true question should be, "Who is Man?" As a thing, the human being is explainable; as a person a human being is both a mystery and a surprise. As a thing, a human being is finite; as a person a human being is inexhaustible. The question "Who is Man?" is a question of dignity, a question of position and status within the order of beings.[6]

It is no wonder that, when we ask "Who is God?," we think immediately of humanity. If the human being as a person is both a mystery and a surprise, and inexhaustible, a person of dignity, position, and status, how much more is this true of God. Since human beings were created in God's image and according to God's likeness (Gen. 1:26, 28; 9:6; James 3:9 NKJV), they inadvertently think of God "according to human likeness." God has created human beings in order that there could be a personal relationship between him and them; therefore, it is obvious to think of God as a person. The fact

---
4. Barth (*CD* I/1, 311 and further); Weber (1981, 386 and further).
5. Cf. Bavinck (*RD* 2:149–50).
6. Heschel (1965, 28).

that Christians believe God to be three persons (see chapter 7), does not prevent them from speaking of the One God as a person as well.

I therefore reject referring to God with impersonal descriptions such as "absolute Being," "highest Being" (Lat. *summum esse*), "Being in itself." These descriptions go back to Greek thinking, were current in scholastic and early Protestant theology, but are also encountered with modern theologians such as Paul Tillich and John Macquarrie. I think also of a description like "absolute Spirit" in the sense of Georg W. F. Hegel, as we find in his theological school of thought (e.g., David F. Strauss). Rather, we refer to God as a person, a true self, an "I-ness," even though he is a person in an infinitely higher manner than human beings are.

As Hendrikus Berkhof put it, we (rightly) attribute to God that in which the world of persons surpasses the world of things: self-consciousness, freedom, the ability of fellowship, in short: being a subject.[7] This must not be taken in the sense of some *analogia entis* ("analogy in being"), in which God and human beings are viewed as participating in the same Being (Gk. *to ōn*) as that which is known first (Lat. the *primum notum*; see §4.8.2). This Thomistic doctrine pulls God under the boundary of the law, instituted between God and creation, or even erases that boundary.[8] The error here is to unite God and humanity in one ontological framework, as if God is *a* being to be classified among *the* beings, more specifically the spiritual beings. In this way, the doctrine of the *analogia entis* could be developed in Thomism on the basis of the supposed ontic continuity between Creator and creature.

I may add here that the fact that we call God "a" being or person does not necessarily mean that God belongs to a *genus proximum* called "being" together with all living organisms,

---

7. Berkhof (1986, 134).
8. Smit (1980, 185); cf. Spykman (1992, 65, 225–26, 288); cf. *EDR* 11:98–103.

or a "person" together with angels and humans.⁹ Therefore, it does not seem correct to me that the KJV, the ASV and other versions render John 4:24 (Gk. *pneuma ho theos*): "God is *a* s/Spirit," instead of "God is s/Spirit," as most translations have it. Thus, Andree Troost also criticized the Belgic Confession Article 1 because it gives a similar description of God: "... there is a single and simple spiritual being, whom we call God" (in the original French version: *une seule et simple essence spirituelle*).¹⁰ German theologian Werner Elert (d. 1954) rightly remarked that the first commandment of the Decalogue is true also for theology, which therefore should never speak of "a" God but only of God.¹¹

Troost also pointed to the theoreticalizing that mars this first Article of the Belgic: no believer, in their practical fellowship with God, would ever express their faith in God in such terms of spiritual beings (in contrast with material beings), to which belong angels and demons, and God as well. This, said Troost, is analogous to someone asking me if I am married, and I answer: Yes, namely, with a two-legged material being (without feathers) that I call woman, and that possesses various good attributes: a good intellect, patience, and so on.

4.2.2 Rationality Over-Emphasized

It is a basic mistake to put God into one ontological framework with humanity. We do not speak of God's personality because of some ontic similarity between God and humanity but rather in the sense of an analogy expressed in an entitary idea, linguistically identified as a metaphor. That is, the idea of a person or personality, referring primarily to the transcendent but finite and created human heart, is used for the equally transcendent but infinite and uncreated God. This is possible only as an approximation, while still yielding rational knowledge about God.

---

9. Cf. Pannenberg (1988, 401), who refers to Joest (1984, 156).
10. Troost (1992).
11. Elert (1956, 201).

The Being of God

This use of the term "person" as an idea with regard to God implies that *not* everything that can be predicated with regard to human beings can be applied to God as well. Therefore, it will not help us very much if we quote a number of modern biological or psychological descriptions of the human personality in order to shed light on God's personality. Rather I suggest that we approximate the latter through ideas that are supplied by the Bible itself. In all these ideas, we are dealing with terms that, for us, point intuitively to a personality as we know it in our human world, usually in clear distinction from the animal world.

Please notice here the inherent multiplicity of the idea of the person, so much different from the definition given by late-Roman Christian thinker Boethius (d. 525): A person is an individual substance of a rational nature (Lat. *persona est naturae rationalis individualis substantia*). Walter Kasper objected to the apparent identification of personality and individuality in Boethius' definition: individuality defines a what, not a who; it describes the nature of the person, not the person as such.[12] He seemed to be happier with the definition by Scottish Christian thinker Richard of Saint Victor (d. 1173): an incommunicable existence of a rational nature (Lat. *naturae rationalis incommunicabilis existentia*). I myself would object to both (and all other scholastic) definitions of person because they limit the idea of person to rationality, or at least they overemphasize the rational. Thus, they ignore the inherent lingual, social, economic, aesthetic, juridical, ethical, and pistical characteristics of personality. Such a limitation is just as one-sided—and thus basically wrong—as the Aristotelian definition of a rational soul (Lat. *anima rationalis*) that is ascribed to Christ as a Man in the Athanasian Creed.

All the more regrettable, then, is the agreement with Boethius's definition of a person by Roman Catholic thinker Edmund J. Fortman (d. 1990), who claimed that this definition

---

12. Kasper (1983, 281).

was accepted by most theologians to this very day. Most of the alternatives that he supplied contained references to rationality, such as "a distinct something, consisting in an intellectual nature" (Thomas Aquinas), "an intelligent being" (Voltaire), and the "carrier and possessor of a rational nature" (Matthias J. Scheeben).[13] In the next section we will consider several other aspects of a person, and of God in particular, is addition to rationality—aspects that are at least as characteristic, and at least as important.

4.2.3 Modal Aspects of Personality

Here are just a few, modally distinct examples of aspects of the very person-like deeds of God.[14]

(a) *Physical.* God acts in great power and with a mighty hand (e.g., Exod. 32:11).

(b) *Biotic.* The living God catches his breath (Heb. *wayyinnaphash*, from *nephesh*, here, "breath") and is refreshed by it (Exod. 31:17); he binds up wounds (Ps. 147:3).

(c) *Perceptive.* God listens to the voice of others, and answers them (Ps. 3:4). He witnesses things (Mal. 2:14). Not only does he see and hear (Ps. 94:9), he also smells (Gen. 8:21). The Bible speaks of his nostrils (Exod. 15:8; 2 Sam. 22:9, 16), and of his lips and his tongue (Isa. 30:27).

(d) *Sensitive.* God's bowels (as the seat of emotions) are troubled (Jer. 31:20 KJV). He is familiar with all kinds of emotions: joy (Isa. 65:19), grief (Ps. 78:40), distress (Isa. 63:9 NIV), fear (Deut. 32:27), wrath (Rev. 14:10), and mocking laughter (Ps. 2:4; 37:13).

(e) *Analytical.* God descends to discover things (Gen. 18:21). He conducts tests (Deut. 8:2; Ps. 7:9; Jer. 11:20; 17:10). He confers with his counselors (1 Kings 22:19–20). As to the cognitive in the broader sense: God can remember (Gen. 8:1; Exod. 2:24) and forget (1 Sam. 1:11; Jer. 31:34).

---

13. Fortman (1972, 295).
14. Bavinck (*RD* 2:99–101).

(f) *Formative-historical.* God builds (Gen. 2:22), and he works (John 5:17).

(g) *Lingual.* God speaks to other persons (Gen. 1:28–29) and gives names (17:5, 15); he writes (Exod. 34:1) and engraves (Isa. 49:16).

(h) *Social.* God meets with other persons (Exod. 3:18), and he visits them (Gen. 21:1; cf. 18:1–2). He speaks intimately with people, as a man speaks with his friend (Exod. 33:11).

(i) *Economic.* God spares no arrows (Jer. 50:14), and he gives abundantly (Deut. 28:11).

(j) *Aesthetic.* God adorns with ornaments (Ezek. 16:11).

(k) *Juridical.* God sits in judgment (Dan. 7:9), he rebukes (Ps. 18:15; 104:7), he judges, he decides with equity, and strikes (Isa. 11:4), and he disciplines like a father (Deut. 8:5).

(l) *Ethical.* He grants motherly care and love (Isa. 49:15; 66:13).

(m) *Pistical.* He en-trusts to people, thus placing his confidence in them (1 Tim. 6:20).

In the *supra-modal* sense, the Bible refers to God speaking of himself as an "I" and addressing people as "you." God speaks of "my Spirit" (Gen. 6:3), "my soul" (Isa. 42:1), and "my heart" (Isa. 63:4). God possesses self-awareness; he is not described by human self-awareness, but he is the One who describes the latter. Following Martin Buber, Heinrich Ott called this the primordial experience of being a person, and applied this to God.[15] In addition, he alluded to Psalm 94:9 when he asked, "He who constitutes and describes the person as a person, would he himself not be a person?"[16] As a person, God is completely free to act, yet at the same time he assumes responsibilities. He addresses, and he himself is addressed. He demands responses, and he himself responds.

---

15. Ott (1974, 41–52).
16. Ott (1972, 105; 1974, 53–54).

4.3   Anthropomorphic? Supra-Personal?
4.3.1   Terminology

In connection with the examples just mentioned, the terms "anthropomorphic" and "anthropomorphism" are commonly used.[17] If we use these terms to mean ascribing a human-like form or human-like attributes to God, they are simply wrong. God does not have a human-like form or human-like attributes, just as human beings are not theomorphic, as if they possessed a God-like form or God-like attributes, or any other meaning parallel to anthropomorphic.[18] God is the infinite God, who completely transcends everything in the created world; and human beings are humans, that is, finite and created. Therefore, it is wise to avoid terms relating to "anthropomorphism," at least if such a term implies that human characteristics are ascribed to God.

Moreover, the term "anthropomorphism" suggests that although we speak of God in this human way, God is actually is very different. I would rather say that modal concepts used to describe the human form and human attributes can be used as modal ideas in order to acquire rational knowledge about what surpasses the boundaries of conceptualization, namely, in this case, the personality of God. God *is* a person, but not a human person, not even with the qualifier "in a manner of speaking."

There is some validity to the statement of Paul Tillich that the being of God is supra-personal, but supra-personal does not mean impersonal.[19] Elsewhere he explained that, ultimately, humans cannot be occupied with anything less than they themselves are, namely, with something impersonal.[20] This supra-personal God transcends everything, as a "God beyond God,"[21] the God of personalistic theology, which (in

---

17. Cf. König (1975, chapter 2); Wentsel (1987, 57–59).
18. Contra Brunner (1946, 144); Althaus (1952, 266); Thielicke (1974, 138).
19. Tillich (1968, 2:13).
20. Ibid., (1:247); cf. Ott (1974, 55–57); Küng (1978, 631–35; 1979, 80–83).
21. Tillich (1968, 2:14).

my words) views God's personality as an image of the human personality. At the same time, we are certainly able to say that God is a person, as long as we use this term in the sense of an idea to refer to the infinite personality of God, who is elevated far beyond finite human personalities.

The term "supra-personal" is not harmless; the thesis that God is supra-personal, says Walter Kasper, really does not say anything because "person" is the highest category at our disposal. We can predicate this category in an analogous way but trying to move beyond this in a higher, supra-personal dimension would imply that we leave behind the domain of meaningful and responsible language. In this way, God's essence would disappear into utter vagueness, indefiniteness, and generality. This would entail a misunderstanding of the biblical God, who has a concrete name.[22]

4.3.2 Concepts and Ideas

Concepts that refer to human persons can be used as ideas to acquire true knowledge of God. God *has* eyes, but useless to ask whether they are brown or blue because they are not human eyes. But they are definitely *eyes*, about which we can obtain true rational knowledge by using concepts referring to human eyes as ideas. Human eyes can see just as God's eyes can see (Ps. 94:9), they can test just as God's eyes can test (11:4), and they can be hurt just as the apple of God's eye can be hurt (Zech. 2:8). God *can* walk (Gen. 3:8; Lev. 26:12) since he has feet (Isa. 66:1; Zech. 14:4), but it is useless to ask about his shoe size (cf. Ps. 60:8), his walking pace, his walking style, or the bones and muscles of his feet. But his walking is genuine *walking*, about which we can obtain true rational knowledge by using concepts referring to human walking as ideas.

I have argued earlier (chapter 1) that rational knowledge is not limited to conceptual knowledge. If we would think otherwise, this would force us to conclude that we can have no rational knowledge of God at all. It might look like an

---
22. Kasper (1983, 155).

attractive alternative to claim that there are matters about which we can have only supra-rational knowledge, as in the case of God. But would there be any knowledge, no matter how elevated, which could not ensnare me in rational formulations (without necessarily being *confined* to them)? If people believe in God, should they not be able to tell us to some minimal extent *what* they believe? And would their reply not necessarily imply certain logical-analytical distinctions, thus displaying (in philosophical terminology) the kernel (meaningful distinction) of the logical-analytical modality of cosmic reality?

If we would deny this rational aspect, this would drive us into the arms of mysticism or negative theology, both of which tell us only what God is *not*.[23] The only reason people shy away from the notion that there could be rational knowledge of God is precisely because they reduce rational knowledge to conceptual knowledge, and thus run into problems. However, there is no conceptual knowledge of God, but only knowledge in the form of ideas, that is, knowledge obtained by using logical terms as ideas.

4.3.3 The Idea of the Person

The objections to the conceptual use of the term "person" with regard to God have led certain nineteenth-century theologians (German theologians Friedrich Schleiermacher, David F. Strauss [d. 1874], and Swiss Alois E. Biedermann [d. 1884]) and philosophers (German philosophers Johann G. Fichte [d. 1814], Georg W. F. Hegel, and Ludwig Feuerbach) to reject the term altogether.[24] Both traditional thinkers and these modern thinkers predicate certain features belonging to the concept of "person" and apply them to God — leading the former to make incorrect statements about God and the latter to conclude that the term "person" is unusable. The latter group understands "person" as a limitation — every person is

---
23. See extensively, Berger (2000).
24. See Althaus (1952, 2670); Berkhof (1986, 135–36).

The Being of God

delimited by and from other persons—whereas God is unlimited. Thus, Fichte argued that, if God is infinite, he cannot be a person in the sense of self-awareness, for the Ego's self-awareness presupposes the non-Ego, by which it is delimited and becomes aware of itself.[25] However, we ought to see that God is not one person among others, and that therefore we cannot speak of God's personality in a conceptual way but only by using the term "person" as an idea. Only in this way will we understand that delimitation indeed belongs to the human person but is not necessarily a constitutive feature of the *idea* of "person," and thus of God.

Therefore, it is inadequate for opponents of the theologians and philosophers mentioned above to define person to include both God's personality and human personality. So for instance German theologian Albrecht Ritschl (d. 1889) defined the person of God this way: "Having all ground of his activity in himself."[26] He was followed by German theologian Paul Althaus (d. 1966), who concluded that therefore only God is truly a person, and human beings are persons only to a certain extent: they are never pure subject, entirely Ego.[27] However, this cannot be the solution. The term "person" is entirely part of our created world; as German theologian Gerhard Ebeling (d. 2001) put it, if God's being is understood as person, God's being is concentrated upon his togetherness with humanity. For we know of no person other than a human person.[28] In other words, God's person can be understood only from the human person, not the other way around, as though God would be more person than humans are. The *idea* of "person" refers to human beings; the same *term* can be applied to God, too, but as an *idea*, which overlaps only partially with the idea of human personality.

---

25. Cf. Uwe Gerber in Ott (1972, 101).
26. Ritschl (1889–90).
27. Althaus (1952, 268).
28. Ebeling (1979, 224).

4.4 Dangers for Theology Proper
4.4.1 Hellenism

First in Judaism (Philo [d. 50]), as well as in early Christianity, theology proper inevitably developed in interaction with Hellenism, the philosophy that blossomed in the countries once conquered by Alexander the Great, consisting of a mixture of Greek thought with thinking indigenous to these various countries. Almost from the beginning, ancient philosophy had been occupied with the question of the true form of the Deity. Judaism and Christianity each in turn presented the knowledge of the true God to the world. They did their best to show that the monotheistic idea of the purely transcendent God whom the ancient philosophers had sought could be found in the Bible. This interaction was a perilous enterprise because the biblical knowledge of God was in danger of being pressed into the mold of contemporary Greek thought.[29] In modern times, this enormous risk has been generally acknowledged, although the evaluation of it strongly differed. In simple terms: the one danger is that theologians wish to explain too much from this Greek influence; the opposite danger is that the influence of Greek thought is played down.

The former danger is seen especially, but not exclusively, where theologians believed that the influence of Greek thought could be identified in the Bible. Thus, the apostle John was thought to have been influenced by Greek *logos* philosophy (Heraclitus), or by (proto-)Gnosticism.[30] In opposition to this, we find traditional theology instead sees in John's Gospel and his first two epistles one of the most powerful attacks upon (proto-)Gnosticism. Another example: Wolfhart Pannenberg saw in the New Testament allusions to philosophical theology, for instance, the natural theology of the Stoics (Acts 17:26–27; Rom. 1:19–20), as well as features of negative theology: God is "*im*mortal, *in*visible" (1 Tim. 1:17), "unsearchable" and

---

29. Cf. Brunner (1950, 254–64); Pannenberg (1971, 296–346); *RGG* 2:1718–22, 1741–42.
30. E.g., Bultmann (1971).

"inscrutable" (Rom. 11:33).[31] He claimed to see in the latter passage a Stoic formula.[32] However, such parallelisms—often quite vague—do not necessarily allude to, and certainly do not adopt, categories of extra-biblical philosophy.

The opposite danger is to minimize the influence of Greek philosophy on Christian theology. It is quite astonishing that Herman Bavinck flatly denied that early dogmatics was a mixture of Christian religion and pagan philosophy.[33] He did so with the simplistic argument that the Christian church was very much on alert when it came to pagan philosophy, and strongly condemned it in Origen. In reality, I feel that Swiss theologian Emil Brunner (d. 1966) was right—even though his terminology was defective—when he said that between, on the one hand, the "unreflected-unsystematic," dispersed, and "theologically naïve" concepts of the New Testament and, on the other hand, the great ecumenical dogmas and creeds of the early church there lay four centuries of the most intensive "dogmatic" work.[34] This work consisted of abstract analytical conceptualization and abstract systematic summaries, such that Greek philosophical terms and thought content foreign to the New Testament itself crept into theology.

Let me give a few examples.[35] Ignatius (d. c. 107) added various negative-theological predicates of God, such as timeless, invisible, incomprehensible, and impassible. Clement of Rome (pope Clement I, d. 99) presented extensive Stoic ideas such as the benevolent providence of the demiurge, and his omnipresence within creation, and linked God's wrath-less love with his benevolence, taken in the Platonic-Stoic sense. The Apologists adopted the theistic proofs from Greek philosophy, which deduced the cause of the world from its form and composition. This cause (Gk. *archē*) was considered to be

---

31. *RGG* 2:1718–19.
32. Pannenberg (1988, 290, 328–29).
33. Bavinck (*RD* 1:104–105, 91, cf. 7–8, 92, 110, 149, 572–75).
34. Brunner (1950, 65–66).
35. Cf. *RGG* 2:1719–21.

necessarily immutable, since whatever is mutable presupposes a cause for its mutation, and therefore cannot be the ultimate cause of things. From this idea of God's immutability (see §7.6), people quickly deduced the notion of God's simplicity, already well-known to Philo (see §7.1.2.). Greek speculation about God's eternity moved between the ideas of eternal simultaneity and timelessness (so already Ignatius; see §§4.11–4.13 below).[36]

Other examples are these. Since the apologist Justin Martyr (d. 165), the righteousness of God was understood in the Aristotelian sense of distributive justice, whereby God the Judge distributes according to merit.[37] In this way, the biblical link between God's righteousness and his covenant faithfulness was largely lost. Under Stoic influence, church father Tertullian (d. c. 230) assumed that the divine spirit had a corporeal character (see §7.10). The notion, arising especially in Alexandrian theology, that the Greek philosophers had acquired their most profound insights from the Jews facilitated the adoption of Greek philosophical notions and views.

4.4.2 Substantialism

In my view, the greatest threat to theology proper comes from substantialism.[38] I will return to this matter in §4.5; for now, I will summarize the most important points with regard to the doctrine of God. Substantialism is the ancient and scholastic doctrine based upon the idea of the (Lat.) *substantia* (Gk. *hypostasis*), which also penetrated Protestant theology.[39] The original substance concept was based upon the empirical fact of the relative constancy of things in spite of exchanges of their component parts and changes in their empirical forms. In order to explain this empirical observation, substantialism sharply distinguished between the *essentia* or (to use the term

---

36. Regarding the timelessness of God, see extensively, Ganssle (2001); Pike (2002).
37. Cf. *EDR* 6:179–80.
38. Cf. Visagie (1982); Strauss and Visagie (1984, 69); Strauss (1991b).
39. See extensively, Dooyeweerd (1943–1946).

of Immanuel Kant) the *noumenal* being of things (Plato: *auto to eidos*; Kant: *das Ding an sich*, "the thing in itself") and their *accidents* or secondary (Kant: *phenomenal*) features. In early Protestant dogmatics, the being of God was vaguely described as infinite spiritual essence (Lat. *essentia spiritualis infinita*) or as the spiritual being existing by itself (Lat. *ens spirituale a se subsistens*), as distinct from his attributes (Lat. *accidentia*).[40]

The error of substantialism consists in placing the practical distinction between constancy and mutability within the framework of a *theoretical antithesis* between the consciousness of the logical subject (the observer) and some objective reality as such. Such a theoretical distancing is entirely foreign to common, everyday experience with its *immediate* orientation toward reality. In this theoretical distancing, thinking continually construes substances through analysis and abstraction, which are subsequently imprinted upon reality. Thus, substantialism originated from absolutizing the theoretical abstract of what is constant. It abstracts essences from the full immanent relationships and coherences in which the Creator has placed them, and then declares these essences to be the true reality. None of the ancient thinkers could have perceived this error because they lacked God's self-revelation. Thus, it is all the more regrettable that so many traditional, orthodox theologians demonstrate their inability in breaking their scholastic bonds with this pagan substantialism. Emil Brunner rightly exclaimed, "What does the substance concept have to do with a Christian theology?"[41] He called the introduction of this concept into the Athanasian Creed a "truly fateful matter."[42]

In this Creed, the term occurs four times: "We worship one God in trinity and trinity in unity, without either confusing the persons, or dividing the *substance* (Lat. *substantia*)" (Art. 3-4). "Our Lord Jesus Christ, the Son of God, is equally

---

40. Althaus (1952, 263).
41. Brunner (1950, 240).
42. Ibid., 254.

both God and man. He is God from the Father's *substance*, begotten before time; and he is man from his mother's *substance*, born in time.... One certinaly not by confusion of *substance*, but by oneness of person" (Art. 30–31, 36)." The Creed even connects the acceptance of these statements with people's eternal salvation: "This is the catholic faith. Unless a man believes it faithfully and steadfastly, he cannot be saved. Amen" (Art. 40). Those who refuse to accept these Greek theoretical constructions have no share in the kingdom of God!

Radical Christian thought necessarily looks in a different direction, and finds the basis for all constancy, and for all changes and variability, within the law-order under which God has placed his creation.[43] The term "constancy" is a modal term; its original sense is found in the kinematic modality. In the view of South African philosopher Daniel F. M. Strauss, the idea of constancy found its first scientific expression in the inertia laws of Italian physicist Galileo Galilei (d. 1642).[44] In opposition to the view current at the time, which held that the movement of an object depends on a causative force, Galileo stated that movement is an original *datum* that cannot be reduced to the physical. In other words, one cannot ask for the physical cause of a movement, but only for the cause of a *change* of movement. This means that the constancy of movement is a condition for causing any change; that is, change exists only by virtue of constancy. Therefore, there can be no polar antithesis between constancy and change, as ancient thought had suggested through dialectically opposing a thing's constant *being* and its changing phenomenal *form*. On the contrary, there is an insoluble coherence between constancy and change, that is, between a thing's alleged essence and its attributes, as established in the divine law-order.

4.4.3 A Christian Philosophical Approach

Let us first see how traditional substantialism deals with the

---
43. See extensively, *EDR* 11:chapter 3.
44. Strauss (1991b, 37).

The Being of God

human experience of the individual thing. Take the famous example of René Descartes: a piece of wax.[45] Its various properties include color, smell, taste, and solidity. Substantialism emphasizes that wax *is* not color, smell, and so on, but merely *has* these properties. That is, these characteristics are ascribed to the actual substance of the wax, which is concealed behind these features. We observe the properties, not the substance. When we cool down this wax, or heat or even melt it, its color, smell, taste, and solidity change, but not its substance. Hidden behind the changing properties lies the unchangeable substance: the wax is and was wax. This is what I would call an "introvert" view: the substance is hidden *within* the thing; it is this unchangeable core that warrants its identity and autonomous existence under all circumstances.

This is very different from the Christian philosophical view that I advocate, and which I would call "extrovert" or "eccentric."[46] That is, the essence of a thing does not lie within it, as is claimed in substantialism, but outside it, namely, in its relationship to the Creator and Law-Giver of all things. There is no room here for any self-sufficient mode of existence, which would sever the thing from its dependence on humanity, and through the latter on the Creator and Sustainer of cosmic reality.

Modern science itself has discredited the entire substance concept, especially since the rise of quantum physics and the theory of the equivalence of matter and energy. In biology and psychology, too, the substance concept has been replaced by a dynamic (holistic) notion of the total structure. Modern scientific functionalism has suppressed earlier substantialism.[47] Physics has no room any longer for the idea that any *material* substance could exist, even a kind of proto-matter that would remain the same under all circumstances. Today, we know that such stable particles as electrons can be destroyed, and

---

45. Cf. Kalsbeek (1970, 181–89).
46. For the use of the term "eccentric" in anthropology, see Plessner (1928).
47. Dooyeweerd (1940b, 43).

in the process produce photons, and that they can also be created from photons. The most stable particles, neutrons, can be destroyed by collision with their anti-particles, and in the process their energy is transformed into light. Matter is not a substance but concentrated energy.[48]

4.4.4 True Essence

In Christian philosophical thought, a thing's essence—if one were to insist using such a loaded term—is primarily sought in its functions (though it is not limited to it). These are not only a thing's subject functions, that is, the modalities in which a thing functions as a subject, or the law-spheres to whose laws a thing is subordinated. This is because, if we enclose a thing's essence within its subject functions, once again we are not far from substantialism. Rather, we look at a thing's subject functions as well as its object functions, that is, the modalities in which a thing functions as an object. For instance, inanimate things, plants, and animals can function as logical, lingual, social, economic, aesthetic, moral, and pistical objects in the lives of human beings.[49] In these very *object* functions, the orientation of these things toward, and their dependence upon, humans—for whom all things were created—become particularly visible. Think again of the piece of wax: God created it as something perceivable (perceptive object function) and analyzable (logical object function), so that it can be sold or bought (economic), worked upon (cultural-historical), and ultimately processed into candles (social and even pistical), cosmetic articles and gramophone discs (aesthetic), and so on.

The identity of the wax is disclosed if we view it in the mutual relationships of the functions, in its orientation toward humanity as creation's crown, and in its total dependence upon the Creator. The wax is not some internal, self-sufficient, autonomous substance that provides warrant for the identity of the piece of wax, but an inner structural principle or law,

---

48. Cf. Ouweneel (1986, 305–306).
49. See Ouweneel (2014a).

instituted by the Creator. It is this "individuality structure" (also called *idionomy*) that arranges the modal functions in such a way that a thing's unique constitution originates.

It is the continuity of this idionomy of the wax that, in spite of all changes, provides warrant for the naïve (i.e., everyday, practical) identity experience. This means that, in spite of extensive processing, we still say, "This is the same piece of matter as the one we started with, although it now looks quite different." And if we implement the same process with a very different piece of wax, even if the two pieces looked identical we would still say, "This is not the same piece." This experience of identity cannot be caught in a concept. Concepts, and in line with them, definitions, always refer to *types* of things. That is, we can define wax, but we cannot define *this* piece of wax. Of the unique identity of *this* piece, even if it looks exactly like thousands of other pieces, we can only form an *idea*.

This Christian philosophical view of the experience of identity, which I have described here in the briefest possible form,[50] may help us to eliminate substantialism from the doctrine of God in its traditional formulation. That is, it helps us to avoid the disastrous dualism of God's substance and God's attributes, or of his absolute (incommunicable) and his relative (communicable) attributes. This view also helps us to free ourselves from the false emphasis upon God's substance by those who deny that he has attributes, and conversely, from the false emphasis upon his attributes by those who, in a Kantian way, deny that his substance would be inaccessible to us, and so on. This view helps us to see that God *is* his attributes so that they cannot be abstracted from him; that he is not something beyond what has been revealed about him, something that he would be truly in himself. We would insist that *all* of God's attributes are absolute (eternal, independent of his creation), and at the same time they are *all* relative because they are all revealed in their meaning for humanity. These

---

50. See extensively, Dooyeweerd (*NC* 3:Part I).

claims may become clearer in the following sections.

4.5 The Damage Created by Substantialism
4.5.1 Dualism

According to the view being presented here, what are the main errors introduced by ancient substantialism into the traditional doctrine of God?[51]

(a) The first error is the Aristotelian *substantialist dualism* between God's being and God's attributes, that is, between God's immutable *substantia* and the mutable *accidentia*. Within the scope of this substantialism, these *accidentia* cannot be viewed as belonging to God's being because of its simplicity (cf. Belgic Confession Art. 1: ". . . there is one only simple and spiritual Being, which we call God; . . ."; see also §4.2.1 above). Therefore, these *accidentia* are thought to refer to his external relationships with the world; thus, they are viewed as attributes only in our reason. However, only some indeterminate "something" would constitute God's being as such. Moreover, we would possess no *self*-revelation *of God*, no revelation *of his being*, but only of his relationships with the world.

In modern (post-Kantian) substantialism, God's immutable *substantia* exists dualistically over against his attributes, even though it does include the relationship(s) of an entity to its substance. In other words, this substantialism ascribes God's relationships with the world, that is, his attributes, to his being. If substantialism itself had been surrendered, this could have led to de conclusion that God's one being and God's multiple attributes are identical, without endangering the unity of God's being (see §4.5.3 below).

4.5.2 Prima Causa

(b) The equally Aristotelian idea of a first cause (Lat. *prima causa*) identified God as the first cause of all causes, a cause

---

51. Cf. the analysis by Kasper (1983, 147–57); cf. Pannenberg (1988, 389–401), who, however, does not criticize substantialism as such.

not itself caused by anything else, and thus the cause of the world as a totality. Of course, this idea as such is undeniable. However, it led to so-called *natural theology*, which tried to derive God's attributes from the creation by arguing back from the creation to its first cause: God (see §§1.1.2 and 2.10). We will return to this when we deal with the three ways of Pseudo-Dionysius (§4.6).

Over against this natural theology, we find the theology that speaks of God's attributes exclusively on the basis of his self-revelation in the Bible. It does not deduce God's attributes from his relationships with the world, but from himself, as he has revealed himself in his Word. The Bible uses terms for God that have been deduced from the created world (King, Shepherd, Father, Judge, etc.), and as ideas that are applied to him.

The *rationalism* of scholastic and early Protestant theology caused people to understand the creational terms that the Bible uses for God as concepts. This has led to various fallacies, such as the idea that God's being and God's attributes can be equated only at the expense of the unity of his being.[52] Indeed, the *concept* of unity conflicts with the *concept* of multiplicity. However, the idea of divine unity does not necessarily conflict at all with the idea of the multiplicity of the divine attributes.

4.5.3 Idealism

(c) The traditional *(conceptual) idealism* along the line of Plato claims that the idea of the divine substance is real, whereas the divine attributes are thought to exist only in our thinking (Lat. *ratione*). However, God's attributes are objectively real, not only *ratione*, and their reality does not differ from that of his being, but is rather proper to it. God's being is his attributes; his attributes are his being.

In our modern, post-Kantian time, idealism has assumed a new form. It has suggested that both God's (unknown)

---

52. Cf. Pannenberg (1988, 391–97).

being and his attributes are hidden behind his empirical cosmic functions, just as the Kantian thing-in-itself (Ger. *Ding an sich*) is hidden behind the perceptions that we receive of it. In practice, this has inevitably led to the projection hypothesis, in which, parallel with the procedure of classical natural theology, these cosmic functions are derived from what we know of the cosmos itself. That is, the cosmic attributes are projected upon the (supposed) deity. Taken one step further, the superfluous hidden, unknown divine being behind these cosmic functions is simply denied. Thus, people end up in pure atheism (cf. Ludwig Feuerbach,[53] and later, Sigmund Freud, §2.3.2 above).

4.6 Scholastic Remnants
4.6.1 Communicable and Incommunicable

Through scholasticism, the disastrous ancient substantialism found its way into theology proper, both in Roman Catholic and in early Protestant dogmatics. It comes to light in the distinction between God's being (or essence, the *ipsum esse* [being itself] defended by Thomas Aquinas) and his phenomenal appearance, a distinction directly related to the scholastic distinction between God's incommunicable and communicable attributes.[54] Compare, for instance, the distinction by the Lutheran Johann Gerhard (d. 1637) between (Gk.) *akoinōnēta* and *koinōnēta*.[55] Actually, Lutheran dogmatics preferred the distinction between relative, operative, or external attributes (Lat. *attributa relativa*, *operative*, or *externa*) and absolute, resting [non-operative], or internal attributes (Lat. *attributa absoluta, quiescentia* or *interna*). This was similar to Martin Luther's distinction between the revealed God (Lat. *deus revelatus*) and the hidden God (Lat. *deus absconditus*), respectively[56] (see below).

---

53. E.g., Feuerbach (1957).
54. Bavinck (*RD* 2:chapters 4–5).
55. Loci theol. II.7.105.
56. Weber (1981, 446–48, 464).

American Evangelical theologian Millard J. Erickson told us that he rejected the speculations of scholasticism.[57] However, he nonetheless uncritically adopted distinctions like those between communicable and incommunicable attributes, or between immanent (intransitive) and eminent (transitive) attributes.[58] This single example out of many illustrates the difficulty of effectively extricating oneself from scholastic thinking.

The distinction between God's incommunicable and communicable attributes is traditionally interwoven with the notion of the incomprehensibility and the unknowability of God.[59] This is the idea that, according to his essential being, his *aseitas* (from *a se esse*, "existing in/by itself"; the term is from Anselm), God is inaccessible to our thinking and elevated beyond our limited human understanding. However, according to his appearance, that is, the way in which, and the extent to which, he has revealed himself in a humanly comprehensible manner, we can understand his communicable attributes to a certain extent. Moreover, they can be communicated in the sense of granted or bestowed upon others; these are the properties that God supposedly shares to a certain extent with humanity.

4.6.2 The Three Ways

The Neo-Platonist (Pseudo-)Dionysius Areopagita argued that it is not permitted to speak of the being of God, and that he is *hyperousios*, that is, elevated beyond the category of being. Interestingly, Abraham Kuyper protested against this argument in a biblicistic way by pointing to Proverbs 8:14 ("Counsel is mine, and sound wisdom" KJV; "I have counsel and sound wisdom" ESV).[60]

This same Pseudo-Dionysius laid the foundation for the

---

57. Erickson (1998, 325–26).
58. Ibid., 292–93.
59. Bavinck (*RD* 2:chapters 1–2).
60. Kuyper (*DD* I.1.128).

distinction between God's communicable and incommunicable attributes through his "three ways" (Lat. *tres viae*).[61] He believed that God could be approached in three ways:

(a) *Via eminentiae* ("the way of eminence"): knowledge of God through *a fortiori* statements (i.e., those expressing "all the more" or "all the more strongly"): if humans are powerful, God is all the more powerful (omnipotent, almighty); if humans have knowledge, God does all the more (he is omniscient, knowing everything), and so on. By magnifying certain known properties of human beings, we can get an idea of certain properties of God.

(b) *Via negationis* or *remotionis* ("the way of negation [denial] or removal"): knowledge of God by telling what God is *not*, in contrast to human beings: human beings are mortal, visible, finite, mutable, God is immortal, invisible, infinite, immutable, and also immeasurable, inscrutable, impassible, incorruptible, incorporeal, and so on. This is the way of so-called "negative theology."

(c) *Via causalitatis* or *attributionis* ("the way of causality or attribution"): knowledge of God through analogous statements: the life and love of human beings issue from, and refer back to, God's life and love. This way has led to the notion of the *analogia entis* (see §4.8.2).

These three ways are a form of pure natural theology: with the help of reason, the transcendent attributes of God are derived from the immanent-empirical world. Nevertheless, this Dionysian method was still followed even in early Protestant theology, for example, by David Hollaz.[62] In more recent times, this doctrine was still defended by, among others, the Jesuit Walter Brugger (d. 1990).[63] In both Roman Catholicism and traditional Protestantism, the doctrine of the three ways has greatly influenced the doctrine of the divine attributes. Emil Brunner pointed to the important parallelism between

---

61. De div. nom. VII.3.
62. Exam. theol. 190.
63. Brugger (1979, 279–86).

these three ways of Pseudo-Dionysius and the three ways of Neo-Platonic mysticism.[64] It is particularly the *via negationis* that corresponds to the mystical way of being separated from what is earthly in preparation for union with the deity.

4.6.3 Divisions

In agreement with the doctrine of the three ways, we can now present some traditional divisions of the divine attributes in the following manner. The distinction between, on the one hand, the first and the third way, and, on the other hand, the second way, can be directly compared with the distinction between positive and negative, or immanent and transcendent, or relative and absolute, or communicable and incommunicable attributes of God. In all these cases, we are dealing with the (supposed) distinction between what God is in relationship with humanity, what he shares with humanity, and what he is in himself alone.[65]

> 1. *Relative* divine attributes, that is, existing only within time, in relationship with the created reality: Creator, Sustainer, King, Shepherd, Judge, and so one.
>
> 2. *Absolute* divine attributes, that is, characterizing God from eternity; these constitute the actual subject of the traditional doctrine of divine attributes. "Absolute" must not be taken here as *sine ulla relatione ad creaturas* ("without any relationship with creatures").[66] When God reveals himself as the eternal, infinite God, (a) this communication as such already implies a relationship, and (b) God does reveal himself to us in this way because of the significance that his eternity and infiniteness have for us. Traditionally, these "absolute" attributes have been divided as follows.
>
> 2.1 Incommunicable attributes: properties that God does

---

64. Brunner (1950, 261–62); cf. Weber (1981, 455); Buri (1978, 671, 682).
65. Cf. Trillhaas (1972, 123–24).
66. Johann Gerhard, quoted by Elert (1956, 230).

not share with (communicate to) his creatures, or *internal* attributes, that is, proper to God's being as such:

2.1.1 *negative*: infinitude, immutability, immeasurability, inscrutability, immortality, unfathomability, and so on;

2.1.2 *positive*: eternity, spirituality (being spirit[ual]), unity, aseity, omnipresence, and so on.

2.2 *Communicable* attributes: properties that God shares with (communicates to) human beings, or *external* attributes, that is, proper to God's relationship with the cosmos; these are always *positive* attributes:

2.2.1 Attributes of *eminence*: properties in which God infinitely surpasses humanity (sometimes called *inimitable*, but this conflicts with communicable): omnipotence, omniscience, and so on (in human beings: power, knowledge);

2.2.2 *Imitable* attributes: love, wisdom, righteousness, holiness, grace, mercy, and so on.

4.7 Concrete Dangers
4.7.1 God's Self-Revelation

Before entering into further philosophical analyses, let me say something about the dangers for faith embedded in distinctions like the ones just mentioned.[67] As we saw, the first danger is that this distinction between communicable and incommunicable attributes produces the notion that faith does not possess a revelation of God *himself*. This is because his non-proper, communicable, external appearance is distinguished from his proper, incommunicable, internal being. Supposedly, we possess revelation only of his external, phenomenal appearance, of the mask that he adopted, which excludes knowing God as he is in himself. In this case, not *God*, but only some external, non-proper properties *of* God, have been revealed to humanity, properties he was pleased to

---
67. Cf. Pannenberg (1971, 320–25).

reveal to us. We would not know God as he really *is*, but only as it pleased him to present himself to us.

Please note that nobody is claiming that any person could know God exhaustively, in every depth of detail. But there is a fundamental difference between, on the one hand, knowing *God* (though not exhaustively), and, on the other hand, knowing only the non-proper aspects that God was prepared to show people. This was precisely the error of John Calvin when he said that God is not being described in Exodus 34:5 ("merciful and gracious, slow to anger, and abounding in steadfast love and faithfulness") as he is in himself but as he is toward us.[68] Similarly, Herman Bavinck asserted, "There is no knowledge of God as he is in himself."[69] In a sense, this is shocking. If we have no revelation concerning *God himself*, Christianity is ultimately meaningless. It was *God* who appeared to Abraham, Isaac, and Jacob (Gen. 12:7; 17:1; 26:24; 35:7, "God revealed himself"; cf. Isa. 22:14, "The LORD of hosts has revealed himself"), not a garment or a mask that he was pleased to put on for the occasion. It is *the Father* who is revealed to the believers (Matt. 11:27; Luke 10:22; John 17:6, 26), not a paternal mask that he adopts for the occasion. It is *God* who revealed *himself*, not just some attributes—non-proper, external properties—*of* God, *of* the Father.

American theologian Gordon Spykman (d. 1993) followed Calvin: "We know God, as Calvin argues, not as he is in himself (*ad intra*), but as he comes out to us in his revelation (*ad extra*)."[70] This is a false contrast, for in his revelation God reveals *himself*. Spykman used this argument to take the "methodological decision not to begin dogmatics proper with a separate discussion of the existence and being of God, or of his knowability and attributes, or even of the doctrine of the Trinity." He was right in saying that these issues must not be reflected upon "apart from their contextualized reality in the

---

68. *Institutes* 1.10.12.
69. Bavinck (*RD* 2:47).
70. Spykman (1992, 139).

biblical doctrine of creation." But Spykman's work contains minimal discussion of the divine attributes or of the Trinity, and he dismisses the proofs of God's existence in one page.[71]

Another Reformed theologian/philosopher, Andree Troost, stated the matter in a far more correct and balanced way:

> As believers, we acknowledge *a priori* that God honestly reveals himself as he, in his divine reality and activity, really *is*, and that, therefore, by faith we (can) really know him as he is. . . . We never ought to speculate about the question who or what God is or does 'in himself,' beyond or apart from his self-revelation, even though we know, precisely through that revelation, that our knowledge of God is *limited* to *what* he reveals of himself in creaturely deeds and words.[72]

The question whether God has revealed himself, or only certain non-proper attributes of himself, must make us very suspicious of the distinction between God's essence and appearance, between his internal and external attributes, between his incomprehensibility and his knowability. All three ways of Pseudo-Dionysius must be fundamentally rejected.[73] This is especially true of the via *negationis* because, as a result of this way, we supposedly would be unable to know anything about God. In opposition to this, I believe that *biblical* attributes, such as God's incomprehensibility, are not understood through some way of negation, but they imdeed tell us something positive about God. As a metaphysical-speculative enterprise, the *via eminentiae* is mistaken because we cannot simply make a superlative of a certain human attribute, thereby to acquire knowledge about God. And the *via causalitatis* is mistaken as well: the person who loves has received this love from God, but this does not mean that such a person

---

71. Ibid., 147–48.
72. Troost (2004, 257); cf. Strauss (2009, 201–204).
73. Cf. Cremer (1917, 23); Elert (1956, 234–35); Trillhaas (1972, 126).

manifests God's own love, in any absolute sense.[74] A certain creational feature does not necessarily refer back in any causal way to any attribute of God; this is the basic error of all traditional theistic proofs (see previous chapter).

4.7.2 Statements about God

The second significant danger for theology proper is that God's communicable attributes, but especially his incommunicable attributes, are treated largely separately from God's redemptive deeds and his Trinitarian being.[75] (The reader will have to judge in how far I myself have fallen into this snare in the coming two chapters.) Of course it is true that, viewed methodologically, the attributes of the Deity, which are shared by all three divine persons, must be distinguished from the questions of the Trinity and of divine salvation. However, such a methodological distinction easily develops into a metaphysical speculation about God's being, apart from his deeds. As German theologian Edmund Schlink (d. 1984) rightly said,

> While the Trinitarian statements of the Apostolic and the Nicene-Constantinopolitan Creeds were cultic confessions, now [i.e., in scholastic theology] their place in dogmatics was taken up by general statements 'about God,' in which human thought expressed itself theoretically, namely, apart from the historically being touched by the word of the cross. Thus, it ran the risk of assuming a viewpoint from which it believed to be able to oversee God and the world, and conceptually relate the one to the other.[76]

The most extreme statements within traditional theology about God's being came from those who wished not to speak about God's attributes at all, and to speak of only his being (or essence). For instance, Philo said, "God is property-less"

---

74. Heyns (1988, 61); of course, we speak here of natural human love, not of God's own love, which he pours out in the hearts of believers (Rom. 5:5).
75. Cf. Rahner (1974, 87).
76. *RGG* 2:1735.

(Gk. *apoios ho theos*).[77] Augustine wrote, "To God belongs no property" (Lat. *In Deum non cadit accidens*),[78] and, "Whatever can be worthily said of God is not quality [property] but essence" (Lat. *Quidquid de Deo digne dicitur non qualitas est, sed essential*).[79] German theologian Johannes Andreas Quenstedt (d. 1688) said, "If we wish to speak in a proper and accurate way, God has no properties, but merely and most simply is essence [being]" (Lat. *Si proprie et accurate loqui velimus, Deus nullas habet proprietates, sed mera et simplicissima est essential.*)[80]

In contrast to these theologians, the nineteenth-century Kantian theologians sharply sensed the dangers of such metaphysical speculation for theology proper. However, they easily fell into the opposite snare, no longer daring to make any statement about God's essence. Thus, Friedrich Schleiermacher's theology proper was limited to statements about religious experience, that of Albrecht Ritschl to statements about God's ethical claim and this activity within history.[81] Ritschl's dogmatics contains no separate doctrine of God.[82] Just as with Kant's *Ding an sich*, statements about God's being seemed no longer possible. In fact, this error was a consequence of the same erroneous distinction between the noumenal and the phenomenal as in ancient and scholastic substantialism. The ultimate consequence of this was the view of Rudolf Bultmann that any speaking about God is possible only as a speaking about ourselves. It was Karl Barth in particular who, in the twentieth century, strongly protested against this development.

Actually, strictly speaking, Immanuel Kant's distinction could not at all be equated with the distinction between God's

---

77. Allegorical Commentary I.13.36.
78. E.g., *De Trinitate* V.5.6.
79. *De Civitate* VIII.6.
80. Theologica didactico-polemica I.8.2. Cf. Brunner (1950, 256); Weber (1981, 452–53).
81. Schleiermacher (1831); Ritschl (1881).
82. Ritschl (1986); cf. Weber (1981, 453–54); Elert (1956, 237–38); Schlink (1983, 738).

being and attributes. God's self-revelation cannot be compared with the Kantian phenomenal form of things because (a) this revelation does not occur primarily under human empirical observation but within the human heart, and (b) it is quite impossible in the first place to abstract some idea of God in himself (Ger. *Gott an sich*[83]) from his revelation. We know God from his works; in no way can his being be abstracted from these works, nor can his being be deduced from his works. For instance, we cannot deduce from suffering experienced by people some attribute of God that leads him to make people suffer,[84] as is attempted nowadays. Faith knows God very differently, despite the phenomenal form of things.

4.8 More on the Being–Appearance Dualism
4.8.1 Negative Theology

Let me say a bit more about the false dualism of God's being versus God's appearance. In classical theology, this dualism has led to two alternative but incorrect doctrines, mentioned before: negative theology (this section) and the doctrine of the *analogia entis* (next section).

As to the former: we saw that the emphasis upon God's inscrutable being (essence) often led to a so-called "negative theology." The essential being of God was considered to be so elevated that it cannot been known by human beings. With regard to this God's being, we can state only what God is *not*. We find this idea already with the Neo-Platonist Plotinus (d. 270).[85] He denied that God had essence, being, or life, and claimed that God was elevated beyond these matters: God is "the being who is above all these things" (Gr. *to hyper panta tauta einai*).[86]

This is de *Deus absconditus* ("hidden God") of scholastic (Roman Catholic and early Protestant) theology.[87] What we

---
83. Elert (1956, 226).
84. Ibid., 229.
85. Bavinck (*RD* 2:35).
86. Enneaden 3.8.9 (352b).
87. Cf. Rahner (1979); Pannenberg (1988, 368).

know of God is supposedly his outer appearance, behind which we must assume his actual, exalted essence, which for us is unknowable, inscrutable, unfathomable, incomprehensible, and inaccessible. Examples of this view in Christian tradition are Justin Martyr, Clement of Alexandria, Athanasius, Origen, Eusebius, Augustine, Anselm, Albert the Great, Thomas Aquinas, and Martin Luther. Herman Bavinck regretted that even "in Reformed theology, too, the significance of God's incomprehensibility was increasingly lost from view," and that it was the (Enlightenment!) philosophers (Immanuel Kant, Johann Gottlieb Fichte) who reminded theology of the "truth of the incomprehensibility of God"![88]

Of course, we can hardly avoid using negative terms about God. We call him *in*visible, *in*scrutable, *im*mutable, *in*finite, *im*mortal, *im*measurable, *un*fathomable, dwelling in an *in*accessible light, and so on, and the Bible itself leads the way in doing so (e.g., Rom. 11:33; Col. 1:15; 1 Tim. 1:17; 6:16; Heb. 11:27; James 1:17). But stating the obvious is not enough. First and foremost, the reply of radical Christian thinking to negative theology must involve the rejection of the entire underlying being–appearance dualism. Second, this thinking must point out that, if God reveals himself in his love, his wisdom, his steadfastness, his omnipotence, his omniscience, his sovereignty, his righteousness, and so on, these and many other attributes describe what God *is*; these are not describing merely the outer appearance of an inscrutable being. This is not a belittling of God, for we hasten to *add* that, *in* his love, wisdom, steadfastness, omnipotence, omniscience, sovereignty, righteousness, and so on, God surpasses the boundaries of our conceptual knowledge, as we have seen. Yet, *this*, and much more, is what God *himself* is. There is not some essence hidden behind these attributes. And by using *creational* terms such as love, wisdom, steadfastness, power, knowledge, freedom, righteousness, and so on, we can acquire *true knowledge* of God's love, wisdom, steadfastness, omnipotence,

---

88. Bavinck (*RD* 2:41–43).

omniscience, sovereignty, righteousness, and so on—that is, *of himself.*

Although I do reject his (later) paradigm, I acknowledge Harry Kuitert's merit of having shown that the so-called "anthropomorphisms" in the Bible with regard to God do *not* imply a kind of accommodation on God's behalf, as traditional theology claimed "from Philo to K[laas] Schilder."[89] Kuitert rightly rejected the consequence of the traditional view—namely, that these anthropomorphisms supposedly reveal nothing of God's *being* ("how he really is")—even if his reasons for doing so differ from mine.[90]

Augustine also claimed that we know with certainty only what God is *not*.[91] And under the influence of Neo-Platonism and of Augustine, Thomas Aquinas, too, was inclined toward a kind of negative theology. The words of Plotinus, that we can say only what God is not, are repeated by Thomas in a similar way.[92] To a certain extent we can sympathize with the challenge of David Hume, who wondered in what sense the mystics, who postulated God's absolute inscrutability, differed from the sceptics or atheists, who claimed that the first cause of all things is unknown and incomprehensible.[93]

Daniel F. M. Strauss summarized the entire problem in the briefest possible way: as soon as we distinguish between conceptual knowledge and concept-transcending knowledge [i.e., in the form of ideas], the vicious circle of a negative theology disappears, for then it is no longer necessary to deny what is factually presented in the form of ideas. In other words, what God, according to negative theology, is *not*, is what cannot be described in the form of concepts but definitely can be de-

---

89. Kuitert (1962, 89; see 88–121).
90. Cf. ibid., 164–88.
91. *Confessiones* IX.20; *De Trinitate* V.10.
92. *Summa contra Gentiles* III.49 (see https://dhspriory.org/thomas/ContraGentiles3a.htm#49) and *Summa Theoogiae* I.1.7, I.13.8, and especially I.13.1(-see https://dhspriory.org/thomas/english/summa/FP.html).
93. Quoted by Macquarrie (1975, 100).

scribed in the form of ideas. [94]

4.8.2 The Analogia Entis

Thomas Aquinas developed his doctrine of the *analogia entis* with regard to God's communicable (knowable and transferable) attributes.[95] In his view, there is an ontic analogy—an analogy with respect to being—between God and humanity. This view is inclined toward a theo-ontological duplication of the creational diversity in God's being in the sense that, according to Thomas, all creational attributes existed *a priori* in God in a more exalted manner, and that all divine attributes exist *a posteriori* in humans. Each attribute appears in a double way, so to speak: first in God, and then, issued from him, in his creatures (Lat. *procedentibus in creaturas ab ipso*).[96] We know God through this analogy with his creatures in the sense that he carries all the attributes of his creatures within himself.

For instance, Thomas wrote,

> So when we say, "God is good," the meaning is not "God is the cause of goodness," or "God is not evil"; but the meaning is, "Whatever good we attribute to creatures, pre-exists in God," and in a more excellent and higher way (Lat. *Cum igitur dicitur: Deus est bonus, non est sensus, Deus est causa bonitatis, vel Deus non est malus; sed est sensus, id, quod bonitatem dicimus in creaturis, praeexistit in Deo; et hoc quidem secundum modum altiorem*.[97]

The background of this view is, according to Thomas, that both human beings and God, in an analogous way, are contained in Being (Lat. *esse*) as the first known thing (Lat. *primum*

---

94. Strauss (2009, 205).
95. See, e.g., Buri (1978, 635–44); Guarino (2005, chapter 8); the latter work is important for various Roman Catholic views of the foundations of systematic theology.
96. *Summa Theologiae* I.13.3 (see https://dhspriory.org/thomas/summa/FP/FP013.html#FPQ13A3THEP1).
97. Ibid., I.13.2 (see https://dhspriory.org/thomas/summa/FP/FP013.html#FPQ13A2THEP1).

notum). Apparently, this Being is the unqualified common denominator of both God and his creation, even though Thomas tries to distinguish ontologically between God, who is both *esse* and *essential*, and humanity, which only *participates* in the *esse*; or between God, who is infinite and uncaused, and humans, who are finite and caused; or between God in whom we see things in their unity, and humanity in which we see them in their diversity.

It is important to carefully perceive the fundamental difference between this view and what I consider to be radical Christian thinking. The former implies that terms with which we refer to certain things in the creation refer at the same time to analogous realities in God. These existed already before and in a more exalted way, namely, in God as a kind of primordial image (*archetype*), of which every creature in its own way is an imprint (*ectype*). For instance, people speak about the Being of God in terms of the ethical modality, especially with reference to his love: "God *is* love" (1 John 4:8, 16). Subsequently, this essence of God is theo-ontologically presented as a primordial image or archetype for creation, from which created must be deduced.[98] Notions that are referred from creation, to God in the form of ideas subsequently become the model *for* creation in a way that is basically Platonic. In this way, God is effectively un-deified because he is reduced to a complex of duplicated creational attributes, an elevated extension of his own creation.

In what I see as a radical-Christian understanding, things are essentially different. In this perspective, God reveals himself in the Bible in terms that are proper to our created reality, simply because we have no other terms at our disposal. These terms are applied to God in the form of ideas. God *is* truly love. Empirically, we know only creaturely love; that is, we know love only because we experience love in our social relationships. We know parental love, matrimonial love, patri-

---

98. So, e.g., Wentsel (1987, 62, 323).

otic love, friendship, and so on. These are forms of love about which we can form concepts. God loves, too; more than that, he is love. However, this is not creaturely, finite, immanent love, or the extension of it. God's love is divine, infinite, eternal; it is elevated infinitely far above any form of human love. Yet, God *is* love, and we can *know* that he is love because in the Bible God has revealed himself as love. God could do this only by using terms adopted from our created reality; what other terms could he have employed that we could have understood?

Of course, humanly speaking, this was a risky endeavor. For if we were to mistakenly understand these terms as *concepts* about God, this would imply an attempt to enclose him within the boundaries of our created, finite world. This, in fact, is what occurs in the doctrine of the *analogia entis*. The ultimate consequence of this doctrine is that it robs God of his deity, and degrades him to the level of his own creatures, no matter how strongly we would emphasize the exaltedness of God's love. To avoid this mistake, we must use these terms as *ideas*, that is, as pointing approximately to something that surpasses the boundaries of our concepts, and surpasses even conceptualization itself. With respect to God, it surpasses even creation as such. In this case, the terms truly tell us what God is in himself, but then only insofar as people can comprehend them.

4.8.3 Further Explanation

As further explanation of this important point, let me add three considerations.

(a) When we say that God is Father, we certainly wish to say that he is and was Father from eternity. The eternal Son in the bosom of the Father (John 1:18) had an eternal Father.[99] Thus, God's Fatherhood existed before human fatherhood. We can easily understand how this fact of the eternal pri-

---

99. This is not to be confused with the Son's Messianic title "eternal Father" in Isa. 9:6.

ority of God's Fatherhood strengthened the idea that God's Fatherhood is the archetype from which human fatherhood was *derived*. This idea seems quite attractive, and is widespread in Protestant circles,[100] but does not find any support in the Bible. It is nothing but a form of ontological idealism, (Neo-)Platonic or otherwise. God was Father from eternity before any human father existed. But this does not change the fact that, within our reality, what God was from eternity—Father—can be expressed only in terms belonging to human immanent-creaturely reality, that is, in terms of human immanent-creaturely fatherhood.[101]

(b) The fact that human fatherhood is not ontically modeled after God's Fatherhood does not stop us from ethically (pastorally, homiletically) using this Fatherhood as a model for human fathers. In his love, his care, his wise admonitions, the Father is a *moral* example for all human fathers. But this is fundamentally different from the idea that the Father would be the *ontic* archetype, the model of which all human fathers would be creational copies, of the same being as the heavenly Father.

(c) The fact that humans were created according to the image and likeness of God is often presented as a proof for the scholastic view that God is the prototype, and humans are the copies. But of course, this is the fallacy of *petitio principii*, assuming as proven precisely what is to be proved. It is a striking example of an age-old malpractice: adducing so-called "proof texts" (Lat. *loca probantia*), which in reality are abused as vessels that are already filled with pagan notions. The claim that human beings are images of God is an exegetical matter that demands interpretation—which has been carried out in various ways[102]—but not a container for importing pagan ideas.

In order to further illustrate how creational terms are used

---

100. See Bavinck (*RD* 2:307).
101. Cf. Chafer (*ST* 1:316).
102. See extensively, *EDR* 3:§§5.1 and 5.2.

as ideas, let us look again at negative theology.[103] It has often been argued that we cannot say anything meaningful about God because he is too exalted; he far surpasses our understanding. Claims like this are simply contradictory, for such statements that God is exalted and surpasses our understanding *are* meaningful, though not necessarily correct, statements about God. If we wonder whether we can apply spatial terms to God, the answer might be, No, God is elevated beyond all spatiality—without realizing that the term "elevated" is a purely spatial term, appealing to our spatial experience of extension and proportionality within creation. How then can such a term be applied to God? Is it "only" a metaphor, which does not express any truth about God? But why would we use the term if in fact it is empty, or even incorrect? Is there an alternative? That is, can we use spatial terms with regard to God *without* eliminating his elevation beyond all spatiality?

The answer is, Indeed we can. For instance, let us look at the following statement by Herman Bavinck who says that, in a certain sense, our knowledge of God is negative, "because we cannot ascribe a single predicate to God as we conceive that predicate in relation to creatures."[104] Everything depends here on the meaning of the word "as." We cannot speak of God's mercy the same way we speak of human mercy, namely, conceptually; but it is equally true that we cannot speak of God's mercy in any terms *other* than creational terms. We can certainly do so in a meaningful way, if only these terms are applied as ideas, not as concepts.

Thus, we can speak of God's exaltedness only in spatial terms because no other terms are at our disposal. Therefore, the Bible too speaks about God in purely creational terms. This is not simply a matter of metaphors; that is, it is not simply a linguistic matter, but it is a reality that definitely belongs to the ontic structure of creation. We can speak in meaningful ways only in creational terms. The very same terms that we

---

103. Cf. Strauss (1977c, 31–33).
104. Bavinck (*RD* 2:48).

use as concepts in order to refer to creational elevation (e.g., in a landscape) can be used as ideas in order to approximately refer to God's elevation above all spatiality. If, for instance, we say that God surpasses his creation, we use a creational (in this case, kinematic) term to indicate precisely that God is *not* creational. This is not problematic at all; we simply don't know any other way of speaking, and God also speaks in this way about himself in the Bible. The same is true for all other modalities, as we will see extensively in the next chapter.

Chapter 5
God and Time

*Before the mountains were brought forth,
or ever you had formed the earth and the world,
from everlasting to everlasting
you are God.*

Psalm 90:2

5.1 The Eternity of God
5.1.1 Lexicographical Aspects

UNDER THE INFLUENCE OF ANCIENT THOUGHT, theological speculation about time and eternity began in church history at an early stage. Before we enter into this, we first try to get an idea of the New Testament use of the Greek term *aiōn*,[1] with some references to Hebrew *colam* in the Old Testament. The essential point to be emphasized at the outset is that the terms *aiōn* and *colam* nowhere necessarily imply a timeless eternity. In the formulations in which *aiōn* is linked with a preposition to indicate an indeterminate past or future, the notions of time and eternity clearly merge. In Luke 1:70 and Acts 3:21, *ap' aiōnos* means "from of old" (or "of long ago"; not KJV, "since the world began"). In Acts 15:18 the meaning could be "from eternity" (NKJV; undesirable is the ERV, "from the

---
1. In addition to the lexicons (*TDNT*; Brown, 1992), see Bavinck (*RD* 2:160–64), and references there.

beginning of *time*"). In John 9:32, *ek tou aionos* can be rendered as "from the age/eternity" (EXB note), or "in all history" (CJB) (undesirable: "from the beginning of time," EHV); with the negation it simply means "never" (or "nobody has ever . . .," EXB). Similarly, in John 13:8 and 1 Corinthians 8:13, *ou… eis ton aiōna* simply means "never," that is, at no point in future time. The phrase *hina aiōnion auton apecheis* (Phlm. 15) means, "that you might have him back forever," or even "as long as you live," according to the original meaning of *aiōn* ("human life span"[2]). Similarly, ^c*ebed* ^c*olam* (Deut. 15:17) means "servant forever" (or, "as long as you live") (cf. LXX, *oiketēs eis ton aiōna*). In all these cases, time, not timelessness, is being implied.

In such phrases, the notion of "eternity," the never ending future, is obvious; see *eis ton aiōna* (e.g., John 6:51), *eis tou aiōna* (Luke 1:33), *eis ton aiōna tou aiōnos* (Heb. 1:8), *eis tou aiōna tōn aiōnōn* (1 Pet. 4:11; also cf. Eph. 3:11, 21). But in these cases as well, the context never demands the introduction of the notion of timelessness, or a ceasing of time. An expression such as *pro pantos tou aiōnos kai nun kai eis pantas tous aiōnas* (lit., "before all eternity [or, before any age[3]] and now and in all the ages [or, forever]" seems to suggest a continual stream of time. The phrase *pro tōn aiōnōn* (1 Cor. 2:7) means "before the ages," that is, from all eternity, or before many and long periods of time, of which the infinite series constitutes eternity (cf. *apo tōn aiōnōn*, "for ages," "through[out] the ages," Eph. 3:9; Col. 1:26; in the latter verse, the suggestion of time is enhanced by the addition *apo tōn geneōn*, "before the generations").

The notions of limited and unlimited time merge in *aiōn*, but nowhere is the idea of timelessness necessarily implied.

---

2. Interestingly, this is also the etymological origin of "world" (from *wer*, "man" [cf. werewolf and Lat. *vir*] and old, a man's age).
3. Indeed, not "before all time," as many have it; any speculation about time, and its assumed beginning or ending, should be omitted here as having no biblical basis.

This is seen most clearly in the remarkable expression *chronoi aiōnioi* ("eternal times," or "times of the ages"), in which "timeless times" would be an inner contradiction (see Rom. 11:26; 2 Tim. 1:9, *not* "before the beginning of time," NIV; Titus 1:2). Also compare *eis hēmeran aiōnos*, "the day of eternity" (2 Pet. 3:18), which again connects the notions of time ("day") and eternity.

One important reason to emphasize that timelessness is not necessarily implied in *aiōn* is that this notion is always seen from the human viewpoint. The long ages past are the ages of human history, which are simply seen as continued in the long ages before this history. The long future ages are the ages of the Messiah, which are simply seen as continued in the long ages after human history. Where the future eternity of *humanity* is meant, this always refers to the everlasting ages that humanity faces. The Bible does not teach the idea that human beings leave a temporal world in order to enter a timeless world or a timeless eternity. Expressions describing physical death, like being "out of time" of "exchanging the temporal for the eternal," are more Greek than biblical.

Human beings are temporal beings, that is, embedded in time and bound to time. There is nothing in the Bible to suggest that this temporal character of humanity will ever be abolished. Such an dissolving of this temporal character lifting would entail that the annihilation of the creaturely character of humanity, and thus of humanity itself. Even in eternity to come, humans will "at all times" be temporal beings. Being elevated above time seems to suggest merging into the Godhead.

5.1.2 Is God Timeless?

The latter claim leads us to reflect about what eternity means in reference to God. Both Genesis 21:33 (Heb. El ᶜ*olam*) and Deuteronomy 33:27 (Heb. *Elohēi qēdem*, many: "the God of old"; CEB, "the most ancient God"; LEB, "the God of ancient time") speak of the "eternal God," each in its own way.

Romans 16:26 describes him as *tou aiōniou theou* ("the eternal God"). German-Australian theologian Hermann Sasse (d. 1976) said of the adjective used here that, "as a predicate of God, *aiōnios* contains not merely the concept of unlimited time without beginning or end, but also of the eternity which transcends time."[4] Similar things could be said of the *pneuma aiōnion* ("eternal Spirit," Heb. 9:14), the *aiōnios doxa* ("eternal glory," 2 Tim. 2:10; 1 Pet. 5:10), and also *zōē aiōnios* ("eternal life") in direct connection with the true God (1 John 5:20).

In 1 Timothy 1:17, the apostle Paul speaks of the *basileus tōn aiōnōn* ("King of the ages"), which is equivalent to *melek colam* (Jer. 10:10, "everlasting King" or "King of eternity" or "king of the future age").[5] As in many such cases, the Greek genitive follows the example of the Hebrew use of the substantive as an adjective, such as "Spirit of holiness" to mean "Holy Spirit" (Rom. 1:4; cf. "mountains of holiness" [Ps. 87:1 Darby] to mean "holy mountains"). It is possible that the genitive not only replaces an adjective here, but, as Jewish tradition claims, also indicates over *what* God is King: he rules over the "aeons," understood as eras *or* as "realms" within the cosmos. Think of the very few times that *aiōn* in the New Testament cannot be translated as "age" but only as "world" (Heb. 1:2; 11:3; in *all* other cases, an excellent translation of *aion* is "age").

What do these considerations mean with regard to the eternity (the eternal existence) of God? The primary meaning clearly seems to be a temporal one: the "God of old," the "God who was there during all times past," the "God of the most ancient times." Compare the interesting expressing *cattiq jomin* (Aramaic, Dan. 7:9, 13), the "Ancient of Days" (GW and

---

4. *TDNT* 1:208.
5. Cf. Talmud: Berachot 60b. In Jewish pseudepigraphic and apocryphal literature, cf. *theos tou aiōnos* (1 Enoch 1:4, "God of the age" or "eternal God"), *theos tōn aiōnōn* (Sirach 36:22 [cf. 1 Clement 55:6], "God of the ages"), *basileus tou aiōnos* (1 Enoch 25:3, 5, 7, see in the text), *basileus tōn aiōnōn* (22:14, "King of the ages"; Lat. *dominus saeculorum* "Lord of the ages"] in Jubilees 31:13); see *TDNT* 1:201.

NOG, "the Ancient One, who has lived for endless years," as one might say: the One who was there since the earliest days. He is the One of whom it is said, "The number of his years is unsearchable" (Job 36:26; cf. 10:5). That is, he did not exist in some timeless eternity; rather, he lived for an endless number of days or years.

In a broader sense, *Elohēi ʿolam* (Isa. 40:28) appears to mean: the God who always was, *and* the God who will always be. This seems to be underlined by expressions such as "I am the LORD, I was there at the beginning; I will be there at the end" (Isa. 41:4 CEV), and: 'I am the first and I am the last" (44:6; cf. 48:12; Rev. 1:8; 22:13). These also describe God's eternity, that is, his having always been (before anything else), and the One who will always be, as expressed in the term "everlasting" (KJV: Gen. 21:33; Isa. 40:28; Rom. 16:26), obviously a temporal expression.

In a similar way, the Bible speaks of *shokēn ʿad*, "(the One) who inhabits eternity" (NIV, "who lives forever") (Isa. 57:15; cf. Deut. 32:40; Rev. 10:6; 15:7), and of *logou zōntos theou kai menontos*, "the living and [always] abiding word of God" (1 Pet. 1:23). In this sense, it can be said, *mēʿolam ʿad-ʿolam attah El*, "from everlasting to everlasting you are God" (Ps. 90:2; cf. 93:3). That is, throughout the ages God has been, and God will be. Before the world was created, he was there, and when the present heaven and earth will have passed away, he will still be there (cf. Ps. 102:25–27; notice the last phrase, "your *years* have no end"). God is *aphthartos* (Rom. 1:23 KJV, "uncorruptible"), *ho monos echōn athanasian* ("who alone has immortality," 1 Tim. 6:16), *ho ōn kai ho ēn kai ho erkhomenos* ("who is and who was and who is to come," Rev. 1:4; cf. 4:8; Exod. 3:14). Hermann Sasse wrote, "Thus the unending eternity of God and the time of the world, which is limited by its creation and conclusion, are contrasted with one another. Eternity is thought of as unending time—for how else can human thought picture it?—and the eternal being of God is represented as pre-existence and post-existence"—that is, as having existed before the world began, and as the One who will exist after the (present) world.⁶

5.1.3 Greek Thought versus the Bible

It was only in later Judaism, presumably under Hellenistic influence, that the attempt was undertaken to create a *contrast* between eternity and time. Thus, 2 Enoch 65:5–6 contains the notion that time was created together with the world: "When all creation . . . shall end, . . . then all time shall perish, and the years, and thenceforward there will be neither months nor days nor hours, they will be stuck together and will not be counted. There will be one *aeon*."⁷ This sounds more like Plato than like the Old Testament. The Bible does not contain the idea that one day time will cease. In the Greek expression *chronos ouketi estai*, "there will be no more *chronos*" (Rev. 10:6), *chronos* does not mean "time" as a universal abstract notion as if "time" would ever cease (cf. KJV), but "delay": there will not be (much) time anymore until the fulfillment of the events announced (CEB, "The time is up").⁸

In ancient Greek, *chronos* refers to time as such, whereas *aiōn* refers to the lifespan assigned to a person, and hence also to "age," or "generation." However, pre-Socratic philosophy needed a term to express the notion of eternity. In his *Timaeus*, Plato distinguishes between *aiōn*, in the sense of timeless, ideal eternity, and *chronos*, in the sense of time originating with the world as a moving image of eternity.⁹ Under Plato's influence, Philo described *aiōn* as *chronou paradeigma kai archetypon* ("example and archetype of time"), as the *bios* ("life") of God and of the *kosmos noētos*, the cosmos insofar as it is accessible to reason, that is, the world of the Platonic ideas, and as the "eternal present"; *chronos* is the *bios* of the *kosmos aisthētos* ("observable cosmos").¹⁰

---

6. *TDNT* 1:201–202.
7. http://www.sacred-texts.com/bib/fbe/fbe172.htm.
8. See Ouweneel (1990, 33).
9. classics.mit.edu/Plato/timaeus.html.
10. E.g., De opificio mundi; see extensively, Runia (1986, 215 and further).

As I said before, in the Bible *aiōn* never necessarily suggests timelessness, nor does the Bible ever say that time began at the creation and will cease at the end of the (present) cosmos. Nevertheless, there are a few passages that do seem to suggest a certain contrast between time and eternity. Thus, 2 Peter 3:8 (cf. Ps. 90:4) says that "with the Lord one day is as a thousand years, and a thousand years as one day." This suggests at least that God has a basically different attitude toward time than human beings do. Actually, Dutch theologian Jan Ridderbos (d. 1960) believed that the sense of Psalm 90:4 is not the same as that of 2 Peter 3:18.[11] Psalm 90 says that for God, who has endless times at his disposal (cf. v. 2), a "thousand years" are what "yesterday" is for us: when the day began, it still seemed so long; but at the end of it, when we look back, it lasted too briefly. Second Peter 3:8 does not necessarily say that God is elevated above time (*contra* Ridderbos) but that God has a different perspective of time.[12]

Second Corinthians 4:18 makes a contrast between the "things that are transient" (Gk. *proskaira*, "lasting for some time, transient," from *kairos*, "time, season") and the "eternal things" (*aiōnia*) (cf. Ps. 90:2 with v. 3). However, this is not a philosophical statement about timelessness as opposed to time.[13] The meaning of *proskairos* can be clearly seen in Matthew 13:21 (= Mark 4:17), someone "enduring for a while," and in Hebrews 11:25, "for a little while" (GNV). The contrast with *aiōnios* is not between time and eternal timelessness, but between what is transient, fleeting, and short-term, in contrast to what is unlimited in time. The latter is not necessary timeless, but neither is it temporary (limited in time), as in the phrase "temporary stay." However, it could certainly mean "temporal" in the sense of embedded in time.

It is important that, in 2 Corinthians 4:18, the term *proskaira* ("transient") is linked with *ta blepomena* ("the things that

---

11. Ridderbos (1958, 398).
12. Blum (1981, 285).
13. Cf. *TDNT* 3:463–64.

are seen"), that is, with the empirical world. It is this world that is bound to time, rooted in time, limited by time, immanent, and therefore transient, fleeting, and temporary. The *aiōnia* are the *mē blepomena*, "the things that are unseen," that is, the world beyond the immanent-empirical, the world of the transcendent.

5.2 Ancient and Scholastic Views
5.2.1 Earlier Views

From the previous analysis we may draw the conclusion that there is an invisible, supra-empirical realm, surpassing all that is temporal — with its connotations of time-bound and transient — but not necessarily surpassing the temporal as if this realm were static and immutable (for all mutation suggests time). What does this imply for God's eternity? Is God's eternity timeless? And if so, what are the implications of this? Immutability? Event-lessness? Or is God simply beyond *our* (created) time? Does he know his own (infinite) time, a kind of time without beginning and without end?

Traditional, scholastic theology has answered these questions under the strong influence of the ancient Greek speculations about time and eternity.[14] Three different ideas were developed, among which the idea of the (Lat.) *aevum* (related to Gk. *aiōn*[15]). The term *aevum* was introduced into philosophy by Boethius, and, following the philosopher Siger of Brabant (d. c. 1282), elaborated by Thomas Aquinas.[16] The latter made the following distinctions:[17]

(a) Eternity as the "measure of permanent Being" (Lat. *mensura esse permanentis*), in which there is no earlier or later,

---

14. Cf. Pannenberg (1971, 338v).
15. Related to Dutch *eeuw* (adjective: *eeuwig*; Ger. *ewig*, but Ger. does not have the concomitant substantive), and with English *eon* and even age (> *edage* > *aetaticum* > *aetas* > *aevum*). The Indo-European root is **aiw-*, "vital strength, (long) life, eternity" (cf. Sanskrit *ayu*, "life"; Old-Persian *ayu*, "age [of a person]").
16. Cf. Dooyeweerd (1939, 2–4; 1940a, 181); Ouweneel (1986, 277).
17. *Summa Theologiae* I qu. 10 a. 5.

but only an "eternal now" (Lat. *nunc aeternum*). This is the "uncreated eternity" (Lat. *aeternitas increata*) of God. This term might suggest that this eternity is something apart from God, or at least something *of* God, which could be distinguished, or even severed, from him. However, this eternity is necessarily God's own mode of existence, inseparable from his being, else eternity itself would be God. Everything that is uncreated is God. Thus, the uncreated eternity is God's own being. God is eternal, but eternity is not God.[18]

(b) Time (*tempus*) as the "measure of transmutable Being" (Lat. *mensura esse transmutabilis*), that is, the type of Being that is characterized by transitions from the one form or state to another. In this Being, there *is* earlier and later. This is the realm inhabited by God's earthly creatures.

(c) The *aevum* as the measure of those things (*aeviterna*) of which the natural Being (*esse naturale*) is not of a transient nature but which do possess (actually or potentially) an "added transmutation" (Lat. *transmutatio adiuncta*; that is, they do not necessarily change, but have the capacity to change), and are measured by time. To put it more simply (in my own terms), the *aevum* is both created and transcending our immanent-empirical world. In itself, the *aevum* (according to Thomas) possesses no earlier or later—it is *aeternitas*, though a "created eternity" (Lat. *aeternitas creata*)—but these can be linked with it.

Thomas mentioned as *aeviterna* the celestial bodies[19] and the angels. We differ from this view in two respects. On the one hand, today everybody will classify celestial bodies as material things embedded in time. On the other hand, Thomas should have consistently assigned the *aevum* also to, as he described it, the immutable "rational soul" (Lat. *anima intellectiva*) as the human-essential form, distinct from matter (the body), and directly created by God. However, no *aevum* can be assigned to such a "rational soul" understood as a hypos-

---
18. Cf. Heyns (1988, 62).
19. Cf. *EDR* 11:474–81.

tasized, rational-ethical complex of human functions; this is because these functions are entirely immanent and temporal. If one would wish to use the term *aevum* at all—as the early Dooyeweerd also did for some time[20]—this can be applied only to the supra-functional, supra-modal, supra-temporal, transcendent I-ness: the humanheart" in its transcendent-religious meaning.[21]

5.2.2 An Astonishing Continuum

It is hardly very useful to follow the story of this view of God's "uncreated eternity" as a entirely timeless "eternal now," as standing over against the notions of "time" and *aevum*, throughout the entire scholastic (Roman Catholic or Protestant) theological tradition. I would mention Friedrich Schleiermacher, who called God's eternity "entirely timeless."[22] With Emil Brunner, there remains a certain tension on this point because, on the one hand, his statement that, for God, things stand "in an eternal present" (Ger. *in ewiger Gegenwart*), reminds us immediately of the timeless *nunc aeternum* of traditional theology.[23] On the other hand, Brunner decidedly rejected the idea of a timeless eternity.[24] Conversely, already in antiquity Boethius's view of God's eternity, which can be traced back to Plotinus, seemed to imply real duration.[25]

For the twentieth century, I again take Herman Bavinck as a primary source.[26] Just as the church fathers had done, following Philo, Bavinck too found his starting-point in the name YHWH (Exod. 3:14), understood as the One who is and will be what he was, the Eternal, Immutable One, perfectly independent in all he is, in all he decides, in all he does, per-

---

20. Dooyeweerd (1936–1939).
21. See extensively, *EDR* 3:§6.4.
22. Schleiermacher (1831, §§52.1 and 2).
23. Brunner (1950, 281).
24. Ibid., 290.
25. Cf. Barth (*CD* II,1, 688); Schilder (*KD* 2:85–117); Pannenberg (1988, 437–38).
26. Bavinck (*RD* 2, 119–34).

fectly autonomous in his thinking, in his will, in his counsel, in his love, in his power, and so on (Ps. 33:11; 115:3; Isa. 46:10; Dan. 4:35; Rom. 9:19; 11:34–35; Eph. 1:5; Rev. 4:11). In traditional theology, this *aretē* (Gk. for "virtue, eminence") of God is called his autarky, his aseity (Lat. *aseitas*, existence-in-himself), omnisufficiency, independence, or magnitude, greatness).

In these respects, there is no essential difference between medieval scholasticism and traditional Protestant theology. Luther described God as the absolute or pure Being, Lutheran theologian Philip Melanchthon (d. 1560) as "spiritual essence." Lutheran theology usually adds that God is infinite, "existing in himself" (Lat. *a se subsistens*), independent. God is the "absolute Being," the "Being One" in the absolute sense, and therefore immutable. In fact, the line can be traced back not only to medieval scholasticism but also to ancient Greek philosophy, for instance, Philolaus (fifth century BC), Aristotle, and later also Philo. They spoke of God as the one, eternal, necessary, immutable Ruler of all things, equal to himself alone, the unmoved Mover, pure Being, absolute form, and so on. God was thought to be necessarily immutable because everything that changes presuppose a cause for such change, and therefore cannot itself be the ultimate cause of things.

Christian theology followed this line of thinking obediently. Irenaeus called God "always the same, equal and similar to himself" (Lat. *semper idem, sibi aequalis et similis*).[27] Augustine spoke of the "entirely immutable and incorruptible God" (Lat. *omnino incommutabilis et incorruptibilis Deus*).[28] His name is "Being" (*esse*), and this is a "name of unchangeability" (Lat. *nomen incommutabilitatis*), for "what is, remains" (Lat. *quod est, manet*).[29] Similar ideas are found with Thomas Aquinas[30] and other medieval scholastics, and with Protes-

---

27. *Adversus Haereses* IV.11.
28. *De Genesi ad litteram* VII.11.
29. *De Trinitate* V.2.
30. *Summa Theologiae* I qu. 9.

tant theologians. It is astonishing how little this view differs from traditional Protestant scholasticism, even as recently as in the twentieth century.

5.3 Bavinck's View
5.3.1 A Traditional Approach

Herman Bavinck defended the traditional approach over against other opinions:

> Nevertheless [in spite of the criticisms], the doctrine of God's immutability is highly significant for religion. The difference between the Creator and the creature hinges on the contrast between being and becoming .... Every change is foreign to God. In him there is no change in time, for he is eternal; nor in location, for he is omnipresent; nor also in essence, for he is pure being. [31]

Bavinck continued by stating that God's immutability — also called his infinity — implies eternity with regard to time, and omnipresence with regard to space. God is infinite in the sense that he cannot be limited by time, and thus is eternal, and he is infinite in the sense that he cannot be limited by place, and thus is omnipresent.[32] God is infinite in a third sense as well, namely, with respect to his virtues: every virtue is present in him in an unlimited way. In this sense, infinity implies infinity of essence, and thus perfection.[33] In Dooyeweerdian terminology: God's infinity is here implicitly linked with the spatial modality (omnipresence, see §7.4), the kinematic modality (immutability; see §7.6), and the economic modality (perfection; see §8.7.1); at the same time, I believe that this infinity must be linked primarily with the arithmetic modality (see §7.2.1).

When it comes to God's eternity, Bavinck tries to combat both deism and pantheism by claiming that this eternity is not

---
31. Bavinck (*RD* 2:156; see 153–59).
32. Cf. Polanus, Syntagma theologiae christianae II c. 10,11; Zanchius, Opera II.90.
33. Cf. Thomas, *Summa Theologiae* I qu. 7.

only partly before (Lat. *a parte ante*) and partly after (Lat. *a parte post*), that is, time that is infinitely elongated both backward and forward.[34] In his view, God's eternity differs from common time in a qualitative and essential sense by not involving some succession of moments, neither earlier, nor later.

In the traditional view, as presented by Bavinck, due to God's immutability, his eternity excludes both a beginning and an end, as well as any form of succession. In agreement with Aristotle, he claimed that time is linked with becoming, and eternity with being. In agreement with Augustine, he claimed that we are dealing with time when the present becomes the past, and the future becomes the present, and that time is a mode of being of creatures, depending on their existence: time began when creation began, and not: creating began when time began.[35] Time is the creature's duration. Because God is immutable, eternal Being, there cannot be in him any earlier or later, no becoming, no duration, no succession. God is an "eternal now," with a past and a future. Or, as Augustine put it, "All is present with God. Your [= God's] today is eternity. God's substance is eternity itself, which has nothing mutable."[36]

5.3.2 A Biblical Basis?

After having quoted Boethius and Thomas Aquinas as well, Bavinck said, "And so [in this way] speak all the theologians, not only the Roman Catholic but the Lutheran and the Reformed as well."[37] At the same time, he was rightly afraid of viewing God's eternity as an immobile moment of time that was eternally static. Therefore, he acknowledged a certain analogy with "the abundant and exuberant life of the cheerful laborer, for whom time barely exists and days fly by."[38] He also stated that God's eternity does not stand above time in an

---
34. Bavinck (*RD* 2:163).
35. *De Genesi ad litteram* V.5; cf. *De Civ.* XI.6.
36. *Confessiones* XI.10–13; cf. *De vera religione* c. 49.
37. Bavinck (*RD* 2:163).
38. Ibid., 163.

abstract and transcendent way but is present and immanent in every moment of time:

> There is indeed an essential difference between eternity and time, but there is also an analogy and kinship between them so that the former can indwell and work in the latter. Time is a concomitant of created existence. It is not self-originated. Eternal time, a time without beginning, is not conceivable. God, the eternal One, is the only absolute cause of time. In and by itself time cannot exist or endure: it is a continuous becoming and must rest in immutable being. It is God who by his eternal power sustains time, both in its entirety and in each separate moment of it. God pervades time and every moment of time with his eternity. In every second throbs the heartbeat of eternity. Hence, God maintains a definite relation to time, entering into it with his eternity. Also, for him time is objective. In his eternal consciousness he knows time as a whole as well as the succession of all its moments. But this fact does not make him temporal, that is, subject to time, measure, or number. He remains eternal and inhabits eternity, but uses time with a view to manifesting his eternal thoughts and perfections. He makes time subservient to eternity and thus proves himself to be the King of the ages (1 Tim. 1:17).[39]

There are beautiful elements in this view. However, the central question is: how much of it can be really accounted for on the basis of the divine self-revelation? How much of these descriptions is more Greek than biblical? We do not demand a biblicistic theology of time and eternity that can be deduced from the Bible, for such a theology does not exist. But we do have to insist on a theology that is rooted in a philosophical view of reality that is congenial to the Bible. According to many, this can be only a philosophical cosmology that fundamentally breaks from the Greek scholastic tradition. Let us try to determine what such a cosmology might look like.

---

39. Ibid., 163–64.

5.4 A New View of Eternity
5.4.1 Eternal and Supra-Temporal

The issue of time, and eternity as its correlate, occupied an important position in the philosophy of Herman Dooyeweerd, primarily, however, not as a theological but as an anthropological problem. I will briefly summarize here the progress of his anthropological development, as I have described it elsewhere,[40] after which I will try to show its theological relevance. Originally, Dooyeweerd saw the unity and coherence of the modal law-spheres in the divine world-plan, that is, God's eternal counsel, understood in the sense meant by Abraham Kuyper.[41] However, this view could not satisfy him because, since humans cannot fathom the divine world-plan, this would render a philosophical view of totality and unity with regard to the modal diversity within the cosmos impossible. Shortly after this, he published for the first time his new view, according to which humanity itself shares in the totality and unity of the cosmos.[42] The central idea was the view of the human heart as the transcendent-religious point of concentration, unity, fullness, and totality of human modal-functional existence.

Insofar as Dooyeweerd, in the publication just referred to, touched upon the question of time, it was in his use of the term "eternal," and this in two respects. First, he argued that the durable unity within the diversity of modal laws lies in their eternal, religious sense, involving humanity's service to God, in obedience to his eternal, religious Law of Love. Since this central Law of Love expresses itself in all the various law-spheres, Dooyeweerd saw the religious sense here still as an *eternal* moment in each law-sphere.[43] Second, Dooyeweerd spoke of the *eternal* essence of any human, that is, the human

---

40. Ouweneel (1986, 261–84; see references there).
41. Dooyeweerd (1926, 63, 65–66).
42. Idem (1928a).
43. Ibid., 31.

heart, through which God works in human temporal life.⁴⁴ The eternal, uncreated God, who is elevated beyond his own laws, works in the eternal but created human heart, which is subject to God's laws.

After 1930, Dooyeweerd usually no longer spoke of "eternal" with regard to the human heart but of "supra-temporal." The transcendent-religious sense is eternal, supra-temporal, integral; the immanent-empirical world is transient, temporal, diverse. From that time on, he saw a strict identity of the modal-functional and the temporal: everything that is modal-functional is temporal, and vice versa. Cosmic time "encloses," so to speak, all the modal law-spheres; the modal aspects are "modalities of time." The modal order is a temporal order, with "earlier" and "later" law-spheres. This implies, for instance, that Dooyeweerd no longer spoke of "eternal principles" because this is a contradiction in terms: a principle implies a beginning (both come from Lat. *principium*), and all beginning is within time. No principle is supra-temporal, except the "eternal, religious meaning of the law."⁴⁵ At the same time, Dooyeweerd felt that the point of concentration, unity, and fullness is necessarily supra-temporal. If everything that is modal-functional-diverse is temporal, then the supramodal-suprafunctional-integral is supra-temporal.

It is interesting that Dooyeweerd did not call the human heart a "window" upon eternity, as if the heart *itself* would still belong to what is temporal-diverse. It is rather the (temporal!) pistical modality, the "highest" or "latest" ("terminal") of all modalities, which he considers to be the human window upon eternity: "According to the order of creation this terminal aspect was destined to function as the opened window of time through which the light of God's eternity should shine into the whole temporal coherence of the world."⁴⁶

---

44. Ibid., 76-77; see also Dooyeweerd (1928b, 425).
45. Idem (1930, 242).
46. Idem (*NC* 2:302).

5.4.2 Further Development

In the period of 1936 to 1940, Dooyeweerd entered far more deeply into the problem of time.[47] Several points strike us here; first his use of Ecclesiastes 3:11, God "has put *Colam* in man's heart." Some render *Colam* here as "eternity" (ESV), others as "the world" (KJV), or "a sense of divine purpose" (AMP), an "awareness/sense of eternity" (CJB), an "awareness of time" (EXB note), a "desire to know the future" (GNT), "the past" (LEB), "the timeless" (NABRE), "thoughts of the forever" (NLV), a "sense of past and future" (NRSV). Dooyeweerd extensively defended the rendering "eternity" because of the implied meaning of this for his view of the heart's supra-temporality.[48] However, the rendering is one many possible meanings, and Dooyeweerd indeed did see that it is risky to hang a philosophical theory on a single Bible verse, one that is capable of multiple interpretations.

Second, we are struck by Dooyeweerd's use of the term *aevum*, or *aeternitas creata* ("created eternity") in contrast to God's *aeternitas increata* ("uncreated eternity").[49] Like Thomas Aquinas, he viewed the *aevum* as an intermediate state between time and eternity, that is, between the creaturely-temporal and God's eternity. As an actual state, this *aevum*, according to him, is nothing but the creaturely concentration of the temporal upon eternity in religiously transcending the time boundary. The *aevum* belongs to the innate structure of our I-ness, which actualizes itself time and again when our self-consciousness is active in religious concentration, even if the *aevum*-consciousness manifests itself in an apostate direction through seeking the eternal within the temporal (cf. Rom. 1:23).[50]

Dooyeweerd must have felt the philosophical and theological risks embedded in a notion—the *aevum*—that is so

---
47. See idem (1936–1939 and 1940a).
48. Idem (1959, 116–17, note 3).
49. Idem (1936, 68–69; 1939, 2–5; 1940a, 181).
50. Idem (1939, 4–5).

heavily loaded with scholastic connotations, for the term no longer appears in his later work. He began to prefer terms such as supra-temporal and transcendent, even if these terms have their own problems in the sense that they are equally applicable to God's eternity. At any rate, Dooyeweerd identified three spheres or realms, which are separated by sharp boundary-lines: the *law* is the boundary between God and his creation, including the *aevum*,[51] and *time* is the boundary between the transcendent, including the *aevum*, and the immanent (modal-functional) order.[52] In this way, the three spheres are established: (a) the sphere of God: beyond time and beyond the law, (b) the sphere of the human heart: beyond time and under the law; (c) the immanent-empirical sphere, which is under time and under the law.

5.4.3 (Trans-)Cosmic Time

In a subsequent article,[53] Dooyeweerd spoke about time as that in which the modal order lies embedded, and explicitly referred to *cosmic* time: time as inherent to the cosmos. In this way, he tried to distance himself from those philosophical views that attempted to distinguish only one temporal *modality*, for instance, absolute mathematical time (Thomas Hobbes, Albert Einstein—the kinematic-physical aspects), the transcendental perceptive form of intuition or sensory experience (Immanuel Kant—the perceptive aspect), the *durée* ("duration," Henri Bergson—the sensitive aspect), historical time (Oswald Spengler, Martin Heidegger—the cultural-historical aspect). With the three spheres just mentioned, we must constantly think of *cosmic* time, thus leaving open the question whether the heart, or even God, possesses its/his own kind of time.

The tension that arose from the notion of the *aevum*, which is eternity (even "creaturely eternity"), is clearly felt in that

---

51. Idem (*NC* 1:99).
52. Ibid., 102.
53. Idem (1940a, 167, 175, 196; cf. *NC* 1:24, 29; see 22–34).

Dooyeweerd in another publication refers to precisely the same thing as "central trans-cosmic *time*" (italics added).[54] This is the crux: does the human heart belong to time (even a time surpassing common cosmic time) or to eternity? One reason why, in the case of the heart, Dooyeweerd does think of a form of time is that things happen also at the trans-cosmic level. We need only remind ourselves of two of the most drastic events in the transcendent heart: the Fall and regeneration, respectively.

Thus, the trans-cosmic sphere is a "sphere of occurrence" too. But again, we run into problems here. This is because of the remarkable fact that, as I will argue below, the same is true of God's eternity. "Occurrence" as such is not a measure for assessing the meaning of time and (timeless?) eternity, respectively. In other words, common, cosmic time is not the measure of this "occurrence," neither in the "created eternity," nor in the "uncreated eternity," or more correctly, neither in the creaturely, nor in the divine eternity.

5.5   Pleni-Temporality
5.5.1   Supra- or Pleni-Temporal

Just as Dooyeweerd, during the development of his thinking, silently dropped the term *aevum*, he did the same with the phrase "central trans-cosmic time" because

> this would lead to a duplication of the temporal horizon in connection with which it would become necessary to use the word ["time"] in two fundamentally different senses. Furthermore, the general explanation "duration determined by the order of succession or simultaneity" would no longer prove serviceable to cover both meanings. I would not know what criterion would have to be accepted for a "trans-cosmic" time. Consequently, the meaning of this term would remain entirely in the dark. For these reasons, I still prefer to reserve the term "time" for the cosmic one and its different modal aspects.[55]

---
54. Idem (*NC* 1:32–33).
55. Ibid.

However, this new view did not answer the question as to how there can be "dynamics," "becoming," and "occurrence" in the *aevum* sphere, without us being allowed to speak of "time." In my opinion, the answer must be that this is possible only in the sense of — not literally *supra*-temporality but — the transcendent *fullness* of time. In order to express this thought, I have coined the term *pleni-temporal* (*plenus* meaning "full").[56] Of course, in itself such a term does not tell us much; terms that are not understood are applied in the wrong way. Therefore, Dooyeweerd, who had earlier dropped the terms *aevum* and "central trans-cosmic time," announced in 1963 that he would drop the term "supra-temporal" because of all the criticism that had been leveled against it,[57] but he would do so without giving up the *idea* behind this term.

Perhaps the term "pleni-temporal" is the least disadvantageous term possible, as I have argued elsewhere.[58] I maintain the term in spite of the criticism of Dutch philosopher René van Woudenberg,[59] because his objection that terms such as "supra-" or "pleni-temporal" would suggest a partition within time is quite removed from Dooyeweerd's (and my) intention. The attempt to interpret Dooyeweerd's view of the duality (not dualism!) of the temporal and the supra-temporal (or, body and heart) in terms of "parts" is so far removed from Dooyeweerd's intention that Van Woudenberg cannot do any justice to it; nor can he do justice to my term "pleni-temporal."[60]

The reason that so many authors have misunderstood Dooyeweerd on the point of "supra-temporality"[61] is that we can speak of the latter only in temporal terms. This is very important for our present investigation because the very same is

---

56. Ouweneel (1986, 284, 379).
57. Begemann (1963–1964, 152 note).
58. Ouweneel (1989b).
59. Van Woudenberg (1992, 175–76).
60. Cf. Ouweneel (1986, especially 354, 363, 370, 402–404, 408); idem (1993).
61. Ouweneel (1986, chapter 6).

true about God's eternity. *Temporal* terms are used here, not as concepts but as ideas, to approximate the *supra*-temporal. Therefore, by definition terms such as *aevum*, "trans-cosmic time," "supra-" and "pleni-temporal" are *all* insufficient to describe the eternal. They will necessarily lead to misunderstandings as soon as people try to analyze them as if they were concepts.

5.5.2   Duality and Dualism

Elsewhere, I have tried to show that Dooyeweerd was never trapped in the snare of postulating a *dualism* of the temporal and the supra-temporal, as his opponents have often suggested.[62] One reason was that his opponents often scarcely distinguished between a duality (a pair) and a dualism (a contrast). However, Dooyeweerd did (inadvertently) give the impression that "supra-temporal" means "non-temporal," because that which surpasses time cannot itself be temporal anymore. He enhanced this misunderstanding, as we saw, by reserving the term "time" for the cosmic, that is, modal-functional, diverse reality, and by claiming that the fullness and unity of reality "is not actually given and cannot be actually given in time."[63] So *can* it be given "beyond" time, that is, in a sphere that itself is in no way temporal anymore? Moreover, Dooyeweerd's speaking of two "spheres," a temporal and a supra-temporal one,[64] has enhanced the impression of a dualism.

Terms such as "supra-temporal" and "spheres" are just indications of the embarrassment caused by the problem of formulating an *idea* of the supra- or pleni-temporal with the help of terms necessarily derived from our *temporal* world. Only the strongest emphasis on the important difference between concept and idea can keep us from attempts to interpret the supra-temporal, as well as God's eternity, in a conceptual

---

62. Ibid.; idem (1989b).
63. Dooyeweerd (*NC* 1:106).
64. Ibid., 31–32, 55.

way.

One aspect of this embarrassment is illustrated by Dooyeweerd's quoted words (see notes 63 and 64). He dropped the term "trans-cosmic time" because the criterion of "duration determined by the order of succession or simultaneity" would not be applicable to it. However, one page earlier he called the supra-temporal "sphere" a "sphere of occurrence" — and does *not* "occurrence" imply "duration determined by the order of succession or simultaneity"? Apparently, we can speak of the supra-temporal (with its "dynamics," its "becoming," its "occurrence") only *in temporal terms*. However, these terms, adopted from our temporal-modal-functional world, can be applied *as ideas* to refer (a) to the "supra-temporal" in the sense of *the temporal in its transcendent unity, fullness and totality*, that is, the "pleni-temporal," and just as well (b) to the "eternal" in the sense of God's eternity, which transcends even the pleni-temporal.

Such arguing seems to suggest that we are dealing with an important matter. That matter is this: whether the human heart is temporal or non-temporal, or whether God's eternity is temporal or timeless, is to an important extent a pseudo-problem. The heart is non-temporal when we refer to time in the sense of the modal-functional diversity. And it is temporal in the sense that the heart deals with the unity and fullness *of* the entire modal-diverse temporality. In other words, we use temporal terms as *concepts* when speaking about time in the sense of the modal-functional diversity, and we use them as *ideas* when speaking about time in the sense of its supramodal-suprafunctional unity and fullness ("pleni-temporality"), and yet we speak of one and the same time.

There is no room here for any dualism, namely, between the pleni-temporal heart and the temporal functions, since the temporal functions are those *of the heart itself*, while the heart is the pleni-temporal concentration point *of the functions themselves*. The pleni-temporal is the temporal in its fullness and unity; the temporal is the pleni-temporal in its diversity.[65] There can be no objection against speaking in this way about time in a double sense, a central and a modal sense. This is because we do exactly the same thing when we speak of faith, love, righteousness, harmony, value, fellowship, communication, history, thinking, and so on, terms that touch upon the kernels of the successive modalities, and always have a central (pleni-temporal) and a modal sense. They also have an eternal sense with regard to God, as we will see.

5.6 A New View of God's Eternity
5.6.1 Is God Timeless?

When it comes to time, the essential difference between the human heart and God is that God transcends time not only in its modal diversity, but also in its fullness and unity. Time is bound to the created cosmos, and the created cosmos is bound to time; if therefore God, the Creator, transcends his own creation, he also transcends time, in whatever sense the term is used. This is eternity in its full sense—I now leave the *aevum*-idea aside—that is, that which transcends time in both its modal-diverse sense and its pleni-temporal sense. However, one thing remains the same: we can speak of God's eternity only in *temporal* terms, which are used not as concepts but as ideas in order to obtain true rational knowledge of God's eternity.

Karl Barth seemed to suggest something similar when he viewed "the concept of eternity in its biblical completeness" as pre-, supra-, and post-temporality.[66] Clearly, we are unable to avoid temporal terms when speaking of God's eternity. Dutch theologian Jan van Genderen (d. 2004) referred to this, although, following Herman Bavinck, he stated that "God is elevated above time," that therefore with him "there is no succession of moments to him and thus no past, present, and future as for us," that "God's eternity is an eternal

---
65. Ouweneel (1986, 143).
66. Barth (*CD* II/1, 716; see 685–722, especially 700–20).

present, for from his perspective everything is in the present, as was pointed out by Augustine already, and because of his eternity, God "can penetrate each moment of time with his eternity."[67] I would ask this simple question: How did he know all this? Does the Bible not speak of God's eternity exclusively in *temporal* terms?

The tension that arises because we can speak of God's eternity only in temporal terms is clearly seen in the biblical use of the terms for "eternal" and "eternity," with regard not only to humans but also to God. As we saw, God is God "from of old," "of ancient times," "the first and the last," the God who will always (at all times![68]) be there, the God of all the past ages (eternities) and of all the coming ages (eternities), and so on. It seems hardly possible to speak of God's eternity without using temporal terms; the term "eternity" itself is originally temporal, both in the biblical and in the modern European languages. (2 Pet. 3:8 and 2 Cor. 4:8 are no exceptions; see §5.1.3).

The conclusion can hardly be avoided that the Bible simply does not contain the idea of timelessness—of God or otherwise—and even less the idea of a static, immutable Being without a past or a future, existing in an eternal, continual "now." Time and again, the Bible refers to God's eternity in terms adopted from our temporal world, even if, at the same time, it implies that God's "time" (or experience, or perspective, of time) is different from ours. American philosopher of religion, Nelson Pike, rightly wondered why the doctrine of God's timelessness ought to have a place in a system of Christian theology.[69] Actually, Pike repeatedly committed the same error as his opponents, namely, the error of a conceptual analysis.

This also seemed to be the mistake of British philosopher

---

67. Van Genderen (2008, 175).
68. Cf. the French *toujours*, the Dutch *altijd*, and the German *allzeit*.
69. Pike (1970, 190).

and theologian Paul Helm,[70] who did defend God's timelessness, apparently in particular because he (rightly) rejected the alternative that he (erroneously) assumed was the only one possible, namely, a God who is drawn within our temporal reality, like the purely historical God of so-called process theology. Helm did not discern the third alternative: God fully transcends our temporal world, yet is not timeless. This was seen more clearly by various other twentieth-century theologians such as Karl Barth, Paul Althaus, Paul Tillich, and Wolfhart Pannenberg, even though they too hardly avoided a conceptual analysis of things.[71]

This is always the core of the matter: we can speak of God's "time" only by means of ideas, not concepts, for he transcends creational time in the absolute sense. As I said, creation is bound to time—time both in its modal diversity and in its pleni-temporality—and time is bound to creation, but God transcends both. Nonetheless, we can hardly speak of God in any other way than in temporal terms.

I could give a large number of examples, and some of them will be dealt with in the next chapters. Here, I limit myself to a few examples. If Psalm 90:2 says, "From everlasting to everlasting you are God," does not *this* expression strongly point to a stream or succession of time? If God was or did something "before the world existed" or "before the foundation of the world" (John 17:5, 24; Eph. 1:4), does this point to a succession in time? How can we say that there is no earlier or later in God if he does some things before or after other things? Connected with his eternity is his immutability; but again, does God not undergo many changes (mutations), each of which presupposes a succession in time?[72] God relents; he regrets having done or announced certain things; in common language: he changes his mind (Gen. 6:6; Exod. 32:10–14;

---

70. Helm (1988).
71. Barth (*CD* II/1); Althaus (1952); Tillich (1968); Pannenberg (1988, 433–43).
72. See extensively, *EDR* 4:chapter 4.

1 Sam. 15:11; Joel 2:13; Amos 7:3, 6; Jonah 3:9–10; 4:2) (see more extensively §7.6.1).

These points do not demonstrate that, in some way or another, God is yet bound to time, for we are aware of only one time. That is the creaturely time in which we ourselves are embedded, and God completely transcends this time. Nor is there some other, analogous time in God's eternity, which would be a kind of primordial image of our own time; as we saw, we do not need such a theo-ontological analogy (*analogia entis*). No, all the points mentioned simply show that we cannot speak of God's eternal being and his eternal actions without using terms adopted from our temporal world, even though these are used not as concepts but as ideas.

5.6.2 Biblical Proof?

The two main Bible verses used as proof texts for the supposed immutability of God are, first, Exodus 3:14, where the name "YHWH" is explained as "I am who I am," or at least as a derivative of Hebrew h-y-h, "to be" ("the Being One," "he who is"; cf. Gk. *ho ōn*, "the Being One, "he who is," Rev. 1:4, 8; 4:8; 11:17). The second passage is James 1:17, where it is said that with God "there is no variation or shadow due to change" (NKJV: "no variation or shadow of turning"; NIV: "who does not change like shifting shadows"). It is a serious mistake to view such passages in a scholastic way, that is, as ontological statements. The absence of any variation or change with God is just as little proof for God's *ontic* immutability or timelessness as his relenting is a proof for his *ontic* mutability or time-boundness. The verses mentioned refer to the faithfulness and benevolence of God, who keeps his promises of redemption and blessing (Exod. 3:14), and whose goodness is like a light that cannot be extinguished, darkened or overshadowed as with the sun (James 1:17).

God is YHWH, the Being One, not so much in the sense of the Eternal One, as Jewish tradition makes of it (under the same Hellenist influence), but in the sense of the Present One, he who is present for his people in all his covenantal faithfulness: "I am there [for you, and with you]" (see further in §8.5.2).

Consistent with its nature, the Bible contains no ontological statements about God's immutability or about his timelessness or time-boundness. The same chapter (1 Sam. 15) tells us without any embarrassment that God "regrets" (vv. 11, 35), *and* that God never "regrets" (v. 29). The one statement refers to his mutability, the other to his immutability—both to be taken in a non-ontological way. The reason for this seeming contradiction, in my view, is that we can speak about both changes in God's ways (not his being!) and his immutable faithfulness only in terms adopted from our temporal world. If such terms were be taken as concepts, they would sometimes inevitably collide because of their inherent limitation.

The entire dilemma whether God's eternity is completely timeless or, in some way, is time-bound[73] was erroneous from the outset because people continually tried to solve it by applying creaturely terms in a conceptual way. In my view, the dilemma can be solved only if we consider in particular the following points:

(a) The Creator cannot be bound to creaturely time.

(b) Bible passages connecting God with time must not be taken in any ontological way.

(c) A theo-ontological analogy involving time inevitably draws God under the boundary between Creator and creation.

(d) We can speak of God's eternity only in creaturely terms.

(e) And in particular, such terms must never be applied as concepts but only as ideas; in other words, not by way of definition but by way of approximation.

To a certain extent, Herman Bavinck was right when he wrote (see the end of §5.3.2): "Time is a concomitant of cre-

---

73. Cf. Bavinck (*RD* 2:163–64).

ated existence. It is not self-originated. Eternal time, a time without beginning, is not conceivable" — if he was describing *cosmic* time. However, he tended to a theo-ontological analogy by asserting just before this: "There is indeed an essential difference between eternity and time, but there is also an analogy and kinship between them so that the former can indwell and work in the latter." And even more dubious is that he founded time upon some "immutable Being" without duration or succession, and called God "pure being" to avoid viewing God as "becoming"[74] — terms adopted directly from ancient thought and foreign to Scripture. Such terms must be radically purged from theology proper.

5.6.3 Once More: Time, Eternity, and Ideas

I have argued that we can speak of eternity only in the form of ideas. But I must add that we can speak of creaturely time as such also only in the form of ideas. Conceptual knowledge of time is strictly limited to terms like "before" and "after," "early" and "late," "soon," and so on, and to the way we measure physical time, that is, terms such as second, minute, hour, day, week, month, year, decade, century, and millennium. However, we can have knowledge of cosmic time as such, or even the way time is manifested specifically in the kernels of the various modalities, only in the form of ideas, namely, by using creaturely terms as ideas, not as concepts. This is even more so when it comes to God's eternity.

In summary, we can conclude, on the one hand, that time and creation are linked together, and that therefore because God is Creator, he fully transcends time, both time in its modal diversity (just as the human heart also transcends this) and the trans-cosmic time (which is the measure of the human heart). On the other hand, the Bible speaks of God's eternity exclusively in temporal terms, that is, terms adopted from our creational reality. Even a term like "eternity" was originally a temporal term (see §§5.1.3, 5.2.1): "eternity" comes from the

---

74. Ibid., 161–63.

Latin *aeternitas* (< *aeviternitas* < *aevum* < *aiw*, "vital strength, [long] life"; the Greek *aiōn* comes from the latter, too. We found something similar in Hebrew ^c*olam*. Therefore, it is not consistent with the spirit of Scripture to speculate about a kind of timelessness or *nunc aeternum* with God, or about a kind of future human eternal timelessness.[75] Human eternity does not exclude human creatureliness, nor human time-boundness, although the latter, like the human body, could be of a new kind. Conversely, God's eternity seems to imply his own unique temporality, his own unique before and after, past, present, and future.

Along with the Bible, we can speak of this temporality of God only in terms adopted from *human* temporality, remembering that these are used not as concepts but as ideas. In other words, there *is* before and after in God; for instance, his counsels are from before the foundation of the world, and their fulfillment is in the future eternity. His ways are after his counsels, his plans precede his actions. However, God's befores and afters cannot be expressed in terms of centuries, years, or minutes; they cannot be pressed into cosmic chronologies. They are "in the beginning" (Gen. 1:1; cf. John 1:1), but this "beginning" cannot be dated; this is different from John 8:44 (the "beginning" of creation), 15:27 (the "beginning" of Jesus' ministry), and 1 John 1:1 (the "beginning" of the Word in its incarnated form).

Where God realizes an "eternal purpose" (Eph. 3:11) this suggests a time of realization, but this time is God's time. It cannot be dated in cosmic time. It belongs to God's eternity, which implies that there was a time that God had *not* yet realized this purpose. It makes sense to say that it was realized before the foundation of the world, that is, before the beginning of cosmic time.[76] But it does *not* make sense to say that the purpose was realized so many centuries, or even an infinite

---

75. Cf. *EDR* 10:chapter 14.
76. There is a contradiction in this phrase only if the terms are used conceptually.

number of ages, before the foundation of the world. This is because in this way we would stretch *cosmic* time infinitely backwards, far before the beginning of the cosmos, and thus far before the beginning of cosmic time. God's purposes are realized in *God's* time, which is the very same as saying that they were realized from eternity, from before the ages of ages.

I refer here to the interesting expression in Jude 25, "before all time and now and forever" (Gr. *pro pantos tou aiōnos, kai nun kai eis pantas tous aiōnas*), literally, "before all the age/eternity, and now, and to all the ages/eternities." This expression seems to point to one continuous stream of time — past ages, the present, future ages — but then as belonging to God's time. I cannot accept the rendering "before all time" here (ESV and many others) because we cannot read into the text some ontological speculation about some beginning of time. On the contrary, we should instead translate it this way: "from all past times to all future times" — where here times are emphatically understood as *God's* times.

Chapter 6
God's Attributes: Introduction

> *O LORD, God of Israel, there is no God like you,*
> > *in heaven above or on earth beneath,*
> > *keeping covenant and showing steadfast love*
> > *to your servants*
> > > *who walk before you with all their heart.*
>
> 1 Kings 8:23

6.1 Attributes and Names: Philosophical Aspects
6.1.1 "Open Windows"

WHEN IN THE NEXT TWO CHAPTERS I discuss God's attributes and names under the viewpoint of the sixteen modalities of our empirical reality, I am not intending to claim that God has (only) sixteen attributes. He is an infinite number of attributes. Actually, "infinity" is a remarkable word in this respect because infinity itself has often been called one of God's attributes, as in the Belgic Confession, art. 1: ". . . eternal, incomprehensible, invisible, immutable, infinite, almighty," and so on.[1] However, God's infinity must always be applied to his other qualities: he is infinite in time, that is, eternal; infinite in space, that is, omnipresent; infinite in wisdom and knowledge, that is, omniscient; infinite in power, that is, omnipotent

---
1. Cf. Heyns (1988, 65).

(almighty). Everything that God is he is in an infinite way: light, love, holiness, righteousness, goodness, and so forth.

God's attributes are infinite in number like the colors of the rainbow: we usually mention seven, but this is (a) because we are so keen on the number seven, and (b) because we have at our disposal so few names for colors; otherwise, we would also give a specific name to the transition between red and orange, or between orange and yellow, and so on. In reality, the number of color shades in the rainbow is in principle infinite. In the next two chapters, the sixteen modalities will function only as hints at the actually infinite number of divine attributes.

As I emphasized before, we can approximate God's attributes only in creaturely terms. We apply these terms not as concepts but as ideas. Such creaturely terms always have their own temporal-modal qualification, and thus the sixteen modalities can function as sixteen different gateways to our investigation of the divine attributes. Using the sixteen modally qualified complexes of creaturely terms as ideas helps us to approximate the supra-temporal, eternal, transcendent riches of God's attributes.[2] Each of these complexes is an open window that enables us to take a glance at God's excellencies.

Just to avoid any misunderstandings, I add that this use of the sixteen modalities does not imply that God is subject to modal laws. As the divine Lawgiver he is above the law; the law has been referred to as the boundary between God and his creation.[3] We will see, for instance, that God's moral attributes are not subject to any ethical law, and yet they are never immoral or amoral. They are supra-moral, so to speak. Nonetheless, we can approximate them morally—and indeed we cannot go any further than approximate—through what the Bible reveals to us about the matter in terms adopted from human morality.

---

2. Cf. Visagie (1979b, 150–51); Strauss and Visagie (1984, 57); Strauss (1991b, 35–36).
3. See *EDR* 11:§3.2.

6.1.2 De-Hellenization

As a second introductory matter, I wish to point out that a significant number of terms from traditional theology proper were originally adopted from ancient Greek and Hellenistic philosophy, or at least they have a background in such thinking. Some examples are God's simplicity, his immutability (unchangeability), and his omnipresence. Other terms as well, which in themselves are fully biblical, such as God's omnipotence and righteousness, are heavily loaded with ancient pagan views. In our investigation, we will have to seek to empty such terms of all ancient Greek notions that are foreign to the Bible. Only then such terms can be used safely.

I hasten to add this caution, however: that a term was not originally adopted from the Bible but was adopted by the early church from ancient pagan thought is an insufficient argument against the use of such terms. Each theological school necessarily adopts from its surroundings contemporaneous terminology, if only because it wishes to be able to enter into a discussion with other schools and thinkers of its own time. However, in cases where Greek (unbiblical) ideas are still (apparently inseparably) implied in certain theological terms, they must be thoroughly examined, and rejected if necessary, or replaced by terms that are more congenial to Scripture.

6.1.3 The Term "Attribute"

For each of the sixteen groups of attributes, I will mention two in the subheadings. This is a symbolic number, indicating that no single description, or even three, five, or ten descriptions, is adequate for expressing who or what God is. The same is true for the term "attribute" itself. It may be criticized, just like other similar terms, such as "appellation," "virtue" (Gk. *aretai*, used for God in 1 Pet. 2:9), property, quality," and "perfection." One main objection has always been that such terms seem to refer to something that is secondary, collateral, whereas they ought to express who and what God *is* in his being. As we saw, this distinction goes back to the difference made by scholastic and early Protestant dogmatics between God's substance (being) and his accidents (attributes) (see §3.4.2),[4] a distinction that continued to be made in the twentieth century, for instance, in Karl Barth's dogmatics.[5]

As long as no rigid distinction or separation is made between God's substance and his accidents, the term "attribute" ("virtue," "property," etc.) can be maintained. God *is* his attributes or properties: he *is* light, he *is* love, he *is* spirit, and so on (1 John 1:5; 4:8, 16; John 4:24; cf. Deut. 4:24; 32:4; 2 Sam. 22:33). Those of old expressed this as follows: God's virtues are his actual being (Lat. *virtutes sunt ipsa essentia*). The will of God must not be deduced to some attribute of God in the abstract sense; he simply *is* the willing God. To some extent, German theologian Horst Stephan (d. 1954) was right in saying that the notion of attributes could better be surrendered because the very same traits of God can be called either attributes or the being of God: "The properties are the traits of his being that are distinctly experienced and imagined, a being that can never be grasped or imagined apart from the properties."[6] However, as soon as the distinction between being and attributes is recognized as only apparent, the argument becomes moot.

Thus, the sharp distinction that Emil Brunner made between God's being (Lord, holiness, love) and God's attributes[7] is artificial because he based it upon what God supposedly is in himself and what he is toward the world, respectively.[8] On the one hand, if we know of God's holiness and love only through his revelation, in which he is holy and loving *toward us*, does this not imply a relationship with the world? And on the other hand, if God's omnipotence, omniscience, righteousness, and so on, are genuine attributes, and therefore identical

---

4. See extensively, Weber (1981, 456–58).
5. Barth (*CD* II/1:chapter 6).
6. Stephan (1941, 95).
7. Brunner (1950, 140–213 resp. 255–322).
8. Ibid., 263.

with his being, do they not genuinely express what and who God is *in himself*, even before the world came into being? The artificiality of Brunner's model is best seen in his discussion of God's eternity and God's glory,[9] both of which he wishes to view as attributes because (a) eternity is not timelessness but correlated with time, and (b) glory is correlated with the revelation of God's Lordship. But, to take one example, why would the fact that God is God "from everlasting to everlasting" (Ps. 90:2) be more creation-oriented than, for instance, his holiness, given that precisely as the Holy One he is the Savior of his people (Isa. 43:3)? And even though glory is indeed God's *displayed* excellency (see §8.8), would the sun not be glorious even if its rays were unobserved?

6.2 The Modal Aspects
6.2.1 Modal Analogies

Without elaborating this subject in the present volume, I point out that, along with the theory of the modal aspects, the theory of the modal analogies is also important. In short, this theory says that each modality returns in each of the other modalities in an analogous (anticipatory or retrocipatory) way. If we say, for instance, that righteousness implies social relationships, we are saying that we are dealing here with the social retrocipation within the juridical modality (see §8.10). And if we say that righteousness is opened up (disclosed, unfolded) in love, we speak here of the ethical anticipation within the juridical modality. In a similar way, there is an ethical anticipation within the logical aspect in the sense that our knowledge of God always involves love (cf. Exod. 2:25 [God's knowing is caring]; Ps. 144:3; Nah. 1:7; John 11:27–28; 1 Cor. 8:3). In the doctrine of the divine attributes, this interwovenness of all modalities is also very important (see §6.2.2). Elsewhere, I have called this type of modal analogies *orientational* analogies because in these examples one modali-

---

9. Ibid., 285–91 resp. 309–13.

ty is oriented toward another modality.[10]

In addition to this, I distinguished the—what I called—*referential* analogies, which are of a more metaphorical character.[11] (I am amazed that few advocates of Dooyeweerd's thinking have picked up this—in my eyes quite essential—distinction.) For instance, when we speak of brainpower we are dealing with a *referential* physical analogy within the logical modality. The term "power" is not being used here in its original physical meaning, but in a strictly logical-analytical meaning.

When we speak of *God's* acumen (brainpower), we use this referential analogy as an idea to approximate the immense wisdom and knowledge of God.

When we speak of the divine persons being close to each other, we are using a spatial analogy within the social aspect as an idea to approximate the relationships between divine persons.

When we speak of the loving relationships within the Trinity, we are dealing with a social analogy within the ethical aspect.

When we speak of God knowing his people in the sense of care and compassion (e.g., Exod. 2:25), we are dealing with an ethical analogy within the logical-rational modality.

6.2.2 Analogies Within Analogies

Actually, some descriptions of divine attributes are themselves based upon modal analogies. Thus, each term ending with "full," such as "beautiful," "faithful," "grateful," "peaceful," or "powerful," is in fact a spatial analogy within (in these cases) the aesthetic, the pistical, the ethical, the aesthetic, and the physical modalities, respectively.

Infinity (having no *finis*, "boundary") is a spatial analogy within the arithmetic modality (see §4.2.2).

---

10. Ouweneel (1986, 65–66).
11. See *EDR* 12:§11.4.

Emotionality (from Lat. *e-movere*, lit. "to move out") is actually a kinematic analogy within the sensitive modality (see §4.8.1).

Sovereignty (from Lat. *superanus*) is a spatial analogy within the cultural-historical modality (see §5.2).

Perfection (from Lat. *perficere*, from *facere*, "to make") is a historical-formative analogy within the economical modality (see §5.5.1).

Light and power are often physical elements in the aesthetic modality, used as ideas to approximate the beauty and glory of God (see §5.6.1).

The term "covenant" (from Lat. *convenire*, lit. "to come together") involves a kinematic analogy within the juridical modality.

Patience (from Lat. *pati*, "to suffer, to endure," cf. long-suffering) is a sensitive analogy within the ethical modality (see §5.8.2).

Wisdom (etymologically related to the verb "to wit") is a rational analogy within the ethical modality (see §5.8.4).

Veracity is a rational analogy within the pistical modality (see §5.9.2).

6.3   Attributes and Names: Theological Aspects
6.3.1   A Christological-Soteriological Approach

An important theological point that must be emphasized at the outset is that traditional theology often investigated God's attributes too abstractly. Dutch theologian Gerrit C. van Niftrik (d. 1972) rightly pointed out that there is an orthodox theology proper that speaks of God, his existence and being, only in an abstract metaphysical way without paying much attention to the risks he has taken in the life of his Son, Jesus Christ, with respect to history and humanity.[12] Such a static orthodoxy ignores the thrilling, dramatic aspects of this life, and of all of redemptive history, which apparently are viewed only

---
12. Van Niftrik (1971, 18–19).

as means and transitional phases to attain the metaphysical end goal. As a reaction to this, a theory like process theology easily arises, in which the reverse takes places and God is subordinated to his own redemptive history. In this way, we fall from one extreme into the other. In the former case, God is too transcendent; that is, he is viewed as too much apart from redemptive history. In the latter case, God is too immanent: little remains of his own personal, eternal exaltedness. He disappears as God, and the result is usually some form of a God-is-dead theology.

In the Bible, God's virtues and perfections are never treated as abstract isolated attributes but always exclusively within the framework of God's *works* in creation and redemption (re-creation) (cf., e.g., the beautiful examples of Ps. 92:1–5 and Ps. 145).[13] Even though the entire discipline of theology always has to start somewhere, and theology proper is a natural starting-point (in theo-logy we start with *theos*) for the discipline, it is essential to keep in mind that each part of dogmatics always presupposes all the other parts of this discipline. Thus, theology proper is necessarily and thoroughly interwoven with Christology (see chapters 6–8) and soteriology, not to mention ecclesiology and eschatology.[14] This is because we could not really know God in all his attributes apart from his self-revelation in sending his Son, apart from the person and work of Christ, and apart from his imminent return.

If this is kept in mind, and if Christology and soteriology (and ecclesiology and eschatology) from the outset pervade the doctrine of the divine attributes, this is a fitting answer to the objection of Otto Weber, for instance, who insisted that we should begin with the doctrine of the Trinity.[15] We then will realize that God's omnipresence, omnipotence, and om-

---

13. See especially Cremer (1917), who linked God's attributes with the historically acting God; cf. Miskotte (1941, 90–97); Rahner (1974); Pannenberg (1988, 398–429).
14. Cf. *EDR* 2 and 6, and the forthcoming Volumes III/2 and III/3 in this series.
15. Weber (1981, 386–88).

niscience, for example, are not intended to constitute a metaphysical theory concerning God, in which they are abstracted from human history. On the contrary, his omnipresence will be viewed as a consolation that God in Christ is always near to his people. His omnipotence is a comfort that God in Christ guides the individual lives of his people, just as he guides the world's history to its consummation. And his omniscience is a consolation that God in Christ knows not only the what and how concerning his people, but he knows *them*, as a man knows his beloved (see the passages mentioned in §6.1.4). We could describe all God's attributes in the same way.

It was particularly German theologian Hermann Cremer (d. 1903) and Swiss theologian Karl Barth who did pioneering work in this respect.[16] Cremer described the attributes in a strictly soteriological way. In each attribute he saw the activity of God's will in order to fight sin, to accomplish salvation, and to attain the consummation of his love. Barth grounded and interpreted each attribute soteriologically in an even more thorough way. He described God's perfections in pairs, each time combining an attribute of God's condescension with one of God's transcendence: grace *and* holiness, mercy *and* righteousness, and so on. Many have followed Barth's approach,[17] although some fell into the other extreme by limiting themselves mainly to God's condescension,[18] again especially in process theology.[19]

6.3.2 Attributes As Soteriology

With respect to the Christological-soteriological approach to God's attributes, German theologian Wolfgang Trillhaas (d. 1995) rightly stated that a doctrine of divine attributes divested of all Greek metaphysics becomes a dogmatics in a nutshell: the doctrine of God's righteousness leads to the

---

16. Cremer (1917); Barth (*CD* II/1:chapter 6).
17. Cf. Brunner (1950); Weber (1981); Trillhaas (1972); Berkhof (1986).
18. Cf. Kuitert (1962).
19. E.g., Hartshorne (1964); Cobb (1966); cf. Berkhof (1986, 121).

doctrine of justification, the doctrine of God's omniscience contains the doctrine of God's providence, the doctrine of God's love leads to the doctrine of atonement, and so on.[20]

As a consequence, the doctrine of the divine attributes by itself asks for a believing response from God's children (cf. Matt. 5:48; Luke 6:36). What is the benefit of speaking about God's love if believers do not love him?[21] Or why speak of God's grace and righteousness if believers do not show grace and righteousness to their fellow humans? "Be imitators of God, as beloved children" (Eph. 5:1). The "new self" is created in true righteousness and holiness "after the likeness of God" (4:24). "As he who called you is holy, you also be holy in all your conduct, since it is written, 'You shall be holy, for I am holy'" (1 Pet. 1:15–16; cf. Lev. 11:44–45; 19:2).

The kingdom of God in its present manifestation is a kingdom of righteousness, peace, and joy (Rom. 14:17). These characteristics are displayed first and foremost in God himself: God is righteous (Ps. 4:1; 7:9, 11), he is the "God of peace" (Rom. 15:33; 16:20), and he is "my exceeding joy" (Ps. 43:4). But in Romans 14, the kingdom is where God's subjects display these very same things: righteousness, peace, and joy, through the power of the Holy Spirit: "Whoever thus serves Christ is acceptable to God and approved by men" (v. 18).

In this context, it is interesting that Gerhard Ebeling considered prayer to be the key to the entire doctrine of God because it is the expression of the relationship (fellowship) between God and people.[22] Thus, Ebeling dealt, for instance, with God's holiness under the heading: the claim to which God is entitled; with his eternity and power under the heading: the praise or glory to which God is entitled; and with his grace and truth under the heading: the loving confidence to which God is entitled.[23]

---

20. Trillhaas (1972, 125).
21. Ibid., 130.
22. Ebeling (1979, §9).
23. Ibid., 241–44.

6.3.3 No Separate Compartments

God's attributes must never be equated to each other, of course; but it is also true that any discussion of them must never be abused to separate them, or even to play them off against each other. In fact, people have traditionally tried to avoid this very danger by speaking of God's simplicity. Actually, this term itself is not unproblematic because it tends to do the opposite: blend all attributes (see further §6.2.1). To some extent, this is also the problem with the early Protestant collective term "perfections" to denote the aggregate of God's attributes, a term used by Karl Barth as well;[24] in my view, God's perfection is but one of many facets of God's being (see §5.5.1).

No matter how we settle this, we must acknowledge that within each of God's attributes all the others are somehow represented.[25] Thus, it is impossible to speak biblically of God's love and mercy without at the same time speaking of God's righteousness and holiness—and vice versa. It is impossible to speak in a meaningful way of a God who inhabits an unapproachable light (1 Tim. 6:16), in blinding splendor, without at the same time speaking of God's gracious, condescending nearness to the believer. It is hardly possible to speak of God's omnipotence without at the same time speaking of God's affliction, which he shares with his suffering people (Isa. 63:9). God's glory is the radiance of his being (cf. Heb. 1:3), but this includes the radiance of his omnipotence, of his righteousness, of his love, and so on. God's love is his being, but as such this is omnipotent, omnipresent, holy, and righteous love. God's being is omnipotence, but this is the omnipotence of his love, of his righteousness, of his holiness. God's being is omniscience, but there is no omniscience without omnipotence and omnipresence. And how could we speak of God's love without speaking of his faithfulness, and vice versa?

It has been the error of nominalist theology to play off

---
24. Barth (*CD* II/1, 362–63).
25. Cf. Cremer (1917, 33).

God's omnipotence and sovereignty against his love and holiness.[26] This is done by treating these terms as *concepts*; of some of these, certain properties are predicated that are viewed as being part of them, which are then rejected, or the other terms are depreciated. However, as soon as one realizes that these terms are used as *ideas* one may recognize that the predicated properties are possibly not part of them at all. In this way, antithetical (contradictory) predication is entirely impossible: God's absolute sovereign freedom and the intrinsic, essential obligations of his love are perfectly harmonious.

Only in this way can the assertion of German theologian Bertram Schuler be correct, namely, that the revelation of God's triple personality may not contain any inner contradiction.[27] That is, if the ideas that are encountered in this revelation are treated as concepts, such contradictions definitely *will* arise. For instance, if it is meaningful to say that God is a person, but also that God is three persons, this is possible only if we use the term "person" as an idea, not as a concept. Conceptually speaking, someone could never be one person and three persons at the same time. But if we use the term as an idea to approximate both God's unity and God's Trinity, the situation becomes very different (see chapters 9 and 10 below).

6.4   Other Theological Aspects
6.4.1   Inherent Antitheses

Another form of simplification is due to a lack of awareness of the antitheses that, according to our limited thinking, are present in most, if not all of God's attributes. He is simple, yet, in a different sense, he is composite.

He is omnipresent, yet sometimes far away (Ps. 22:1, 11, 19).

He is transcendent, yet condescending.

He is unchangeable, yet he sometimes changes his mind

---
26. Cf. Elert (1956, 236, 239, 241, 244).
27. Schuler (1961, 13).

(Exod. 32:14; 1 Sam. 15:11; Jonah 3:10).

He is almighty, yet he allows his divine Son to be crucified "in weakness" (2 Cor. 13:4).

He is the living and life-giving God, yet he sometimes puts to death (Gen. 38:7; Exod. 13:15; 1 Chron. 10:14).

He is the spiritual God, yet he has many body parts.

He dwells in eternal bliss, yet he knows sorrow, grief, affliction, and distress.

He has a sovereign will, yet he sometimes wishes certain things to happen that do not happen, or things not to happen that do happen (Matt. 23:37; 1 Tim. 2:4; 2 Pet. 3:9).

He is the speaking God, yet he is sometimes silent (1 Sam. 28:6; Zeph. 3:17).

He is the God of fellowship, yet he sometimes drives people away from his fellowship.

He is the God of peace, yet he sometimes wages war.

Consider more deeply one of the examples mentioned: he is the God of love, yet he sometimes hates (Ps. 5:5; 11:5; Prov. 6:16–19). The fact that he is love does not mean that he always *must* love, as if any person could force him to do that. We could also say: God always loves, but his love is not always accepted, and in such a case hate is sometimes the only thing that remains—without, paradoxically enough, his love diminishing. God is infinite, and thus his steadfast love endures forever (Ps. 136). Yet, at the same time it is finite, for he shows his mercy to whomever he wills (Rom. 9:18), and his mercy toward the sinner lasts only until the day of judgment.

6.4.2 Too Little Attention?

It may seem that while the attributes of God have received much attention from many authors, his names have received far too little. Therefore, Emil Brunner began his theology proper with a treatise on the divine name, YHWH,[28] and criticized

---

28. Brunner (1950, 121–140).

all systematic theologians who did or do not do so.[29] Immediately following his chapter on the name of God, he dealt with God's Lordship, because, in the Septuagint (and hence also often in the New Testament), the Greek word *Kyrios* is the rendering of YHWH. (That is, in Old Testament quotations, YHWH is rendered as *Kyrios*, but in the New Testament *kyrios* is not always the rendering of YHWH.)

Next, Brunner dealt with the holiness and love of God before entering into the matter of the Trinity and the attributes of God. However, already here we have a difference of opinion; I will deal with God's holiness and love as attributes, which in my view does not constitute a difficulty because I do not separate God's being and God's attributes in any way.

Some wish to make a distinction between essential, absolute attributes and names of God that are eternally true for him, apart from creation, and names that are relative, that is, involve God's relationship to the world. However, besides the appellative "God" (Heb. *Elohim*, Gk. *theos*, Lat. *deus*),[30] the question is what (other) essential names there are for the Godhead (of course, other than the distinct divine persons: the names Father, Son, and Holy Spirit are indeed eternal, essential, and absolute). Otto Weber thought the traditional view impled that the names of God are the immediate expression of his being, whereas the biblical predicates are the expression of his attributes.[31] Weber himself argued, more correctly, that the name *par excellence*, YHWH, is bound not only to creation but to the Old Testament, as may be clear from the fact that, in the New Testament, the name is not even quoted once.[32] This is certainly remarkable, because the New Testament does contain the Hebrew word *Sabaoth* (Rom. 9:29; James 5:4 KJV), which in the Old Testament is *YHWH Tsebaot*,

---

29. Ibid., 134–137.
30. On the question whether "God" is a name, see Durrant (1973b, chapter 1).
31. Weber (1981, 458–59).
32. Ibid., 461–62.

"LORD of hosts."[33]

It is true that the tetragrammaton seems to express primarily what God is in relation to his people of Israel: "I am there [for you]" (see §6.2.1). And a name like "Most High God" (Heb. *El ᶜeljon*, Gk. *ho hypsistos*, Lat. *altissimus*) seems to presuppose the existence of other gods,[34] who are created (and fallen) angels. Precisely with respect to God's essence, little can be said about his names because this essence hardly comes to expression in any name. Here we recall what the Angel of YHWH told Manoah: "Why do you ask my name, seeing it is wonderful?" (Judg. 13:18; cf. Gen. 32:29), and what the Messiah is called, whose names begin with "Wonderful" (Isa. 9:6, assuming this name is not to be joined with the following name: "Wonderful Counselor"; the translations differ on this point).

6.5 Multiplicity of God's Attributes
6.5.1 Examples of Classifications: Until 1950

Our approximation of God's being and attributes through the gateways of the sixteen modalities of our immanent-creaturely world may prevent us from any attempt to divide the attributes over just a few categories. In addition to the traditional classification into metaphysical and ethical attributes, each systematic theologian has their own way of classifying, and thus, each approach is questionable.[35] A few examples may suffice to illustrate this point.

The English Puritan Stephen Charnock (d. 1680) wrote a massive work on God's being and attributes,[36] in which the latter are summarized under eleven headings: God's spirituality, eternity, immutability, omnipresence, knowledge

---

33. Actually, in Rom. 9:29 and James 5:4 the phrase "Lord of hosts" is an inaccurate rendering, because the non-Greek word Sabaoth should be left untranslated.
34. Cf. "God of gods" (Deut. 10:17), "Who is like you, O LORD, among the gods?" (Exod. 15:11; cf. Ps. 86:8; 89:8).
35. Cf. Schilder (*KD* 2:46–49).
36. Charnock (1996).

(omniscience), wisdom, power (omnipotence), holiness, goodness, rule, and patience. Why these? Why not love, grace, mercy, and righteousness?

Abraham Kuyper distinguished only two broad categories.[37] First, the *virtutes per antithesin* (virtues that form an antithesis to God's image, that is, humanity; these are his incommunicable attributes), divided into (a) eternity and omnipresence, (b) simplicity, unity, infinity, immutability, and immeasurability, and (c) absolute sovereignty. Second, the *virtutes per synthesin* (virtues that are reflected in humanity as God's image, that is, his communicable attributes), divided into (a) intellectual virtues (corresponding to the human prophetic office): wisdom and omniscience, (b) ethical virtues (corresponding to the human priestly office): goodness, grace, holiness, righteousness, truth (both verity and veracity), and (c) dynamic virtues (corresponding to the human royal office): omnipotence. My main problem with this (rather artificial) type of classification is the distinction between communicable attributes and incommunicable attributes, which I discussed earlier.

Hermann Cremer distinguished between the attributes that *open up* in God's revelation (holiness, righteousness, goodness, wisdom, mercy) and those that beforehand are *contained* in the notion "God" (omnipotence, omnipresence, omniscience, immutability, eternity).[38] The former presuppose God's fellowship with humanity, the latter do not. I have explained earlier why I think this is the same false contrast between God's communicable and incommunicable attributes.

Herman Bavinck divided the incommunicable attributes into God's *aseitas*, immutability, infinity (eternity and omnipresence), and the unity of simplicity and multiplicity. He divided the communicable attributes into (a) God's spiritual nature (spirituality, invisibility), (b) attributes of intellect knowledge, foreknowledge, wisdom, trustworthiness),

---
37. Kuyper (*DD* I.1.286–418).
38. Cremer (1917).

(c) moral attributes (goodness, holiness, righteousness), (d) attributes of sovereignty (will, omnipotence), and (e) perfection, blessedness, and glory.[39]

Just like Abraham Kuyper, Karl Barth distinguished only two broad categories,[40] which in fact correspond to the ancient, but objectionable, classification into communicable and incommunicable attributes: the perfections of the divine *love*, divided into (a) grace and holiness, (b) mercy and righteousness, (c) patience and wisdom; and the perfections of the divine *freedom*, divided into (a) unity and omnipresence, (b) constancy and omnipotence, (c) eternity and glory.[41]

Emil Brunner spoke separately of God as (1) the Lord, (2) the Holy One, and (3) Love, and then, of the attributes of (a) omnipotence, (b) omnipresence and omniscience, (c) eternity, immutability, faithfulness, and righteousness, and (d) wisdom and glory.[42]

6.5.2 More Recent Examples of Classifications

Dutch theologian Klaas Schilder (d. 1952) distinguished between God's autarky, *aseitas*, eternity, infinity, immutability, personality, spirituality, identity, transcendence, blessedness, immeasurability, freedom, omnipotence, and omniscience.[43]

Paul Althaus distinguished between (a) freedom and rule (including [1] *aseitas*, immutability, sufficiency, [2] personality, [3] unity and simplicity, [4] omnipotence, omniscience, omnipresence, eternity), (b) love and righteousness, and (c) holiness, glory, blessedness.[44]

Swiss theologian Fritz Buri (d. 1995) distinguished between the "transeunt properties of being" ([a] *aseitas*, unity, *actus purus* ("pure act," implying God's perfection and

---

39. Bavinck (*RD* 2:chapters 4–5).
40. Adopted by Weber (1981, 445–50, 463–508).
41. Barth (*CD* II/1:chapter 6).
42. Brunner (1950, 121–322).
43. Schilder (*KD* 2–4).
44. Althaus (1952, 264–98).

omnipotence), [b] immutability, eternity, omnipresence, [c] simplicity, spirituality, inscrutability, invisibility) and the "immanent properties of essence" ([a] vitality, omnipotence, "all-wisdom," [b] love, righteousness, faithfulness, [c] wisdom, holiness, glory).[45]

Walter Brugger distinguished between God's *entitative* attributes (perfection, infinity, simplicity, unity, inscrutability, omnipresence, immutability, eternity), and God's *operative* attributes (knowledge, will, omnipotence).[46]

Edmund Schlink distinguished between the Lord ([a] omnipotence, [b] omnipresence, [c] eternity, [d] glory or freedom), the consuming God ([a] unavoidable, [b] ranting), and the God giving himself ([a] love, [b] righteousness, [c] wisdom, [d] constancy).[47]

Wolfhart Pannenberg distinguished[48] between the attributes that are mentioned of God on the basis of his acting (goodness, mercy, faithfulness, righteousness, patience; in brief: love[49]), and those determining the "object" of these mentions as such (infinity, holiness, eternity, omnipresence, omniscience[50]).

British theologian Gerald Bray distinguished four categories in God's properties, namely, in relation to *time* (uncreatedness, incorruptibility, immortality, eternity), *space* (infinity, unlimitedness, omnipotence), *matter* (simplicity and multiplicity, uncorporeality), and *quality* (impassibility, immutability, invisibility).[51]

Under the title "Transcendence and Immanence," American theologian Donald G. Bloesch (d. 2010) spoke of the pair "infinity and spirituality," the pair "immutability and impas-

---

45. Buri (1978, chapter 13).
46. Brugger (1979, 277–427).
47. Schlink (1983, 762–87).
48. Pannenberg (1988, 424–29).
49. Ibid., 456–77.
50. Ibid., 429–56.
51. Bray (1993, 81–82).

sibility," the pair "power and wisdom," and the pair "holiness and love" (including righteousness).[52]

American theologians Beverley Clack and Brian R. Clack limited themselves to God's eternity, his omnipotence, and his omniscience because they viewed these attributes as the most philosophically significant.[53]

6.5.3 Summary

If we gather all these together, we have the following divine properties (in alphabetical order, without any claim to completeness and without giving much heed to possible overlaps): *actus purus*, *aseitas*, autarky, awareness, blessedness, eternity, faithfulness, glory, goodness, grace, holiness, identity, immeasurability, immortality, immutability (unchangeability, constancy), impassibility, incorruptibility, infinity, inscrutability (unfathomability), invisibility, knowledge, love, mercy, multiplicity, omnipotence, omnipresence, omniscience, patience, perfection, personality, power, ranting, righteousness, rule, simplicity, sovereignty (freedom), spirituality (incorporeality), sufficiency, transcendence, truth(fulness), unavoidability, uncreatedness, unlimitedness, unity, vitality, will, and wisdom.

The enormous differences between all the approaches mentioned seem to indicate that classifying the divine attributes is not very fruitful. Therefore, my approach will be a different one. People might argue that mine is still another one in a long series of attempts, and thus no guarantee that I will succeed any better. But there is a difference. The classifications mentioned, which were very different, were human-made, and thus often arbitrary. They tell us more about the creativity of the theologian making them than about God's real essence. Of course, the Dooyeweerdian theory of the modal aspects of reality is precisely that: just another theory. Yet, together with Dooyeweerd and Vollenhoven, and many

---

52. Bloesch (1995, chapters 4–6).
53. Clack and Clack (2008, 54–69).

congenial thinkers of younger generations, I believe this theory to be the best approximation of the modal diversity within created reality formulated so far.

Dooyeweerd's model was not at all designed as a model for approximating the being of God—that use of his model is nothing but my own personal application of it. But if it is true that we speak of God in no other terms than those adopted from created reality, applied to God in the form of ideas, then I know no more appropriate way of approximating God's attributes than through the theory of cosmic-modal diversity. Whether this view possesses any truth or plausibility may be evaluated on the basis of the next two chapters.

Chapter 7
God's Attributes: (Natural Modalities)

O LORD, God of Israel, there is no God like you,
   in heaven above or on earth beneath,
   keeping covenant and showing steadfast love to your servants
      who walk before you with all their heart.

1 Kings 8:23

7.1   The Arithmetic Modality: God's Unity
7.1.1   The Unity of Singularity

A TYPICAL APPLICATION OF AN arithmetic term, used as an idea, is found in our speaking of God's unity (his being-one).[1] "YHWH our God, YHWH is one" (Deut. 6:4; see §7.1.4), not in the sense of an intrinsic unity within his being (*unitas* Dei, "unity of God") but in the sense that there is no other besides him (*singularitas Dei*, "singularity of God") (Deut. 4:35, 39; 32:39; 2 Kings 19:19; Ps. 18:31; Isa. 44:6; 45:21–22; Zech. 14:9; cf. Mark 12:29; John 17:3; Rom. 3:30; 1 Cor. 8:6; 1 Tim. 1:17; 2:5). God is unique (from Lat. *unus*, "one"); of his "kind" there is only one. However, we must add two notes to this statement:

---

1. Barth (*CD* II/1:498–501.

(a) The unity of God must be placed immediately beside the Trinity doctrine. This is because the apostle Paul, who tells us that there is "one God and Father of all," says in the same passage that there is "one Spirit" and "one Lord" (Eph. 4:4–6), who, to him, all three together are one God (see, e.g., Rom. 9:5; 1 Cor. 2:10–11; 12:4–7; 2 Cor. 3:17; 13:13; 1 Tim. 3:16; Tit. 2:13). This is already clear from the fact that, in passages on the "one God," he applies the title *kyrios* to Christ, a title that in the Septuagint stands for YHWH (also see 1 Cor. 8:6; 1 Tim. 2:5).[2]

(b) The Bible, which tells is that God is one, also says that there is no one *like* him (Exod. 8:10; 9:14), which suggests that he is the *primus inter similibus* ("first among the similar ones"). In the term *primus* we find another arithmetic term, used as an idea. In his battle against the "gods" of Egypt (Exod. 12:12; 18:10–11; Num. 33:4; 2 Sam. 7:23; cf. Isa. 19:1), God is the "number one." About the significance of the relationship between God and the "other Gods" I have written elsewhere.[3]

Traditional theology distinguishes between the *unitas singularitatis* ('Unity of singularity") and the *unitas simplicitatis* ("unity of simplicity"). The former refers to God's uniqueness, his *unicitas*, as just described: of his kind there is only one. This is an "exclusive, numerical unity,"[4] which underlines the arithmetic character of this way of speaking of God, even though Bavinck does not distinguish between using these arithmetic terms as concepts or as ideas.

Friedrich Schleiermacher objected that, strictly speaking, unity cannot be an attribute of something.[5] Allegedly, unity and multiplicity are no qualities but belong to the category of quantity. Even the *unitas singularitatis* can be predicated of God only if it is implied that he is one among several. To this I reply:

---

2. Cf. Weber (1981, 395).
3. *EDR* 10:§1.4.
4. Bavinck (*RD* 2, 141.
5. Schleiermacher (1831, §56,2, followed by Pannenberg (1988, 478v).

(a) Why could a quantity not be a quality? Does the unity or multiplicity of a thing not express an aspect of its *qualitas*, its "being so-and-so"? At any rate, it is viewed like this in the doctrine of modalities, in which the arithmetic is considered to be one (even the first) qualitative mode of the cosmic reality, and as such is seen as presenting a noetic window to the unity of God.

(b) In a sense, the Bible does describe God several times as one (the unique One) among many, the "God of gods" (Deut. 10:17; Ps. 136:2; Dan. 2:47; 11:36), the "Most High God" (Gen. 14:18–22 etc.; Num. 24:16; Deut. 32:8; cf. 1 Cor. 8:5–6).

(c) The objections mentioned are basically lifted as soon as it is grasped that, indeed, we cannot speak of God's unity in a conceptual way. Wolfhart Pannenberg rightly pointed to God's *unitas absoluta* ("absolute unity"),[6] a term that is acceptable if it is used as an arithmetic idea (not concept) of God's unity. That is, God's unity does *not* necessarily imply that he would or should be *unus inter pares* ("one among equals"), or that he would be only a "something," and never "all in all" (cf. 1 Cor. 15:28; Eph. 1:23; 4:6), and so on.

7.1.2 The Unity of Simplicity

The second mentioned term of traditional theology, *unitas simplicitatis* ("unity of simplicity"), is less harmless,[7] even though it was still defended by, for instance, Dutch theologians Klaas Schilder and F. Gerrit Immink.[8] The term is a direct fruit of Greek-metaphysical speculation about the "simplicity" of God. The philosophers Johan Visagie (South Africa) and Andree Troost (Netherlands) referred to Greek philosopher Xenophanes (d. c. 478 BC), who asserted that the Godhead is *entirely* eye, *entirely* mind, and *entirely* ear.[9] God

---

6. Pannenberg (1988, 478v.; Cf. Cusanus, De docta ignorantia I.5.14.
7. Cf. Bavinck (*RD* 2, 144–49); Barth (*CD* II/1:501–18); Pannenberg (1971, 322 and further; 1988, 389–401).
8. Schilder (*KD* 2:28–38); Immink (1987); idem in Van den Brink and Sarot (1995, 98–116).
9. Visagie (1982, 8–9); Troost (1992a, [2–3]).

is not "simple" like we speak of a "simple man," but in the sense that there is no multiplicity in him. God is not both this and that, but entirely this and entirely that; what he is, he always is totally.

Under the influence of arithmetic speculations, Xenophanes was also the first to apply to the Godhead the notion of "that which is one" (Gk. *to en*). Thus, Greek thought arrived at viewing "multiplicity" as "non-essential" (i.e., telling us nothing about the essence), for it implies "difference from that which is one" (so, e.g., Plotinus). This line of thinking was adopted by the church fathers. They emphasized that God is not a "composite" (viz., of many different attributes) but that God's attributes, expressed as substantives, are identical with his being. For instance, God is not just both wise and good, both holy and righteous, but God *is* (entirely) wisdom, goodness, holiness, righteousness.

As long as this idea only aimed at combating certain heresies, I see little difficulty with it. Thus, it is impossible that the Son and the Spirit would possess certain divine attributes without sharing in the essence of God, as Socinians taught, or that something that is in God[10] does not necessarily belong to God, to his essence, as some Arminians taught. God is not a set of parts, he is not in a process of development toward higher perfection, has no latent capacities that would not have developed yet, has no attributes that would describe his being more fully than other attributes, and so on.[11] At the same time, some of the problems of such a speaking of God's "simplicity" immediately come to mind:

(a) If God indeed is identical with wisdom, goodness, holiness, and so on, how can we avoid the conclusion that all that is wise, good, or holy — as some people are — is divine?

(b) If God is "simple" (i.e., non-composite), how can we

---

10. Notice that the Bible does say many times that believers are "in Christ" (as Man), who himself (as the Son) is "in the Father" (John 10:38; 14:10–11), but never that believers are "in the Father."
11. Heyns (1988, 40).

avoid the conclusion that his wisdom is identical with his goodness, his goodness identical with his holiness, and so on?

The answer must be that we can speak of God only in creaturely terms, used as ideas:

(a) If we say that God is wise, we do not mean that all wisdom would be divine, or that human wisdom was modeled after God's highest wisdom (theo-ontological duplication), but that God is something special that we can approximate only by using the creaturely term "wise," not as a concept—which would turn God into a creature—but as an idea, in order to refer to something that surpasses the conceptual, and in this case even the immanent and temporal.

(b) The notions wisdom, goodness, holiness, and so on, directly refer to certain modes of being (modalities) within our immanent reality. These are notions that we know exclusively in their creaturely diversity, and which we necessarily maintain in their diversity, even if we apply them as ideas to God. We can approximate their coherence in God by referring to the creaturely coherence of the immanent modalities, and to their unity, fullness and integration within the human heart. However, we can speak of them only in their diversity. We can speak of the intrinsic unity, fullness and integration of all God's attributes in his being. But it is Greek speculation to assert that *each* attribute as such is totally identical with God's *being* in a way that would exclude all multiplicity.

7.1.3 Further Complications

In the sense just described, it cannot be any problem to speak both of God's simplicity and of his multiplicity, as long as we do not understand such terms as concepts, because in this case they would lead to logical contradictions. We rather use them as arithmetic *ideas* in order to approximate both the intrinsic unity of God's being and the multiplicity of his properties; or rather, in order to avoid any possible dualism: both the unity and diversity of his being, and both the diversity and unity of his properties.

Also Herman Dooyeweerd seemed to have retained a piece of ancient "simplicity" metaphysics in saying:[12] "The fullness of meaning of love, as revealed in Christ's cross, is at the same time the fullness of justice. If we assign a higher place to Divine love than to Divine justice, this procedure necessarily detracts from God's holiness." The latter is true—but I object to the "is" in the first sentence. The fact that God *is* love (1 John 4:8, 16) and that God *is* light (1:5), does not imply that love and light are identical. Dooyeweerd's "is" seems to suggest such an identification. In God, his love and light are one, but not the same, just like in a man, for instance, authorship and fatherhood can be united in one person—I *am* an author, and I *am* a father—while yet not being identical. It is true that God *is* love; it is equally true that God *has* love, *bestows* love, as one of his many characteristics.

It is remarkable that Herman Bavinck calls God's "simplicity" a "property."[13] On the one hand, it is argued that God does not *have* attributes, but that he *is* his attributes. On the other hand, this identity of God's being and his attributes—that is, his simplicity—is called itself an attribute of God. Thus, one peculiar attribute of God is that he has no distinct attributes! Of course, this is a contradiction only if, again, terms are used here as concepts. In that case, the kinds of embarrassment arise that Bavinck describes.[14] On the one hand, we must appreciate the intentions of traditional theology, which wished to emphasize that there is nothing "in God" that is not truly God, that he is not a composition of parts, that he does not possess any latent, not yet actualized potencies, and so on.[15] On the other hand, the Greek-scholastic term "simplicity" has introduced terms into theology foreign to the life of faith, and overlooking that we can speak of God only in creaturely terms applied not as concepts but as ideas.

---

12. Dooyeweerd (*NC* 2:157).
13. Bavinck (*RD* 2, 145).
14. Bavinck (*RD* 2, 145v).
15. Cf. Bavinck (*RD* 2, 147v.; Heyns (1988, 40).

God's Attributes: (Natural Modalities)

The Bible speaks of God's "simplicity" only once, but in a very different way. James 1:5 says that God "gives generously to all"; the Greek *haplōs*, literally "simply" (cf. Segond: *simplement*; Luther 1545: *einfeltiglich*; cf. EHV, LEB: "without reservation").[16] This verse is not about some "ontic" simplicity of God, but about a so-called "moral" simplicity.[17] Those who feel bound to the Belgic Confession (art. 1, God is a "simple" being) are in no way hindered to refuse the ontological idea of simplicity, even though Guido de Brès no doubt had this in mind. Jan van Genderen acknowledged the latter implicitly;[18] after this, he spoke of God's simplicity in a practical way[19] that certainly was not intended by De Brès. This is no problem; every reader is free to think in Article 1 of the moral "simplicity" of which James 1:5 speaks. Or, if one so chooses, one could think of the view of Karl Barth,[20] who rejected the traditional view, and noticed that God "is so simple that, in his glory, he can be near to the simplest knowing, and also can mock the greatest profundity and acumen."

7.1.4 Names of God

Here, we think again of the famous *Sh'ma^c* in Deuteronomy 6:4, *Sh'ma^c Yisraēl YHWH Elohim YHWH echad*, with the remarkable third (cayyin) and last consonant (dalet), which are written large in the Masoretic text, and together form the word ^c*ēd*, "witness." The text can be rendered in several ways (which hardly need any further comments):

"YHWH our God, YHWH is one" (cf. ESV)

"YHWH our God is one YHWH" (cf. KJV, ASV)

"YHWH is our God, YHWH is one" (cf. WEB)

"YHWH is our God, YHWH alone" (cf. ISV, TLB)

"YHWH our God is an only (unique) YHWH" (Segond,

---
16. The HSV rendering of "overvloedig" is the least successful.
17. Cf. Troost (1992a, [2v.].
18. Van Genderen (2008, 165).
19. Ibid., 173.
20. Barth (*CD* II/1:515).

Luther 1545)

"YHWH is our God. He is the only YHWH" (cf. ICB)

"YHWH our God, YHWH is unique" (cf. LEB)

"YHWH is our God, YHWH is the only [God]" (cf. ERV, GW).[21]

7.2 The Arithmetic Modality: God's Infinity
7.2.1 Two Kinds of Infinity

In my opinion, also the *infinity* of God must be dealt with under the viewpoint of the arithmetic modality, even though it has often be viewed from a spatial (omnipresence), kinematic (immutability), or economic viewpoint (perfection).

Since ancient Greek philosophy, Western thought, including mathematics, has made a distinction between the *potentially* or *incomplete infinite* and the *actually* or *completely infinite*. The former refers to what is "without end," such as certain mathematical series; the latter refers to what in all its parts is fixed and determined, while at the same time surpassing each finite magnitude.[22] Aristotle denied the existence of the actually infinite, and even asserted that his form-giving godhead (the *nous*) was finite. In his wake, Origen taught that God cannot be infinite (unlimited), for if he were, he would not be able to "delimit" himself, and thus would not be able to understand or know himself. Plotinus, however, in agreement with his view of eternity as the timeless present (Lat. *nunc aeternum*; see §§5.2.1, 5.2.2, and 5.6.3), considered "that which is one" (Gk. *to en*, i.e., God) as infinite. Augustine saw God as the actually infinite, and viewed the creation as finite.[23] German scholar Nicolaus Cusanus (d. 1464) also saw God as the actually infinite, but the creation as endless.[24] Baruch Spinoza, who identified God with nature, viewed the universe as

---

21. Cf. De Groot and Hulst (1952, 56–59).
22. So, e.g., the German mathematician Georg Cantor (d. 1918); see Strauss and Visagie (1984, 57–58); Strauss (1989, chapter 2; 1990, 32; 2009, 190–92).
23. *De Civitate* XII.19.
24. De docta ignorantia I.13–17.

actually infinite, too.[25]

In mathematics, the idea of the actually infinite was made fruitful by German mathematician Georg Cantor (d. 1918) and others. In the twentieth century, however, this idea was fiercely combated by the intuitionist school in mathematics. Under its influence, Dooyeweerd, too, rejected the notion of the actually or completely infinite, and only acknowledged the potentially or incompletely infinite.[26] Daniel Strauss, however, pointed out that Dooyeweerd's own doctrine of the modalities offers a gateway in order to speak in a responsible way of the actually infinite, which Strauss called "the simultaneously infinite," in distinction to the "successively infinite" (above called the potentially infinite).[27]

On the law-side of the arithmetic modality as such, we no doubt only find the numerical order of succession, which determines each (countable) successive-infinite set (e.g., the infinite series of the integers, the whole, and the rational numbers). However, if we also take into account the spatial anticipation within the arithmetic modality, we see how, on the law-side, the arithmetic order of succession approximates the spatial order of simultaneity, and on the subject-side, we see an uncountable, continuous set as that of the irrational numbers (such as $\sqrt{2}$, π, and e) that clearly anticipates spatial-continuous simultaneity.[28] Thus, "simultaneous" infinity cannot be understood in purely arithmetic terms but seems to involve the anticipation to the spatial order of simultaneity and continuous extension.

7.2.2 Application

The considerations just described seem to give us a useful gateway to an understanding (in the form of ideas) of God's infinity as actual ("simultaneous") infinity, in agreement with

---

25. Strauss (1989, 29; 1990, 30–31).
26. Dooyeweerd (*NC* 2:92).
27. Strauss (1989, 51–55; 1990, 38–39); cf. Strauss and Visagie (1984, 57–59).
28. Stafleu (1989, 41).

Augustine, Cusanus, and others. Friedrich Schleiermacher wished to understand God's infinity not primarily as unlimitedness (cf. the potentially successively infinite) but as that which stands over against the finite, that is, that which is partly determined by other things.[29] Wolfhart Pannenberg called this a *qualitative* determination of the concept of the infinite, to be distinguished from the *quantitative* determination of the mathematic-infinite.[30] Apparently, the latter is understood in the sense of the successively infinite, the "infinite series," including "the indefinite succession of finite magnitudes in time and space," that is, realized "by unlimited addition of endless steps." In opposition to this, Pannenberg saw "the basic determination in the concept of the infinite" in "the contrast with all that is finite," that is, with all that is delineated by other things and is corruptible. This seems to agree entirely with the idea of the actually or completely or simultaneously infinite.

Please note that God's "simultaneous" infinity does not necessarily imply timelessness (see chapter 5). On the contrary, notions such as "simultaneous" and "at the same time" do imply a certain form of time. Thus, the mathematical "simultaneous infinity" helps us to form an idea (not a concept) of God's own "temporal" order of "simultaneity," which far surpasses all modal-functional idea of time.

7.2.3 Names of God

If the total number of God's plans is already "countless" (Ps. 139:17 CEB; "How vast is the sum of them," ESV), how infinitely great the Lord himself must be. If God's understanding is "beyond measure" (Ps. 147:5; KJV: "infinite"), how boundless must he then be himself. The book of Baruch says, "O Israel, how great is the universe in which God dwells! How vast is all that he possesses! There is no end to it; there is no way to measure how wide or how high it is" (3:24–25). If

---

29. Schleiermacher (1831, §56,2).
30. Pannenberg (1988, 430).

there is "no end" to everything that God possesses, then even less is there any end to his own greatness.

Therefore, Psalm 150 calls upon us to praise him for his "surpassing" greatness" (v. 2 NIV etc.; many: "excellent greatness"). "By this power he can do infinitely [NIV: immeasurably] more than we can ask or imagine" (Eph. 3:20 GW). Genuine divine names are not encountered here, but what we find does suggest a name such as the Overwhelming One, the All-Surpassing One. In this, we partly hear already spatial terms (see the next sections).

7.3 The Spatial Modality: God's Elevation
7.3.1 Supratemporal, Surpassing

We already found various modal-spatial expressions that, if used as ideas, tell us something of God. God is "supra"-temporal, and such in an even more emphatic sense than in the case of the human heart. Actually, the human supratemporality is rather pleni-temporality (§5.5); it never surpasses creaturely time in any absolute sense. But God does. Terms such as "supra" ("above," a spatial term) and "surpass" ("transcend," a kinematic term) really tell us something about God's "elevation" (another kinematic term, from Lat. *e-levo*, "lift," i.e., above [!] time and creation).

These are not "just" metaphors; that is, it would be impossible to say anything meaningful about God's elevation other than in spatial or kinematic terms. This is no problem at all—the Bible also necessarily uses such terms—as long as such terms are not used conceptually. Only in the latter case, such foolish questions come up as this one: how can God dwell "above" us, and at the same time also "above" our antipodes?

If we accept that spatial terms can be used as ideas only, we can understand how the law can be called a "boundary" between God and his creation. A boundary does suggest two "domains" separated from each other, but this does not make God spatial in any creaturely sense. We use spatial terms here only as ideas in order to point "beyond" the modal-spatial.

In a similarly way, we can understand that, on the one hand, God is described as the One who is "in heaven" or "in the heavens" (Deut. 26:15; Ps. 11:4; 115:3; Isa. 63:15; Matt. 5:34; Eph. 1:20; Rev. 4:1–2), whereas, on the other hand, Solomon recognizes that "heaven and the highest heaven cannot contain you" (1 Kings 8:27; 2 Chron. 2:6; cf. Isa. 66:1; Acts 17:24). "Do I not fill heaven and earth?" (Jer. 23:24). All these statements truly tell us something about God; we can obtain true, even rational knowledge of God through them, be it knowledge in the form not of concepts but of ideas.

7.3.2 The Spatial Modality: God's *Aseitas*

Some other terms that we have discussed in connection with God's eternity can be viewed as being of a modal-spatial origin as well. The Latin term *aseitas* (see §4.6.1) was derived from *ens a se*, "being on (or, in, out of) oneself." It is quite difficult, if not impossible, to express such a "standing by itself," "being on one's own," in any other way than with the help of spatial terms. "On," "in," and "out of" are spatial prepositions.

Also the Latin term *magnitudo* (God's "magnitude"), which I suggest as an alternative for *aseitas* and independence (German *Selbständigkeit*, Dutch *zelfstandigheid*, "standing on one's own"), is basically a spatial term. It refers to the measurements (dimensions) of a physical thing, here applied as ideas. Newer theology seems to prefer a term such as *absoluteness* (not the least because of Georg W.F. Hegel), deduced from Latin *ab-solvo*, from *ab*, "off, away from," and *solvere*, "to loosen, untie, release, detach," in which we clearly recognize a spatial aspect.

7.3.3 Names of God

In various ways, the Bible alludes to God's greatness (magnitude): "O LORD my God, you are very great!" (Ps. 104:1); "praise him according to his excellent greatness" (150:2). If God's "understanding is beyond measure" (147:5), how much beyond measure must he be himself. The apostle Paul speaks in Ephesians of "the immeasurable greatness of his power" (1:19), "the immeasurable riches of his grace" (2:7), and "the unsearchable riches of Christ" (3:8). Isaiah 40:26 speaks of "the greatness of his might." Real divine names do we not find here either, but the qualities just mentioned do suggest a name such as the Infinitely Great One, the Immeasurable One, the One Delimited By Nothing (also see §7.2).

7.4 The Spatial Modality: God's Omnipresence
7.4.1 Historical Background

The most important modal-spatial term that is used as an idea with respect to God is his *omnipresence* (Lat. *omnipraesentia or ubiquitas*; cf. *immensitas*).[31] Be it not the term, at least the idea frequently occurs in Scripture: God "is actually not far from each one of us, for 'In him we live and move and have our being'" (Acts 17:27-28). "Am I a God at hand, . . . and not a God far away? Can a man hide himself in secret places so that I cannot see him? . . . Do I not fill heaven and earth?" (Jer. 23:23-24). The well-known passage in Psalm 139:7-10 tells us that, wherever we go, God is there as well: "Where shall I go from your Spirit? Or where shall I flee from your presence? If I ascend to heaven, you are there! If I make my bed in Sheol, you are there! If I take the wings of the morning and dwell in the uttermost parts of the sea, even there your hand shall lead me, and your right hand shall hold me."

If we would interpret such passages in a conceptual way, we will easily find, here again, many (apparent) contradictions. For instance, God will put the wicked "away from the presence of the Lord" (2 Thess. 1:9). How is this possible if God is omnipresent? Or how can the name of YHWH "come from afar" (Isa. 30:27) if he is always near? How can God be driven "far from" his sanctuary (Ezek. 8:6) if he is omnipresent? How can David pray, "Be not far from me" (Ps. 22:11; cf. vv. 1, 19) if God is always near? This is what we must now

---

31. Barth (*CD* II/1:518–51).

investigate.

In the development of the notion of God's omnipresence, Stoic thought about the benevolent providence of the demiurge, and his presence within the created reality, presumably played a role already in the thought of Clement of Rome. However, the notion was not simply adopted; the idea was already clearly present in the Bible itself. Moreover, other than the Stoa did the Apologists connected the idea of God's omnipresence with his transcendence, as we will see. Thus, they protected this idea against pantheism, in which God and the cosmos are thought to coincide. Still, the notion of God's omnipresence did not remain free of Greek influences. Thus, as we saw, God's eternity was traditionally viewed as his immutability with respect to time, and his omnipresence as his immutability with respect to space (see §5.3.1).[32]

This time–space dualism cannot be maintained in a radically Christian philosophy. The latter views time as the cosmic framework for the entire modal diversity; that is, time expresses itself in *all* modalities, also in the spatial modality, in each modality in its own way. In contrast with this, the spatial modality is only one out of many different modalities within the immanent reality.

7.4.2 Conceptual Misunderstandings

Most problems with the term "omnipresence" arise if the term is not used as an idea but as a concept. Wolfgang Trillhaas rightly noticed that an "abstract [which, in my terms, amounts to conceptual] omnipresence" of God is by definition pantheism,[33] Conversely, if we take the Bible passages that speak of God's "absence" in any absolute sense (in my terms: take them conceptually), we land in atheism. Let me give a practical example. We can say that energy is present everywhere in the cosmos. Is, therefore, cosmic energy omnipresent, at least within the cosmos? Yes, namely, in a strictly

---

32. Bavinck (*RD* 2, 129); Althaus (1952, 276).
33. Trillhaas (1972, 129); cf. Brunner (1950, 274).

conceptual sense, just like oxygen is omnipresent on the surface of oceans and continents. At each point determined by mathematic coordinates in the cosmos, there is energy; it is "omni-spatial." However, can we speak in the same way of God's omnipresence?

This was exactly what Augustine imagined during his Manichean period:[34] he saw God as a kind of fine ether, spread throughout the world and infinite space. Afterwards he described God as *unique totus* ("everywhere entirely") and *nusquam locorum* ("at no single place," nowhere localizable).[35] Martin Luther uttered a similar reproach with respect to Ulrich Zwingli, claiming that the latter viewed God as a "large, wide being filling the world."[36]

God's omnipresence can in no way be defined geo- or cosmographically. If it were otherwise, God would be subjected to arithmetic (algebraic) and spatial (geometrical) laws. Such a view would draw him under the boundary of the law between Creator and creation. As Augustine rightly said, *Si in aliquo loco esset, non esset Deus* ("If he would be at any [specific] place, he would not be God").[37] Anselm saw this danger of conceptually speaking about God's omnipresence when he argued that it is better to say that God is *cum tempore et loco* ("[given] with a [certain] moment of time and a [certain] location") than *in tempore et loco* ("at a [certain] moment of time and a [certain] location").[38] Karl Barth rightly warned against the false conflict between a spacelessness of God and a kind of "all-spatiality."[39] I myself would prefer expressing it as follows: God *is* spatial, but not in the sense of a concept but of an idea. Therefore, for instance, heaven is not a "spatial image";[40] it is spatial but not in the sense of a concept but of

---

34. *Confessiones* VII.1.
35. *Confessiones* VI.3; *De civitate* VII.30; cf. Bavinck (*RD* 2, 137–38).
36. WA 26, 339.
37. Enarrationes on Ps. 74.
38. Monologion 22.
39. Barth (*CD* II/1:527–28).
40. Pannenberg (1988, 446).

an idea.

We can speak of God's omnipresence only by using spatial terms as ideas, that is, as referring to matters that surpass the modal-spatial.[41] Strictly conceptually, it is impossible that God at the same time is "nearby" and is "far away" from something. However, if we use such terms as ideas, both his "nearness" and his being "far away" supply us with some truth about him. I can form for myself a concept of my nearness to my desk at the time of my writing; I can even express it in inches. But of God's simultaneous "nearness" to a person as well as his "turning away" from that person if the latter begins to walk in evil I can only form an idea. Please note again that I am not speaking of metaphors, for these speak by way of comparison. God's "nearness" is not just imagery; he truly *is* "near," even if I cannot express this in inches.

7.4.3 Ambiguity

In the way just described, we can also understand in a rational way a certain ambiguity in the Bible, flowing from the embarrassment, very familiar to us, that arises when we speak—and cannot do else than speak—about non-creaturely things in creaturely terms. On the one hand, the Bible does not hesitate to use spatial-geographical terms when speaking of God; he is in heaven (Ps. 115:3, 16) and in hades (Ps. 139:8), on the land (see below) and in the sea (Ps. 77:19), in the light and in darkness (2 Chron. 6:1; Ps. 139:11–12).

On the other hand, the Bible clearly shows that God surpasses cosmic space: "But will God indeed dwell on the earth? Behold, heaven and the highest heaven cannot contain you" (1 Kings 8:27). Amos 9:2 even says that, if people climb up to heaven, God will bring them down from there—as if he himself is not there, but down here. Such a free usage of spatial terms is possible because God surpasses all our conceptual images of space. Yet, if spatial terms are used as ideas they certainly do tell us something about both God's presence and

---

41. Cf. L. J. van den Brom in Van den Brink and Sarot (1995, 85).

his absence, and even about his omnipresence.

Thus, for instance, God is omnipresent, yet his presence or "dwelling" is linked in particular with heaven (Ps. 115:3, 16; Matt. 6:9), Bethel (Gen. 28:16-17), the burning bush (Deut. 33:16), Mount Sinai (Exod. 24:16), the tabernacle (29:42-46), Zion (Isa. 8:18), especially the temple (1 Kings 8:12-13 [but cf. v. 27]), more concretely, the ark (Ps. 80:1-2); further, the individual believer (Isa. 57:15; John 14:23; Rom. 8:9, 11; 1 Cor. 6:19), and especially Jesus Christ (John 14:10; Col. 1:19; 2:9), and subsequently through his Spirit in the Church (1 Cor. 3:16; 2 Cor. 6:16; Eph. 2:20-22).

Heaven is in particular the "where" of God's existence, and the "whence" of his works, not simply a "place," but a dynamic indication of divine presence and divine works, not on the basis of his revelation or incarnation but of his being.[42] Traditional theology has tried to distinguish between God's omnipresence and his dwelling at a certain location by means of the terms *general* and *special presence*.[43]

It is wise to avoid, here again, all ancient-metaphysical speculation about God's omnipresence. What does it add to our understanding of God if we say that he is both somewhere and nowhere (Philo, Plotinus)?[44] If this is understood conceptually, it is a vacuous, purely contradictory statement, which will appeal only to people who love irrational (mystical) knowledge of God. However, if we understand it in the sense of ideas, I consider it to be completely meaningless to say that God is "nowhere." Bavinck is mistaken in suggesting that, because speaking of God's *ubi* ("where") is not conceptually possible, we could speak of God's "nowhere" in a meaningful way, because, if we do the latter conceptually, we simply land in the same error. The answer to the problem that we cannot conceptually speak of God's "where" is not conceptually speaking of God's "nowhere" but speak of God's

---
42. Weber (1981, 497); Schlink (1983, 765–66); Heyns (1988, 45).
43. Wentsel (1987, 494).
44. Cf. Bavinck (*RD* 2, 138).

"where" in the form of ideas.

7.4.4 Names of God

Some spatial analogies are based upon the fact that God can be viewed as a "place" where one can hide: he is a "stronghold," a "fortress," "my rock, in whom I take refuge," a "shelter," a "refuge," a "hiding place," and a "strong tower" (Ps. 9:9; 18:2; 46:7, 11; 59:9, 17; 61:4; 62:8; 94:22; 119:114; Prov. 18:10). God is also the God who is "near" (Deut. 4:7; Ps. 75:1), and who sometimes is, or seems, "far away" (Ps. 22:1, 11, 19).

The most important spatial name is *El ᶜelyon*, "God the Most High" (Gen. 14:18-22; Num. 24:16; Deut. 32:8; Gk. *ho hypsistos*, Mark 5:7; Luke 1:32, 35, 76, etc.; Lat. *altissimus*); *ᶜelyon* is derived from the root *ᶜ-l-h*, "to go up, to rise" (which actually is kinematic). Literally speaking, also the name Sovereign belongs here since this name was derived from Latin *superanus* (super = above), but I will deal with this name in §8.3.

7.5 The Kinematic Modality: God's Transcendence
7.5.1 Transcendence and Immanence

I refer here again to some expressions already mentioned, especially the term *transcendence*.[45] The doctrine of God's transcendence is very important over against pantheism: God is not identical with his creation but surpasses it. The doctrine of his immanence is equally important, this time over against deism: God has not detached himself from his creation, but remains concerned with it.

Latin *trans-cendere* is "to rise beyond, to surpass," just like *immanere* means "to remain in." God is the only One who in the most absolute sense is "in" the world (immanence) but not "of" the world (transcendence) (cf. John 17:11-16).[46] If we, therefore, say that God "transcends" or "surpasses" our cosmic reality, we basically mean something different from

---

45. Cf. Wentsel (1987, 277–85).
46. Heyns (1988, 43–44).

a rocket rising beyond our atmosphere. The latter is a kinematic phenomenon that can be expressed in terms of speed, distance and time and for which geographical coordinates and flight altitudes can be indicated, expressed in arithmetic numbers. Nothing of this is true for God's "trans-cending" because nothing of God can be enclosed in purely creaturely concepts. (Actually, the same is true for the human heart, which is indeed creaturely, but transcendent as well.) Yet, we can speak about the "movements" of God (and of the human heart) only in creaturely terms, simply because we have no other at our disposal. These terms are used as ideas, regulative border-concepts, which direct our thinking toward what cannot be captured in a concept, a "definition," since it surpasses any defining (delimiting, delineating).

Much of what was said in §§7.3 and 7.4 about spatial ideas, can, *mutatis mutandis*, be repeated here. The Bible speaks without any problem about God's "descending" and "ascending" (see the next section), about his coming and going, his walking and resting, but never in a conceptual way, because God's "movements" are not bound to spatial coordinates, not subject to laws of speed, and so on.

7.5.2 Descending and Ascending

When thinking of God's "descending" we are reminded in particular of God's *condescendence*, so strongly emphasized by Hendrikus Berkhof. It is the necessary correlate of his transcendence; both terms are derived from Latin *scandere*, "to climb." In fact, it is more emphatically such a correlate than God's immanence, a term that philosophically is heavily loaded, and always implies the danger of pantheism.[47] Berkhof pointed to Karl Barth's approach of theology proper,[48] who, in his distinction between the freedom and the love of God, did not continue the ancient dualism of being and attributes (or incommunicable/absolute and communicable/relative

---
47. Berkhof (1986, 111–15).
48. Barth (*CD* II/1).

attributes, etc.). Rather, he viewed God's condescendence as the disclosure and realization of God's transcendence or being. Indeed, this has become quite an influential view,[49] and the counterpart of Paul Tillich's ontological approach of God as the "ground of all being," "Being itself."[50]

It is true that God surpasses cosmic space and the kinematic laws; yet, his descending and ascending are *real* in the sense that such creaturely terms *really* tell us something about God's "movements." Even though we know that God's "movements" are not like our movements (cf. the parallel thought in Isa. 55:8),[51] yet the Bible shows us that God "moves," and that we can speak of it—and are even not able to speak of it in any other way—in creaturely terms. This is quite fascinating in the case of Jesus Christ, who was "a man with a nature[52] like ours" (cf. for this expression James 5:17). About his movements, insofar as these are not meant metaphorically, we can speak conceptually, in kinematic terms. At the same time, as God the Son he "moves" in a supra-kinematic way. On the one hand, his ascension to heaven a literal kinematic going up, a being "taken up," which could be observed by his disciples until a cloud took him out of their sight (Acts 1:9–11). On the other hand, it was a supra-kinematic being "taken up in glory" (1 Tim. 3:16), a "going into heaven" to sit down at God's right hand (1 Pet. 3:22; Heb. 1:3; 4:14; 9:24). The two things should not be confused in any way. If Jesus had been "taken up" purely kinematically, he would not yet have reached the boundaries of the universe, even if he moved with the speed of light. If he had been "taken up" purely supra-kinematically, the disciples would not have seen him ascending.

---

49. Cf. Weber (1981, 439–450).
50. Tillich (1968).
51. Cf. the Christian hymn, "God Moves in a Mysterious Way" (William Cowper, 1773).
52. Cf. the Dutch States Translation: van gelijke bewegingen als wij ("of like movements to us").

7.5.3 Names of God

We already saw (§7.4.4) that El celyon literally means, "the God who ascends (rises above all others)." He transcends both the realm of humans and the realm of angels. No real names but certainly allusions to God as the "moving" God we find, for instance, in his "coming down" to see Babel (Gen. 11:5), and to see Israel in Egypt (Exod. 3:8), his "coming down" on Mount Sinai (19:20; Neh. 9:13), his "descending" to show himself to Moses (Exod. 34:5), and so on (Num. 11:25; 12:5; 2 Sam. 22:10 [= Ps. 18:9]; Ps. 144:5; Isa. 64:1, 3; Micah 1:3; Acts 7:34; cf. 14:11).

Of special interest is Genesis 17:22, where God "went up" from Abraham; further, 35:13, where God "went up" from Jacob; and Judges 13:20, where the Angel of YHWH "went up" from Manoah and his wife. In all these cases, there seems to be a purely kinematic aspect (the people involved saw something of someone coming down or going up) as well as a supra-kinematic aspect (God coming down from, or going up to, heaven). Also compare Psalm 47:5, "God has gone up with a shout," and 68:18, "You ascended on high."

7.6 The Kinematic Modality: God's Immutability
7.6.1 Changeable and Unchangeable

Of God's immutability or unchangeability (Lat. *immutabilitas*) we can also form an idea by using modal-kinematic terms. This is because immutability is closely related to *constancy*, of which the original sense can be found in the kinematic modality.[53] As said before (§4.4.2), we know since Galileo Galilei that the constancy of movement is a condition for bringing about any change. No change without constancy. Thus, there cannot be any polar contrast between constancy and change, as ancient philosophy claimed by placing a thing's constant "essence" dialectically over against its changing appearance. On the contrary, there is an inseverable coherence between a thing's constancy and its change, and thus also between its

---
53. Cf. Strauss and Visagie (1984, 68–70).

ostensible essence and its properties. As we saw, in theology proper a distinction was made between God's "essence" and his appearance, which is closely related to the distinction between God's incommunicable and his communicable attributes, and with the concomitant distinction between God's inscrutability and his knowability (see chapter 4).

We can speak safely of God's immutability only if we sever it completely from all Greek-scholastic substantialism with its idea of God's "immovability": God as the "unmoved Mover" (Aristotle: *ti ho ou kinoumenon kinei*, "something that moves [other things] without being moved [itself by something else]"; Lat.: *primum movens omnino non motum*), the first and uncaused cause (Lat. *prima causa non causata*). We encounter this idea in Thomism, but also with a Reformed theologian such as Franciscus Junius (François du Jon, d. 1602).[54] However, there is no constant *substantia* standing in opposition to changing *accidentia*. The constancy of God's identity (cf. "I am who I am"; see §7.6.3), of his counsels and promises, his goodness, wisdom and holiness, are equally true of him as the changes in his thoughts and ways, his "relenting" (e.g., Gen. 6:7; Exod. 32:14; 1 Sam. 15:11, 35 (cf. v. 29!); Jer. 18:8–10; 42:10; Joel 2:13; Amos 7:3, 6; Jonah 3:10),[55] his being persuaded by prayers (Gen. 18:23–32; Exod. 32:10–14; Judg. 10:15; 2 Chron. 33:13; cf. Ezek. 22:30; Luke 18:1–8).[56] Both about God's constancy and about his changes we can only speak in creaturely terms used as ideas, while thus definitely obtaining genuine rational knowledge about God.

Of course, this is not a plead for the modern tendency, especially due to Hegel's dialectic philosophy, to emphasize the changeability of, and changes in, God. Thus, Dutch theologian Bram van de Beek described God as capricious and volatile,[57]

---

54. See Van Genderen (2008, 176); cf. Barth (*CD* II/1, 552–87); Pannenberg (1971, 327–32); Wentsel (1987, 408–13).
55. On this, see A. Vos in Van den Brink and Sarot (1995, 57–58).
56. See §5.6.1 above and *EDR* 4:chapter 4.
57. Van de Beek (1984, 252–66).

and Hendrikus Berkhof spoke of God as "Changeable Faithfulness,"[58] which is just as one-sided as the traditional emphasis upon God's immovability. I do appreciate, however, Berkhof's protest against the traditional view: "God is going to resemble [here] the awesome ice crystal which, according to Ezekiel, he precisely was not (1:22)."[59]

7.6.2 Being and Becoming

In the nineteenth century, the greatest breakthrough in the thinking about God's immutability came with the study by the German theologian Isaak August Dorner (d. 1884).[60] He linked the question of God's immutability *versus* his mutability with God's love and his unchangeable ethical purpose over against free and changeable humanity. In agreement with Dorner, Karl Barth developed his view of God's constancy,[61] that is, his loving-in-freedom as well as his life: pure immutability is death. He underscored the changes in God's attitudes and works, which in his view, however, do not affect God's essential immutability. After Barth, this is the very point that has been criticized, especially in process theology, which views God as essentially involved in an "unpredictable process of becoming."[62]

Berkhof described this process, and concluded:

> It would be blasphemy to say that this history [of ours] left him unmoved. But it would also be blasphemy to say that he, with us, is incalculably extradited to this history. He is in this process what we are not: the "Rock" whose "work is perfect" [Deut. 32:4]. But he is not such in a far, unmoved eternity, but as our ally on the way through time, with all its turnings and surprises.[63]

---

58. Berkhof (1986, 143–49).
59. Ibid., 145.
60. Dorner (1883).
61. Barth (*CD* II/1:552–87).
62. Whitehead (1929); Hartshorne (1964); Cobb (1966).
63. Berkhof (1986, 147–48).

This can be placed alongside the work by Eberhard Jüngel (subtitle: *God's Being in Becoming*):[64] "... It is not about a 'God who becomes.' God's being is not equated to God's becoming; rather, God's being is ontologically localized."

Even though, in my view, Berkhof went very far into the direction of God's "changeability" — "He allows himself to be made a victim"[65] — he rightly warned against the Scylla of Hengel's changing, becoming God and the Charybdis of Aristotle's "unmoved mover." The distinction between God and humanity, and within God himself, cannot be captured in terms like "being" and "becoming." On the one hand, there is ontic constancy in humans in the sense that, if we could not recognize certain *constant* properties in humans and their behavior, we would never be able to recognize them as specimens of the species *Homo sapiens*. On the other hand, there is "becoming" in God; there is an abundance of Bible passages describing God as "*becoming* angry (sad, impatient, jealous)," and stopping being so (e.g., Exod. 4:14; Num. 11:1, 33; Deut. 33:5; Judg. 10:16; 2 Sam. 7:24; Joel 2:18; partly ERV). Above all: "The Word [who is God] became flesh" (John 1:1-2, 14). God *became* Man.[66] Playing off "being" against "becoming" is of an objectionable Greek-scholastic origin. It gives a misleadingly one-sided picture, both in the scholastic emphasis on God's being and in de modernist-relativistic emphasis on the "becoming" God.[67] There is much "becoming" in eternity — more than some people seem to think — and there is much "being" within time, more than some people seem to think. This does not create any problems as long as we do not understand such terms conceptually. In the summary of American philosopher Jay W. Richards,[68] God is immutable in those respects that are relevant to his essential perfection

---

64. Jüngel (1976, vii).
65. Berkhof (1986, 148).
66. Cf. Ott (1974, 26).
67. Cf. Brunner (1950, 289–90).
68. Richards (2003, 212).

and *aseitas*, but mutable[69] with respect to certain contingent properties because of his freedom.

7.6.3 Names of God

The word *nētsach* in 1 Samuel 15:29 comes from the root *n-ts-ch*, "to excel" or "to be everlasting," and thus means something like Splendor, Glory, Eminence (AMP) or the Enduring One (CEB) or Eternal One (CJB). Some Dutch translations have "Unchangeable One," which is not accurate; the fact that God is everlasting does, as such, not necessarily imply that he is immutable.

The name *par excellence* that is based upon the constancy of God's identity seems to be the tetragrammaton, YHWH. In Exodus 3:14, YHWH describes himself as *ehyeh asher ehyeh*, "I am who I am." Because of this, it has been assumed that the name YHWH is derived from the root *h-y-h*, "to be." At least four interpretations are conceivable:

(a) The name is a reference to God's eternity; compare the alternatives in AMPC and CJB: "I will be what I will be" (cf. Luther and the Dutch States' Translation), and even CEV: "I am the eternal God." From this view stem well-known renderings of this name as "the Eternal One," especially popular among Jews, but also in the French translation of Louis Segond or John N. Darby: *l'Éternel*.

(b) Traditionally, the name has often been interpreted as "highest being" (Lat. *summum esse*) in the Greek-scholastic sense. The Septuagint has furthered this rendering by translating in Exodus 3:14 *ego eimi ho Ōn* ("I am the being One"), presumably for apologetic reasons in opposition to Hellenism. Augustine explained this such that God would be immutable Being itself.[70] However, in my view such Greek ontology is entirely foreign to the Old Testament.

---

69. In the sense that such properties could be different, even though there is in fact no time t at which they actually change (Richards).
70. Cf. Van Genderen (2008, 136–37), who, however, does not do justice to Gispen (1932, 54).

(c) Karl Barth and Emil Brunner believed that God not only reveals but also hides himself in the name YHWH.[71] "I am who I am" would thus mean: "I am he whose actual name no one repeats" (Barth), the "undefinable, unnamable One" (Brunner).[72] However, I agree with Jan van Genderen that [d] is a more satisfactory explanation than that by Barth and Brunner.

(d) In my view the best interpretation—given the context of Exodus 3 and 4—is the one that sees in the name a reference to God's constancy, not that of some Absolute Being in any metaphysical sense but that of God's faithfulness to his promises. Compare God's own explanation of the name: "YHWH, YHWH, a God merciful and gracious, slow to anger, and abounding in steadfast love and faithfulness, keeping steadfast love for thousands, forgiving iniquity and transgression and sin" (Exod. 34:6–7). "I am who I am" would thus mean: "I remain the same, always faithful to my promises," and also: "I am there," namely, always for you (German: *Ich bin da*, as in the Tanakh translation by Martin Buber and Franz Rosenzweig). An excellent and extensive study is that by Dutch theologian Benne Holwerda (d. 1952).[73] He concludes that the name YHWH speaks of God's work in history,[74] and links the "I am who I am" with God's promises to the fathers: "I do what I promise."[75]

7.7 The Physical Modality: God As Causa Sui
7.7.1 God's Independence

In this section I return to an attribute of God mentioned before: his independence. This word comes from Latin *dependere*, "to hang from/down," for instance in *dependere ex umeris*, "to hang down from the shoulders." Hence follows the fig-

---

71. Barth (*CD* I/1, 335, 339–40); Brunner (1950, 125).
72. Also cf. Thielicke (1974, 132); Berkhof (1986, 111).
73. Holwerda (1971, 200–64).
74. Ibid., 264.
75. Ibid., 242; also cf. the extensive exposé by Wentsel (1987, 258–98, especially 263–67).

urative meaning: to "hang" on something or someone, and thus become "dependent" on this or him. This clearly seems to go back to a modal-physical term, especially if it is linked with an expression that is well-known from ancient and more modern philosophical schools (Lactantius, Synesius, Jerome): God is *causa sui* ("his own cause").[76] Jerome wrote, *Deus qui semper est nec habet aliunde principium et ipse sui origo est suaeque causa substantiae* ("God who always is, and has no beginning from elsewhere, and is the origin of himself, and the cause of his substance"). He understood this such that God did exist by himself but not that he had ever called himself to life. From eternity, God is his own carrying ground; he "depends" on himself alone.

Usually, theology has avoided the expression *causa sui* because it may create the error that God would have had a beginning in time. If properly understood the expression does not need to mean anything else than that God finds his "ground" or "foundation" within himself. It is here the same as with the "eternal generation of the Son by (or from) the Father" (see the next volume in this series): the latter did not take place either at some time t in past eternity but is "from eternity," and lasts forever.

Whether the expression *causa sui* approximates the biblical way of speaking about God is another matter. Actually, the term is linked too much with the traditional theistic proofs, especially the cosmological argument, which is based upon the contingency of the world.[77] Certain scholastics "stumbled" over the world's contingency, and "found rest" in some Necessary Being, which has caused everything, and is even its own cause. Some more modern thinkers do not find any "rest" in this idea at all. They argue that such a *causa sui* is "necessarily" contingent itself, and as such implies the summit of meaninglessness (Jean-Paul Sartre; §3.3.3). With the decline of the theistic proofs, the entire idea of a *causa sui* seems

---

76. Cf. Bavinck (*RD* 2, 125–27).
77. Cf. Pannenberg (1988, 423–24).

to have lost its attractiveness.

The point that is of special interest right now is that speaking of God as *causa sui* is possible only by appealing to our immanent reality. I refer here to our experience of the physical modality of cosmic reality with its kernel of energetic interaction. It is only within the framework of the physical aspect that we find the relationship of cause and consequence in its original sense.[78] We would not be able to speak of God as the cause of himself or of created reality if we were not familiar with causes and consequences *within* this created reality itself. By using such terms as ideas, we obtain knowledge of God's "resting" in himself, is being "carried" by a foundation that lies in himself, his eternal "causing" himself, through which he is also eternally his own "consequence."

7.7.2 Names of God

First, the description of Christ as the "beginning" comes to mind here (Gk. *archē*, Col. 1:18; Rev. 3:14), and the statement by God or Christ, "I am the beginning" (Gk. *archē*, Rev. 21:6; 22:13), and, "I am the Alpha and the Omega" (Rev. 1:8; 21:6; 22:13; Gk. *to Alpha kai to ō*,[79] i.e., the first and the last letter of the Greek alphabet; thus, materially identical with "the beginning and the end"). Of course, this does not mean that Christ *had* a beginning (as Jehova-Witnesses conclude from such verses), but that he himself *was* and *is* the beginning of all things.

Further, we note the use of some special Greek prepositions here. All things were made "through" (*dia*) the Word (John 1:3). From (*ek*) God and through (*dia*) God and to (*eis*) God are all things (Rom. 11:36). All things are from (*ek*) God the Father—and we for (*eis*) him—and they are through (*dia*) his Son, Jesus Christ (1 Cor. 8:6). All things were created in (*en*), through (*dia*), and for (*eis*) the Son, and hold together in

---

78. Cf. Strauss (1991b, 31).
79. Please note the remarkable fact that the alpha is written as a complete word, whereas the omega is referred to only by the letter involved.

God's Attributes: (Natural Modalities)

(*en*) him (Col. 1:16–17). The "from" refers to God as the root and source, the "through" to the means by which all things have come to be, the "in" to the place of force where things find their origin and existence, and the "to" or "for" refers to the purpose for which all things were created. Everything is the "consequence" of God, the cause of all things.

7.8 The Physical Modality: God's Omnipotence
7.8.1 Potentiality and Actuality

The most important term of a modal-physical origin with regard to God is "omnipotence."[80] We immediately meet here with a conceptual problem. Within God's omnipotence, Paul Althaus distinguished between God's *potentialitas* (what God *can* do—"he can do as he likes") and his *actualitas*, that is, what God actually does:[81] "All that is real [in creation] is there through God's willing and working." However, Emil Brunner wished to exclude any idea of the *posse* (what God is able to do, but not does).[82] That is, the Bible does not teach that God is able to do everything but that he possesses power over everything; or, God is able to do everything *he wants.*

Indeed, the idea of the *posse* has led to the many absurd-speculative questions about what God "can" do, and what he "cannot" do, such as: Can God make the past to have never occurred? Can God make what he does not make? Can he improve what he has made? And so on.[83] A classical example: can God make a stone that is so heavy that he cannot lift it himself? If we say Yes, then God is not omnipotent because there are stones he cannot lift. If we say NO, God is not omnipotent either because there are certain things he cannot do. Or speaking of "power," if Jesus says, "All power . . . has been given to me" (Matt. 28:18 NLV), this is indeed power over everything—but is it also *all* power over everything? As

---

80. See extensively, Barth (*CD* II/1:587–685); further, e.g., Van den Brink (1993); Bloesch (1995).
81. Althaus (1952, 274–75).
82. Brunner (1950, 265).
83. Thomas (*Summa Theologiae* I.25.4 and further).

Matthew 19:26 says, "With God all things are possible." But Brunner interpreted this such that the verse does not say that God could do all things that he might wish (but perhaps not wishes) but rather is a statement that he can do what he (actually) wishes.[84]

We must keep in mind here the distinction between power and authority (the word that many translations prefer in Matt. 28:18; Gk. *exousia*). "Power," "strength," "force," and "energy" are physical terms, but "authority" is a historical-formative term. Power is based upon the application of energy in the sense of the ability of doing a certain work. Authority involves controlling and influencing other people. (Of course, the terms are not always clearly kept apart; we may speak of the "power" that influential people have over other people.) Some people have enormous physical power, yet have little authority over others, and vice versa. God as well as Christ have both power and authority, that is, he has unlimited energy and abilities, and he exerts unlimited authority over the universe. These two elements are both present in God's omnipotence but are often hardly properly distinguished.[85]

I will deal with the aspect of historical-formative "authority" in §8.3, and will limit myself now to a few remarks concerning God's "power." In the expressions "the greatness of his might" and "strong in power" (Isa. 40:26), we obviously have to do with a use of physical terms as ideas. The same is true for passages telling us that nothing is "too hard" for the Lord (Gen. 18:14; Jer. 32:17, 27; cf. Zech. 8:6 DRA), that no plan of his can be "thwarted" (Job 42:2), and that "with God all things are possible" (Matt. 19:26; cf. Luke 1:37; 18:27). God is able to do many things, even to raise up children for Abraham from stones (Matt. 3:9). "Our God… does all that he pleases" (Ps. 115:3; cf. Isa. 46:10). When it is a matter of the resurrection of Christ (and that of the believers), the apostle Paul even uses the strongest (!) expression: "… the exceeding greatness of his

---
84. Brunner (1950, 270).
85. Cf. Bavinck (*RD* 2, 215–19).

power [Gk. *dynamis*] towards us, who believe according to the operation [*energeia*] of the might [*kratos*] of his power [*ischys*, strength], which He worked in Christ" (Eph. 1:19–20 DLNT).

God's power is absolute and unlimited; he is *al*-mighty (omni-potent). Yet, there are definitely things that God is *not* able to do. Ability is not always physical power, and non-ability is not always a lack of physical power; sometimes it is a moral impossibility. Thus, the Bible tells us that "it is impossible for God to lie" (Heb. 6:18; cf. Titus 1:2; Num. 23:19), that "he cannot deny himself" (2 Tim. 2:13), that "he is not a man that he should have regret" (1 Sam. 15:29 [but cf. vv. 11 and 35]); his promises cannot be revoked (cf. Rom. 11:29); God "cannot be tempted with evil" (James 1:13), and he "cannot look at wrong" (Hab. 1:13). In none of these examples of what God "cannot" do it is a question of a lack of what we, in creaturely terms, would call God's "strength." They have to do with God's intrinsic impossibility to sin.

If God were "able" to do sin, he would not be God. This is not a restriction of his "physical" strength but only expresses the *one* thing that God cannot do: stop being God; that is, do anything that is in essential contradiction with his own being. Augustine has emphasized that this is not a lack of power but rather true, absolute omnipotence;[86] for it would be a *lack* of power—not *omni*- but *impotence*—if God were able to err, to sin, to lie, and so on. This is the chief argument against those nominalists (William of Ockham [d. 1347] and others) who postulated a *potential absoluta* ("absolute power") in God in the sense of pure arbitrariness, pure, vacuous potency, which *is* nothing and can *become* anything.[87] God's omnipotence is intrinsically bound to his moral being, his virtues, his consistency. God can do everything, except ceasing to be God.

7.8.2 Power and Weakness

In the twentieth century, God's omnipotence was heavily

---

86. Sermons 213, 214; *De Civitate* V.10.
87. Cf. Weber (1981, 446–49, 485–88, especially on Calvin, 448–49).

discussed for several reasons.[88] Sometimes, it was (largely) limited to God's redemptive-historical power,[89] which manifested itself in Jesus' *powerlessness* on the cross (cf. 2 Cor. 13:4, "crucified in weakness"). In the words of German theologian Dietrich Bonhoeffer (d. 1945):[90] "God drove himself out of the world to the cross, God is powerless and weak in the world, and precisely and exclusively in this way he is with us and helps us." Hendrikus Berkhof believed that we can speak of God's omnipotence only in the eschatological sense, but that we cannot use the term for the present.[91] At present, God is "defenseless," as is seen most strikingly on the cross. However, this is not the defenselessness of powerlessness but of a higher, be it non-violent power; thus, Berkhof spoke of the "Defenseless Supremacy." One day, this superiority of love will overcome all resistance, and then reach its omnipotence.

To my mind, terms like omnipotence and powerlessness, strength and weakness, are played off against each other here because they are used as if they were concepts. The Bible knows nothing of God's omnipotence as suffering under the freedom granted to humanity by God, or as suffering under human rebellion. Therefore, Dutch theologian Gijsbert van den Brink did maintain the possibility of uniting divine omnipotence and human freedom in his discussion of the views of David and Randall Basinger, William E. Mann, Wolfhart Pannenberg, Charles Hartshorne, David R. Griffin, and others.[92] The Bible continually presents God as ruling over humanity, resisting its rebellion, carrying out his counsels, and attaining his purposes in a sovereign way. The Man who was "crucified in weakness" (2 Cor. 13:4) was at the same time the omnipotent God, who had to give power to the wood and the iron to keep him nailed to the cross. Also on the cross he was

---

88. Cf. Van Genderen (2008, 181–83), and especially the extensive study by Van den Brink (1993).
89. Barth (*CD* II/1:681–85).
90. Bonhoeffer (1964, 342).
91. Berkhof (1986, 136–142).
92. Van den Brink (1993, §4.2); also cf. Wentsel (1987, 480–84).

the One who upheld "the world by the word of his power" (Heb. 1:3); even then, it was in him that all things held together (Col. 1:17). These are things that cannot, and must not, be theoretically unraveled but must be reverently admired in awe.

I repeat, terms like omnipotence and powerlessness must not be used as if they were concepts. Thus, Theo de Boer referred to the Jewish Dutch philosopher Baruch Spinoza, who ultimately reduced all things to God's absolute *potentia*.[93] De Boer argued that he could understand the objections of the rabbis against Spinoza (d. 1677) because the God of the Scriptures has identified himself with the vicissitudes of a homeless nation. This allegedly is not the attitude of an absolute *potentia*, which has as its highest aim guaranteeing its own existence. I wonder, however, how much in this argument comes from the seventeenth-century rabbis, and how much of the twentieth-century De Boer, and whether both do not suffer by this conceptual confusion. It is only when we use terms like power and weakness as concepts that contradictions arise between God's omnipotence and his equally essential powerlessness on the cross. De Boer's quotation of French philosopher Jean-François Lyotard (d. 1998)[94] — "It is in conflict with power to allow oneself to be led by weakness" — seems to me a perfect example of such a conceptual (ab)use. The same is true *par excellence* for De Boer's assertion that those two concepts of power, omnipotence and defenseless supremacy, contradict each other.[95] Only if the terms involved are used as ideas, they can help us to approximate both God's omnipotence and his impotence.

7.8.3 Names of God

Some typically physical names of God (and Christ) are Rock (e.g., Deut. 32:4, 15, 18, 30–31, 37), Sun (Ps. 84:11; Mal. 4:2),

---

93. De Boer (1989, 55).
94. Lyotard (1979, 101).
95. De Boer (1989, 84).

Star (Num. 24:17), Morning Star (Rev. 22:16), Light (Ps. 27:1; Rev. 21:23), Fire (Deut. 4:24; Heb. 12:29), Fountain (Ps. 36:9; Jer. 2:13), Shield (Gen. 15:1; Ps. 84:11), Banner (Exod. 17:15), Way (John 14:6), and Temple (Rev. 21:22). A name such as *monos dynastēs*, "only Sovereign" (1 Tim. 6:15), clearly refers to the physical aspect of *dynamis*, but will be dealt with in §8.10.

Of course, *the* name that must be mentioned here is "God Almighty" (Heb. *El Shaddai*, Gen. 17:1; 28:3; 35:11 etc.; Gk. *theos pantokratōr*, 2 Cor. 6:18; Rev. 1:8; 4:8 etc.). The meaning of the name's Hebrew version is unclear:

(a) A literal translation of *shaddai* would be "my breasts" (Heb. *shad*, "breast"), where "my" might refer not to the woman but to the baby: God is the One who feeds me and cares for me[96] (cf. Gen. 28:3; 35:11; 49:25). Savina J. Teubal read "God of the breasts," and wished to see in it a reference to a pre-Israelite fertility god or hermaphrodite god.[97]

(b) Others have rendered the name as "God of the mountains," or "God of the open plains," renderings of which it is difficult to see the sense (cf. 1 Kings 20:23, 28).

(c) Others again have referred to the root *sh-d-d*, "to destroy," the more so because passages such as Isaiah 13:6 and Joel 1:15 suggest a link between "destruction" and *Shaddai*.

(d) A fourth explanation suggests a link with Hebrew *dai*, "enough," and renders *Shaddai* as the "(All-)Sufficient" (see GNV in Gen. 17:1 etc., and further in §[5.5.2]).

(e) The most important reason to render *El Shaddai* as "God Almighty" is the rendering in the Septuagint: *theos pantokratōr*, the God who has power over everything.[98] Hence the Latin *Deus omnipotens* (lit., "able to all), which entered into English (*omnipotent* besides *almighty*) and into all Romanic languages: *on(n)ipotente, tout puissant, todopoderoso*.

---

96. See, e.g., www.deadsoulsyndrome.com/el_shaddai.htm.
97. Teubal (1984).
98. Exception: in Ps. 91:1 the Septuagint reads "God of heaven."

7.9 The Biotic Modality: God's Vitality
7.9.1 The Living God

It is remarkable to see how often the Bible uses the expression "the living God" (Deut. 5:26; Josh. 3:11; 1 Sam. 17:26, 36; 2 Chron. 19:4, 16; Ps. 42:2; 84:2; Isa. 37:4, 17; Jer. 10:10; 23:36; Dan. 6:20, 26; Hos. 1:10; Matt. 16:16; 26:63; John 6:57; Acts 14:15; Rom. 9:26; 2 Cor. 3:3; 6:16; 1 Thess. 1:9; 1 Tim. 3:15; 4:10; Heb. 3:12; 9:14; 10:31; 12:22; Rev. 1:17; 7:2). Also compare: "As I live, says the Lord" (Rom.14:11; cf. Isa. 49:18), as well as "the Author (or, Prince; Gk. *archēgos*, also: Origin) of life" (Acts 3:15). God is the one who in himself has life in its original sense, the Father giving this life from eternity to the Son (John 5:26). Hence, God is from eternity the Life-Giver (Father) as well as the Life-Receiver (Son). God is the One "who lives forever and ever" (Rev. 4:9–10; 10:6; 15:7). It is he "who alone has immortality" (from Lat. *mors*, "death"; Gk. *athanasia*, from *thanatos*, "death") (1 Tim. 6:16). He also gives life (John 5:21), he is the fountain of life (Ps. 36:9), he is the One making (others) alive (John 6:63; 1 Cor. 15:45, Gk. *zōopoioun*), he is the Lord of life and death (Deut. 32:39; Job 34:14; Ps. 104:29–30; Luke 12:20; 2 Cor. 1:9; James 4:15).

God's "life" entails notions such as "vitality" (Lat. *vita*, "life") and "nature" (Lat. *natura*, 2 Pet. 1:4), just like organisms such as plants (Rom. 11:21, 24), animals (2:12; James 3:7) and humans (Rom. 2:27; Gal. 2:15; Eph. 2:3) have a "nature" (Gk. *physis*). This "life" of God also includes the "higher" manifestations of (organismal) life, such as perception, feeling, thinking, willing (see the next sections). It is the self-conscious, perceptive, sensitive, affective, considering, knowing, inventing, designing, willing, loving life of God; in all these cases, we have to do with anticipations in the biotic modality used as ideas. It is the life as life principle "in" God, but also the life that he "leads," his "way" of life, the life "atmosphere" in which he "breathes."

God's emotional "life" is sometimes linked with his "intestines" in a rather dramatic-biotic way. Isaiah 63:15 (KJV) speaks of the "sounding of thy bowels" (ESV: the "stirring of your inner parts"). In Jeremiah 31:20 (KJV), God says of Ephraim, "[M]y bowels are troubled for him." Also in the case of common people we find this kind of imagery (Gen. 43:30; 1 Kings 3:26; Job 30:27; Song 5:4; Isa. 16:11; Jer. 4:19; Lam. 1:20; 2:11; Phlm. 7, 12, 20; also see the KJV). The great difference is that humans do have literal intestines, and God has not. The imagery occurs frequently; thus, we read of Jesus several times that he was "moved with compassion" (Matt. 9:36; 14:14; 15:32; 20:34; Mark 1:41; Luke 7:13 KJV); the Greek verb used here is *splangchnizomai*, derived from *splangchna*, "bowels, intestines" (lit., e.g., in Acts 1:18).

Again, it is important to understand in what way the Bible speaks of the "living" God. It is not human life in some "higher" form, nor is it "original" life after which human life would have been "modeled" (which would imply a theo-ontological duplication of primordial image and copy or imprint). Terms like life, vitality, nature, are all necessarily creaturely terms, and *exclusively* creaturely terms. If they are used conceptually with respect to God, we change him into a biotic organism, and thus into a creature. At the same time, we have no other terms than creaturely ones to describe the life of God. We do not use them as concepts, but not irrational-mystically either in order to convey some mysterious knowledge concerning God, to be grasped by the initiated only. On the contrary, they convey *rational* knowledge concerning God, be it not in the form of concepts but of ideas, in order to refer to something real—the life of God—that cannot be enclosed in concepts because it surpasses all conceptualization (logical objectification).

7.9.2 God's Eternal Life

Divine life is one of God's attributes that, in the redemption, are transferred to humans, be it without ever making him divine. As the "fountain" of life, God can give life, and this life is his own life. We may find this in the clearest way in 1 John 5, "God gave us eternal life, and this life is in his Son. Whoever has the Son has life" (vv. 11–12); "we know that the Son of God has come and has given us understanding, so that we may know him who is true; and we are in him who is true, in his Son Jesus Christ. He is the true God and eternal life" (v. 20).

The fact that Christ, who is eternal life in his own person, can communicate himself as such to us,[99] has become possible because the Word has become flesh (John 1:14). God has become human (1 Tim. 3:16), has partaken in flesh and blood (Heb. 2:14). However, this life of God was not the natural, human life of Jesus Christ; in the person of the Man Jesus, too, the divine life always fully transcends the natural-human. It remains divine, not human. The believer "receives" this life, but with an important difference: Jesus *is* the true God and eternal life, whereas the believer can only "share" in it.

This formulation is important given the cumbersome expression in 2 Peter 1:4, "become partakers of the divine nature [Gk. *genēsthe theias koinōnoi physeōs*]." I take it that this can be approximated as follows:[100] becoming "partakers" of (or, receive a share in) divine *life* without also becoming *divine*. As I see it, the divine nature does not become the nature of the believers; they only become "sharers" in something that, as such, always remains "outside" themselves. As Paul says, "Christ your life" (Col. 3:4 NABRE), but at the same time this life is "hidden in God." The leaf has the life of the tree in it; but it *is* not the tree, and will never be it, and will never "possess" the tree's life apart from the tree. Pull it off the tree, and it will die. The Son has "life in himself" (John 5:26), the believers have it only "in him" (1 John 5:11–12). God became human, and remains God; humans can receive eternal life — become partakers of the divine life — but remain humans. The first Adam became a living soul (Gen. 2:7 KJV etc.), the last

---

99. See more extensively, *EDR* 6, §§4.1–4.2; Vol. III/4.
100. Cf. *EDR* 6, 322–23, 337–38, 344–45.

Adam became a life-giving spirit (1 Cor. 15:45).

7.9.3 Names of God

The appellation "the living God" (Heb. *Elohim chayyim, Elohim chai, El chai*, Gk. *[ho] theos [ho] zōn*, Lat. *Deus vivens*) can almost be viewed as a name. Some other references to God that appeal to our modal-biotic experience are Vinedresser (John 15:1), Shepherd (Ps. 23:1), and Healer (Exod. 15:26). God even compares himself to a beekeeper and a barber (Isa. 7:18, 20).

As far as eternal life is concerned, in 1 John 5:20 the expression "eternal life" could almost be viewed as a name of God the Son, just like the equivalent expression "true God."

The most important name of God, derived from the earthly-human notion of biotic begetting, is Father. It occurs several times in the Old Testament, be it usually in the sense of Origin (Deut. 32:6, 18; 2 Sam. 7:14; Isa. 63:16; 64:8; Jer. 3:4, 19; 31:9; Mal. 2:10). It also occurs many times in the New Testament, especially in John's books, primarily in the sense of the eternal Father of the eternal Son. These two meanings must be sharply distinguished; see, for instance, "your Father" in Matthew 5:16–7:11 (eleven times in the classical-Jewish, that is, Old Testament sense[101]) and "your Father" in John 20:17, where the eternal Father of the eternal Son for the first time is called the Father of the believer as well. If none less than the eternal Son of the eternal Father is the believers' "life," then the Father of this Son has become the believer's Father — in a far loftier sense than the "Father" in the Sermon of the Mount.[102]

7.10 The Perceptive Modality: God's Spirituality
7.10.1 God Is Pneuma

As we saw, we read of God that he sees, hears, and smells. God has eyes, ears, a nose (even nostrils), a mouth, a tongue

---

101. Basically, there is nothing in the Lord's Prayer that an orthodox Jew could not pray as well; in fact, it is not a typically Christian prayer at all.
102. See extensively, *EDR* 2, chapter 8; Vol. II/3.

(§4.2.3). His personality also includes complete self-awareness, self-consciousness, self-observation. Conversely, we can "perceive," "observe" God. He can be "seen" with spiritual eyes (John 14:9; Eph. 1:17–18; cf. Exod. 24:10–11; 1 John 3:2), but he cannot be "physically" seen, for his glory would consume us (Exod. 33:20, 23; Judg. 13:22; 1 Tim. 6:16). The words of his mouth can be heard—although even his words in principle can be deadly (Deut. 5:24)—and it can even be "tasted" that he is good (Ps. 34:8; 1 Pet. 2:3).

Although God's seeing, hearing and smelling are *real*, we can, as we saw, speak of it only in the form of ideas, not concepts. This is related to the so-called "spirituality" of God. Many organs that we know in the human body are ascribed to God, although it is never said explicitly that he "has" a body.[103] If a heart, and also bowels (see §7.9.1), are ascribed to him, this is not because he is supposed to possess a blood circulatory system and a digestive system. On the contrary, the Son "partook" of flesh and blood (Heb. 2:14), which implies that, before this, he had no flesh and blood, in spite of the Bible speaking many times of God's heart (Gen. 6:6; 8:21; 1 Sam. 2:35; 13:14; 2 Sam. 7:21; 1 Kings 9:3; 2 Kings 10:30; 1 Chron. 17:19; 2 Chron. 7:16; Job 7:17; 10:13; 34:14; 36:5; Ps. 33:11; Isa. 63:4; Jer. 3:15; 7:31; 19:15; 23:20; 30:24; 32:35, 41; 44:21; Ezek. 28:2, 6; Acts 13:22).

The clearest statement about God's spirituality is John 4:24, Gk. *pneuma ho theos*, "God is spirit." (In my view, rather not "*a* spirit," as if God is a spirit just like many others.) This is not the Holy Spirit (one of the three persons in the Godhead), but a statement about the being of the (Triune!) God. It is not easy to describe what this entails, for even the term *pneuma* was originally derived from natural-creaturely life: "wind" (cf. John 3:8; Heb. 1:7) or "breath" (Matt. 27:50; 2 Thess. 2:8). Even of such a typically divine things as God being "spirit," we can speak only in creaturely terms used as ideas. The

---

103. Bavinck (*RD* 2, 69, 149); cf. *EDR* 3, §5.2.2.

relationship between God and humans is like that between spirit and flesh; compare Isaiah 31:3, "The Egyptians are man [Heb. *adam*], and not God, and their horses are flesh, and not spirit." Man is to God as flesh is to spirit.

7.10.2 Is God Incorporeal?

Traditionally, God's spirituality has been equated with "immateriality, incorporeality."[104] Such an identification was radically rejected by Dutch theologian Jelier R. Wiskerke (d. 1968).[105] He saw the origin of it in the Greek-scholastic anthropology with its dualism of the lower, material body and the higher, spiritual, "immaterial" soul.[106] Subsequently, this dualism supposedly was projected in the doctrine of God: his spirituality was viewed to be in agreement with the human soul/spirit, and therefore necessarily immaterial. Wiskerke rightly rejected each parallelism between God's spirituality and the Greek-scholastic idea of the human soul/spirit. God is "spirit" in an absolutely unique way. I may *add* to this that the *term* "spirit," as adopted from creational reality, can be used as an idea to tell us something about God, but only if this term is severed from all Greek-scholastic connotations, such as the rationalistic identification with the nous ("mind").[107] Only if we do this, we will begin to grasp that many "corporeal" terms are just as appropriate to give us an idea of God as "spiritual" terms.

Of course, I do not plead for a falling into the other extreme, and to emphasize a certain "corporeality" of God, as occurs in modernist theology.[108] In a sense, this is just as much a depreciation of God's being as denying all his "corporeal"

---

104. So, e.g., Bavinck (*RD* 2, 152): "immaterial substance"; Schilder (*KD* 3:91); Pannenberg (1971, 318–20; 1988, 401–16); Wentsel (1987, 63–66); Heyns (1988, 41, 46); Van Genderen (2008, 173).
105. Wiskerke (1978, 93–161, especially 154); cf. König (1975, 78); Kamphuis (1982, 23).
106. Cf. Ouweneel (1986, 294–312).
107. Pannenberg (1988, 402–06, 413 and further).
108. Cf. Kuitert (1967, 199vv).

properties, as occurred in traditional theology. God's "corporeal" properties, such as his eyes, hands, and bowels, cannot be understood conceptually, but the very same is true for his spirituality. If tradition speaks of "anthropomorphisms" when it is a matter of God's eyes and hands, it must consider that, in this case, God's spirituality is just as much an "anthropomorphism." Both "spiritual" and "corporeal" are terms that, if used as ideas and not as concepts, may cast light upon the being and the attributes of God.

For many, this has been difficult to accept. Tertullian ascribed a *corpus* ("body") to God,[109] although he apparently only meant this in the sense of *substantia*. Also Melito, the bishop of Sardis (d. 180), seems to have ascribed a body to God.[110] In the fourth century, this "anthropomorphism" was taught by many Christians,[111] and much later it was adopted by the Socinians. Mainstream traditional theology always rejected this view, although if often fell into the other extreme by speculating about God's "immateriality." The great danger in any speculation about whether God is "material" or "immaterial" is that in both cases the terms are used as concepts, so that both approaches run into the sand. The answer to the dilemma can only be that we speak of God exclusively in terms derived from our *material* world; strictly speaking, even "wind" and "breath" are, as dislocations of air, material phenomena. However, our speaking of it must be in the form of ideas, not of concepts, that is, as pointing beyond the material to the divinely "spiritual."

7.10.3 Names of God

God *is* light (1 John 1:5), and God *is* love (4:8, 16), and therefore light and love could almost be called names of God. Similarly, "spirit" can almost be called a name, for God *is* spirit (John 4:24; not *a* spirit, as I have argued before). (Actually,

---

109. Adversus Praxean 7.
110. Melito, *Peri tou ensōmaton einai ton theon*.
111. Cf. Cyrillus' Contra anthropomorphitas.

there is a verb, Gk. *estin*, "is," in 1 John 1:5 and 4:8 and 16, but not in John 4:24.)

In a more literal sense, God's names are appellatives, that is, names by which God is *addressed* by human beings. (Angels addressing God are very rare; cf. 1 Kings 22:21–22.) So far, we found the names YHWH (thus addressed by a human, e.g., in Gen. 15:2; also cf. the seraphim in Isa. 6:3), "Father" (e.g., Isa. 63:16), "Most High (God)" (e.g., Ps. 9:2), "Almighty (God)" (cf. Job 13:3; 31:35; also see celestial powers in Rev. 4:8; 11:17; 16:7; 19:6).

7.11 The Perceptive Modality: God's Invisibility
7.11.1 The Contemplation of God

Directly connected with God's spirituality is his invisibility, to which the Bible refers many times (e.g., Exod. 33:20; John 1:18; 6:46; Rom. 1:20; Col. 1:15; 1 Tim. 1:17; 6:16; Heb.11:27; 1 John 4:12, 20). In the Bible, this invisibility finds its counterpart in the *visio Dei* ("contemplation of God") by believers here on earth. A fascinating question that has been much discussed in traditional theology is the nature of this "seeing" of God, as in the case of the elders of Israel (Exod. 24:9–10), Moses (33:23; 34:6), Manoah and his wife (Judg. 13:22), Isaiah (Isa. 6:1), Ezekiel (Ezek. 1:26–28), Daniel (Dan. 7:9), and John (Rev. 4:2–3).

Most theologians were of the opinion that this was a mediated *visio*, that is, a seeing in the form of a vision or in a form in which the glory of God had veiled itself.[112] Therefore, more interesting is the question whether, in the *status gloriae* ("state of glory"), there will be a true *visio Dei per essentiam* ("a seeing of God according to his essence").[113] Herman Bavinck discussed the various views of his time on this matter.[114] The Lutherans were inclined to accept such a *visio*, not only *mentalis* ("in the mind") but even *corporalis* (with the eyes of the glorified body). Most Reformed theologians re-

---

112. Cf. Bavinck (*RD* 2, 155).
113. See *EDR* 10, §14.5.1.
114. Bavinck (*RD* 2, 155–58).

jected this with an *a fortiori* argument based upon Ephesians 3:19 and Philippians 4:7: if even the love of Christ "surpasses knowledge," and the peace of God "surpasses all understanding" — and is a *visio per essentiam* not a form of *comprehensio* ("understanding")? — how much more will the intrinsic glory of God surpass the believers' perception. Moreover, God is infinite, and humans remain finite, even in the glory. Therefore, even if humans will see God's infinite glory to some extent, this seeing will always be finite (limited).[115]

7.11.2 Seeing God Through Christ

I would put the matter just discussed as follows: if, in the eternal bliss, a *visio Dei per essentiam* would be possible, it would mean that humans would then be able to observe in super-creaturely categories, and thus would be divine. If, also in eternity, the believers will be and remain creatures — and they will — then God can never be known other than in creaturely categories, no matter how much more perfect this will be than it is the case today. On this standpoint, believers will forever have knowledge of God in creaturely terms, used as ideas.

I therefore wonder whether their contemplation of God will ever reach any further than what Jesus himself has indicated in John 14:9, "Whoever has seen me has seen the Father." In other words, will they ever see the Father apart from the Son, that is, apart from the incarnated Word? Even today, since the resurrection and glorification of Jesus — the *fullness* of deity dwells in Jesus Christ *bodily* (Col. 2:9). That is, the "fullness" of (the Triune!) God dwells in the glorified body of the Son of *Man*, who *is* himself the Son of God. Will the believers ever perceive the deity apart from its manifestation in the *body* of the incarnated Son? If the answer must be negative, one could say that also God's invisibility is a genuine attribute of his, which in fact, in the absolute sense, will also be maintained in eternity.

---

115. Cf. Heyns (1988, 63).

1 John 3:2 ("we know that when he appears we shall be like him, because we shall see him as he is") offers us little help here. As more often in 1 John, the author sometimes (deliberately) mixes references to the Father and the Son. In 2:28 the "he" who "appears" is the Son, for John speaks of "his coming." But in verse 29 he means "God," for believers were born of God (John 1:13). In 1 John 3:1 the apostle speaks of "the Father," in verse 2a of "God," but in verse 3b he says again, "when he appears," referring to the Son. The One who is "seen" is he who "appears," that is, he who "comes," that is, the incarnated Son of God.

7.11.3 Names of God

A peculiar name of God is *El ro'i*, "God of seeing," that is presumably, the "God who sees me," or the "God who looks after me." This name was preserved in the name of a well, *B'ēr lachai ro'i*, which played a role in the lives of the patriarchs (Gen. 16:14; 24:63; 25:11), "Well of the Living One who sees me (watches me, looks after me)." Several commentators, however, prefer the rendering:[116] "the well where God has been seen [and the beholder still lives]," or, "the well of the living One of vision," that is, of God, who appeared there. In the former case, it is God seeing the person, in the latter case it is the person seeing God.

7.12 The Sensitive Modality: God's Emotionality
7.12.1 Anthropopathisms?

As we saw (§4.2.3), the Bible ascribes every possible emotion to God. It gives numerous examples of God's joy (Isa. 65:19), bliss (1 Tim. 1:11, "blessed"=blissful, felicitous), grief (Ps. 78:40), distress (Isa. 63:9 NIV), fear (Deut. 32:27), disappointment (Isa. 5:4), anger (Rev. 14:10), zeal (2 Kings 19:31), relenting (Exod. 32:14), hate (Amos 5:21), compassion (Deut. 32:36), and so on. We could hardly mention an emotion that could not be part of this list. This biblical speaking is all the

---
116. E.g., see https://biblehub.com/genesis/16-14.htm.

more remarkable because the early Christian writers taught that God was not capable of suffering, and of emotions in general. Ignatius wrote to Polycarp that God is "impassible,"[117] and Origen believed that God's perfection excludes all passions, especially rage.[118]

This is very different from what we read, for instance, in Isaiah 63:9, "In all their affliction he was afflicted" (CSB etc.: "In all their suffering, he suffered"). Or in Exodus 32:10, where God, so to speak, angrily pushed Moses aside with the words, "So now do not stop me. I am so angry with them that I am going to destroy them" (EXB). An expression like "the fury of his wrath" (Rev. 16:19) cannot simply be pushed aside because ostensibly it does not fit our conceptualized presuppositions concerning God's immutability or perfection. In our time, some love to speak of unfounded, primitive "anthropopathisms" in cases where the Bible speaks of God's fury. Emil Brunner rightly responded to this that those arguing like this do not know the *holy* God and the *Lord* God of Scripture.[119]

Self-evidently, God's "emotionality" is not subject to glandular secretions or dependent on the activation of the sympathetic nervous system. His emotionality is not of a creaturely nature but surpasses it, just like the Creator surpasses his creation. However, *we* can speak of God's emotions only in creaturely terms, but not through any conceptual use of such terms, which inevitably would draw God under the boundary between Creator and creature.

A special problem of this subject is that we can hardly imagine some of the emotions mentioned without the involvement of sin in human life. Our fears, anger (cf. Eph. 4:26), jealousy (cf. Prov. 6:34; 27:4; Eccl. 4:4), regretting—what we usually regret, or repent of, is sin!—and hate are mixed with sin just too often. Thus, we have a double difficulty in

---

117. Letter to Polycarp 3.
118. Peri Archon 1.1.6; Contra Celsum 4.72; in Homilies 6.6.3, however, he does speak of the sufferings of God and of the pre-existent Savior.
119. Brunner (1950, 167–68), contra Julius A.L. Wegscheider.

understanding God's feelings and sentiments: first, in his case they are completely without sin, and second, they surpass our creaturely emotionality, whereas we can still speak of them only in creaturely terms.

7.12.2 Pathos or Apatheia?

God's so-called "pathos" has received special attention through the work of Polish-American rabbi Abraham J. Heschel (d. 1972).[120] He even called the preaching of the biblical prophets "pathetic theology," and believed it to stand in opposition to the early-Christian view of the *apatheia*[121] of God, adopted from Plato and the Stoa: God is "impassible," unable to suffer.[122] If this is meant to say that God is free and independent of humans, human influences, and human circumstances, everything is fine. However, the Greek view of the "apathetic" God also implied that God would be insensitive to, or not concerned with, human affairs, and would not need any partners (people "feeling" with him). This was not the God preached by the prophets: theirs was not an unconcerned, neutral God but One who deeply cared for his people, also in the sense that we refer to as "emotionally involved."

We deduce from Scripture God's independence and freedom, but also his intensely moved concern with his people. It is only a conceptual use of such terms that can create any contradictions between them. God is the God who, so to say, can decide freely and autonomously to be passionately concerned with his people. In no way does God's sorrow, and even relenting, with regard to his people touch his power and freedom.

In the sixth century, this idea that God essentially cannot suffer gave rise to the so-called *theopaschitic* conflict: if God

---

120. Heschel (1936); see more recently Sarot (1992); Idem in Van den Brink and Sarot (1995, 117–37).
121. Cf. the derived word "apathy," which however refers especially to passivity, whereas apatheia means "not suffering" or "not being able to suffer."
122. Cf. Küng (1970, 622–31); Moltmann (1993, 255 and further); König (1975, 111–24).

cannot suffer, and Jesus is truly God, how then could Jesus suffer and die on the cross?[123] In other words, could Jesus on earth suffer only according to his human nature, or also according to his divine nature?[124] If the idea that God could not suffer is given up, this problem disappears. To me, this seems to be a better way of solving the problem than by making the distinction between the two natures of Christ diffuse, as South African theologian Adrio König actually did.[125] In a sense, Karl Barth made himself guilty of the same by fully equating the history of Jesus Christ with the history of God:[126] Christ's suffering is God's suffering, Jesus' self-sacrifice is God's self-sacrifice. Dutch theologian Gerrit C. Berkouwer (d. 1996) rightly pointed out that Barth blurred the relationship between Jesus and God.[127] In this way, we neglect the fact that Jesus delivered himself up to God (1 Pet. 2:23), suffering under the striking hand of God (Zech. 13:7), as the Mediator between God and humanity (1 Tim. 2:5). This did not mean, however, that Berkouwer wished to deny that Jesus suffered also according to his divine nature, or that Jesus himself was God the Son.[128]

7.12.3 Names of God

Various names mentioned in §7.9.3 deserve a place here as well, because they are rooted not only in the biotic modality but also include the notions of care and affection, such as Shepherd, Healer, and in particular Father. Let us restrict ourselves to mentioning here some names of birds and mammals (sensitively qualified beings) that have been used as metaphors for God or Christ:

- Eagle (Deut. 32:11; cf. Isa. 31:5),
- Hen (Matt. 23:37 and parallel sections),

---

123. See more extensively, *EDR* 2, 217–18, 318–19.
124. See Küng en Moltmann in note 122.
125. König (1975, 117–18).
126. Barth (*CD* IV,1, §59).
127. Berkouwer (1954, 294–307).
128. Ibid., 359 and further.

- Lion (Isa. 31:4; Lam. 3:10; Rev. 5:5),
- Bear (Lam. 3:10; Hos. 13:8), and especially
- Lamb (Isa. 53:7; John 1:29, 36; 1 Pet. 1:19; Rev. 5:6–14).

7.13 The Sensitive Modality: God's Beatitude
7.13.1 Beatus and Benedictus

A very special "sentiment" is God's beatitude or bliss. As Paul Althaus expressed it, God's beatitude not only refers objectively to a state of perfection but also subjectively to the awareness of it, the experience of joy.[129] In the Old Testament, the Hebrew root *'-sh-r* literally means "to be/go/make right," and hence "to make/call blissful (happy, felicitous)" (the proper name Asher was deduced from it). The ideal state of the person is the blissful (happy, felicitous) state, the state of beatitude.

Unfortunately, the Dutch States' Translation (1637) did not make a difference between "to make blissful [*(geluk)zalig*]" (the original verbs mean "to save, to redeem") and "to make blissful [*(geluk)zalig*]" in the sense of making happy. Both in Hebrew and in Greek we have to do here with very different roots and terms. When somebody is saved, he indeed is made happy (blissful, felicitous), but that does not change the fact that these are quite different word meanings. The rather recent revision of this Dutch translation failed to correct this error. In passages where we find the two meanings next to each others, this creates confusion, for instance, in Titus 2:13, "… waiting for our *makarian* [*gelukzalig*, blissful, happy, felicitous] hope, the appearing of the glory of our great God and *sōtēros* [*Zaligmaker*, Blissful-Maker] Jesus Christ."

The English does not fare much better here. "Blissful" ("happy, felicitous") is traditionally rendered as "blessed,"[130] which is misleading because the original word is not derived from a verb "to bless." There may be a relationship between

---

129. Althaus (1952, 296).
130. Interestingly, we are told that "bless" and "bliss" are not etymologically related (https://www.etymonline.com/word/bliss).

blessing and happiness—just as the above mentioned link between salvation and happiness—yet these are different matters. More modern translations venture to use the colloquial "happy," for instance, in the verse mentioned (Titus 2:13), "... as we wait for the happy fulfillment of our hope" (NET). The meaning is *beatus* ("happy, blissful, felicitous," Gk. *makarios*, Ger. *[glück]selig*, Fr. *bienheureux*), not *benedictus* ("blessed," Gk. eulogētos, Ger. gesegnet, Fr. béni). The point is not "blessing" but "happiness, felicity, well-being, intense joy." The latter may follow from the former, but that does not make the latter equal to the former.

From '-sh-r, *ashrē* was derived, a plural *status constructus*, which is the introductory term of a "beatitude": "Blissful (felicitous, happy) is he (or, the man)..." (e.g., Deut. 33:29; Job 5:17; Ps. 1:1; 2:12; 32:1-2, 12). This term is never used for God. The corresponding term in the New Testament is *makarios*, used frequently for people, for instance, in the "Beatitutes" (Matt. 5:3-11). It is used only two times for God, and this in one and the same book: "... the gospel of the glory of the blissful (felicitous, happy) God" (1 Tim. 1:11), and, "the blissful (felicitous, happy) and only Sovereign" (6:15). Titus 2:13 ("the blissful [felicitous, happy] hope") comes close to this in that it refers "to the sphere of the incorruptible and blessed [read, blissful, felicitous, happy] God."[131] Originally, the term refers to the transcendent happiness of a life beyond sorrow, distress and death, especially the blissful state of the gods beyond earthly sorrows and afflictions, and then concerning humans, the state of God-like bliss in the realms of the felicitous.[132]

Apart from the Bible passages mentioned, *makarios* and related forms refer to a great extent to the special religious joy that is bestowed upon humans because of their share in the bliss of the kingdom of God,[133] both in the Septuagint and

---

131. *TDNT* 4, 370.
132. Ibid., 362.
133. Ibid., 367.

in the New Testament. It is very important that God's bliss differs from that of the pagan gods in the sense that it never implies some elevation above, and a consequent disinterest in, human circumstances. God's bliss cannot be severed from his love and mercy, in which an emotional dimension is clearly observable as well (see above). Only in cases where both God's bliss and his concern with human fortune are understood conceptually, contradictions will arise. Thus, German theologian Albrecht Ritschl asserted that we should not speak of the sufferings of Jesus' soul under the human burden of sin because this would not agree with his bliss.[134] This is nothing but the pagan view of the divine bliss as being lifted above human vicissitudes.[135] Emil Brunner made the opposite mistake by denying God's bliss—he argued 1 Timothy 1:11 and 6:15 away—because this would conflict with his compassionate care and concern.[136]

7.13.2 Perfection, Knowledge, Love, Joy

One of the true aspects of both God's love and God's bliss is that he can be fully compassionate with people, and yet be perfect in his bliss. There can be no true mercy of God without this dimension of compassionate emotionality; but God would not be God either without his continually unshaken bliss. If terms like compassion and bliss are understood conceptually, one can easily create contradictions between them; for how can someone suffer intensely *and*, at the same time, be intensely happy?[137] However, if the terms mentioned are used as ideas, they may help us to approximate both God's transcendent-lofty bliss and his immanent concern with human suffering.

---

134. Ritschl (1890,III, 521 and further).
135. Althaus (1952, 298).
136. Brunner (1950, 313).
137. Actually, it has been witnessed of some martyrs that they seemed to have reached the highest state of bliss in their worst sufferings. But this was a bliss that was rather a consequence of their sufferings, not a state in which they dwelt in spite of their sufferings, as was supposed of God.

Herman Bavinck saw three elements in God's bliss:[138]

(a) Absolute perfection, for bliss is the part of each being that lives perfectly, without any disturbance from the in- or from the outside. In this sense, eternal life is eternal bliss, both for God and for his children.[139]

(b) God absolutely knows his own absolute perfection, and loves it with an absolute love. There is no perfect bliss without perfect knowledge and perfect love.

(c) God finds joy in himself, rest in himself, suffices himself, all in the absolute sense; it is eternal joy, eternal, undisturbed rest.

What troubles me most here is the scholastic formula, quoted by Bavinck, that God loves himself with an absolute love.[140] In my view, this is more neo-Platonic than Christian.[141] Where we can speak of God's love only with the help of creaturely terms used as ideas, the highest criterion for love is not self-love,[142] but the love toward others. I believe that, here again, we can easily go beyond Scripture, unless we bring in the Trinity here. If we do so, God's eternal, perfect bliss, including his eternal, perfect love, must be primarily understood as the love *between* divine persons, the bliss of undisturbed, perfect, peaceful, harmonious, felicitous fellowship. What is central here is not "self-love": the miracle of God's bliss is that the Father loved the Son before the foundation of the world (John 17:24), and *vice versa*, which also includes the "love of the Spirit" (Rom. 15:30).

7.13.3 Names of God

The description "the blissful (felicitous, happy) God" (Gk. *ho makarios theos*) can almost be understood as a name. "Bliss"

---

138. Bavinck (*RD* 2, 220–22).
139. See extensively, *EDR* 6, chapter 4; Vol. III/4.
140. Bavinck (*RD* 2, 221).
141. Althaus (1952, 297).
142. See Bavinck (*RD* 2, 201) in reference to God, following Augustine, *De Trinitate* IX.2.

is here an attribute of God just as much as "life" is so in the expression "the living God," or "glory" in the expression "the God of glory" (i.e., "the glorious God," Ps. 29:3; Acts 7:2), "mercy" in "the merciful God" (so literally in Rom. 9:16; cf. Luke 6:36; 2 Cor. 1:3), or like "light" is such in the expression "the Father of lights" (James 1:17), "love" in the expression "God of love" (2 Cor. 13:11), "peace" in the expression "the God of peace" (Rom. 15:33 etc.), and so on.

Chapter 8
God's Attributes:
(Spiritive Modalities)

*"Who is a God like you, pardoning iniquity
and passing over transgression for the
remnant of his inheritance?
He does not retain his anger forever,
because he delights in steadfast love."*

Micah 7:18

8.1 The Logical Modality: God's Rationality
8.1.1 Higher Thoughts

WE HAVE SPOKEN EARLIER OF God's "rationality," which actually is supra-rational, if we understand the word "rational" in its strictly modal-logical sense: "For my thoughts are not your thoughts, neither are your ways my ways. . . . For as the heavens are higher than the earth, so are my ways higher than your ways and my thoughts than your thoughts" (Isa. 55:8–9). Of course, such a Bible word is not a philosophical statement about the nature of God's rationality. Rather, it is of a practical-ethical nature: we cannot fathom, not perceive, not scrutinize God's thoughts: "Can you find out the deep things of God? Can you find out the limit of the Almighty? It is higher than heaven—what can you do? Deeper than Sheol—what can you know? Its measure is longer than the earth and broader than the sea" (Job 11:7–9). "Behold, God is great, and we know him not; the number of his years is unsearchable" (36:26).

In the Psalms we read, "You have multiplied, O LORD my God, your wondrous deeds and your thoughts toward us; none can compare with you! I will proclaim and tell of them, yet they are more than can be told" (40:5). "How great are your works, O LORD! Your thoughts are very deep!" (92:5). "How precious to me are your thoughts, O God! How vast is the sum of them! If I would count them, they are more than the sand" (139:17–18).

God's thinking surpasses our rationality, that is, the extent of our own thinking; hence the word supra-rational. Baruch Spinoza was right to some extent when he remarked that speaking of a divine intellect in principle is just as metaphorical as, for instance, speaking of God as the "rock" of our salvation (Deut. 32:15; 2 Sam. 22:47; Ps. 89:26; 95:1), or as the "light" on our path (Ps. 119:105).[1] However, this does not mean that God's thinking would be non-rational, irrational, or extra-rational. It is rational, but in a way that we cannot capture in concepts, as we can to some extent with our own rationality. I say to some extent, for even the kernel of the logical-analytical modality as such can be captured only in ideas, not in concepts. In other words, like all modal kernels this kernel cannot be "defined."

8.1.2 Reasoning Together

The rationality of God's thinking comes to expression, among other things, in the way in which he, through the prophets, "directly" addresses the Israelites, and appeals to *their* rational thinking. Well-known is Isaiah 1:18, "Come now, let us reason [or, dispute] together" (ESV, KJV etc.; Vulgate: *venite et arguite me*, "come and argue with me, exchange arguments with me"; ERV etc.: "Come, let's discuss this"; NLV: "Come

---

1. Quoted in Pannenberg (1988, 410).

now, let us think about this together"; MSG etc.: "Let's argue this out"). The Hebrew *w'niwak'chah* comes from the root *y-k-ch*, "to decide, to judge, to prove," and hence "to be right," and mutually: "to argue, to discuss." God challenged his people to enter into a debate with him in order to establish who of the two was right on the basis of the arguments available.

In a similar way, believers bring their "cause" to the Lord God with the confidence that, when he will hear their arguments, he will put them to the right: "To God would I commit my cause" (Job 5:8). "I desire to argue my case with God" (13:3). "Vindicate me, O God, and defend my cause against an ungodly people" (Ps. 43:1). "Plead my cause and redeem me" (119:154; also see 1 Sam. 24:15; Ps. 35:23; 119:154; Jer. 11:20; 20:12; Lam. 3:58; Micah 7:9).

If we could not trust that God is open to rational arguments, it would make no sense if a person would plead his case before him. God's supra-rationality does not exclude his rationality, but includes it. Job challenged both his friends and God to refute with arguments: "Behold, I have prepared my case; I know that I shall be in the right. Who is there who will contend with me? For then I would be silent and die" (Job 13:18–19; cf. v. 3). " Oh, that I knew where I might find him, that I might come even to his seat! I would lay my case before him and fill my mouth with arguments. I would know what he would answer me and understand what he would say to me. Would he contend with me in the greatness of his power? No; he would pay attention to me. There an upright man could argue with him, and I would be acquitted forever by my judge" (23:4–7). Elihu reproached Job that he accused God of false arguments: "Behold, he finds occasions against me [ERV, found an excuse to attack me; MSG, God keeps picking on me; NABRE, he invents pretexts against me]." In all these cases, a common frame of thinking is presupposed, in which God and humans reason together according to the same logical laws, even though believers know at the same time that God cannot be captured under these laws but surpasses them.

It is remarkable that Herman Bavinck associated God's "rationality" with the metaphorical meaning of "light."[2] In the expression, "God is light," especially the "intellectual" meaning, or the notion of "knowledge," supposedly is prominent. I would rather say that, in the Bible, "light" — primarily a physical term — seems to possess in particular the ethical connotation of holiness, and also the sensitive connotation of joy, bliss, and the aesthetic one of splendor, beauty, glory. This is the clearest in passages that pronounce explicitly that God is "light"; see for the notion of holiness, 1 John 1:5–6 (cf. John 3:19–20; Eph. 5:8–14; 1 Tim. 6:16); for the notion of bliss, Psalm 27:1 (cf. Ps. 4:6–7; 36:7–9; 97:11; Isa. 9:2; 60:19; 1 Pet. 2:9–10); and for the notion of splendor, luster, Deuteronomy 33:2 (cf. Ps. 50:1–2; 80:1; 94:1). At the same time, it is true of course that the light that God introduces into the souls and lives of people cannot be severed from knowledge, and that knowledge can never be considered apart from the logical-analytical modality (see especially 2 Cor. 4:6).

8.1.3 Names of God

We just considered the fact that God is called "light." God is also Judge (e.g., Gen. 18:25; Judg. 11:27; 1 Sam. 24:16; Job 9:15; Ps. 7:11; 75:7; Isa. 33:22; Jer. 11:20; 2 Tim. 4:8; Heb. 12:23; James 4:12; 5:9), and although this fact appeals first and foremost to the juridical modality (see §8.10), God's rationality is enclosed in this as well, namely, as a logical analogy within this juridical modality. God "reasons" with people in judicial cases, as we saw. God's judgments are underpinned by logical arguments: "The dead were judged by what was written in the books, according to what they had done" (Rev. 20:12). See further the next sections on the *Logos*.

---

2. Bavinck (*RD* 2, 158).

8.2 The Logical Modality: God's Omniscience
8.2.1 Knowing All, Yet Acquiring Knowledge

True knowledge involves meaningful distinction and identification: recognition of differences, similarities, and connections. This refers back to the kernel of the logical modality. Therefore, God's perfect knowledge, his *omniscience* (his "knowing everything"), must be dealt with under the logical modality. We can acquire knowledge about God's knowledge through using as ideas terms that appeal to our everyday experience and knowledge in the immanent-modal-functional sense.

If we understand terms concerning God's knowledge conceptually, we soon land in contradictions. For how, on the one hand, can God be omniscient, and, on the other hand, *obtain* knowledge?[3] Thus, in Genesis 11:5 he "came down to see the city [of Babel] and the tower, which the children of man had built." In 18:21 he says, "I will go down to see whether they have done altogether according to the outcry that has come to me. And if not, I will know." In Deuteronomy 8:2 Moses says, "You shall remember the whole way that the LORD your God has led you these forty years in the wilderness, that he might humble you, testing you to know what was in your heart, whether you would keep his commandments or not." And in 13:3, "The LORD your God is testing you, to know whether you love the Lord your God with all your heart and with all your soul." In Psalm 139:23-24, David invites God to (come to) "know" his heart and his thoughts.

Scripture shows that God sometimes tries to "find out" something, and at the same time it is true that he knows all things, and that nothing can be added to his knowledge: "Who has measured the Spirit of the LORD, or what man shows him his counsel? Whom did he consult, and who made him understand? Who taught him the path of justice, and taught him knowledge, and showed him the way of understanding?"

---
3. Cf. *EDR* 4, 90–91.

(Isa. 40:13–14). Both matters contradict each other irreparably if the terms involved are understood conceptually, but they do not necessarily so if they are used as ideas.

The terms used are necessarily derived from our creational reality: "He who planted the ear, does he not hear? He who formed the eye, does he not see? He who disciplines the nations, does he not rebuke? He who teaches man knowledge—the LORD—knows the thoughts of man, that they are but a breath" (Ps. 94:9–11). God knows the hearts of all people (1 Kings 8:39; Jer. 17:9–10; 20:12; Ezek. 11:5; Luke 16:15; Acts 1:24; Rom. 8:27), all their sins (Ps. 69:5) and all their actions (139:2–3; Jer. 32:19); he knows all future things (1 Sam. 23:10–13; Isa. 42:9; 46:10; cf. 41:22–23). However, this knowledge is not just dry-intellectual knowledge ("being aware of," "being informed about"); it is perfect knowledge *concerning* creation but also *to the benefit of* creation: "The eyes of the LORD run to and fro throughout the whole earth [this is *his* omniscience], to give strong support to those whose heart is blameless toward him [this is *their* benefit]" (2 Chron. 16:9). He knows all the needs of his children, and provides for them (Matt. 6:8, 32). In this, several analogies within the logical modality come to light, such as the sensitive and the ethical analogy: "God saw the people of Israel—and God knew [i.e., took heed of them, was concerned about them]" (Exod. 2:25; cf. Amos 3:2; John 11:27–28; 1 Cor. 8:3).

There is also the juridical anticipation: "No creature is hidden from his sight, but all are naked and exposed to the eyes of him to whom we must give account" (Heb. 4:13), that is, God's omniscience is in view of people's repentance and conversion.

8.2.2 Prescience in God?

Traditional theology distinguished within God's knowledge between *scientia naturalis* or *necessaria, simplicis intelligentiae* ("natural" or "necessary knowledge," that of "simple intelligence") and the *scientia libera* or *contingens, visionis* ("free" or "contingent knowledge," that of "vision"). This amounts to self-awareness and world-awareness, inwardly and outwardly oriented knowledge, respectively. Herman Bavinck rightly objected to a sharp division between the two,[4] yet used himself various scholastic expressions. Here are some examples.

(a) Bavinck accepted the Platonic idea that, "from the infinite fullness of ideas that are present in his absolute self-consciousness," God chose some ideas "in order to realize them outside himself."[5]

(b) He maintained the Greek-substantialist idea that the *cognitio naturalis* ("natural knowledge," i.e., God's self-knowledge) cannot be revealed to creatures, and that this relates to the *cognitio libera* ("free knowledge," i.e., God's knowledge of the world) as archetype relates to ectype (see §§1.7.1, 1.7.2, 1.10.3 and 4.8.2).[6]

(c) Bavinck denied that there could be in God factually something like *prescience*, because with him there is no *differentia temporis* ("difference in time," i.e., no before and no after).[7] Even if he can appeal to some church fathers here, it is an evident mistake. A theory concerning God rules here over the clear testimony of Scripture,[8] which freely speaks of God's *fore*knowledge, his *pre*destination, his preparing beforehand, his acting "before the foundation of the world" (Rom. 8:29–30; 9:23; Eph. 1:4–5, 11; 1 Pet. 1:2, 20; John 17:5, 24). The theory says that God is both omniscient and timeless; "therefore," references to time in relation to God cannot

---

4. Bavinck (*RD* 2, 162–63).
5. Ibid., 162; cf. 171–74.
6. Ibid., 162–63.
7. Ibid., 163–64.
8. This is something that Bavinck (*RD* 2, 208) condemned himself: "Alle wetenschap is gebonden aan haar voorwerp; zij mag de verschijnselen, die zij waarneemt, niet ter wille van eenige vooropgezette theorie vervalschen of ontkennen. Zoo is ook de theologie ten strengste gebonden aan de feiten en getuigenissen, welke God in natuur en Schrift haar kennen doet. Zij moet deze laten staan, onverzwakt en onverminkt. Als zij ze niet verklaren kan, heeft zij hare onwetendheid te belijden."

be "factually" true. Yet, temporal references to God are just as clearly biblical as references to his omniscience, which is apparently beyond time. Which theory wishes to establish which of these two categories of references is "factually" correct, and which one is only "metaphorical," or something similar? As always, the underlying misunderstanding is that temporal-creaturely terms are viewed as concepts. As a consequence, contradictions arise, which must necessarily be solved, and this is done by declaring one of the two categories to be "factually incorrect."

Bavinck objected to making a distinction within God's omniscience between *praescientia* ("foreknowledge," viz., in the past, or in the present with regard to the future), *scientia visionis* ("knowledge of vision," viz., in the present), and *reminiscentia* ("reminiscence," viz., in the present with regard to the past, or in the future with regard to the present) with the argument that this is "altogether a human representation."[9] This is perfectly correct. But the point that Bavinck overlooks is that we *have no other way* of considering God's omniscience; as always, we can speak of such matters only in creaturely terms. This is no problem at all—Scripture is our great example in this—as long as we apply such terms not as concepts but as ideas.

8.2.3 Divine Foreknowledge and Human Responsibility

Along the same lines, another problem of traditional theology must, and can, be solved. It is the important question how God's foreknowledge can be harmonized with the notion of human responsibility. If God, as Scripture seems to teach very clearly, surely and infallibly knows everything beforehand, how can any room be left for human freedom and contingency of acting? And how can the idea be avoided that God would be the author (origin) of sin, and that even his own actions are of a "necessary" nature (because they are fixed since the foundation of the world)? Let me mention various solutions

---

9. Bavinck (*RD* 2, 164).

that theology has offered for this problem.[10]

(1) Relativizing or minimalizing God's foreknowledge (Marcion, Socinians; today the "Open Theists"). To me, this seems to conflict with the absolute way Scripture speaks of God's foreknowledge.[11]

(2) Distinguishing between God's prescience and his predestination of people, as is done in Romans 1:29 (this was already Origen's view). Augustine, however, objected that, if God foreknows as a certainty that something will occur, this *must* necessarily occur.[12] If it were otherwise, God's foreknowledge would fall apart.

(3) Augustine's own solution was that the human will, with its entire nature and all its "free" decisions, was enclosed in God's foreknowledge, and is not annulled by it, but rather posited and maintained.[13] This line was generally followed by scholastic theology.

(4) The Jesuites, Spanish scholar Luis de Molina (d. 1600) in particular, introduced the notion of a *scientia media* ("middle knowledge") "in between" God's *scientia necessaria* and his *scientia libera*; this is God's foreknowledge of what is conditional-future. This means that God knows all future possibilities, and everything he will do if and when a certain possibility will become reality. In a sense, this was a return to Origen's solution (see [2]). Both the Lutherans and the Arminians sympathized with it, whereas Reformed theology kept to Augustine's line. Thus, for those who reject "Open Theism," there are two alternatives on the table: that of Origin and that of Augustine.

Bavinck ardently defended the latter option,[14] but I am

---

10. Cf. Bavinck (*RD* 2, 164–70); Weber (1981, 487–93); also see Dekker in Van den Brink and Sarot (1995, 162–83).
11. Cf. *EDR* 4, §2.4, 4.2, 5.1.2 in connection with "Open Theism"; also see Vol. III/1.
12. De libero arbitrio III.4.
13. Ibid., III.3; *De Civitate* V.9.
14. Bavinck (*RD* 2, 167–70).

convinced that both solutions must be rejected. They both suffer of the same shortcoming, namely, the attempt to unite God's absolute foreknowledge and human responsibility (and freedom of acting) within one *conceptual* framework. Through the contradictions that inevitably arise in this way we cannot do justice either to the one, or to the other pole, or even to both poles. The Remonstrants (Arminians) could not do full justice to God's foreknowledge and predestination, the Contra-Remonstrants (strict Calvinists) could not do full justice to human responsibility and freedom. Both sides did not, or not sufficiently, see that we have to do here with matters that surpass all conceptualization, that is, that cannot be enclosed in definitions based upon logical-analytical distinction and identification, as we do in cases of immanent-modal-functional matters. Everything that surpasses the immanent-modal-functional also necessarily surpasses conceptualization and defining.

8.2.4 Logical Errors

The fact that, as we saw, we can speak of divine "fore"-knowledge and human responsibility only in creaturely terms, easily causes misunderstandings. This is because theologians time and again, consciously or unconsciously, concluded from this that we "therefore" can speak of such matters in a conceptual way. In this manner, we saw the rise of so many contradictions, which have been solved neither by Origen, nor by Augustine and their respective successors. Origen could not fully maintain God's foreknowledge and predestination, and Augustine could not fully maintain human responsibility and freedom. However, as soon as we give up our attempt to combine these notions in one logical-conceptual framework, we are free to do justice to the biblical speaking both concerning God's foreknowledge and predestination, and concerning human responsibility and freedom. We do so in creaturely terms—we have no other terms at our disposal—which we do not use as concepts but as ideas. What, on the level of concepts, is necessarily contradictory is not so on the level of ideas. This is because we realize that such an idea-like use of creaturely terms only yields a human *approximation* of divine truth.

This is the manner in which Scripture itself reveals such truths. It is never occupied with the possible *conceptual* contradictions between such truths; it freely reveals both God's foreknowledge and human responsibility. It is only theologians who create contradictions between such notions by understanding them conceptually. Some of them, just like Bavinck (see above), say that the Bible says A, but "actually" means non-A, because A cannot be true according to their self-construed conceptual frame of thought. However, it is this frame of thought that is mistaken. As soon as we give it up, and approximate divine truth through creaturely terms used as ideas, we can fully accept both God's foreknowledge and human responsibility without any *conceptual* contradictions. It is mere hybris to assert that we could treat foreknowledge and responsibility as conceptual systems, of which each property could be predicated.

This perpetual confusion between concepts and ideas also explains how traditional theology can commit the basic error of claiming that the Bible "as word of God [is binding] not only in its literal words but also in what can be legitimately deduced from it."[15] The latter statement would be correct if biblical terms were always used conceptually. However, in the (many) cases in which Scripture uses certain terms as ideas it would be very wrong to predicate certain properties that would belong to these terms *only if they were concepts*. For instance, if eternal election were dealt with conceptually, it would necessarily lead to the conclusion that there must also be an eternal reprobation. If God's sovereignty were dealt with conceptually, it would necessarily lead to the conclusion that there is no room for genuine human freedom. If Jesus is

---

15. Ibid., 262.

God, then Mary is the mother of God, and God died on the cross. And so on. Traditional theology is full of examples of such logical errors.

To conclude: Bavinck also dealt with *wisdom* (Lat. *sapientia*) as one of the virtues of God's intellect. But he admitted that wisdom greatly differs from knowledge in the logical-rational sense. When it is a matter of God's wisdom in his work of creation the logical-analytical element is predominant (Ps. 104:24; Prov. 3:19-20; Jer. 10:12), just like in his work of re-creation (Rom. 11:33; Eph. 3:10). There is also an ethical dimension in God's wisdom—particularly the wisdom of the Torah that he gave to his people; see further in §8.14.

8.2.5 Names of God

The name that comes to mind here is the Greek name *Logos* ("Word"), from which words such as "logic" and "logical" were derived.[16] The name "Logos" is assigned to the pre-incarnate Son, but with the addition that the Word was "God" (John 1:1; cf. vv. 14, 18). The Logos, as the word seems to imply, is the perfect expression of who, what and how God is—and he can be so because he is himself God. I do not think that we go too far when we say that the Logos is the perfect expression of the *Trinity* because he himself is one of the three hypostases within the Trinity.

Actually, although the term "Logos" is related to "logic," the lingual meaning of *Logos* is more important. Greek *logos* is "reason" in the sense of "intellect," but also in the sense of "speech, talk, address"; the word comes from the verb *lego*, "to speak [thinkingly]"; cf. Dutch *rede*, which means both "speech" and "intellect" or "reason"). We will come back to this in §8.4.

---

16. Cf. *logos* in the meaning of "ground" or "reason" in Matt. 5:32; Acts 10:29; 18:14.

8.3 The Historical-Formative Modality
8.3.1 God's Sovereign Will and Arbitrariness

We now come to God's absolute, sovereign power over all created reality.[17] This sovereignty includes his will: "He does according to his will among the host of heaven and among the inhabitants of the earth; and none can stay his hand or say to him, 'What have you done?'" (Dan. 4:35; cf. Exod. 33:19; Job 9:4; Matt. 20:15). This will of God is the basis for his counsel (Rom. 9:22–23; Eph. 1:5, 9, 11), for his creational work (Rev. 4:11), for his government (Ps. 115:3; Prov. 21:1), his work of redemption (Matt. 26:42), the acceptance of believers (Rom. 9:15–18), regeneration (James 1:18), the sanctification of the believers (Phil. 2:13), their sufferings (1 Pet. 3:17), their lives and destinations (Acts 18:21; Rom. 15:32; 1 Cor. 4:19; Heb. 6:3; James 4:15), the charismata in the church (1 Cor. 12:11), and even the smallest things (Matt. 10:29). God's sovereignty implies that he does not have to give account to anyone (Job 33:13). People are in his hands like the potter's clay (Job 10:9; Isa. 29:16; 30:14; 64:8; Jer. 18:6; Rom. 9:21). People can undertake against God just as little as the axe can against the person hewing with it, or as the rod can against the person wielding it (Isa. 10:15; cf. Job 9:3; 11:10; Isa. 45:9).

Theological thinking about God's sovereign will was strongly influenced by ancient (Plato, Aristotle, Stoa, Plotinus) and humanistic thinking (René Descartes, Georg W.F. Hegel, Friedrich Schelling, Arthur Schopenhauer, Eduard von Hartmann). Herman Bavinck claimed the significance of the latter three thinkers for "theism" because they supposedly refuted rationalist and idealist pantheism.[18] To me, however, such philosophies seem dangerous allies for a theology that wishes to think along the lines of Scripture.

Philosophers have sometimes argued that "willing" is a desiring and a striving, and therefore points to imperfection, dissatisfaction, which are not found in God. Why willing if

---
17. Cf. Bavinck (*RD* 2, 197–219).
18. Bavinck (*RD* 2, 200).

you are perfect, and you have everything? Thus, they have sometimes simply denied God's will, as mysticism has often done as well. Bavinck replied to this that willing is not just a desiring something not yet attained or obtained, but also an active resting in, and enjoying, what *has* been attained or obtained.[19] I wonder, however, whether this is a sufficient reply, for, as long as God has not yet attained or obtained a certain thing, how can he be self-sufficient or satisfied[20] with respect to that thing? To me it seems that, here again, two different groups of terms, one pertaining to God's sovereign will and the other concerning his self-sufficiency, are understood in a conceptual way. This necessarily leads to contradictions, which subsequently must be argued away. Even if it is emphasized that God's *propensio in creaturas* ("propensity toward [his] creatures"), as distinct from his *propensio in se ipsium* ("propensity toward himself"), is always for his name's sake (cf. Prov. 16:4),[21] I still maintain that all attempts to reconcile this with his self-sufficiency are only a hybristic word play as long as such notions are used as concepts instead of as ideas.

Many other speculations concerning God's sovereign power and will suffer from the same error. Thus, William of Ockham asserted that God's *potestas absoluta* ("absolute power"), as distinct from his *potestas ordinata* ("ordinary power"), might just as well have willed an egotistic morality because his will is after all completely free. We cannot prescribe to him what he, according to our moral ideas, "ought" to have willed. Therefore, claimed William, the Decalogue is necessarily a product of divine arbitrariness. Creation, incarnation, atonement through satisfaction, good and evil, true and untrue — it could all have been very different if God had wished so.

---

19. Ibid., 200–01.
20. Cf. Gk. *autarkēs*, Phil. 4:11; in Flavius Josephus, *Contra Apionem* 2.190, with regard to God.
21. Bavinck (*RD* 2, 201–02).

In opposition to this view, we notice, first, that within immanent reality the notion of "power" can be understood only as an idea within the coherence of all modal aspects, and this means that God's power and will, too, can be understood only as an idea within the coherence of his entire being: his love, his holiness, his righteousness, and so on. There is no ("amoral") divine power "as such," only loving power, holy power, righteous power, merciful power, and so on.

Second, speaking of God's supposed arbitrariness presupposes a *norm* by which we can determine what is arbitrary, and what not. This implies that God, or his behavior, are submitted to a law; in this way God is drawn under the law-boundary between Creator and creation.[22] God's will cannot be subjected to norms; he is absolute. God gives account to himself alone so to say, not to an (alleged) law outside himself. Even if we would say, as Bavinck does,[23] that God cannot ever want something unless it is good in itself or because of something else, we draw God under the law-boundary, as if there were a norm outside God determining what is God, or what God can want and what he cannot want. *If* we would at all speak of a "norm" here, this can be only a norm within God's being itself. That is, God does not call something good because this thing is after all good in itself, nor does he do so arbitrarily — as if he could just as well chosen to call it evil — but because *he himself* is good.

8.3.2 God's Sovereign Will and Evil

As far as God' will is concerned, there is a special difficulty present in the subject of evil. Traditionally, theology makes a distinction between God's *prescribing* will concerning what people are supposed to do (Matt. 7:21; 12:50; John 4:34; 7:17; Rom. 12:2; 1 Thess. 4:3), and God's *descriptive* will, namely, as describing what God himself does and will do (Ps. 115:3;

---

22. Kalsbeek (1970, 69); cf. Bavinck (*RD* 2, 206 and further).
23. Bavinck (*RD* 2, 215), with a quotation from Gisbertus Voetius, *Disputationes Selectae* I.387.

Dan. 4:17, 25, 32, 35; Rom. 9:18–19; Eph. 1:5, 9, 11; Rev. 4:11).[24] Sometimes the two resemble each other very strongly, like in the prayer, "Your will be done," in Matthew 6:10 and in 26:42. Yet, in my view the former passage belongs to the first category ("Let people do your will on earth"), whereas the latter belongs to the second one ("Carry out your counsel").

We find this distinction at many places. God's wants Abraham to sacrifice his son (category 1: commandment to a person), and in the end makes sure that this does not happen (category 2; Gen. 22:2, 12). He wants Pharaoh to let the Israelites go (category 1; Exod. 4:22), but hardens his heart, so that he does not do it (category 2; Exod. 9:12, 16). He wants people not to condemn an innocent person (category 1; Exod. 23:7; Deut. 19:10; 27:25; Prov. 6:17; Isa. 59:7; Jer. 7:6; 22:3, 17), yet, according to his counsel, he delivers Jesus into the hands of the sinners (category 2; Acts 2:23; 3:18; 4:28; cf. Matt. 17:22–23; 20:18–19). God does not want evil (see, e.g., Hab. 1:13), yet he allows it (Josh. 11:20; 2 Sam. 16:10; Rom. 1:24–26; 2 Thess. 2:11 and so on), and sometimes even seems to bring it about (Isa. 45:7; Amos 3:6). He wants all people to get saved through their conversion and faith (Ezek. 18:23, 32; 33:11; Luke 13:34; 1 Tim. 2:4; 2 Pet. 3:9), yet he has mercy on whomever he wills, and he hardens whomever he wills (Rom. 9:18), and he has made the wicked for the day of disaster (Prov. 16:4).

In order to explain this paradox, theology made a distinction between two kinds of God's "will." Tertullian spoke of a lower, lesser, and a hidden, higher will.[25] Augustine stated that God often realizes his good will in spite of, or even through, the evil will of people.[26] Scholasticism spoke of the *voluntas beneplaciti* (the "will of [God's] good pleasure"; or *arcana, decernens, decretive*, "hidden, discerning, decretive will") and the *voluntas signi* (the "will of [God's] signs," viz., commandment, exhortation, chastisement; or *revelata, praecipiens,*

---

24. See Bavinck (*RD* 2:210 and further).
25. De exhortatione castitatis 2–3.
26. *Enchiridion* 101.

"revealed, anticipating will"), respectively.[27] Many Reformed theologians (e.g., John Calvin, Wolfgang Musculus, Zacharias Ursinus, Amandus Polanus) adopted this view.

However, Roman Catholics, Lutherans and Arminians preferred a distinction between the *voluntas antecendens* ("preceding will"; or *absoluta*, "absolute will") and the *voluntas consequens* ("consequential will"; or *conditionata*, "conditional will"), respectively. The *former* is the factual will of God, implying that God does not want sin, even if he allows it; that he wishes the salvation of all, offered to all, and that, if a person has come to a decision, God follows that decision, having determined beforehand what he wants: salvation for all those who believe, and destruction for all those who refuse to believe. The *latter* will is the will that "follows" upon, and depends on, a person's decision; it is not the factual, absolute will of God, but God's acting as a consequence of people's acting. The Reformed theologians rejected this distinction. They viewed the *voluntas beneplaciti* as the factual, absolute will of God, which is always realized, entirely independent on human will and decisions. In this case, a person's being saved or being lost depends exclusively on God's will. The *voluntas beneplaciti* must only be distinguished from God's *voluntas signi*, his prescribed will in law and gospel, as the norm for human behavior.

In my view, both theological approaches must be rejected again. The two combat each other by dealing with the opponents' view as a conceptual system, of which certain properties are predicated such that both an A and a non-A follow. On this basis, one (rightly) rejects the opponents' system, and (wrongly) accepts one's own system as the only correct alternative, without realizing that one's own system suffers from exactly the same errors.

8.3.3 Bavinck's Example

A striking example of the situation just described is found in

---

27. E.g., Thomas van Aquino, *Summa Theologiae* I qu. 19 art. 11–12.

Herman Bavinck's dogmatics, with its Augustinian-Calvinist system over against the Pelagians.[28] We already met with the procedure that he followed. Bavinck explained that, in certain cases, the Bible says A, but "actually" means non-A. Thus, the *voluntas signi* is not the "actual" will of God, because in it he does not tell us what *he* will do. It is not a law for *his* actions, it does not prescribe what *God* must do, only what *people* must do. Therefore, this supposedly would only be *voluntas Dei* in a "metaphorical sense."[29] Thus, Bavinck told us that God does *not* wish all people to be saved, in flagrant contravention of 1 Timothy 2:4 ("God who desires all people to be saved") and 2 Peter 3:9 ('… not wishing that any should perish, but that all should reach repentance").

This is the consequence of taking one's own system in a conceptual way, and deriving contradictions from it on whose basis one can claim that, when the Bible says A, it "actually" means non-A. Those who think this way always reject the thought systems of their opponents on the basis of their inner contradictions, and also their being at variance with the Bible, but they do not see the contradictions in their own systems. If such theologians solve the latter by asserting that, when the Bible says A, it "actually" means non-A, they should show somewhat more tolerance toward the systems of their opponents, where the same kind of problems occurs, and where the same kind of pseudo-solutions is offered.

In my own approach this problem does not occur; therefore, I believe it to be more congenial with the Bible. I understand terms regarding God's will *not* as concepts but as ideas, so that *not* all kinds of properties can be predicated that lead to contradictions. Therefore, without any reticence I can speak of God's "absolute" (irresistible) will in order to maintain his absolute sovereignty, *and* of God's "conditional" (resistible) will in order to maintain human responsibility and freedom, that is, his high position as the image and likeness

---

28. Bavinck (*RD* 2, 213).
29. Ibid., 214.

of God. In both cases, we have to do with idea-like *approximations* of God's will, which surpass all conceptualization, and thus also all logical contradictions that arise between conceptual systems. In this way, we can still speak *rationally* of God's will—for our rational knowledge is not limited to conceptual knowledge—but only in the form of ideas. Only in this way we can rationally live with apparent contradictions, which really exist only if we try to speak of God's will in a conceptual way.

How easily people can overestimate their theological "models"—the theologians involved prefer to speak of "truths"!—is evident from Bavinck's statement "that Scripture, though theologically emphasizing the voluntas beneplaciti, yet also maintains in the voluntas signi how and in what way [God] does not want sin."[30] Of course, Scripture is not "theologically emphasizing" anything; it does not supply us with theological models or theories. People's theological models, such as the distinction between the *voluntas beneplaciti* and the *voluntas signi*, are always designed by theologians and imposed upon the biblical data, not *vice versa*.

Traditionally, God's sovereignty is viewed as manifesting itself particularly in what is called his *omnipotence* (see §7.8). The fact that God is "omnipotent," or "almighty," comes to light in all his creational works and in their sustenance, in his providence, in world history, in redemption and consummation.[31] One of the chief problems regarding God's omnipotence of which theology, and also philosophy, was continually aware, is the relationship between this omnipotence and God's absolute love. It has been asserted that, if God is really almighty, he cannot be absolute love, for if he were love, his omnipotence would not allow any human suffering. Conversely, if God is really love, given the enormous amount of human, innocent suffering in the world he cannot possibly be really almighty. God cannot be absolute power and absolute

---
30. Ibid.
31. Ibid., 215v.

love at the same time; we cannot have both.

This subject, which takes up a central place in each philosophy of religion and is the theme of many *theodicies* ("vindications of God," especially in view of human suffering), cannot be extensively dealt with here.[32] But at least we can say that, here again, contradictions are created between God's omnipotence and his love in speaking of them in terms that are used as concepts. Here again, the solution is using these terms not as concepts but as ideas. Thus, we can continue speaking unlimitedly of both God's omnipotence and God's love, since both manners of speaking are *approximations* of God's being, which surpasses all conceptualization. Such speaking also surpasses all (supposed) logical contradictions because these can arise only through using the terms involved as concepts. Thus, we can speak *rationally* of both God's omnipotence and God's love, as long as we use the terms involved as ideas. It is only in this way that we can rationally live with the paradoxes mentioned. In my opinion, here lies the key to a theodicy that is really in line with the spirit of Scripture.

8.3.4 Names of God

The primary name, or rather appellative, that comes to mind is Hebrew *El*. Probably related to it are the forms *Eloah* and the plural *Elohim*, if at least the ground meaning of *El* is "strong, powerful, eminent"; not every specialist is convinced of this, however.[33] We can also think here of *Adon* and *Adonai*, and their Greek equivalent *Kyrios* in the Septuagint and the New Testament, with the ground meaning "powerful, dominant, ruling," and hence, "lord, commander, master [of slaves]," and so on.

It is peculiar that, according to Emil Brunner, the Septuagint properly represented the tetragrammaton (YHWH) as *kyrios*.[34] First, *kyrios* is in no way the meaning of YHWH, in

---

32. See *EDR* 4:197–201, and Vol. III/1 of this series.
33. Cf. *TDNT* 3, 84–85.
34. Brunner (1950, 142).

spite of Brunner's reasoning. Second, the reason for the Septuagint to render the name this way was not because the translators thought that *kyrios* is the meaning of YHWH but because YHWH was traditionally read as *Adonai* (because of an exaggerated application of Exod. 20:7).

In Exodus 15:3, YHWH is a "man of war" (Heb. *ish milchamah*; cf. Ps. 24:8, "the LORD, mighty in battle"), in Psalm 78:65 (NIV etc.) "warrior" (*gibbor*), in Zephaniah 3:17 (NIV etc.) even "Mighty Warrior" (*gibbor*), in Isaiah 1:24 and at other places the "Mighty One [*abir*] of Israel." Also remember the name *El Shaddai*, Greek *pantokrator* (§7.8.3), "God Almighty," or rather, "the mighty God over everything." Also the description *YHWH Tsebaot*, "the LORD of hosts" (1 Sam. 1:3 etc.), which is very frequent in the prophetic books (eighty-eight times in Jeremiah alone), is rendered in the Septuagint as (*theos*) *pantokrator*. The "hosts" are the armies of Israel (1 Sam. 17:45), the celestial bodies (Gen. 2:1), and the angelic powers (1 Kings 22:19). God rules them all, and as such, he delivers and protects his people (cf. Ps. 46:7, 11).

Some other names containing a historical-formative dimension, such as King, Judge and Master, will be dealt with below.

8.4 The Lingual Modality: the Speaking God
8.4.1 The Word and the Words

God is the *speaking* God, as I have explained in Volume I/1.[35] Therefore, God the Son is called the *Logos*, "Word" (John 1:1, 14). Through the activity and the power of the Logos, the entire creation exists; that is, by his speaking it was brought about (cf. ten times "and God said" in Gen. 1), and by his speaking it is sustained (Heb. 1:3). The Logos is not so much the intellectual Ratio, as ancient thought claimed, but the expression of God, speech of God (from Gk. *lego*, "to speak"). When God reveals himself, it is in a speaking way so to speak. This is true for his creational word, for his providential word,

---
35. Vol. I/1, §7.2.1 and passim; see there for details and footnotes.

for his inscripturated Word, and for the incarnated Word of God (see again Volume I/1).

God *speaks*—in order to create, to sustain, to redeem, to restore—that is, he expresses himself, his inner thoughts, in his Word, and ultimately this Word is the Son. The Son is able to be such because he himself is God, namely, God the Son; he is "the only God… at the Father's side" (John 1:18; this daring verse was easily changed by the scribes into "the only[-begotten] *Son*"; see KJV etc.). The Son is the eternal Logos because it was and is in him that God has expressed and revealed himself in the most perfect way.[36] Christ *is* the Revelation of God both in his person and in his work. And because also God's law has word character—his law is speech, his *torah* ("instruction, teaching") is Logos ("word")—Christ is in the same sense the eternal Torah, for God's Word is always Commandment of God.[37] In Christ, the Logos, all claims ("commandments") of God regarding his creation have been revealed.

We have seen in Volumes I/1 and I/2 that, in its transcendent fullness, the law is one, but in its immanent "refraction" (think of the prism metaphor) it diverges into many different commandments. Similarly, in the concrete "refraction" within immanent reality, the one, eternal Logos diverges into many immanent *logoi* (oracles of God). We can hear the "Word" only in the many different "words" addressed to us by God, or by Christ, or by God's Spirit. Thus, within immanent reality, the one, eternal Torah reveals himself on Mount Sinai in ten "words" (so literally in Exod. 34:28; Deut. 4:13; 10:4), commandments for *immanent* life, which find their converging integration in the *transcendent*, even *eternal* Torah, the eternal Logos.

8.4.2 Speech and the Trinity

Just as we saw in the case of God's love (see §7.13.2), the full meaning of God as the speaking God is disclosed only if we

---

36. *EDR* 2, 243–48.
37. See extensively, Vol. I/2.

bring in the Trinity here.[38] If God for showing his love would depend on other beings outside him, he could not have been the loving God before the foundation of the world. At best he could have been the potentially loving God, or the God who loved future beings. In this case, what sense would it make to say that God *is* love (1 John 4:8, 16)? The only solution would have been self-love; but, as we saw, we can hardly imagine that God's *self*-love could ever be the moral criterion for *human* love. This is because, ultimately, love is considered to be *sacrificing* love; it is the love that gives to the other one.

Indeed, the notion of God's eternal love is disclosed only if we understand that the three persons of the Deity have loved *each other* from eternity. In a parallel way, God is from eternity the speaking God in the sense that the three persons spoke *together*. Similarly, God is the God practicing fellowship, the God doing justice, the God who is faithful. We cannot say that the compassionate God, the merciful God, the condescending God, and so on, from eternity found his first realization as such within the Trinity; these properties presuppose lowly, and even afflicted, beings. But we *can* say that, from eternity, the three persons in the Deity maintained perfect communication, perfect fellowship, perfect justice (doing "justice" to each other), perfect faithfulness and perfect love among the three of them.

Edmund Schlink put it this way:[39] "From eternity, God is not a lonely God, but unity and community at once—not an isolated Ego, but an eternal over-against of I and Thou, and thus eternally I and We at the same time. God became the loving, speaking and glorifying One not for the first time through the over-against of creation, but from eternity he is the loving One, the beloved One, and the One-loving-in-return— the speaking One, the Word and the Responding One—the glorifying One, the glorified One, and the One-glorifying-in-

---

38. See *EDR* 2, 80, 278; Chafer (*ST* 1:291–95) developed from this even a rational "proof" for the doctrine of the Trinity.
39. *RGG* 4:1037.

return in the unity and community of the Father, the Son and the Holy Spirit."

"From the beginning," and even "from eternity," there has been a spoken, and in a sense even written Word of God: "Behold, I have come; in the scroll of the book it is written of me" (Ps. 40:7). These prophetic words were fulfilled "when Christ came into the world" (Heb. 10:5; cf. 1 Pet. 1:20). The apostle John speaks of "everyone whose name has not been written before the foundation of the world in the book of life of the Lamb who was slain" (Rev. 13:8), and of "the dwellers on earth whose names have not been written in the book of life from the foundation of the world" (17:8). God "declares" and "tells" new things "before they spring forth" (Isa. 42:9). God is the One "declaring the end from the beginning and from ancient times things not yet done, saying, 'My counsel shall stand, and I will accomplish all my purpose'" (46:10; cf. 48:3). "Your eyes saw my unformed substance; in your book were written, every one of them, [namely,] the days that were formed for me, when as yet there was none of them" (Ps. 139:16). The names of the righteous are also written in a book (Exod. 32:32–33; Ps. 69:28; Isa. 4:3; Dan. 12:1; Luke 10:20; Phil. 4:3; Heb. 12:23; Rev. 13:8; 17:8; 20:12, 15), although this does not always seem to involve the same book metaphor.

8.4.3 Names of God

The lingual name of God that comes to mind most prominently is *Logos*, mentioned before. The Greek word *logos* is derived from the verb *legō*, "to speak."[40] It is what is spoken, but not like the word *rhēma*, which we find, for instance, in Hebrews 1:3. Perhaps we may explain the difference as follows: in *rhēma* the emphasis is on the word spoken, in *logos* the emphasis is on the inner thought that is outwardly expressed. God the Son being the Logos means that in and through him is expressed what was and is in God, that is, the Triune God. The

---

40. *TDNT* 4, 124–36; see John 1:1–2, 14; 1 John 1:1; Rev. 19:13; cf. 1 John 5:7 (KJV etc.).

Logos *can* be the perfect expression of what is in God because he himself is God. It is God (the Son) revealing what is in (the Triune) God. It is God the Son, who is at the side of God the Father, by whom and through whom *God* has revealed himself (cf. 1 John 1:18).

8.5 The Social Modality (1)
8.5.1 God Practicing Fellowship

God is not only the "communicating" God (cf. the lingual modality) but also the "communing" God — not only the God speaking to others but speaking *with* others, keeping company with them, having fellowship with them. It is possible to speak without practicing fellowship, but, conversely, the human world does not know any true communion with lingual communication. The latter can be non-verbal communication; yet, the latter is lingual in the broader sense of the word; compare the expression "body language." What I just said implies that the social modality presupposes the lingual modality, not the other way around.

It is only in creaturely terms, adopted from human fellowship, that we can speak — in the form of ideas — about the God practicing fellowship. The Word of the speaking God is directed to shaping and enhancing fellowship between God and people, and between person and person, a fellowship that is an extension of the intertrinitarian fellowship: "...the word of life we proclaim also to you, so that you too may have fellowship with us; and indeed our fellowship is with the Father and with his Son Jesus Christ" (1 John 1:1, 3). The "horizontal" and the "vertical" fellowship merge here.

Genuine divine attributes are only those that from eternity belong to God.[41] This is the answer to the age-old question what God "did" before he created the world. The answer is (a) that all God's genuine attributes are eternal, (b) that all his attributes have been eternally active, (c) that this eternal activity of his attributes is *God's* work, and (d) that it therefore has

---
41. Cf. Chafer (*ST* 1:291–92); Bavinck (*RD* 2, 302–03).

been active from eternity. This implies two things. (1) With respect to God's attributes: from eternity God is the speaking, fellowshipping, justifying, loving and faithful God, namely, regarding the fellowship between the three divine persons. (2) With respect to God's eternal "works": from eternity the Father generates the Son, from eternity the Son is born of the Father, from eternity the Holy Spirit proceeds from the Father (and, according to western tradition, from the Son).[42]

God did not become the fellowshipping God after he had created humanity. From eternity he was the fellowshipping God because of the eternal fellowship that existed, and exists, between the three persons within the Deity. The Syrian scholar John of Damascus (d. 749) introduced the Greek term *perichōrēsis* (perichoresis, Lat. *circumincessio*) to describe the intimate fellowship between the persons in the Deity (*communio personarum divinarum*), which goes so far as entirely pervading each other.[43] None of the three persons can exist, or act, apart from the other two persons. Therefore, the Council of Florence (1439) stated that, because of this fellowship, the Father is entirely in the Son and in the Spirit, the Son is entirely in the Father and in the Spirit, and the Holy Spirit is entirely in the Father and in the Son.[44]

The term "perichoresis," literally referring to a continual "turning around" of the three persons, as a kind of dance (Gk. *choros*, "dance"; cf. the term choreography), is not ideal. The Western church preferred a "spatial" to such a "kinematic" image, and tried to express this in terms such as *circuminsessio* ("dwelling in each other"; one letter differing from *circumincessio*), *immanentia* ("remaining in each other"), or *inexistentia* ("existing in each other"[45]), spatial terms used here as ideas. However this may be, the terms were all designed to underscore the strict unity within the Trinity.

---

42. See extensively, *EDR* 2:283–88; and Vol. II/2 in this series.
43. Ekdosis I.8 and 14; cf. Barth (*CD* I,1, 390–92, 417, 509).
44. Van Genderen (2008, 153–54); see *EDR* 2:100, 126.
45. Barth (*CD* I,1, 390).

As soon as humans had been created, God extended his fellowship to them. This is clear already in Genesis 1. Polish rabbi Benno Jacob (d. 1945) pointed to a remarkable difference between animals and humans:[46] God blessed the animals, "saying, 'Be fruitful'" (v. 22), but of the humans it is said, "And God blessed them. And God said *to them*, 'Be fruitful and multiply'" (v. 28). The "saying" (Heb. *lēmor*) in verse 22 means hardly anything more than: "God blessed them with the words…" It was not a real *addressing*. However, in verse 28, the subject of the sentence, God, is repeated with a new consecutive imperfect and the repetition of the object: "And God said to them" (*wayyomer lahem*). God did and does not address the animals, but he did and does address humans. He stretched his hand out to the latter so that they would become his *socii*, his companions, partakers, partners, allies, friends. In this way he also came to them after the Fall: he came to Adam, "walking in the garden in the cool of the day," and asked him "where" he was, that is basically, where he was in relation to God (Gen. 3:8–9).[47]

8.5.2 Names of God

In §§7.1.1 and 7.1.4 I briefly dealt with the name YHWH. On the basis of Exodus 3:14 I see a clear "social" element in it: "I am who I am" may be taken to mean, "I remain the same, always faithful to my promises." It is not an abstract-ontological "I am," but "I am *there*" (Buber-Rosenzweig: *ich bin da*), namely, for my people. Notice the remarkable "I am" in John 6:20 (CEB etc.; other rendering: 'It is I"), when Jesus comes to his disciples in their distress, but also the majestic "I am" over against his opponents (John 18:5–6, 8; also cf. 8:24, 28, 42; 13:19).

Also in Jesus' seven well-known "I am" statements in John's Gospel, the central point is always what Jesus is in relation to, and in fellowship with, his people; or broader, in

---

46. Jacob (1974, i.l.).
47. See extensively, Ouweneel (2018, chapter 8).

relation to humanity:

(1) "I am the bread of life" (6:35, 41, 48, 51).
(2) "I am the light of the world" (8:12; 9:5; cf. 1:9; 3:19; 11:9; 12:46).
(3) "I am the door of the sheep" (10:7, 9).
(4) "I am the good shepherd" (10:11, 14).
(5) "I am the resurrection and the life" (11:25).
(6) "I am the way, the truth and the life" (14:6).
(7) "I am the true vine" (15:1, 5).

8.6   The Social Modality (2)
8.6.1   The Covenanting God

After the Flood, God made his covenant with Noah and his descendants after him, and extended it to all creatures (Gen. 9:9–17). After this, he made his covenant with Abr(ah)am (Gen. 15 and 17), and renewed it with Isaac (Gen. 26) and Jacob (Gen. 35 and 46). Subsequently, he made his covenant with their descendants, the people of Israel (Exod. 6:1–13; 19:5; 24:1–8), and renewed it many times.

In this fact of God being the covenantal Partner with humans, the social element in God's being comes to light in a very special way. The kinematic element of constancy in God's name, YHWH (Exod. 3:14), is extended here to God's covenantal faithfulness, in which we encounter a social, an in particular also a pistical element (§8.15). From the beginning, God was going to be known to Israel in quite a peculiar way, not known to the patriarchs (Exod. 6:2–3), in that he was going to show to them the blessing of his immediate and continued presence among them, as implied in his name, YHWH. It is only when there is a redeemed *nation* that the social dimension in God's being comes to light most fully because he expresses the desire to dwell in their midst. On the very first day of their redemption, this nation speaks, led by God's Spirit, of a "holy abode" (Heb. *n'wēh qodchecha*), a "dwelling" (*nachalt'cha*), a "sanctuary" (*miqdash*), in which God will dwell

God's Attributes: (Spiritive Modalities)

in the midst of his people (Exod. 15:13, 17).

After Moses had climbed Mount Sinai, the very first thing that the Lord God told him was that the Israelites had to make him a "sanctuary" (*miqdash*), so that he could "dwell" (*sh-kh-n*) in their midst (Exod. 25:8). The very first sacrifice that is described, the daily burnt offering "at the entrance of the tent of meeting before the LORD," immediately mentions as the motive: "… where I will meet with you [plural: Israel], to speak to you [singular: Moses] there. There I will meet with the people of Israel… I will dwell among the people of Israel and will be their God. And they shall know that I am the LORD their God, who brought them out of the land of Egypt that I might dwell among them. I am the LORD their God" (Exod. 29:42-46).

God's *sociabilitas* is seen in a special way when his people pass through times of affliction. When Israel is in the "iron furnace" (Deut. 4:20), God "comes down" in order to redeem them (Exod. 3:8). He says so himself when speaking to Moses from the burning bush, of which Moses says later that God "dwelled" in it, that is, in what was the very sign of that fiery furnace (Deut. 33:16; cf. Dan. 3:25). It is a wonderful illustration of Isaiah 63:9, "In all their affliction he was afflicted !, and the angel of his presence saved them; in his love and in his pity he redeemed them; he lifted them up and carried them all the days of old." Here, the social element merges with the sensitive and the ethical element.

It would carry us too far to continue this thought throughout Scripture.[48] I only wish to point out how the New Testament applies this to the church: "We are the temple of the living God; as God said, 'I will make my dwelling among them and walk among them, and I will be their God, and they shall be my people'" (2 Cor. 6:16; cf. 1 Cor. 3:16; Eph. 2:19-22; also see 1 Tim. 3:15; 1 Pet. 2:5; 4:17). And about the status *aeternus* (the "eternal state") we hear: "Behold, the dwelling place

---
48. See extensively, *EDR* 7, §§4.2 and 5.1.

[or, tabernacle] of God is with man. He will dwell with them, and they will be his people, and God himself will be with them as their God" (Rev. 21:3). Thus, the notion of the fellowshipping God stretches from almost the first to almost the last page of the Bible. And what is even more important: God was such from eternity, if we think of the Trinity. Similarly, God was from eternity the speaking God, the righteous God, the good and loving God, and the faithful God, since there was perfect mutual communication, fellowship, justice, love and faithfulness between the three persons of the Deity.

This important point is of special significance in a time when God's immanence and condescension are emphasized at the expense of his transcendence. It is the time when the fact that God is the "Partner" of humans, and humans are the "partners" of God (with an appeal to, e.g., 1 Cor. 3:9), is emphasized so strongly as if God would "need" humans, and would not manage without them. In so-called process theology, God is made to depend on, and is viewed as changing with, the world process.[49] Such a view belittles God, and does not acknowledge the fact that God existed from eternity before he created humanity, and that in this eternity he was perfect in his self-sufficiency, and in his Trinitarian fellowship and love. The idea that God "needs" humans can be correct only if we firmly maintain that God himself *sovereignly chose* to "need" humans, in which statement the term "needing" is actually bereft of its power.

8.6.2 Names of God

The well-known reference to the "covenantal God" ("God of the covenant") in Reformed theology does not occur in the Bible, but it is certainly congenial with it. God is "the God of Abraham, Isaac and Jacob, the God of our fathers" (Acts 3:13; cf. Exod. 3:6, 15; Matt. 22:32; Acts 7:32). He is such due to his covenants with the fathers, just like he is the "God of Israel" (so many times from Exod. 5:1 to Luke 1:68) due to his cove-

---

49. See about this Wentsel (1987, 173–74); Erickson (1998, 304–08).

nants with Israel. He is "our God, the great, the mighty, and the awesome God, who keeps covenant and steadfast love" (Neh. 9:32).

The social as well as ethical dimension in God being the covenantal God comes to light especially in expressions like these: "The friendship of the LORD is for those who fear him, and he makes known to them his covenant" (Ps. 25:14). "My steadfast love I will keep for him forever, and my covenant will stand firm for him" (Ps. 89:28).

8.7 The Economic Modality
8.7.1 God's Perfection

Herman Dooyeweerd described the kernel of the economic modality approximately in terms of "saving," "frugality,"[50] and hence as "balanced," "effective," "efficient." I link this with God's perfection, just like I wish to associate the next, aesthetic modality with God's *glory*. Just like aesthetic harmony presupposes economic balance, God's glory seems to presuppose his perfection.[51] There is no disharmony in God because all his attributes, all his properties, all his virtues, are in perfect equilibrium.

Matthew 5:48 tells us that God the Father is *teleios* ("perfect"). This word was derived from telos, "end, goal." The verb *teleioō* means "to bring to an end" or "to its goal" or "purpose," and hence "to complete," "to bring to its fullness," "to perfect." Interestingly, *telos* sometimes has an economic meaning in the strict sense of the word "economic," namely, "toll" (Matt. 17:25; Rom. 13:7b), and *teleō* sometimes means "to pay"(Matt. 17:24). This meaning is based upon the element of "duty, liability, obligation" contained in the original meaning of *telos*. I mention this just in passing because naturally I do not attach particular value to this specifically economic meaning of the term. What is intended in Matthew 5:48 is rather the ethical element of love in God's perfection. Therefore, the

---
50. Dooyeweerd (*NC* 2, 66).
51. Cf. Bavinck (*RD* 2, 178v.,219–25).

MSG renders the last part of Matthew 5:48 as follows: "Live generously and graciously toward others, the way God lives toward you." Also notice the parallel text in Luke 6:36, "Be merciful, even as your Father is merciful."

The fact that perfection sometimes specifically means reaching a certain goal is supported magnificently in the case of the Son of God, who, as God, was perfect from eternity, as a Man was ethically perfect, yet in a certain sense had to be brought to "perfection." As we read in Hebrews 2:10, "It was fitting that he [i.e., God]... in bringing many sons to glory, should make the founder of their salvation perfect through suffering" (cf. 5:9, "being made perfect, he became the source of eternal salvation to all who obey him"; 7:28, "a Son who has been made perfect forever"). "To make perfect" means here as much as "to lead to the perfect end of a course" and/or "to bring someone into a perfect position that makes this person fit for a certain office." This is the office of "founder of their salvation" (2:10): the leader who went before the others, experienced all the sufferings of believers, knows them thoroughly well, can sympathize with them, and can safely help them through as a compassionate high priest.[52] One day, the believers too with reach the "perfection," namely, the glory of the Messianic kingdom (11:40; 12:23).

8.7.2 God's Sufficiency

A specifically "economic" element in God's perfection is his sufficiency in the sense of God being "sufficient" in and to himself (Gk. hikanos). He does not really "receive" from his creatures in the sense that he would "need" from them anything or any person. On the contrary, from his own sufficiency he gives to others (cf. this notion in Ps. 50:9-13; Isa. 40:28-29; Phil. 4:19). When a person compares himself with God (or Christ), he must say, ouk eimi hikanos (Matt. 3:11; 8:8), "I am not worthy," literally, "I am not enough" or "sufficient." Compare again the economic element: "my value is not high

---

52. Ouweneel (1982,I, 38–41).

enough."⁵³ The person who witnesses to Jesus that his own value is not high enough thus confesses that God, or Christ, has all value or worthiness. Paul confesses of himself the same in relation to the glorified Christ (1 Cor. 15:9), and says, "Not that we are sufficient in ourselves to claim anything as coming from us, but our sufficiency (Gk. *hikanotēs*) is from God" (2 Cor. 3:5). John the Baptist says, "After me comes he who is mightier than I, the strap of whose sandals I am not worthy (*hikanos*) to stoop down and untie" (Mark 1:7).

Following Thomas Aquinas, Herman Bavinck explained the notion of divine perfection from the Platonic notion of Greek *idea*, and called God pure *eidos* (Lat. *actus purissimus*).⁵⁴ I already rejected this ancient way of speaking about God; it is foreign to the spirit of Scripture. Bavinck indeed did see the danger of it. He said, "A creature is perfect… if the idea, which is the *norma* for it, has been fully realized in it," and added, "And thus, God is perfect too because the idea of God completely agree with his being."⁵⁵ However, he hastened to tell us that there cannot be such an authoritative *norma* "above" God with which he would have to agree, and that therefore in this sense there is no "idea of God."⁵⁶ But why then at all bring in the Platonic notion of *idea* with respect to God? Why *add* that "the idea of God has been derived from God himself"? What insight does this give us if the notion of a "norm," implied in "idea," in God's case must be left out? Can we use the term "idea" as a concept for humans, and as an idea for God? Or should we not rather say that each notion linked with ancient substantialism ought to be banned from our thinking?

In my opinion, the notion of God's eternal sufficiency refutes each "idealistic" view of God. According to this view, God would have to enter into history in order to arrive at

---

53. Cf. *TDNT* 3, 294.
54. Bavinck (*RD* 2, 178, 219–20).
55. Ibid., 219.
56. Ibid., 220.

himself: the noumenal (i.e., the "idea") must become phenomenal (the terminology is Immanuel Kant's). However, the Bible does not know anything of any necessity of history for God. He *is*, he does not have to *become* anything, even though he *can* become, and sometimes does become; especially, "the Word *became* flesh" (John 1:14). He carries all perfection in himself; he is sufficient to himself.[57] Again, this is best understood from the doctrine of the Trinity. From eternity to eternity God is sufficient to himself in the eternal mutual loving, mutually practicing fellowship, and mutually communicating of the three persons in the Deity. In himself, God is a sufficient "universe"; he has no necessity to create the world. If he nonetheless does so, he does so as a free, sovereign act, not from some inner necessity. I repeat, *if* we can say at all that God "needs" the world, it is because he has freely and sovereignly chosen to "need" it, that is, he has chosen to create the necessity of it.

I may *add* here that God's perfection implies, among other things, that he has no "character," such as people have: a complex mixture of good and less good qualities, stronger and weaker ones, which characterize an individual and distinguish it from other such individuals. First, there is no individual with whom God can be compared; of the *species* "God" there is only one (the "gods" are only created angels[58]). Second, there is no property in God that is more prominent than others, as is the case with humans: the unique combination of stronger and weaker features gives to each of them his specific "character." All God's attributes are in perfect equilibrium with each other because each attribute is present in hem in absolute perfection.

8.7.3 Names of God

If "saving" is an essential element in the kernel of the economic modality, we can say that God as the "Savior" is

---

57. Cf. Althaus (1952, 265, 694).
58. See *EDR* 11, §§14.1 and 14.4.

the "saving" (2 Sam. 22:3; Ps. 106:21; Isa. 43:3, 11; 45:15, 21; 49:26; 60:16; 63:8; Jer. 14:8; Luke 1:47; 1 Tim. 1:1; 2:3; Titus 1:3; 2:13; 3:4; 2 Pet. 1:1; Jude 25) or "sparing" God (Exod. 12:27; Neh. 13:22; Isa. 31:5; Ezek. 20:17; Joel 2:17; Mal. 3:17). God is the God who "saves" his people from judgment, that is, "spares" them in judgment (notice in English the link between "Savior" and "savings"). Being "spared" stands in contrast with being judged (Jer. 13:14; 21:7; Ezek. 24:14; Amos 7:8; 8:2; Jonah 4:11; Zech. 11:6; Rom. 11:22; 2 Pet. 2:4–5). God did not "spare" his own Son in order to be able to "save" his people (Rom. 8:32; cf. the contrast in Mal. 3:17).

"To redeem" means, among other things, "to buy for a price" (1 Cor. 6:20; 7:22; cf. "ransom" in Matt. 20:28 and parallel passages; 1 Tim. 2:6). In this metaphor we also find enclosed the value that the thing that is bought has for the buyer (cf. Matt. 13:44–46). I also refer here again to the name *El Shaddai* (see §8.3.4) because some have suggested a link with Hebrew *dai*, "sufficient"; the name would thus mean, "God the (All-)Sufficient."

8.8 The Aesthetic Modality: God's Glory
8.8.1 Splendor and Magnificence

Traditional theology tells us that God's perfection (§8.7.1) intrinsically is the ground for his bliss (§7.13.1), and outwardly implies his glory.[59] We could describe God's glory as the display of God's excellence; compare Psalm 145:5, where we literally read of the "splendor of the glory or your majesty" (LEB) (cf. Isa. 2:10, 19, 21). This element of "display" is essential for the notion of God's glory; to it belongs the fact that it is observed. God's glory "shines" (Ezek. 43:2; Luke 2:9; cf. Deut. 33:2; Matt. 17:2; John 1:14; 2 Cor. 4:4, 6).[60] We may speak here of the perceptive retrocipation in the aesthetic modality, used as an idea here to approximate the glory of God.

---

59. See Bavinck (*RD* 2, 222); a standard work is still Von Gall (1900); cf. Barth (*CD* II,1, 362 etc., 722–64).
60. Cf. Althaus (1952, 293–94).

And where the Bible, in connection with God's "shining" glory, tells us that God is "light" (1 John 1:5; cf. Ps. 118:27; Isa. 9:2; 60:1; John 1:5), we speak of a physical retrocipation in the aesthetic modality, used again as an idea. Where reference is made to God as "light" in a certain moral context (as in 1 John 1), we have to do with an ethical anticipation in the aesthetic modality. Not an ethically qualified notion, for the aesthetic remains the primary idea: God's light is far more than only his moral purity. It is beaming beauty, brightness, grandeur, splendor, luster, magnificence, majesty, brilliance, effulgence, radiance, resplendence.

This glory is the glory of God's being; it is God himself. God *is* light. In Psalm 102:15 and Isaiah 59:19, the glory of YHWH even stands in parallelism with his person or his name. In the Old Testament, the *kabod* YHWH ("glory of the LORD") is what comes to light from God when he manifests himself in an exceptionally impressive way.[61] This can be in a thunderstorm, as is suggested by Psalms 29 and 94. In Exodus 24:15-16, the glory of God is like a consuming fire in a cloud on the mountain (cf. 19:16). Though the expression is not mentioned in Judges 5:4-5, we hear here of God's magnificent appearance, which is accompanied by a trembling earth, clouds from which the rain is gushing, and quaking mountains. In Ezekiel 1, God's glory appears in a storm, a cloud, in fire, lightning, and the sound of roaring water. Deuteronomy 33:2 says, "The LORD came from Sinai and dawned from Seir upon us; he shone forth from Mount Paran; he came from the ten thousands of holy ones, with flaming fire at his right hand." Habakkuk 3:3-6 speaks even more strongly, "His splendor covered the heavens, and the earth was full of his praise. His brightness was like the light; rays flashed from his hand; and there he veiled his power. Before him went pestilence, and plague followed at his heels. He stood and measured the earth; he looked and shook the nations; then the eternal mountains were scattered; the everlasting hills sank

---

61. Cf. *TDNT* 2, 238-39.

God's Attributes: (Spiritive Modalities)

low. His were the everlasting ways."

Of course, these things never imply that the thunderstorm, the flaming fire, the water currents, and so on, *are* the glory of the YHWH. His glory can never be equated with any natural phenomenon. On the contrary, at other occasions, God's glory manifests itself *not* in a strong wind, an earthquake, or a fire, but in "the sound of a low whisper" (1 Kings 19:11-12). In all situations described, the natural phenomena are only of an outward, accompanying nature, according to God's own sovereign choice.

8.8.2 Goodness and Beauty

In Exodus 33:18-19, the glory of YHWH manifests itself in his *tob* (or *tov*), "goodness," a word that can mean "splendor" here (GNT) (cf. *tob* in Exod. 2:2; Judg. 15:2; 1 Sam. 16:12; 1 Kings 1:6; Dan. 1:4). Another word with this meaning is *no-ᶜam*, which is used for God in Psalm 27:4 and 90:17. A suggestion of God's beauty is given in Exodus 24:10 in the collateral phenomenon of "a pavement of sapphire stone" under God's feet, "like the very heaven for clearness."

Already Augustine liked to speak of the *pulchritudo Dei* ("beauty of God"); he called God the highest beauty because in his being there is absolute unity, measure and order.[62] In brief, God is absolute harmony, this term being in our creational reality a good description of the kernel of the aesthetic modality.

The fact that God's glory or beauty is linked with heaven is also clear from Psalm 19:1, "The *heavens* declare the glory of God." In particular it is linked with the "meteorological" phenomenon of the cloud, which first rested on Mount Sinai (Exod. 24:15-17), then on the tent of meeting (40:34-35), and especially between the cherubim on the mercy-seat (Num. 7:89; 2 Sam. 6:2; Ps. 80:1). The way the prophet Ezekiel speaks of the glory of YHWH also reminds us of the pillar of the cloud

---

62. De ordine I.26; II.51; De beata vita 34; Contra Academicos II.9; cf. Bavinck (*RD* 2, 224–25).

(Ezek. 10:4, 18; 11:22-23; 43:2-5). He had the privilege of contemplating God's beauty in a very special way: "Above the likeness of a throne was a likeness with a human appearance. And upward from what had the appearance of his waist I saw as it were gleaming metal, like the appearance of fire enclosed all around. And downward from what had the appearance of his waist I saw as it were the appearance of fire, and there was brightness around him. Like the appearance of the bow that is in the cloud on the day of rain, so was the appearance of the brightness all around. Such was the appearance of the likeness of the glory of the LORD [*kabod* YHWH]" (1:26b-28; also cf. Dan. 7:9).

Isaiah speaks of the glory of YHWH as a light that comes to the fore like the sun at morning dawn (Isa. 58:8; 60:1-2; cf. Mal. 4:2, "sun of righteousness"). In the New Testament, this image of the sun returns three times with regard to Christ: Matthew says that Jesus "was transfigured before them [i.e., the disciples], and his face shone like the sun" (17:2). Paul says, "I saw on the way a light from heaven, brighter than the sun, that shone around me" (Acts 26:13). And John says that "his [i.e., Jesus'] face was like the sun shining in full strength" (Rev. 1:16).

8.8.3 Glory and Light

The technical term for "glory" is Greek *doxa*, here in the unique meaning—not known in secular Greek (though found in the writings of Flavius Josephus)—of "shining," with regard to God more specifically "divine and heavenly shining," God's "splendor," "glow" or "lustre." German theologian Gerhard Kittel (d. 1948) even spoke of God's "(mode of) being"; glory constitutes his essence.[63] *Doxa* comes from *dokeo*, "to seem" (cf. the term "Docetism") or "to shine."[64] The word occurs many times in the New Testament; I limit myself to some ex-

---

63. *TDNT* 2, 237, 247.
64. Interestingly, German scheinen and Dutch schijnen mean both "to shine" and "to seem."

amples thought to be helpful.[65]

Of primary importance are the associations with light, mentioned before: "… the glory of that light" (of the appearance of the glorified Jesus; Acts 22:11 KJV etc.). In Revelation 21:23, it is the glory of God that gives "light" to the new Jerusalem, and its "lamp" is the Lamb. In Hebrews 1:3 the Son is the "radiance" of the glory of God. In 2 Peter 1:17, the "Majestic Glory" is that of the "bright cloud" in Matthew 17:5, reminding us of the pillar of the cloud and the pillar of fire in the Old Testament (Exod. 13:21–22; 14:24; Num.14:14; Neh. 9:12, 19). In Revelation 15:8 the heavenly temple is filled with "smoke from the glory of God and from his power." This is the smoke of the judgment that will be poured out on the earth by (and for) the glory of God (cf. Rev. 9:2; 14:11; Ps. 18:7–9; Isa. 6:3-4), but also reminds us of the cloud that filled the tabernacle (Exod. 40:34–35) and the temple (1 Kings 8:10–11).

As explained before, "light" is the physical retrocipation in the aesthetic modality, just like power is another physical retrocipation in this modality (cf. John 2:11; Rom. 6:4; Col. 1:11, where glory and power closely belong together). A third physical retrocipation is found in the fact that Hebrew *kabod*, "glory," literally means "weight." Paul seems to allude to this in 2 Corinthians 4:17, "For this *light* momentary affliction is preparing for us an eternal *weight* of glory beyond all comparison." The original meaning of *doxa* is "opinion" (cf. the related term *dogma*; *dokeo* suggests here, "it seems to me that…"). This aspect of "opinion" involves a logical retrocipation within the aesthetic modality.

Many have been the speculations about the glory of God.[66] Rabbinical tradition saw the *Kabod* YHWH as a *created*, visible radiation, a "body of light," through which God made known his presence within creation.[67] This idea was adopted by theosophy (Jakob Boehme). In 1493, the Greek-Orthodox Church

---

65. Also cf. Bauer (1971, 403–04).
66. Bavinck (*RD* 2, 223–24).
67. Cf. Scholem (1976, 251–73).

accepted the doctrine of an uncreated, divine light, distinct from God's being, without explaining how something can be uncreated without belonging to the being of God. Early Lutheran theology speculated about the question whether God is light in a factual or in a figurative sense—a consequence of not distinguishing between using the term "light" as a concept or as an idea. God *is* light (1 John 1:5), even though we can approximate that which is God only in creaturely terms—physical light—which we use, however, not as concepts but as idea. How "close" the idea of the literal physical light is can be seen in Psalm 104:1-2, where we read that God covers himself with light as with a garment.

8.8.4 Names of God

Several times God is called the "God of glory" (Ps. 29:3; also in Acts 7:2, where it is the "God of glory" who appears to Abram; 2 Thess. 1:9 speaks of the "presence of the Lord" and of the "glory of his might"). Such a designation underscores the fact that glory constitutes God's being insofar as he actually displays his being. God is "the most beautiful [matter]" (*das Schönste*, a neuter, not a masculine term), as a hymn by the German Pietist Paul Gerhardt (d. 1676) tells us, even though Emil Brunner could hardly appreciate this notion.[68]

Dutch theologian Ben Wentsel put special emphasis on the beauty of God, and pleaded for a corresponding aesthetic of the liturgy.[69] British songwriter Tim Hughes wrote the song "Beautiful One"; verse 2 says, "Powerful, so powerful, Your glory fills the skies, Your mighty works displayed for all to see. The beauty of Your majesty awakes my heart to sing. How marvelous, how wonderful You are." And the chorus says, "Beautiful One I love, beautiful One I adore, beautiful One, my soul must sing."

---

68. Brunner (1950, 313–14).
69. Wentsel (1987, 464–67).

8.9 The Aesthetic Modality: God's Peace
8.9.1 Harmony, Order, Rest

Above, I have claimed that, presumably, the kernel of the aesthetic modality can be expressed most adequately in the term "harmony." The notion of harmony is clearly encountered in the notion of peace (Heb. *shalom*, Gk. *eirēnē*, Lat. *pax*). Other such elements in the notion of peace are order and rest. God is the God of piece (see next section), of harmony, of order and rest, and therefore he is the enemy of disorder, that is, everything that is disobedient to his law-order (1 Cor. 14:33, "God is not a God of confusion [or, disorder] but of peace"). The "rest" that Jesus grants to the people who follow him (Matt. 11:29) hardly differs materially from "my peace" that he gives to his own as his personal inheritance (John 14:27), of from the "peace of Christ" that the apostle Paul refers to as the peace that ought to rule the believers' hearts (Col. 3:15).

True peace, harmony, rest and order are elements of God's being. Gideon built an altar that he called YHWH *Shalom*, "The LORD is peace"(Judg. 6:24). Though the Hebrew does not contain a copula, the description expresses quite well one of God's attributes. The same is true for the appellation "God of peace," the God characterized by peace (see §8.9.2). Only once, God is called the God of joy (Ps.43:4 GNV etc.), or "God, my exceeding joy" (ESV), and this in a very personal sense ("*my* joy"), but he is called the "God of peace," in a general sense, many times.

8.9.2 Names of God

The designation "God of peace," which can almost be considered to be a name of God, occurs several times in the New Testament (Rom. 15:33; 16:20; 1 Cor. 14:33; Phil. 4:9; 1 Thess. 5:23; 2 Thess. 3:16; Heb. 13:20; "the God of love and peace," 2 Cor. 13:11). It means both the God who is characterized by peace and the God who grants peace. He *is* peace, and he *gives* peace.

Of aesthetic significance is also the fact that God is

"designer and builder" (Heb. 11:10), although Greek *technitēs* also clearly contains a historical-formative element (cf. the English word "technician"); the *technitēs* of Acts 19:24 is both artist and artisan.

8.10 The Juridical Modality
8.10.1 The Righteous God

The fact that God is the righteous God and that his acts are righteous is testified in the Bible many times (see "righteous" as an adjective or predicate with God, e.g., in Exod. 9:27; Deut. 32:4; 2 Chron. 12:6; Ezra 9:15; Neh. 9:8; Ps. 7:9, 11; 11:7; 112:4; 116:5; 119:137; 129:4; 145:17; Lam. 1:18; Dan. 9:14; Zeph. 3:5; John 17:25; Rom. 3:26; 2 Tim. 4:8; 1 John 1:9; 2:29; 3:7; Rev. 16:5). God is "the One who is infallibly consistent in the normative self-determination of His own nature, and who maintains unswerving faithfulness in the fulfilment of His promises and covenant agreements."[70] This description implies using as ideas several analogies within the juridical modality, such as kinematic ("consistent"), historical-formative ("self-determination") and pistical analogies ("faithfulness"). When Swiss theologian Gottlob Schrenk (d. 1965) spoke here of God's "normative self-determination," it was in the sense that God himself is the norm, not that God would stand under a norm "outside" himself.[71] If Hebrew *tsedeq* describes someone's state as agreeing with a law,[72] it is of special importance to mention this since God is beyond all laws and norms. If anywhere, we see here how necessary it is to emphasize that, even though we can speak of God and his righteousness only in creaturely terms, these terms must never be applied as concepts but as ideas. Each conceptual usage fails here since God's judicial acts cannot be measured according to any *dikē*, any judicial norm, except the supra-normative *dikē* of his own being.

---

70. *TDNT* 2:185.
71. Ibid., 195.
72. Bavinck (*RD* 2, 189–90).

It is important to comprehend the biblical connection between God's righteousness and his covenantal faithfulness, as we just found it in Schrenk's description. The reason is that already late Judaism[73] and the Apologists (Justin Martyr) viewed God's righteousness too one-sidedly as "distributive" righteousness.[74] This is the justice in the Aristotelian sense of a God who, as Supreme Judge, "distributes" to every human what he or she deserves. The same view is also found in Roman law as the *ius suum cuique tribuendi* (distributing to each one his right, as the Roman lawyer Ulpian called it around AD 200); it has heavily influenced the theology of Augustine and the Scholastics. Thomas Aquinas claimed that God's righteousness can be known in that he gives to each person what he deserves.[75]

It was this view that formed a tremendous stumbling block for the young Martin Luther.[76] The Reformation began with a man who discovered that God's righteousness does *not* mean that God only attributes to each human what he or she deserves, but that it primarily entails that God acts righteously according to the promises of the gospel.[77] However, early Protestant theology, for instance German theologian Johann Gerhardt (d. 1676), quickly re-introduced the ancient view. Yet, even some of the church fathers, such as Ambrosiaster (fourth century), discerned the proper key to especially the meaning of God's righteousness in Romans. In Greek *dikaiosynē theou* (e.g., 1:17), the genitive is not a *genitivus auctoris*, as Augustine thought (a righteousness coming from God, but possessed by humans); rather it is a subjective genitive. That is, it is God's *own* righteousness that is revealed in the gospel, a merciful righteousness on behalf of which God fulfills his promises toward the sinner on the basis of Christ's redemp-

---

73. Cf. Eichrodt (1962, 126).
74. Cf. Pannenberg (1971, 339; 1988, 469–70).
75. *Summa Theologiae* II–II qu. 61.
76. See extensively, *EDR* 6:chapter 7; and Vol. III/2 in this series.
77. Berkhof (1986, 130–33); Van Genderen (2008, 184–87).

tive work (cf. 3:26, God is "just [righteous]" when he "justifies [makes righteous]" the believing sinner; 1 John 1:9, God is "just" when he forgives the believers' sins).[78]

"Righteousness" entails a relationship: a person can be righteous toward himself but the point is especially being righteous toward others.[79] This is the social retrocipation within the juridical modality. Just as a person is righteous when he meets certain claims that another person has on him on behalf of their relationship, God's righteousness, too, is primarily his covenantal rule in fellowship with his people.[80] But this is not the whole story. If righteousness entails only God's righteous attitude toward his creatures, in what sense can we call his righteousness a genuine attribute of his, that is, an attribute that he already possessed before the world existed, when there was not yet any question of creatures? I see two answers:

(a) In past eternity, there was absolute righteousness in the relationship between the three persons of the Trinity in giving to each other what was right (proper, reasonable) on the point of love, respect, affection, appreciation. Each of the three did "justice" to the other two.

(b) In past eternity, God's righteousness also came to expression in his counsel and promises. God is faithful not only in keeping his promises but also in granting them. Titus 1:2 speaks of such a promise, namely, that of eternal life (cf. 1 John 2:25). Of course, God's promises from before the foundation of the world are gifts of his pure grace (cf. 2 Tim. 1:9), but also of his righteousness, namely, as that which God "owes" (see next section) to the redemptive work of Christ, accomplished in the fullness of time (cf. Gal. 4:4), but predestined — and therefore perfectly certain (cf. Rev. 13:8b) — before the

---

78. Barth (*CD* II/1, 422–57); Brunner (1950, 321–22); Althaus (1952, 283–85); Weber (1981, 473–84); Wentsel 987, 414–28); see further extensively, *EDR* 6, chapter7; Vol. III/2.
79. Cf. Eichrodt (1962, 121–23).
80. *TDNT* 2, 195.

foundation of the world (cf. 1 Pet. 1:20).

8.10.2 The Justifying God

The legal-juridical element in God's righteousness clearly comes to light in Bible passages such as Job 9:14–15, 19–20, 32–33 and Isaiah 43:9, 26; 50:8–9, where the situation of the law court is depicted. God is the Judge, who executes judgment, and in doing so condemns the one and acquits the other (see §8.10.3). As such, he is the perfect example for all earthly judges (Exod. 23:7; Deut. 1:17). Besides this judicial usage, "righteousness" in a more general sense is being "right" in a dispute; as people say, "he was right in the matter" (Gen. 30:33; 38:26; 1 Sam. 24:18). This is true of God in the universal and absolute sense. He is always "right," always has justice on his side (he is "justified" or "vindicated" in all that he does). This is true, both when he condemns the wicked and unrepentant sinners (justice *in malam partem*) and when he saves repentant and believing sinners (justice in bonam partem). Herman Bavinck gave many biblical examples of this,[81] which are important over against the many modernist theologians who reject the notion of a retributive divine justice.[82]

This righteousness of God is the particular subject of Paul's doctrine of justification.[83] I only repeat here that Greek *dikaiosynē theou* is a possessive or subjective genitive—it involves God's own righteousness—as is underscored by the Old Testament examples, especially in Isaiah, where God's righteousness manifests itself in his redemptive actions (Ps. 98:1–2; Isa. 46:13; 51:5–8; 54:17; 56:1; 61:10–11; 62:1). Thus, it is not the righteousness that proceeds from God to humans (e.g., Frederick B. Meyer), or the *human* righteousness that is approved of God (e.g., John Calvin), or that is valid before God (Friedrich A. Philippi).[84] It is righteousness as an attri-

---

81. Bavinck (*RD* 2, 192–94).
82. Ritschl (1890), and many after him.
83. See extensively, *EDR* 6, chapters 7–10; Vol. III/2.
84. See Murray (1968,I, 30).

bute of God's being. Romans 1:17 refers to something of *God himself* that is revealed.

In opposition to Scottish-American theologian John Murray (d. 1975),[85] I wish to emphasize the juridical element in this "righteousness" (although this is certainly not the only element that counts in Paul's doctrine of justification). God is righteous when he redeems repentant and believing sinners—not only bestowing love, not only gracious and merciful. He redeems because he is love, but also because he judicially "owes" this redemption to the redemptive work of Christ. In God's righteousness, the point of the matter is that God is *righteous* (not only gracious) when he justifies (declares righteous) the one who has faith in Jesus (Rom. 3:26). "If we confess our sins, he is faithful and *just* [*righteous*, not only gracious] to forgive us our sins and to cleanse us from all unrighteousness" (1 John 1:9). "Dikaiosynē is an expression of grace, but of such a kind that the justice of God is also displayed."[86]

However, we must realize again that we are not dealing here with forensic *concepts*. Otherwise, an expression such as "judicially obliged" could be easily misunderstood, as if God would stand under a law that he would have to obey. But this "obligation" of God is not imposed upon him from "above"; implicitly, he took it upon himself when he did not spare his own Son but gave him up for people into death (Rom. 8:32). We are dealing here with forensic terms used as ideas, especially over against the conceptual approach of Anselm's forensic doctrine of justification. It is only in emphasizing this idea-like use of forensic terms that we can be kept from the hopeless discussion between a more "forensic" and a more "ethical" doctrine of justification.

If we, similarly, use the term "law" too much as a judicial concept, we understand the entire law-order under which God has placed his creation[87] too one-sidedly as a judicial order.

---

85. Ibid.
86. *TDNT* 2, 204.
87. See extensively, Volume I/1, chapter 3.

God's Attributes: (Spiritive Modalities)

Thus, Herman Bavinck spoke indeed of a "judicial order,"[88] though warning himself that not too many divine attributes should be put under the heading of God's righteousness.[89] All the other elements in this law-order, which we can approximate by using as ideas other modally qualified terms, are then easily neglected. Conversely, the judicial and the ethical should not be identified, as Bavinck did to some extent by calling the former a "piece" of the latter.[90] As far as this matter is concerned, a careful distinction between the various irreducible modalities (and their modal analogies), and using modal terms not as concepts but as ideas, can keep us from many dangers.

8.10.3 Names of God

We saw that, in the Bible, God is often called a "Judge" (e.g., Gen. 18:25; Ps. 75:7; 94:2; James 4:12; cf. the creaturely use in Deut. 25:1). Daniel 7:9–10 says, "As I looked, thrones were placed, and the Ancient of Days took his seat; his clothing was white as snow, and the hair of his head like pure wool; his throne was fiery flames; its wheels were burning fire. A stream of fire issued and came out from before him; a thousand thousands served him, and ten thousand times ten thousand stood before him; the court sat in judgment, and the books were opened." We can *add* to God being Judge the fact that he is also Lawgiver (James 4:12; Isa. 33:22; cf. 51:4).[91]

Some titles contain both a historical-formative and a juridical element (see §8.3), such as King (an Oriental king was both supreme ruler and supreme judge), Master (Heb. *baʿal*, Hos. 2:17; Gk. *despotēs*, Acts 4:24; Rev. 6:10), Lord (Gk. *kyrios*, if used in the sense of Owner, e.g., Matt. 9:38; Luke 10:2), and the only Sovereign (*monos dynastēs*, 1 Tim. 6:15). A special juridical name is YHWH *Tsidqēnu*, "the LORD our righteous-

---

88. Bavinck (*RD* 2, 196).
89. Ibid., 195–96.
90. Ibid., 197.
91. "Lawgiver" in Gen. 49:10; Num. 21:18; Ps. 60:7; 108:8 (KJV etc.) is "ruler's staff" or "scepter."

ness" (Jer. 23:6; 33:16).

It is remarkable that so many people in the New Testament called Jesus "the Righteous One": Pilate's wife and Pilate himself (Matt. 27:19, 24 KJV etc.), Peter in Acts 3:14 and in 1 Peter 3:18; Stephen in Acts 7:52; Ananias in 22:14; John in 1 John 2:1; according to some, also James in James 5:6 (notice the capital letters in DRA, EHV and NTE).

8.11 The Ethical Modality: God's Love
8.11.1 Love from Eternity

All God's attributes are necessarily equally important and to the same extent expressions of God's being; this is the consequence of the "economic" balance of God's perfection (§8.7.1). Nonetheless, his moral attributes, God's love in particular, have always drawn special attention. German philosopher Ludwig Feuerbach was afraid that, if, in the phrase "God is love," love is viewed as a predicate and not as subject, God might be viewed as a subject in itself, apart from his love.[92] The Danish theologian Regin Prenter (d. 1990) stated that 1 John 4:8 and 16 ("God is love") point not only to an attribute of God but to his being or essence, which is love.[93] However, both views contain a false dilemma. God's being can never be considered apart from his attributes; his being *is* his attributes, and his attributes are his being. The underlying misunderstanding is the traditional, false distinction of ancient substantialism between *substantia* and *accidentia* (see §§4.4.2 and 4.5.1). Indeed, God *is* love; but God is also righteousness (cf. Jer. 23:6; 33:16), he *is* his own glory (cf. "God of glory"), he *is* peace (cf. "God of peace"), and so on, without these attributes being identical.

What immediately strikes us in God's ethical attributes is their multiplicity. We have to do not only with God's love, but also with his goodness, his grace, his mercy, his patience, his loving-kindness, and even with the ethical element in his

---
92. See the discussion by Jüngel (1976, 430–53).
93. Prenter (1971), quoted by Pannenberg (1988, 458–59).

holiness and his wisdom. However, this multiplicity is somewhat misleading. First, love and goodness are closely related: God's love manifests itself in his benevolence and well-doing ("well" is the adverbial form of "good", and bene- is the same in Latin: *benevolentia*, *benefactor*). Second, grace, mercy, patience and loving-kindness are mainly the way in which God's love manifests itself within time for people, especially after the Fall.[94] Third, where love manifests itself in the desire to do good, holiness manifests itself in the desire to avoid evil. God's love toward doing good finds its counter-balance in his hate toward evil.

"Love" and its derivations (from the Heb. root '-h-b and Gk. *agap*-) contain a strongly sensitive element (warm affection; a sensitive retrocipation within the ethical modality), as is illustrated, for instance, by Jeremiah 31:20 (KJV), "my bowels are troubled for him" (others, "my heart longs [or yearns] for him"). But more important is the element of self-surrendering, a selfless attitude that is fully taken up with the desire of the other's well-being (cf. Luke 19:18, 34); *how* fully is indicated by Deuteronomy 6:5; 13:3b, 4 (cf. Mark 12:30, "with all your heart and with all your soul and with all your mind and with all your strength").[95] Love is primarily love for people, although, in a weaker sense, there is also love for animals, things and acts. But even love for what is good (Amos 5:15) is in fact the love to do good to others, or love for what is good *for* others, or love for good people. God is love, that is, he loves. This is the eternal love between the divine persons within the Trinity (John 17:24b; cf. Mark 12:6, and conversely John 14:31), and subsequently for creatures.

8.11.2 Types of Love

There is a "circle" of love in which divine persons dwell eternally, and into which believers enter to dwell there (John 15:9–10; 17:24; 1 John 4:16). In the words of Paul

---

94. Cf. Wentsel (1987, 395–408).
95. *TDNT* 1, 22v.

Althaus,[96] "... It means that the eternal love between Father, Son and Spirit is the ultimate reality. God's loving is from eternity loving in itself, and yet no self-love... The confession of the eternal essential Trinity offers the safe boundary against all pantheism. God is eternally love. If we confess this, but refuse to acknowledge the Trinity, we need [in our thinking] an eternal world as object of God's eternal love." That is, if, in past eternity, there were no other divine persons to love, an eternal world was necessary that God *could* love—otherwise he could not have been love since eternity.

The eternal love between the divine persons is the same love that God had for the patriarchs (Deut. 4:37; 10:15), for the people of Israel (7:7-8, 13; 23:5; 2 Chron. 2:11; Isa. 43:4; 63:9; Jer. 31:3; Hos. 11:1, 4; 14:4; Zeph. 3:17; Mal. 1:2-3), for the tribe of Benjamin (Deut. 33:12), for Solomon (2 Sam. 12:24-25; Neh. 13:26), for Persian king Cyrus (Isa. 48:14), for individual believers (Ps. 127:2; John 14:23; 16:27; 17:23; Rom. 5:5, 8; 8:39; 2 Thess. 2:13, 16, etc.), for the righteous one (Ps. 146:8; Prov. 15:9), for the sojourner (Deut. 10:18), for the world (John 3:16; 1 John 4:9-10), and so forth.

In our immanent societal relationships, we are familiar with love in many forms: parental love, matrimonial love, patriotic love, and so on. Various ones of these forms are used in the Bible as ideas to approximate God's love. His love is fatherly (Deut. 1:31; Ps. 103:13; Hos. 11:1-4), and in a sense "even" motherly (Isa. 49:15; 66:13; Luke 13:34); this love resists punishing a beloved child, even if this is necessary for its education (Prov. 3:12; Hos. 11:8-9; Heb. 12:5-11).

God's love for his people is also that of a bridegroom and a husband (Isa. 54:5-8; 61:10; 62:4-5; Ezek. 16:8; Hos. 2:15, 18-19; 3:1; cf. Song 8:6-7); it is also a suffering love if this matrimonial love is not answered (Isa. 50:1-2; Jer. 3:6-13; Ezek. 16:15-58; Hos. 2:1-13). The metaphor is limited insofar as all religious eroticism in this matrimonial love is lacking

---

96. Althaus (1952, 694); also cf. Pannenberg (1988, 456–66).

(which is true only if one does not wish to see in the Song of Songs [also] the relationship between God or Christ and his people[97]):[98] "The love of God for Israel (Dt. 7:13) is not impulse but will; the love for God and the neighbour demanded of the Israelite (Dt. 6:5; Lv. 19:18) is not intoxication but act." The notion of the sovereign "will" (cf. Hos. 14:4, "I will love them freely") is the historical-formative element in God's love; the notion of obedience is the judicial element in the human love for God (that is, we have to do here with corresponding retrocipations within the ethical modality).

Even the element of "patriotic love" is not absent in God; think of his love for Mount Zion and the city of Jerusalem with its gates (Ps. 78:68; 87:2). The Holy Land is *his* land (Lev. 25:23), and the mountains in it are *his* mountains (Isa. 14:25; 49:11; 65:9; Ezek. 38:21).

8.11.3 Agapē

Already in the ancient Greek world, the verb *agapaō* "relates for the most part to the love of God, to the love of the higher lifting up the lower, elevating the lower above others."[99] Thus, it is "condescending love," which in John's Gospel and in his first Epistle assumes the character of "a heavenly reality which in some sense descends from stage to stage into this world."[100] Therefore, the New Testament never uses the word *erōs* or derivations of it, which "seeks in others the fulfilment of its own life's hunger."[101] It does use *philia* and its derivations, which in the ancient world "signifies for the most part the inclination or solicitous love of gods for men, or friends for friends."[102] However, this word is seldom used for the love of God (John 5:20; 16:27a; *philanthrōpia* in Titus 3:4). Thus, *agapē* and its derivations are by far the best Greek expression of the

---

97. Cf. Ouweneel (1973).
98. *TDNT* 1, 38.
99. *TDNT* 1, 37, with reference to Plotinus, Enneads V.1.6.
100. *TDNT* 1, 53.
101. Ibid., 37; also see Nygren (1930–37); Barth (*CD* IV,2, §68,1).
102. Ibid., 36.

divine love, just like in Latin *caritas* and dilectio in contrast with *amor*. This is the love that is first present in God himself, and is subsequently reflected in the believers.

It has often drawn people's attention that, originally, *agapē* was an extremely rare word in the ancient world, and moreover a weak, rather colorless word. It was only through Hebrew *ahabah* that it received in the Septuagint the rich and strong significance that we know from the New Testament.[103]

The agapē is the love that loves because it *is* love, cannot do anything else than love, and does so without obligation, undeservedly, freely (cf., e.g., John 3:16; Rom. 5:8; 9:25; 1 John 4:9–10). It does not love because of the lovability of its object, but on grounds that it finds purely in itself. It is no inclination to the lovable, as in the case of natural-human love, but it creates the lovable because of love.[104] In the words of Martin Luther:[105] *Ideo enim peccatores sunt pulchri quia diliguntur, non ideo diliguntur quia sunt pulchri* ("For sinners are beautiful because they are loved, they are not loved because they are beautiful").

When Herman Bavinck speaks of God's "moral attributes," he takes his starting-point in God's goodness because this can be "attributed" to God in an absolute sense. God is goodness in himself, and then, secondarily, good for others, which is expressed in loving-kindness, mercy, grace and love. Yet, God is never called "goodness" in the Bible, but he *is* called "love" (1 John 4:8, 16). And God *is* love in himself, not only in relation to others, because love is the essence of the relationships between divine persons.[106]

Therefore, I would rather take my starting-point in God's *love*, while viewing his goodness as one of the characteris-

---

103. Ibid., 36,39; also cf. Brunner (1950, 209–13). Because of the vowels and the central guttural and labial, *agapē* and *ahabah* exhibit a remarkable similarity, which must be accidental.
104. Cf. Althaus (1952, 279).
105. WA 1, 365.
106. Cf. Lewis (1944, 25–26); see extensively, Lewis (1960).

tics of it. Moreover, to speak of God as the *summum bonum* ("supreme good"), as does for instance Augustine,[107] the *bonum in se* ('what is good in itself"), or the *bonitas metaphysica* ("metaphysical goodness"), tastes too much like pagan-Greek thought; only compare the Platonic notion of God as the idea of the good. In the Bible, God is seldom called "good" in some absolute sense (Matt. 19:17 and parallels; Gk. *agathos*). Only once the Greek kalos is used for divine persons, namely, for the Man Christ, in the expression "good shepherd" (John 10:11, 14). This does not mean "lovely" shepherd in some idyllic sense, but the "true, genuine" shepherd in contrast with the many false ones.[108] Also compare the "honourable [*kalos*] name" of God in James 2:7.

Bavinck discerned in God's "absolute goodness" in particular—what I call—the economic element of the sufficiency and perfection, and the sensitive notion of bliss. However, in my view it is obvious that God's goodness in the Bible almost always refers to his goodness toward creatures (Num. 10:32; 1 Chron. 16:34; 2 Chron. 5:13; Ps. 25:7; 34:8; 54:6; 65:11; 69:16; 73:1; 86:5; 100:5; 106:1; 107:1; 109:21; 118:1, 29; 119:68; 135:3; 136:1; 145:9; Jer. 33:11; Lam. 3:25; Nahum 1:7; Acts 14:17, etc.).

8.11.4 Names of God

The divine names of which one might think here—Father, Bridegroom, Husband—have all been dealt with above. In 1 John 4:8 and 16, "Love" is almost a name of God because it is not viewed here simply as a predicate that can be attributed to God ("God is "loving, affectionate"") but as the expression of his being: he is altogether love, he is love all over.

8.12 The Ethical Modality: Other Features
8.12.1 Lovingkindness, Patience, Mercy

A second characteristic of God's love, besides his goodness, is his "loving-kindness," Hebrew *chesed* (ground-meaning:

---

107. *De Trinitate* VIII.3; Enarrationes in Psalmos 26; De doctrina christiana I.7.
108. *TDNT* 3, 548.

solidarity, trustworthiness, reliability, loyalty; in the ESV rendered as "steadfast love"; others, "mercy, grace/graciousness, compassion, faithful love, loyal love"). The word occurs very frequently in the Old Testament; an example is the beautiful expression *ki le^colam chasdo*, "for his *chesed* endures forever" (many times, e.g., 26 times in Ps. 136). Because the Bible also speaks of the *chesed* of humans ("piety, godliness"; cf. the noun *chasid*, the "godly one"), the question comes up whether a rendering of *chesed* could be found that is true for both God and humans. Perhaps, the term is "loyalty," especially "covenantal loyalty": God is *chesed* because he always remains loyal to his covenantal promises; a human being is *chesed* if he remains loyal to the covenant in the sense of obeying its commandments.

The Greek parallel of *chesed* is *chrēstotēs*, "kindness, goodness, generosity, bountifulness" (with respect to God, see Rom. 2:4; 11:22; 2 Cor. 10:1; Eph. 2:7; Titus 3:4).

A third characteristic of God's love is his "patience" (from Latin *patior*, "to endure"; cf. "endurance"). The Hebrew term is quite different: *erek affim* literally means "making one's anger long," that is, postponing the outbreak of this anger; in many translations: "slow to anger" (ASV, WEB etc.), "not easily angered" (GNB) (see Exod. 34:6; Num. 4:18; Neh. 9:17; Ps. 86:15; 103:8; 145:8; Joel 2:13; Jonah 4:2; Nahum 1:3). The Greek parallel is *makrothymia*, "longsuffering," literally: "being great of mind" (Rom. 2:4; 9:22; 1 Tim. 1:16; 1 Pet. 3:20; 2 Pet. 3:1).[109]

Remarkably, this not only means that he postpones his anger but also that he can postpone his love for his chosen ones: "Will not God give justice to his elect, who cry to him day and night? Will he delay long over them?" Others read, "... though he bear long with them," or "suffer for them," or, "Is he slow to help them?" and so on. The opinions on this phrase differ greatly.[110]

---

109. Barth (*CD* II,1, 457–75).
110. Cf. Geldenhuys (1951, 448); Green (1997, 642).

A fourth characteristic of God's love is his "mercy" (pity, compassion); this is God's goodness as it expresses itself toward those who are in miserable circumstances (cf. Lat. *miseria* and *misericordia*, "mercy").[111] It is remarkable to see how freely the Bible uses anthropopathisms here. Hebrew *rachum* comes from *rechem*, "womb," just like Greek *splangchna*, "compassion," literally means "bowels" (cf. §7.9.1). Similarly, *misericordia* comes from *cor*, "heart" (cf. Jer. 31:20; Hos. 11:8). These terms, together with *eleos* and *oiktirmos* and their related forms, occur many times in the Bible. Mercy is a typical feature of God's love that presupposes a certain (desperate) condition of humans, and therefore is less a genuine attribute of God's own being than his loving-kindness, and also his grace.

8.12.2 Grace

Grace, this fifth characteristic of God's love (Heb. *chen*, Gk. *charis*, and related forms), often presupposes people who, through sin, have forfeited all right to blessing. This is the common way many Christians speak of grace. Yet, "grace" does not always presuppose sin.[112] Even without the Fall, humans would at all times for each blessing have depended on God's grace, or favor, since they have no rights of themselves. They freely receive everything; they deserve nothing.

Seen from this viewpoint, one might think that grace is an attribute of God because it does not necessarily presuppose sin. Yet, God's loving-kindness, mercy and grace always involve a relationship to other persons, whereas they can hardly be used to describe the relationship between divine persons within the Trinity (at best in the sense of benevolence). Therefore, we can call love and goodness (aspects of) God's being, whereas his loving-kindness, mercy and grace seem to be the effects of his being upon humanity, according to its condition and needs. Thus, it is understandable that, in

---

111. Barth (*CD* II,1, 413–22).
112. Cf. Ibid., 394–402.

traditional theology, grace was not primarily viewed as a divine virtue. Rather, theologians spoke of God's benevolent *acts* of grace, which therefore were not dealt with in the doctrine of God (*theologia propria, locus de Deo*) but in soteriology (the doctrine of salvation).[113] This is still the case in Roman Catholic dogmatics.[114]

8.12.3 Names of God

Otto Weber has emphasized that the name Father—not so much in the sense of the eternal Father of the eternal Son but the Father who, already in the Old Testament, takes care of the people that he has generated (Deut. 32:6, 18; 2 Sam. 7:14; Ps. 103:13; Isa. 63:16; 64:8; Jer. 3:4, 19; 31:9; Mal. 2:10; cf. Exod. 4:22; Deut. 1:31; 8:5)—is the summary of God's love, grace, mercy, faithfulness, and loving-kindness.[115] A genuine father is not only the one who generates the child, but who also protects it, takes care of it, and educates it.

An expression that comes close to a name for God is "Father of mercies" (Gk. *patēr tōn oiktirmōn*) in 2 Corinthians 1:3. This is as much as the "merciful Father" or the Father characterized by, or forming the source of, mercy. It is one of the best-known appellations of Allah in the Koran and Muslim tradition: "Allah, the compassionate, the merciful." The Arabic word is *rachman*, which reminds us of the Hebrew *rechem* (§8.12.1).

8.13 The Ethical Modality: God's Holiness
8.13.1 Is Holiness a Divine Attribute?

As surprised as some may be that God's grace was often not treated as an intrinsic virtue of God, the more surprised may some be that this is also true for God's holiness (or sanctity, Lat. *sanctitas*).[116] Italian-French scholar Peter Lombard (d. ca. 1162) as well as Thomas Aquinas did not mention it as a divine

---

113. Bavinck (*RD* 2, 182).
114. Cf. the comments by Althaus (1952, 280–81) and Weber (1981, 469–73).
115. Weber (1981, 466–68).
116. Bavinck (*RD* 2, 184).

attribute. Protestant theologians often reckoned it to God's perfection, his righteousness, his goodness, his truthfulness, his wisdom, his sovereignty and power, his majesty, and so on, or they viewed it as a purely relational notion, not as an essential quality of God.[117] How hard it is to maintain such a view can be immediately concluded from a Bible passage as Isaiah 6:3, where seraphim praise God as the Thrice Holy — the well-known *Trisagion* — and this returns in the song of the four living creatures in Revelation 4:8. It is even important to emphasize the holiness of God in its very connection with his love because the two are inseparable.[118] Already the Apostolic Fathers seemed to have neglected this because they linked the love of God with the Stoic notion of God's general benevolence. As Clement of Rome wrote (1 Clement 19:3), "Let us behold him in our mind, and let us look with the eyes of our soul at his long-suffering will. Let us note how free from anger he is towards all his creatures." Such a statement could easily be abused to ignore or underestimate God's holiness.

In the twentieth century, thinking about God's holiness was heavily influenced by the famous work written by German theologian Rudolf Otto, in which he described what is divinely holy as *mysterium tremendum* and *fascinans* ("awesome [horrifying, therefore repellent]" and "fascinating [attractive, charming] mystery").[119] To some extent, Karl Barth distanced himself from this by placing the Holy One over against the holy matter as Otto had described it.[120] However, Emil Brunner and Paul Althaus, along the lines mapped out by Otto, used Isaiah 6:3 and other Bible verses to point out that God's holiness is not just one of God's many attributes, which moreover supposedly would be a purely ethical attribute.[121] In this respect, they stood over against the overwhelm-

---

117. Diestel (1859).
118. Cf. Brunner (1950, 196–99); Bloesch (1995, chapter 6).
119. Otto (1958).
120. Barth (*CD* II,1, 405); see extensively, 402–13.
121. Brunner (1950, 161–82); Althaus (1952, 289–92).

ing majority of Roman Catholic and Protestant dogmaticians. They viewed holiness as a reference to God's *essence* proper; according to Althaus actually just like God's glory and bliss. Thus, the Spirit is the *Holy* Spirit, not because holiness is one of many attributes but because the term expresses God's being. What is holy is what is lofty, splendid, shining, beaming, resplendent, majestic, awesome, unfathomable, mysterious, inscrutable—and this in a much broader sense than *morally* inscrutable.

Althaus and Brunner certainly had a point here. Yet I wonder whether this is not simply a problem with *all* so-called attributes (see §6.1.3). Is love, or light, or spirituality just one attribute out of many? God *is* all love, all light, all spirit, but in the very same way he is all holiness, bliss, glory, majestic power, and so on. Yet, his love, his spirituality, his righteousness, his holiness, and so on, do not coincide, although they are never at variance either. Because of this terminological embarrassment, we keep speaking of distinct "attributes." I feel supported in this approach by the fact that the Bible does place God's being "holy" alongside other attributes; see, for instance, John 1:11, 25 ("righteous"; cf. Mark 6:20; Acts 3:14; Rom. 7:12; Eph. 4:24); Revelation 6:10 ("true").

8.13.2 The Holy and Sanctifying God

In the Old Testament, the root *q-d-sh* mainly points to cultic aspects; it involves what is distinct from the secular, severed from all profane usage, put apart for, and dedicated to, God.[122] It is remarkable that this root can also be used for what is dedicated to the false gods, and therefore in fact is very *un*holy. Thus, the term as such does not contain a value judgment: what is consecrated to God *or* to the gods is *q-d-sh*. Thus, the *qadēsh* (femin. *q'dēshah*) is the consecrated temple prostitute, male or female (both in Deut. 23:18).

In the positive sense, a place is called "holy" if the peculiar presence of YHWH is connected with it: the ground

---

[122]. Von Rad (1957, 204–06); *TDNT* 1, 90.

around the burning bush (Exod. 3:5), Gilgal (Josh. 5:15), Jerusalem (Neh. 11:1, 18; Isa. 48:2; 52:1), the location of the temple (Isa. 11:9; 56:7), the temple itself (1 Chron. 29:3; Ps. 5:7; 79:1; 138:2; Isa. 64:10). Because God himself is separated from all that is secular or profane he is holy (Isa. 5:16; 6:3; Hos. 11:9). Where God is manifested, presented or praised in his holiness, he is "hallowed" (sanctified), that is, his holiness (sanctity) is brought to light (Num. 20:12-13; Isa. 5:16; Ezek. 20:41; 28:22, 25; 36:23; 38:16; 39:27; cf. Matt. 6:9; Luke 11:2). Because God is holy, that which expresses his being, his name, is holy (Lev. 20:3; 22:2; 1 Chron. 16:10, 35; Ps. 33:21; 103:1; Ezek. 36:20-23). His Word (Ps. 105:42) and his Spirit (Ps. 51:11; Isa. 63:10-11) are holy because they stand over against all that is creaturely and secular. Isaiah calls God twenty-nine times the "Holy One of Israel," in relation to both judgment and redemption.

Hermann Cremer emphasized that holiness is not primarily a relation from below to above, but from above to below, and must be primarily attributed to God, and subsequently, in a derived sense, also to creatures.[123] Creatures are not holy of themselves, and cannot sanctify themselves. All holiness and sanctification proceed from God. He can sanctify things or persons, that is, set them apart from the profane, but he alone is holy in himself. Also where people "sanctify" things, this is because God told them to; God is and remains the criterion of holiness. It is this very attribute that, in each revelation of God, impresses people with his deity. If God swears by his holiness, it is the same as swearing by himself (Amos 4:2; 6:8). His holiness manifests itself in redemption, consolation, faithfulness, but also in chastisement and punishment.[124]

In the New Testament, the use of Greek *hagios* largely corresponds with that of *q-d-sh* in the Old Testament. God is the "Holy Father" (John 17:11), the "Sovereign Lord, holy and true" (Rev. 6:10). In 1 Peter 1:15-16, God is called holy in line

---
123. Cremer (1917), quoted by Bavinck (*RD* 2, 187).
124. See extensively, Bavinck (*RD* 2, 188–89).

with Leviticus 19:2. Besides this, God is *hosios*, a word that means "holy" too (Rev. 15:4; 16:5; cf. Heb. 7:26), but then, if we follow the Septuagint, as a rendering of Hebrew *chesed*, never of *qadosh*; the word has connotations such as "pure, clean, righteous." Much more clearly than in the Old Testament, the God who is *hagios* is in the New Testament the God of sanctification, the God who is holy and makes holy, who separates humans from the domain of sin and consecrates them to himself.

8.13.3 Names of God

In the Bible, God is sometimes briefly called the "Holy One" (2 Kings 19:22; Job 6:10; Ps. 78:41; 89:18, etc.), in Isaiah in particular also the "Holy One of Israel" (25 times), not only in connection with judgment but also with redemption (41:14; 43:3, 14; 47:4; 48:17; 54:5). The latter is quite important: God redeems his people, not (only) in spite of his holiness but (also) because of his holiness: "I will not execute my burning anger; I will not again destroy Ephraim; *for* I am God and not a man, the Holy One in your midst, and I will not come in wrath" (Hos. 11:9).

Jesus Christ is sometimes called the "Holy One of God" (Mark 1:24; Luke 4:34; John 6:69), or the "Holy and Righteous One" (Acts 3:14), or simply the "Holy One" (1 John 2:20; Rev. 3:7). In Luke 1:35 we find a remarkable neuter, which is hard to render in English: "that Holy Thing" (KJV, ASV, GNV).

Qadosh and *hagios* are both used for the Holy Spirit of God, *qadosh* in Psalm 51:11 and Isaiah 63:10–11, and *hagios* numerous times from Matthew 1:18 to Jude 20.

8.14 The Ethical Modality: God's Wisdom
8.14.1 Moral Aspects of Wisdom

Let us return here once more to God's wisdom (Heb. *chokmah*, Gk. *Sophia*), this time to look at the ethical elements in this term (cf. §8.2.4).[125] There is a logical-analytical (cognitive) element in this wisdom in the sense that God through his divine wisdom has created the world (Prov. 3:19–20; 8:22–31). However, both in Proverbs 3 and in Proverbs 8, the very same wisdom of God is presented to humans as their ethical standard of life. God reveals himself as wise not only in the way he prepared the world but also in the commandments and prohibitions that he presented, and presents, to created humanity. Humans in their turn are truly wise if they keep God's commandments (Deut. 4:6; Ps. 19:7). "Behold, the fear of the Lord, that is wisdom, and to turn away from evil is understanding" (Job 28:28; cf. Ps. 111:10; Prov. 1:7; 9:10; 15:33).

Wisdom is the ability through which humans know how to distinguish between good and evil (cf. the prayer of the young Solomon, 1 Kings 3:9–12), that is, know to discern the way of obedience to God's commandments. Wisdom is for the "perfect" (Gk. teleioi, here, the "spiritually mature") (1 Cor. 2:6); the "mature" (*teleioi*) are "those who have their powers of discernment trained by constant practice to distinguish good from evil" (Heb. 5:14; cf. Isa. 7:15). This is the property that we find perfectly manifested in God himself in relation to his holiness. It is no wonder that, in Christ, God's wisdom is connected with his righteousness, sanctification and redemption (1 Cor. 1:30). God's wisdom stands over against human foolishness, which manifests itself in wickedness (1 Cor. 1:18–31; Rom. 1:22–23).

8.14.2 Names of God

In Romans 16:27, God is described as the "only wise God." Jesus Christ, who is God manifested in the flesh (1 Tim. 3:16 KJV etc.), is in his person the "wisdom of God" (1 Cor. 1:24; cf. v. 30). He is not only wise, he *is* the divine wisdom in his own person, just like God *is* spirit (John 4:24), light (1 John 1:5) and love (4:8, 16).

In Proverbs 8, Wisdom is personified in such a way that

---

125. Barth (*CD* II/1:475–95).

the ancient rabbis thought here of the Torah, but the early Christians thought here of the Logos, Christ.[126]

8.15 The Pistical Modality
8.15.1 God's Faithfulness

Emil Brunner made the interesting remark that, although God's faithfulness plays a foundational role in the Bible, it has hardly a place in the traditional doctrine of the divine attributes.[127] He saw the origin of this in the speculative idea of the Absolute with its timeless immutability, which leaves no room for God's faithfulness since the latter would thus be nothing but a synonym for this immutability.[128] What use would it have to speak of the faithfulness of an immutable God in the traditional ontological meaning of the term "immutability"?

However, the living, loving God of the Bible is totally different from the God of philosophical speculation, the God who by definition is "immutable." The God of the Scriptures is faithful in the sense that he realizes his counsel (this is the historical-formative element in his faithfulness), that he suffers together with humans (this is the sensitive element), and that he loves them (the ethical element). The moment we perceive that the God who can "change his mind" is just as biblical as the immutable God (§7.6) the term "faithful" is meaningful and important. If God can change his ways with humanity it becomes important to emphasize that God remains faithful to his counsel and promises.[129]

If we now have arrived at the pistical modality as a gateway to understanding God's faithfulness more profoundly, we realize that the term "pistical" comes from Greek *pistos*, "faithful," and that we are told several times that God is *pistos* (1 Cor. 1:9; 10:13; 2 Cor. 1:18; 1 Thess. 5:24; Heb. 10:23; 11:11;

---
126. See extensively, Ouweneel (1998, 59–62).
127. Brunner (1950, 292).
128. Also cf. Wentsel (1987, 406–13); Pannenberg (1988, 471–72).
129. See extensively, *EDR* 4, chapter 4, and Vol. III/1, on the difference between God's counsel and God's ways.

1 Pet. 4:19; 1 John 1:9). The same is said of Jesus Christ (2 Thess. 3:3; 2 Tim. 2:13; Heb. 2:17; 3:2). In all these cases, the significance of the matter is that God, or Christ, is absolutely faithful to himself and to others. He is the One who is thoroughly reliable; people can count on him, trust him, place their confidence in him. Similarly, God's *pistis* is his faithfulness; thus in Matthew 23:23 (at least if *God's* faithfulness is meant here; KJV and others read "faith") and Romans 3:3 (in opposition to *apistia*, "unbelief").

We see here that *pistis* can mean both "faith" and "faithfulness"; the same is true for Latin *fides*, from which "faith(-fulness)" was derived (cf. French *fidélité* [faithfulness] and *foi* [faith]). When God's *pistis* is involved, we consistently render it as "faithfulness"; when it is human *pistis*, we usually render it as "faith," but sometimes as "faithfulness" (I only speak of the noun): Matthew 23:23 (if related to humans); Galatians 5:22 (part of the fruit of the Spirit; KJV etc. "faith"); 2 Thessalonians 3:2 (English translations have "faith," but the rendering "faithfulness" is just as conceivable; cf. the contrast with v. 3); Titus 2:11 (the slave's faithfulness to his master; some render it as "faith" or "fidelity"). In the believer's faithfulness, God's faithfulness is reflected.

One of the most important Bible verses on God's faithfulness is 2 Timothy 2:13, "If we are faithless, he remains faithful — for he cannot deny himself." That is, God cannot become unfaithful toward himself; he is not able to act in a way that is inconsistent with his own divine being. The verse can be read in two ways: even if his people are unfaithful, the Lord remains faithful to the promises that he once gave;[130] or, God remains faithful to his holiness when he must chastise his people for their unfaithfulness.[131] The corresponding element is that, in both cases, God remains faithful to *himself*.

---

130. Ridderbos (1967, 207–08); Towner (2006, 512–14).
131. Bouma (1937, 144–45).

8.15.2 God's Truthfulness

Also in the Old Testament God is called the Faithful One. Here this occurs by means of the Hebrew root '-m-n and its derivations (Deut. 7:9; 32:4; Neh. 9:33; Ps. 33:4; Isa. 49:7). These terms can also be rendered as "truth" or related words. Where the KJV often has "truth," ESV (and others) has "faithfulness. "Truth" and "faithfulness" seem to be very different concepts, but this is mainly because of our Western ears. "Faithful" is "reliable, truthful, trustworthy." The English words "truth" and "trust" are related to Dutch *trouw* and German *Treue*, which both mean "faithfulness."[132] The fact that God is "trustworthy" means that he does what he says, but also that he always speaks the truth. He tells us how things really are; we can trust him for that. Literally we read that God even *is* "truth" (Ps. 31:5; Jer. 10:10; cf. Rom. 3:4, 7) in the sense that he is totally reliable in what he says and does, worthy of our unconditional and dedicated trust (confidence). He shows "truth" to humans, that is, trustworthiness, faithfulness (Gen. 24:27; Ps. 57:3; 61:7; 89:14, etc.; compare for each verse KJV and ESV). All God's words, ways and works are "truth," that is, truthful, trustworthy (2 Sam. 7:28; Ps. 19:9; 25:10; 33:4; 111:7; 119:86, 142, 151; Dan. 4:37). He is even *abounding* in faithfulness (or, truth) (Exod. 34:6); it extends to the clouds (Ps. 36:5). Humans, too, must be "truth" (trustworthy, faithful) (Exod. 18:21; Neh. 7:2; Ps. 45:4; 51:6; cf. Rom. 3:7).

Thus, in Hebrew *emet* both the notion of "truth(fulness)" and that of "faithfulness" are implied, while in Greek *pistis* lies enclosed both the notion of "faith" and that of "faithfulness." Truth(fulness), faithfulness and faith (or confidence [from the same Latin root *fides*]) all three characterize the relationships between God and humans on the transcendent-religious level. Through words of the same root '-m-n it can be said that, because God is faithful, he confirms or establishes his word, that is, makes it come "true" (1 Kings 8:26; 1 Chron.

---

132. Cf. *TDNT* 1, 21–35, 233–51; 6, 174–82, 197–228.

17:23–24; 2 Chron. 1:9; 6:17; Ps. 89:28; Isa. 55:3; Hos. 5:9; see the Hebrew text).

German theologian Alfons Weiser underscored how much terms such as "truthful" and "faithful" refer to God's being:[133] "The root meaning [of *emet*] is 'the essential,' that is, 'what makes God God'." Truth is the truth concerning God: concerning that which constitutes the being of God. What is "true" of God is his essence.

It is amazing that Herman Bavinck concluded so easily that, because *emet* means both "truth" and "faithfulness," God's "veracity" is both a virtue of the understanding as a virtue of the will.[134] In my view, what he should have said in his own words is what in my words sounds as follows: in *emet* there is surely both a logical-analytical and a historical-formative element. But first, this is the case in *all* modalities, and second, *all* the other modal analogies are present in the pistical modality as well. Is there not a spatial element when it comes to the size, and a kinematic element when it comes to the firm constancy of God's promises? (In fact, '-m-n means "to be firm/established.") Is there not a physical element in the strength of this faith- and truthfulness? And a perceptive element in the self-awareness of this faithfulness? And a social element in the relationships that are presupposed in God's faithfulness toward humans? And is there not an aesthetic element in the inner harmony of God's faith- and truthfulness, and in his attitude to wavering humans? And a judicial element in his faith- and truthfulness manifesting itself in both judgment and redemption? And an ethical element in the love that is presupposed in his faith- and truthfulness toward humans?

Consequently, is God's faith- and truthfulness the sum of all these elements? No, these are only analogous elements within something that is irreducible to any other modal idea. God's faith- and truthfulness cannot be expressed either in purely logical, or in purely historical-formative terms (of the

---
133. *TDNT* 6, 185.
134. Bavinck (*RD* 2, 174).

will), or in both; it is essentially irreducible. It could just as well be asserted that God's love or God's righteousness is, for instance, a "virtue of the will"; for what would love or righteousness be if there is not a will to practice them toward humans! But it is overlooked here that the element of the will is only one in the totality of God's love, righteousness or faithfulness. Love, righteousness, holiness, faithfulness, and so on, are not specifically "virtues of the will"; they are just as much "virtues of feeling," or "virtues of the understanding," or "virtues of fellowship," and so on.

All God's attributes contain such historical-formative, sensitive, logical-analytical, social elements, and so forth, which can all be viewed as analogies within the juridical, the ethical, the social, the pistical modality, and so on. However, love, righteousness, holiness, faithfulness, and so on, can never be *reduced* to such analogous elements. The kernel of the historical-formative, the sensitive, the logical-analytical, the social modality, and so forth, is by definition irreducible; if it would turn out to be otherwise, it would follow that people have incorrectly distinguished them as separate modalities. Therefore, the Dooyeweerdian doctrine of the modalities is a tremendous — and as far as I know so far unsurpassed — aid in discerning the modal and analogous aspects and to obtain insight into the various attributes of God.

8.15.3 Names of God

The New Testament says several times, "God is faithful" (1 Cor. 1:9; 10:13; 2 Cor. 1:18; 1 Thess. 5:24; cf. Heb. 10:23; 1 John 1:9). In 1 Peter 4:19 God is called the "faithful Creator." The Christ appearing in the skies bears the name, "Faithful and True" (Rev. 19:11; cf. 21:5; 22:6). He is faithful to his promises, faithful to his people, and above all faithful to himself.

What perhaps comes closest to a divine name is Jeremiah 10:10, *YHWH Elohim emet*, which can be rendered in several ways: "YHWH is the true God" (cf. KJV, ESV etc.), or, "the God of truth" (GNV etc.), or, "The Lord God is the Truth"

(JUB). Also compare the expression the "true" (or "truthful") God (John 17:3; 1 John 5:20; cf. John 3:33; Rom. 3:4). In Psalm 31:5, *YHWH El emet* is a vocative, to be rendered as follows: "Oh YHWH, God of truth," or, "faithful God." In Deuteronomy 32:4, God is the "God of faithfulness" (or, "truth"), and as such the "Rock" — a firm foundation on which humans can build their confidence in God.

Chapter 9
The Doctrine of the Trinity

> *"Go therefore and make disciples of all nations,*
> *baptizing them in the name of the Father*
> *and of the Son*
> *and of the Holy Spirit."*
>
> Matthew 28:19

9.1 The Unitarian Challenge
9.1.1 Introduction

IN THE PRESENT VOLUME, on the eternal God, and in the next Volume, on the eternal Christ, there is necessarily an amount of overlap. This is because Jesus Christ is, as the early church already confessed it, true Man *and* true God, and this in one person. As far as Jesus, as the eternal Son of the Father, is part of the Trinity, he is also part of the last two chapters of this book. However, the arguments *why* we call him God, namely, God the Son, must wait until the next Volume, and the same holds for the arguments why we call him true Man. In other words, the Trinitarian aspects are being dealt with in the present Volume, whereas the Christological aspects will be treated in the next Volume.

In the meantime we do realize that these are the most important, but also the most complicated, and perhaps the most controversial, subjects of Christian theology. The doctrine of the Trinity is complicated because our mind cannot grasp right away — or not grasp at all — how the Father is God, the Son is God, and the Holy Spirit is God, and yet there is only one God. Christology is complicated because our mind cannot grasp right away — or not grasp at all — how Jesus can be fully God, and at the same time can be fully Man, and yet be one single person. I once visited the Visitors' Center of the Mormons at Salt Lake City, where the guide told us that Mormons believe that Jesus "is fifty percent God and fifty percent Man" — which, of course, will not do, for a half God is no God, and a half Man is no Man. If one insists on using mathematics, Jesus is hundred percent God and hundred percent Man, which seems just as implausible and incredible as saying that a person is hundred percent a man and hundred percent a woman.

Similarly, the doctrine of the Trinity is *a priori* just as hard to believe. It is walking on the razor's edge here. It is like the relationship between God's sovereignty and human responsibility, which seem to exclude each other: it is either God who has determined, and determines, all things, or it is humans who at least determine *some* things (i.e., make choices in their lives, for which they are fully responsible). Theologians have *always* been tempted either to overemphasize God's sovereignty, and neglect human responsibility, or to do the reverse. It is similar with the doctrine of the Trinity: theologians have *always* been tempted either to overemphasize the *oneness* of God, at the expense of the three distinct hypostases within the Deity, or to to do the reverse: overemphasize the three hypostasis — three "persons" in the modern sense: three independent individuals — at the expense of the oneness of God: there is one God, not three Gods. (I may add that the same occurs in the Christological area: theologians have *always* been tempted either to overemphasize the deity of Christ at the expense of his humanity, or to do the reverse.)

9.1.2 The Double Sense of "Father"

The doctrine of the Triune God is the most essential of all Christian doctrines. Thus, it is no wonder that, after his discussion of the Word of God as the criterion of dogmatics, Karl Barth opened his treatise concerning God's revelation immediately with a presentation of the Trinity.[1] Paul Tillich called this a mistake because he viewed the doctrine of the Trinity not as the "pro-," but as the "postlegomena" of dogmatics.[2] Following Friedrich Schleiermachter, various dogmaticians placed this doctrine at the very end of their dogmatics.[3] As a contrast, Gerrit van Niftrik divided his dogmatics according to the three persons of the Deity, which led to the unacceptable situation that God's attributes were dealt with exclusively under the heading "God the Father." The underlying error, occurringly very frequently but hardly ever openly expressed, is that the Father is God in any "actual" sense. We observe this already in the Apostolic as well as in the Nicene-Constantinopolitan Creed: it is the Father who is called almighty and the Creator, not the Triune God. Different again is the view of Edmund Schlink, who called the doctrine of the Trinity noetically the last, and ontically the first part of dogmatics.[4]

The idea that God is Triune briefly means that there is one God, and yet there are three divine persons: Father, Son, and Holy Spirit. Yet there are not three Gods—there is only one God. The being, the attributes and names of God are far less specific of Christianity because the views on these matters agree to a large extent with those of Jews, and to some extent even those of Muslims. But when it comes to the doctrine of the Trinity, the ways of Christians, Jews and Muslims part. This doctrine is *the* obstacle in any "dialogue" between these religions. Christ crucified is a stumbling block for Jews and a

---
1. Barth (*CD* I,1, 311–514).
2. Tillich (1968,III, 303–04).
3. Besides Tillich, e.g., Herrmann (1925), Stephan (1941), Althaus (1952), Van Niftrik (1961), and Buri (1978).
4. Schlink (1983, 754); also cf. Kasper (1983, 311–14).

folly to Gentiles (1 Cor. 1:23). Buth the idea that the crucified Christ was and is at the same time God the Son, equal to the Father, and that yet there is only one God—this is at least as much a stumbling block in any dialogue with "the others," but even for many people who do call themselves Christians, who misunderstand, misrepresent, or overtly reject the doctrine of the Trinity.

It would be very wrong to suggest that Christians "at least" have the notion of God the *Father* in common with unitarians such as Jews and Muslims, as well as with Christian unitarians.[5] This is an error because the unitarian idea of God as "Father" at best entails the thought that this Father is the Creator of humanity, or in a special way of his own people, and that he cares for them and loves them. Nothing more than that. There is nothing wrong with this description as such; it clearly occurs in the Old Testament (Ps. 68:5; 103:13; Prov. 3:12; Isa. 63:15–16; 64:8; Jer. 3:4, 19; 31:9; Mal. 1:6; 2:10). However, the point is that he who, in the Old Testament, is called "Father" (in the sense of Creator, Caretaker, Redeemer), is, just like YHWH, *not* just the first person within the Trinity *but the Trinity itself*. The "Father" (i.e., Creator, Provider and Protector) in the Old Testament reveals himself in the New Testament as the eternal Father *and* the eternal Son *and* the eternal Spirit. Many problems arise when *this* is not grasped, as we will see time and again in the last chapters of this book.

Thus, the *New Testament* idea of God the Father is primarily that he is the eternal Father of the eternal Son, an idea that we will extensively investigate but that is rejected by all kinds of unitarians ("Christian," Jewish, Islamic). Even where God today is the Father of his children, this may be taken in the Old Testament sense. But it is much more than that; it means emphatically that the eternal Son of the eternal Father is their life (1 John 5:11–13), and thus therefore it is the eternal Father *of the eternal Son* who is their Father—in that quality (cf. Jesus'

---

5. Cf. Chafer (*ST* 1:311–12).

proclamation in John 20:27 to Mary Magdalene, "my Father and your Father").

9.1.3 A Spiritual Battle

Both orthodox Jews and Muslims have argued time and again that God is absolutely one, and therefore he cannot have a Son, at least not in the sense of a divine person who is co-equal with that other divine person: the Father.

According to Jewish expositors, the Tanakh excludes the idea that the Messiah in any divine way were, or could be, the Son of God. As we read in John's Gospel: "This was why the Jews were seeking all the more to kill him, because not only was he breaking the Sabbath, but he was even calling God his own Father, making himself equal with God" (5:18). "The Jews answered him, 'It is not for a good work that we are going to stone you but for blasphemy, because you, being a man, make yourself God'" (10:33). Today, Jewish expositors can even appeal to liberal-Christian theologians,[6] who consider the Trinity dogma to be a pious invention of the early Church, inspired and pervaded by ancient philosophy, but not by Scripture (see below). Such theologians may accept to some extent the "divinity" (not "deity") of Christ. But for the rest, they seem to essentially agree with Jews, Muslims and Christian Unitarians (a) that there is, and can be, only one God, whom Jews and Christians call "Father," (b) that the Holy Spirit is God in his own person, or rather, the power or working proceeding from him, and (c) that Jesus is at best Son of God in the sense of a specially chosen en blessed human being, adopted by God, as this was the case with every Davidic king (Ps. 4:7, and the quotation in Acts 13:33 and Heb. 1:5; 5:5; also cf. Ps. 45:6–8). We call this view "adoptianism."

One of the best known advocates of classical adoptianism was Paul of Samosata (third century), who viewed Jesus as a Man who was "indwelled" by the eternal Logos (see the next Volume on this and many related matters, which at this point

---

6. So, e.g., many times in *SBB*.

are only touched upon). Adoptianists begin with the Man Jesus, who subsequently is viewed as animated by the Holy Spirit (at his birth or at his baptism), or by the eternal Logos. In opposition to this, the official church doctrine begins with the eternal Logos, who subsequently partakes of flesh in the person of Jesus. The former view deifies Jesus, or — even worse — believes that Jesus was deified by the early church. The latter view believes that the eternal, divine Word became flesh.[7] Shorter: either a Man was made God (so the modernists), or God was made Man.

Each theology in the twenty-first century that wishes to do justice to Scripture sees itself confronted here with tremendous challenges, both from the inside and from the outside. For various reasons, it is clearly impossible to simply repeat here the age-old answers.

(a) Our answers must enter into the challenges of today, not those of, for instance, the fourth or the eighteenth century. Our answers to these challenges may be rather similar, but the questions may be very different.

(b) The age-old answers themselves, as formulated especially by the Ecumenical Councils, are subject to criticism in several respects. To a certain extent, there *were* indeed more Hellenistic than biblical, and this ought to be a serious handicap for a critical theology.[8] We must avoid here the three greatest threats for any theology:

(1) *biblicism* or *fundamentalism* (which, in a positivistic way, piles up "biblical proofs" for the Trinity without being aware of the Trinitarian "glasses" one is wearing from the start);

(2) *scholasticism* (the approach of traditional Roman Catholic and early Protestant theology, in which the Greek-philosophical influence was *a priori* legitimized), and

---

7. Hengel (1995, 368, 374).
8. Although we should not exaggerate this: the word homoousios "did not Hellenize the faith or burden it with an alien philosophy. On the contrary, it captured in a stable formula exactly what had emerged as incomparably new and different in Jesus' way of speaking with the Father" (Ratzinger [2007, 355]).

(3) the *anti-supernaturalist*, anti-"metaphysical" elements in Enlightenment theology.[9]

9.2 The Existential Background
9.2.1 Practical and Theoretical

We must strongly emphasize that we have to do here with *theological* problems. For Christian faith, which transcends all theory building, and which is certainly rational but especially existential, there are no "problems" in the theoretical sense of the word. It is true, not every believer is able to *express* everything that he or she believes in a rational-lingual form. But whatever way of expression one may find, it will at least strongly differ from the modal abstraction and distancing that are characteristic of theoretical "problems" and "problem solving."[10] To faith, it is as clear as the day that the Father is God, that the Son is God, and that the Holy Spirit is God; that Father, Son and Spirit are not identical but distinct; and that nevertheless there is only one God.

For instance, see how the Heidelberg Catechism (Q and A 25) answers the question why we speak of three persons, the Father, the Son, and the Holy Spirit, whereas there is yet only one God.[11] It does not give us a long argument, but says in an almost snippy way, "Because that is how God has revealed himself in his Word: these three distinct persons are one, true, eternal God." That's why. Period.[12] We believe in God—and this God is Father, Son and Spirit. In this simple sentence, the doctrine of the Trinity is indeed the center, not only of Christian theology, but of Christian faith itself.

I say this *contra* Emil Brunner,[13] although he was right in saying that, as soon as we ask about the precise relationships between Father, Son and Spirit, the *theological problems*

---

9. See Ouweneel (1995, §1.2).
10. See extensively,, Ouweneel (1995) and Vol. V/1 in this series.
11. Ouweneel (2016, ad loc.).
12. Cf. Troost (1992).
13. Brunner (1950, 213–14).

begin.¹⁴ He rightly criticized Karl Barth because the latter did not cleary distinguish between faith and theological reflection, and as a consequence fell into "theologism," in contrast with the Reformers.¹⁵ Johan Heyns rightly warned that theology does not possess any "revelational quality";¹⁶ it is occupied with "revelational truths, *but the systematic reflection and logical formulation has as such no revelational significance*. A single example: it has been revealed that God is Father, Son and Holy Spirit. But that this Trinity is described as *one Being and three persons* (una substantia tres personae) was not revealed, but is the result of scholarly reflection. Therefore, at a later stage this may be formulated in a more correct way."

Gerrit van Niftrik¹⁷ pointed to a sermon by Luther, in which the latter stated that the simple confession, "I believe in God: Father, Son and Holy Spirit," should actually be sufficient for us. To faith this is what the truth of the Trinity is: nothing less and nothing more. And this faith functions in a vital way only in a soteriological context.¹⁸ The Father whom the believer worships is the Father who gave his only Son for him so that he would not perish. The Son whom the believer worships is the Son who, as a Man, gave himself on the cross for him as the latter's substitute under God's judgment. And the Holy Spirit whom the believer worships is the Spirit who made him spiritually alive, and renews and sanctifies him also further. He worships the Triune God, not only because he admires his majesty but because he has an existential relationship with him; that is, because he is *his* God. This "God of *my* salvation" (Ps. 88:1; cf. 27:1; 38:23; 62:1–2, 6–7; 88:2; 89:27), who therefore is "*my* exceeding joy" (43:4), is the God who through faith is known and worshiped.¹⁹

---

14. Ibid., 216.
15. Ibid., 252–53.
16. Heyns (1977, 78).
17. Van Niftrik (1961, 420).
18. *EDR* 2, §1.1.3; cf. Berkouwer (1952, 80–83); Rahner (1974, 87).
19. *EDR* 2, §1.1.1.

9.2.2 A Confession of the Heart

Faith believingly accepts the many biblical witnesses regarding the deity of Christ (see the next Volume), and has no problems with the many distinct personality features that the Bible assigns to the divine Spirit.[20] Yet, it realizes, even without any theological reflection, that there cannot be three Gods, for the Bible clearly testifies at many places that there is only one God (e.g., Deut. 4:35, 39; 6:4; 1 Cor. 8:4; Eph. 4:6). Faith simply accepts this, not because it would not have many questions; also "simple" believers may wonder how there can be three divine persons, and yet one God. However, such a question is the admiring wondering of faith; the theoretical thinking-attitude is foreign to faith in its transcendent-existential sense. I may even *add* here that this existential and doxological aspect of the Trinity doctrine must govern all theological reflection, so that the latter will not lose itself in idle speculation and dry orthodoxy.

German theologian Helmut Thielicke (d. 1986) described the difference between practical Trinitarian faith and theoretical Trinitarianism as that between (a) the "object" of faith, by which we are "encompassed" when we believe, and (b) the believing (and, moreover, *theoretical.* WJO) "reflection" upon this object.[21] In the former sense, faith has a "revelational ranking" because it involves the *intention* of the Trinity doctrine, that is, expresses the way in which God as Father, Son and Holy Spirit is "our God." In the latter sense, faith has no "revelational ranking" because it involves the *form* of the Trinity doctrine, that is, it is expressed "in systematic figures of our thinking," in order to protect it against the autonomous consequences of our thinking, and thus honor the mystery of God's divinity.

We must carefully maintain the balance here, in order to create no gaps between existential faith and doctrinal matters. Jesus' question, "What do you think about the Christ [i.e., the

---
20. See Ouweneel (2007, 74–75); and Vol. II/3.
21. Thielicke (1974, 208).

Messiah]?" (Matt. 22:42), is certainly an existential question, that is, a question that appeals to the believing heart. However, the continuation of the question is not some subjective, "What does he mean to you personally? Do you personally know him? Do you realize that he is going to die for you?" and so on, but: "Whose son is he?" The other questions just mentioned are not worthless, on the contrary; but the question mentioned last is not either. A believer could hardly say that Christ died and rose for him or her, if he or she does not know or acknowledge whose Son he is: the pre-existent Son of God, who as such was David's Lord, to mention just one aspect (vv. 43–45). Conversely, it is not very worthwhile if one acknowledges him as the Son of the living God without knowing him personally as Savior and Lord.

In Matthew 16:16, Simon Peter does not proclaim some formal creed but airs the conviction of his heart, brought about by the Father himself (v. 17).[22] This confession does not primarily bring to light that Peter is "orthodox" but that he is *makarios* (v. 17), that is "blissful, felicitous, happy." Of course he is "blessed," as the translations commonly render the term, but that is not the point; a man making such a confession is a *happy* man (cf. §7.13.1). Being orthodox and being happy can go together of course, but as such they are very different things. It is difficult to be happy in any biblical-spiritual sense without being orthodox—but unfortunately it is quite possible to be orthodox without being happy in any biblical-spiritual sense.

If believers confess the doctrine of the Trinity, it is not (primarily) because they would be more intelligent than anti-Trinitarians. Rather, it is because the existential "necessity is laid upon them" (cf. 1 Cor. 9:16). If they have any knowledge of this doctrine it is because they have received "the Spirit of wisdom and of revelation in the knowledge of him," and "the eyes of their hearts enlightened" (cf. Eph. 1:17–18).[23] They

---
22. See *EDR* 2, §1.1.1.
23. Cf. Berkouwer (1952, 8,1 1, 146–48).

wish to know more about the subject, not (only) out of intellectual curiosity (although there is nothing wrong with this as such), but (also) because they *love* the Triune God. They wish to know more about him like the young man who is in love wishes to know more about the beloved.

9.3   In Conflict with Scholasticism and Liberalism
9.3.1   Ontology and Axiology

The balance mentioned is disturbed by, on the one hand, the speculation of scholastic Trinitarianism and, on the other hand, by the modernist resistance to all supposed "metaphysics" in the doctrine of the Trinity. As far as the latter point is concerned, in particular German theologian Albrecht Ritschl must be mentioned here, together with his pupils, Adolf von Harnack (d. 1930) and Friedrich Loofs (d. 1928). They all rejected traditional Trinitarianism as "metaphysics," which supposedly seeped in from ancient philosophy.[24] They claimed that (metaphysical) *ontological* statements must be replaced by (ethical) *axiological* statements. They did their utmost to find all kinds of pagan origins of the Trinity doctrine, and overlooked the plain fact that traditional orthodoxy — apart from unfortunate speculations that indeed went beyond Scripture — had always based the ground-elements of Trinitarianism on the statements of Scripture itself.

Only if it could be shown that the doctrine of the Trinity is a foreign element in the Bible, it would be justified to search for extra-biblical sources where this doctrine might be found. As things look now, such a quest seems to be largely based upon the Deistic, rationalistic, anti-supernaturalistic and anti-"metaphysical" prejudices of Enlightenment thinking. Such biases claim the doctrine of the Trinity *a priori* to be an "impossibility," and function as a covering up of the biblical testimony.

In his *Loci Communes*, the first systematic theology of

---
24. Cf. Berkouwer (1952, 15–16, 77–78); Tillich (1968,III, 305–06).

Lutheranism, Philip Melanchthon said,[25] "We do better to worship the mysteries of the Godhead than to investigate them." He also argued that it is more important to know God's good gifts than the exact difference between Christ's two natures, and the ways of his incarnation.[26] Many theologians, especially in the nineteenth century, appealed to such statements in order to underpin their existential approach and their rejection of the "metaphysical" approach. However, Melanchthon's *Loci Communi* very clearly defend the traditional doctrine of the Trinity and of the two natures of Christ.[27] At the same time, Melanchthon did his best to maintain the balance by rejecting many scholastic speculations, and emphasizing the necessity of a redemptive relationship with the Trinity. Otherwise, all theological knowledge of Trinitarianism and Christology will be of no avail for humans.[28]

Careful balance must be maintained here. It is true, on the one hand worshipping God is more important and more fruitful than analyzing God. But on the hand, who is the God one is worshipping? Without gathering profound knowledge about what the Bible reveals us about God, we are like the Samaritans of whom Jesus said, "You worship what you do not know" (John 4:22), and like the Athenians who worshipped an "unknown god" (Acts 17:23; cf. Deut. 29:26).

9.3.2 Trinitarianism and Faith

A little more must be said here about the transcendent-existential element of faith in Trinitarianism. Theology may enrich our knowledge of the Trinity doctrine, but it cannot grant to us the faith knowledge of the Triune God. Jesus literally says, "[U]nless you believe that I AM [Gk. *Egō eimi*] you will die in your sins" (John 8:24). On the profoundest level, I take

---

25. Quoted in Ford and Higton (2002, 209).
26. Vgl. Barth (*CD* I/1, 437; Berkouwer (1952, 78); Schlink (*RGG* 6:1034).
27. A replacement of ontological by axiological statements cannot be based upon statements of the Reformers; Berkouwer (1952, 78–79).
28. Cf. Barth (*CD* I/1, 437–40), who referred to similar statements in Calvin's and Luther's writings.

this to mean that everyone who does not recognize Jesus as the great I AM will die in his sins. Besides the seven I AM's followed by one or more nouns (John 6:35; 8:12; 10:7, 11; 11:25; 14:6; 15:1), there are two more impressive I AM's in John's Gospel: the reassuring I AM of chapter 6:20 ("It is I" is again Gk. *Egō eimi*) and the threatening I AM of chapter 18:5, 8.

Another example of the supra-rational character of the Trinitarian faith is that Jesus does not appeal to our intellect but to our will when he says, "If anyone's *will* is to do his [i.e., the Father's] will, he will know whether the teaching is from God or whether I am speaking on my own authority" (7:17). It is not just a matter of the intellect but of the will. The apostle John writes, "Everyone who goes on ahead and does not abide in the teaching of Christ, does not have God. Whoever abides in the teaching has both the Father and the Son. If anyone comes to you and does not bring this teaching, do not receive him into your house or give him any greeting" (2 John 1:9–10). Such a heretic does not simply have a different theological opinion. Rather, he is an enemy of God: "Happy are those who don't stumble and fall because of me" (Matt. 11:6 CEB) — fall because they are not prepared to accept the truth about him — not just theological truth but the truth of faith.

In this connection, it is remarkable to see how the doctrine of Christ, and in a broader sense the doctrine of the Trinity, is presented in the New Testament. It is hardly ever mere teaching as such, as a purpose in itself. The clearest verse in which the Trinity is mentioned is this one: "Go therefore and make disciples of all nations, baptizing them in the name of the Father and of the Son and of the Holy Spirit" (Matt. 28:19). This verse does not present the Trinity as an object of teaching but as the name in (or, unto, Gk. *eis*) which people must be baptized. The remarkable passage in 2 Corinthians 8:9, about the pre-existent Christ who, "though he was rich, yet for your sake he became poor," stands in the midst of an exhortation concerning generous giving. There is the even more remarkable Christological passage in Philippians 2:6–11 ("... Christ

Jesus, who, though he was in the form of God, did not count equality with God a thing to be grasped, but emptied himself, by taking the form of a servant, being born in the likeness of men," and so on) is not given as a piece of Christological teaching as such, but as a motivation to brotherly love and humility.

The interesting enumeration of the three divine persons in 1 Corinthians 12:4–6 does not primarily aim at unfolding to us the doctrine of the Trinity but at offering us very practical teaching concerning the functioning of the Spiritual gifts in the church. And the similar enumeration of the three divine persons in 2 Corinthians 13:14 has a very practical purpose as well, namely, to bring us under the blessing of the Triune God. None of this is theology as such. It is divine preaching to our souls. Theology has its own, very different, specific task, into which we must now enter a little further.

9.4 Positing the Theological Problem: Exegetical Ground-Questions
9.4.1 Theoretical and Practical

As soon as we turn to the theological reflection upon the dogma of the divine Trinity, the problems are numerous. German theologian Friedrich Meyer (d. 1891) even ventured to say,[29] "People generally agree that there is no Trinity doctrine in the New Testament." This is correct insofar as the New Testament does not contain a complete, fully elaborated theological theory concerning the Trinity. But this is true for *any* New Testament based theological theory. The Bible simply does not contain theories, and even does not contain "doctrines," if we understand by this the systematic, rounded-off doctrines of any dogmatic handbook.

Wolfgang Trillhaas said,[30] "It must always be called the strongest argument in favor of the Trinity doctrine that it en-

---
29. Meyer (*RGG* 6:1024); cf. Barth (*CD* I/1, 330–31); Trillhaas (1972, 111–12); Pannenberg (1988, 327–30).
30. Trillhaas (1972, 112).

deavors to interpret the Bible passages involved in the language of ancient ontology." My answer to this is that, on the one hand, it can be no merit at all if ancient (Hellenistic) ontology would have penetrated Trinitarianism. On the other hand, insofar as the Trinity doctrine tries to interpret the relevante "data" with the help of a specially designed academic terminology, it does not otherwise than what *all* theological, and even *all* scientific theories do. British theologian Arthur W. Wainwright rightly said that there is no formal presentation of the Trinity doctrine in the New Testament but an answer to the problem of the Trinity.[31] But even such a description contains the danger of viewing Scripture as supplying answers to *theoretical* problems. The Bible writers are not concerned about Trinitarian "problems," they simply present Trinitarian truth.

I repeat, this truth is that, on the basis of the New Testament, no believing reader can seriously doubt that there is one God, and that the Father is God, the Son is God, and the Holy Spirit is God. Indeed, the New Testament does not contain a Trinity *doctrine* in any *theological* sense of the word. On the contrary, the Trinity is a practical matter here. At the end of many church servicies, the blessing of 2 Corinthians 13:14 is heard concerning the grace of the Lord Jesus Christ and the love of God and the fellowship of the Holy Spirit. And over all Christians, some already very shortly after their birth, the testimony of Matthew 28:19 is proclaimed, that is, the one divine name, which belongs to the Father *and* to the Son *and* to the Holy Spirit. This is how the doctrine of the Trinity practically functions in church life.

The objection by Berkhof against the use of Matthew 28:19 as evidence for the Trinity doctrine because it is supposed to be "so clearly a product of later reflection" seems to me begging the question.[32] Apart from the anti-supernaturalist prejudice, there is no *a priori* reason why the Trinitarian

---
31. Wainwright (1969, 265).
32. Berkhof (1986, 348).

confession should presuppose a theological development that could not yet have taken place within the life of Christ itself.[33]

9.4.2 Main Theoretical Problems

In my view, as to the theoretical-theological elaboration of the Trinity doctrine, we could enumerate the main problems as follows:

(a) Is there indeed an unambiguous New Testament image of God and of Jesus? Can "biblical data" be tied together just like that, whereas the Synoptic Gospels present an image of Jesus that is very different from that of John's Gospel, the apostle Paul having his own picture of Jesus? Can we indeed distill from all these different images of Jesus a coherent and consistent New Testament picture of Jesus? In my view, the answer is yes; but the matter will be mainly dealt with in the next Volume in this series.

(b) Is there indeed only one God? Does the Bible not often speak of many other "gods"? I have extensively discussed this matter elsewhere.[34] The "gods," or rather, "idols," in the Bible are fallen angels, that is, demons (cf. Deut. 32:17; 1 Cor. 10:20; Rev. 9:20). If the text refers to them, God can be called the "God of gods" (Deut. 10:17; Josh. 22:22; Ps. 50:1; 136:2; Dan. 2:47; 11:36). However, there can be no question of "gods" that are on one line with, or are even comparable with, YHWH (Deut. 32:39; 2 Sam. 7:22; 1 Kings 8:23; 2 Kings 5:15; 1 Chron. 17:20; 2 Chron. 6:14; Ps. 77:13; Isa. 43:10; 44:6, 8; 45:5, 21; 64:4; Hos. 13:4), even though some texts may seem to suggest such a comparability (Num. 21:29; Judg. 11:23–24).

(c) Does the New Testament not often distinguish Jesus and the Spirit from "God," as if the former two were not God (1 Cor. 12:4–6; 2 Cor. 13:14)? If God (as such) is the Father of Jesus, how could Jesus himself be God (2 Cor. 1:3; Eph. 1:17)? The significance of these questions is this: if indeed it could be shown that the Son is a "god" (in whatever sense), well dis-

---
33. Cf. Van Genderen (2008, 145); see the arguments by Wentsel (1987, 360–61).
34. Ouweneel (2003, §2.1,2 and Appendices 2–4).

tinct from the God of gods (see, e.g., John 10:34–36), the entire Trinitarian paradox seems to go up in smoke: the Father is then the only and Most High God, the Son is a "god" in some lower sense (in whatever, probably some angelic, way), and the Spirit might also be such a "god," or simply the "Spirit" (the mind, the power, the activity) of the Father. This point is closely related to the following one.

(d) Jesus Christ is often called the "Son of God" (from Matt. 4:3 to Rev. 2:18). Does this not suggest that this Son must be distinguished from "God"? Is he a human adopted by God? Or is he divine (in whatever sense: he might have divinity but not deity)? Or is he both? And if (also) divine, is he truly "God"? And if so, is he only "a god" (see point [b]), or is he God just like the Father is God? In other words, is he a creature or Co-Creator? In still other words, is he lower than the Father, or co-equal with the Father? And if the latter, can he be called YHWH? And if so, how can it be that Jesus' humanity is stressed so often in the New Testament, even so strongly that he clearly distinguishes himself, not just from the Father, but from God, as if he were not himself God? The full treatment of these questions must wait again until the next Volume, because the Christological aspects are predominant here. We can state already now that the most important basis for such questions is the fact that Jesus is both God and Man. The Trinitarian problem and the Christological problem—both already complicated enough in themselves—are strongly interwoven, which makes the entire matter even far more complicated.

(e) If Jesus is the Messiah announced in the Old Testament, how can we explain that the latter seems to have no knowledge at all of the divinity of the Messiah, whereas in the New Testament this is self-evident? Here again, we must refer the reader to the next Volume (but I may already point to, e.g., Micah 5:2 (NKJV), where it is said of the Messiah that his "goings forth have been from of old, from everlasting," Heb. *umotsa'otaw miqqedem, mimē ᶜolam*). I mention the point here because several New Testament scholars made a comparison with the many Hellenistic myths that spoke of a divine son who appeared on earth, died and lived again.[35] If the Old Testament contains nothing of the kind, could it be that the "Jesus myth" is of an outer-biblical, namely, Hellenistic origin? In other words, how can be accepted that Jesus is the divine Messiah if the notion of a *divine* Messiah is unknown in the Old Testament? This question in itself legitimizes the entire problem of the nineteenth-century *Leven-Jesu-Forschung* ("investigation into the life of Jesus")—although its anti-supernaturalist Enlightenment prejudice was *not* legitimized beforehand. It is an established fact that, during the theological development of Trinitarianism and Christology in the early church, various ancient-philosophical (Hellenistic) elements sneaked in. How can we be sure that this was not the case already within the New Testament? See again mainly the next Volume.

(f) Is it at all possible, after centuries of Trinitarian and Christological theory building, to objectively reconstruct the New Testament's own teaching? Are we still able to look at the New Testament through pre-Nicene glasses? In other words, can we manage to be sufficiently unprejudiced to check whether the Councils of Nicea (AD 325), Constantinople (AD 381), and Chalcedon (AD 451) did sufficient justice to the New Testament? This is not a plea for biblicism; seeing how the pre-Nicene and pre-Chalcedonian fathers wrestled with Trinitarian and Christological questions, no present-day person can imagine to re-invent the wheel and the fire all by his own power. Yet, this does not take anything away from the demand, even long after "Nicea," "Constantinople," and "Chalcedon," to go back to Scripture time and again.

When I was still quite young, a Roman Catholic professor in philosophy—so much older and wiser than me—said to me, "At least we stand on the common ground of Nicea together." In youthful arrogance I answered, "Yes, but you believe the

---

35. See extensively, Ouweneel (2003, especially chapters 2 and 3, as well as Excurs 2–4).

Nicene Creed because it is invested with the authority of the church—I believe it because, and insofar as, it corresponds with Scripture." It was not a very friendly reply—but I cannot help still agreeing with it. I might have given the same answer to traditional Protestants who believe in Creeds, Confessions and Catechisms first and foremost because of their authority.

We are just dwarfs standing on the shoulders of the giants of the past; and yet as theologians we have the duty to re-think all dogmatic statements of the past. Every new generation of Christian theologians should be like Paul's Berean listeners who "received the word with all eagerness, examining the Scriptures daily to see if these things were so" (Acts 17:11). The Bereans did so with the words of the *apostle Paul*; we must all the more do so with all the lesser ones: Athanasius, Augustine, Anselm, Thomas Aquinas, Luther and Calvin. And we do so hoping that newer generations will do the same with our own words (if they still think them worthwhile).

9.5 Trinitarian Problems
9.5.1 An Introduction

Besides the exegetical and biblical-theological questions, the fully developed Trinity doctrine contains its own, typically theoretical problems. In my view, some of the most important ones are the following five. I present them here by way of introduction, because they will be dealt with in the last two chapters of the present, and in the next Volume.

(a) What exactly do we *mean* by the Trinitarian terminology? In particular, what do we mean by the term "person": one God, three persons, but in a sense we can also speak of *God* as a person (§§4.2 and 4.3). Can both statements be true at the same time? In how far does the term "person" mean here the same thing as what it means in our modern human "psychologized" world? How can persons be distinct, and still constitute one being?

(b) What do we mean by the term "nature" (Jesus Christ is one person and two natures)? How can a person have two "natures"? How do they relate to each other, and how do they relate to Christ as one "person"?

(c) According to what *scientific criteria* do we determine the distinction or identity, or the equality or inequality, of divine persons, given the fact that the New Testament does not make any direct statements about such questions? The same is true for the question whether Jesus Christ is one or two "persons," or whether he possesses one or two "natures." (Almost all options have found their ardent defenders: one person, one nature; two persons, two natures; one person, two natures.)

(d) How can such terms, which seem to be strictly bound to our creaturely world, be at all used for divine persons, who transcend our created world? (We have discussed this point several times: we can speak of God only in terms derived from our creaturely world.)

(e) Is theology at all capable of speaking rationally of the Trinity, or of the two natures of Christ, or should it rather confess here some *docta ignorantia* ("learned ignorance")? Is theological theory building concerning such mysteries *a priori* possible, or do such mysteries surpass the possibilities of theory building?

These matters will be mainly dealt with in the next Volume. The reason why I mention them here is that these are not only Christological but also Trinitarian matters, and as such they touch upon the doctrine of God in the broadest sense.

Let me make here another point. In the present "Eternal" series, I time and again refer to the paradigmatic determinedness of all our theological investigation. It is not true that the exegetical biblical data are collected in some "neutral, objective, unprejudiced" manner; rather theologians select and interpret them on the basis of their transcendent, existential faith in the one God and the three divine persons, *or* on the basis of their disbelief concerning these matters. Not only we, but also the fiercest opponents of the Trinity doctrine can interpret the biblical data only through the "glasses" of their own aprioric beliefs. No single theologian can escape here from his "ultimate commitment."[36] We never get here outside our "hermeneutical circle."[37] The exegetical data determine what theological theories we prefer, but it is equally true that the theories we prefer determine what exegetical data we prefer to take into account, and how we interpret them (e.g., which ones we wish to view as "authentic," and which we do not). However, this hermeneutical circles never rules out our responsibility to account for our theological views as thoroughly and accurately as possible.

9.5.2 Is Further Theological Development Possible?

Because, to a large extent, we have to do with theological *theories* (or *models*, if one so prefers) in Trinitarianism and Christology, theologians must observe here the greatest modesty. Some of the theological views that, since many centuries, have been solidified in Creeds and Catechisms as self-evident matters, and have been imposed upon church people with force, were not self-evident at all for the Apostolic Fathers and for the Apologists — and these were men for whom we have the greatest respect. On the contrary, it took centuries before certain notions, such as the "eternal generation" of the Son and the Christological doctrine of the "two natures" (see the next Volume) had received their definitive shapes. This was because the views concerned are not explicitly dealt with in Scripture, but were the result of extensive and complicated theological reasoning.

This does not mean at all that such views are necessarily wrong, but they are not necessarily correct either. I believe that Christians may criticize each other when the fundamental beliefs of Christianity — take as an obvious example the Apostolic Creed — are at stake. But I even more firmly believe that no theological *theory* (i.e., any theoretical-theological elaboration of that doctrine of faith) ever ought to be imposed

---

36. See extensively, Ouweneel (2005a, chapters 7–8; 2007, chapter 13).
37. See Vol. I/1, §§1.7 and 6.6.3.

upon Christians, or ought to be invested with ecclesiastical authority (whatever the latter may mean, for this is a problem of its own).[38]

It was therefore correct that, for instance, Dutch theologian Kornelis H. Miskotte (d. 1976)[39] asked the question whether we must stop at Chalcedon—that is, is the Christology since the Council of Chalcedon (451) forever fixed and determined?—apart from Miskotte's own motives.[40] He asked this question in opposition to theologians, such as the Dutch Frederik W.A. Korff (d. 1942),[41] who gave to the confession of Chalcedon—"Christ is one person with two natures: a divine and a human one"—the character of a terminal point in the ecclesiastical Christological development, and condemned all confessional development after and beyond Chalcedon. What is true of Chalcedon, is also applicable to the Councils of Nicea (325) and Constantinople (381), which involved the essential equality of the Father and the Son, and the deity of the Holy Spirit as well as the Trinity doctrine, respectively.[42]

Take the example of the fourth Ecumenical Council, that of Ephesus (431), which proclaimed that Mary was *theotokos*, that is, the one who had given birth to God; in more popular terms, Mary is the mother of God. In spite of the fact that this was the verdict of an Ecumenical Council—on the same level as Nicea, Constantinople and Chalcedon—Protestant theologians have often expressed that they are unhappy with it. Mary is the mother of Jesus according to the latter's human nature. The fact that Jesus is both Man and God does not give

---

38. Ouweneel (1995, §3.3).
39. Miskotte (1941).
40. Cf. Berkouwer (1952, 65–76).
41. Korff (1940, 196).
42. Brown (1994a, 25) depicts the relationship between "Nicea" and "Chalcedon" as follows: in the former Council, the issue was Jesus as the "true God from the true God," in the latter Council the issue was Jesus as "true God and true Man." Also cf. 150–152: if the former were not true, we still would not be able to truly know God; if the latter were not true, we would not know the depth of God's love, namely, the love of his self-emptying.

us the right to claim that his human mother was the mother of God. We cannot go any further than this: Mary is the mother of the Man Jesus, and this Man is also God—but God as such does not have a mother.

Similarly, many non-Lutheran theologians do not like to say that God died on the cross, as many Lutherans do.[43] The former believe that we cannot go any further than this: the Man Jesus, who died on the cross, is also God—but God as such cannot die. Jesus died according to his human nature. Yet we cannot separate the natures. In the next Volume, we will come back to the tension that arises here. Notice the similiarity: the Trinitarian tension between the oneness and the threeness is comparable with the Christological tension between Christ's divinity and his humanity.

9.5.3 Criteria

To come back to Miskotte and Korff, already before the latter, the Dutch dogmatician Anthonie G. Honig (d. 1940)[44] had written that the doctrine concerning the person of the Mediator, as established by the church, is not receptible to any further development, and has already been formulated to its full extent. Other traditional theologians have accepted a more nuanced point of view. Take one simple example, which will be dealt with in these last chapters: does the notion of a "person" have for us the same meaning as it had for the fathers of the fourth and the fifth centuries?

The answer is strongly negative. Since the rise of modern psychology, and in fact already since the Enlightenment, the notion of the "person" has undergone an important development. To us, a person is a far more independent individual than it ever was in earlier ages. In other words, if we say today that God is three "persons" (three independent individuals) we run the danger of positing the idea of a tritheism (the belief in three Gods), which is totally different from the faith

---

43. Cf. Moltmann (1993, title: *The Crucified God*).
44. Honig (1910, 74).

of the church fathers.

In other words, there is, and there even must be, room for a critical evaluation of "Nicea," "Constantinople" and "Chalcedon." As I said, each generation of theologians must reconsider the creeds and confessions involved. But the central question is this. If we do accept the possibility, and even necessity, of a further "development" of the Trinity doctrine, in what way and to what extent is this possible? What criteria are to be applied here? For it is obvious that by far the most post-Chalcedonian "developments" on the point of the Trinity doctrine have been rejected by traditional theologians — and often rightly so.

Insofar as "Chalcedon" has formulated in human words the practical faith of millions of common Christians it was the faith based upon a reverent acceptance of the biblical testimony. It is the firm belief that Jesus Christ was and is true God and true Man, and yet one individual. This faith is unassailable. It is not open for further "development" because it is hardly anything more than repating the clear statements of Scripture. The person who believes that the New Testament is part of the infallible Word of God cannot possibly deny that Jesus was, and is, a true Man (John 1:14 etc.). And he or she cannot doubt either that Jesus was, and is, God (John 1:1, 18; 5:18; Rom. 9:5; Titus 2:13; 2 Pet. 1:1; 1 John 5:20).

However, the doctrinal conclusion of Chalcedon also involves a complicated theological *theory*, in which terms as "person" and "nature" play a great role — and these are terms that, in the meanings given to them, do not occur at all in the Bible, as we will see below. Such theories can never acquire the status of infallibility, no matter what the ecclesiastical authority may be with which they have been invested, for this authority is not infallible either (and from an ecclesiological viewpoint doubtful in itself). Therefore, on this *theoretical* level there is the possibility, and even the obligation, to come to further development, even if it were alone for this reason: do

The Doctrine of the Trinity

the terms that are used (hypostasis, substance, essence, nature, person, etc.) still have the same meaning for us as they had for the church fathers, and even the Reformers? The *faith* in the Trinity and in the God-Man Jesus Christ is unassailable. But all theological practice, reflection, discussion and theory building is not only disputable, but also constantly on the move.

9.6 The One and the Three
9.6.1 Ancient Formulation

Let us try to offer a formulation of the traditional Trinity doctrine that is as concise and accurate as possible.[45] There is one God (no other gods are comparable with him), and this God is one (single) in his substance or essential being. The former is a numerical unity (of his kind there is only one), the latter is an indivisible unity (within the Deity, there are not several Gods).

This one and only God *is* three divine persons, or three hypostases, called the Father, the Son and the Holy Spirit. These are not three Gods, who would be "one" only within some generic unity, that is, just like people are "one" in the unity of the species *Homo sapiens*, or in the unity of a marriage or a family. Nor are the three hypostases "one" only in some moral unity, like people of the same moral nature and motivation are "one," which does not mean much more than being unified, unanymous, in unison.[46]

The three hypostases are distinguished as existing within the numerical and indivisible unity of God. These three are

---

[45]. Cf. quotations from Hermannus Venema, Samuel Harris, E. A. Pack, and J. Pye Smith in Chafer (*ST* 1:277, 283–85). Fortman (1972) gave a good survey of the history of the doctrine of the Trinity; cf. also Durand (1985, chapter 1); Lonergan (1976) described the development of Trinitarianism until Nicea (325).

[46]. Moltmann (1981, 215–20) picked up this misleading parallel with a human community, and developed from is a social Trinitarianism, in which the Trinitarion community is presented as a model for a "humane," non-patriarchal, non-authoritarian society.

not just three different manifestations of God, but distinct hypostases, three eternal, co-equal entities with the one essence of God, each with its own distinct properties, which yet are not separate essences, but one essence, each possessing all divine attributes (omnipotence, omniscience, omnipresence, holiness, glory, and so on).

The Athanasian Creed expresses this as follows:[47] "[T]he catholic [i.e., universal-Christian] faith is this: that we worship one God in Trinity, and Trinity in Unity; neither confounding the Persons [as if the three are identical after all], nor dividing the Essence [as if the unity is a threeness after all]. For there is one Person of the Father; another of the Son; and another of the Holy Ghost. But the godhead of the Father, of the Son, and of the Holy Ghost, is all one; the glory equal, the majesty co-eternal. Such as the Father is, such is the Son, and such is the Holy Ghost. The Father is uncreated, the Son is uncreated, and the Holy Ghost is uncreated. The Father is unlimited, the Son is unlimited, and the Holy Ghost is unlimited. The Father is eternal, the Son is eternal, and the Holy Ghost is eternal. And yet they are not three eternals but one eternal, as also there are not three uncreated, nor three infinites, but one uncreated, and one infinite," and so forth.

9.6.2 Analysis of the Terms Used

We must carefully distinguish and describe the terminology that is used here.[48]

As to the *one God* (Lat. *unitas*, "unity"): there is one essence or substance (Gk. *ousía*, Lat. *essentia* and *substantia*), that is, one divine nature (Gk. *physis*, Lat. *natura*). The traditional doctrine of the Trinity rejects the thesis that there would be three divine substances, three essences, or three divine natures, for this would amount to tritheism, that is, the belief that there are in fact three Gods.

Originally, *essentia* was an uncommon Latin word. Au-

---
47. https://en.wikipedia.org/wiki/Athanasian_Creed.
48. On *ousia*, *physis*, and *hypostasis*, see also MacLeod (1998, 46–48).

gustine gave it its common Trinitarian meaning.[49] He preferred it to *substantia* because this word was heavily loaded with Greek substantialism. Through him, the scholastic Christian thinkers, and later the Reformers, accepted formulas such as these: in God there is *una essentia, unitas naturae* ("one essence, a unity of nature"), and there are *tres personae, trinitas personarum* ("three persons, a trinity of persons").[50] Ultimately, terms such as substance, essence, nature, and so on, can all lead to misunderstandings. In a certain sense they are even superfluous, as we will see. Karl Barth rightly said that the "being of God" is nothing but the "*Godhead* of God" (Ger. *Gottheit Gottes*). We may indeed wonder whether some other term is at all necessary or desirable besides this biblical *theotēs* (Col. 2:9; Lat. *deitas*).[51]

As to the *three divine persons* (Lat. *trinitas*, "trinity"): there are three persons (sing.: Gk. *prosōpon*, Lat. *persona*), that is, three hypostases (sing.: Gk. *hypostasis*), which are all three eternal as well as co-equal (Gk. *homo-ousios*, Lat. *consubstantialis*[52]). The traditional form of the Trinity doctrine rejects the thesis that there would be one divine person or one divine hypostasis, for this would amount to unitarianism or modalism; this is the view that Father, Son and Holy Spirit are not different persons or hypostases, but "just" three modes in which God reveals himself, sometimes as Father, sometimes as Son, sometimes as the Holy Spirit. Supposedly these are just three "faces" of the one Deity.

Traditional Trinitarianism has rejected this view just as decidedly as the opposite of it: tritheism, the belief that makes Father, Son and Holy Spirit so independent of each other that this amounts to the belief in three distinct Gods. The former view emphasizes one-sidedly the oneness of God at the expense of the threeness; the latter view emphasizes

---

49. Cf. Durrant (1973, chapters 3–4).
50. Bavinck (*RD* II, 264).
51. Barth (*CD* I,1, 369).
52. See on this term Berkouwer (1952, 46–48) and Weber (1981, 416–17).

one-sidedly the threeness of God at the expense of the oneness.

9.7 New Testament Use of Terms
9.7.1 *Ousía*

The four Greek terms used here occur all in the New Testamen, but not (always) necessarily with the same meaning, or actually hardly at all.

Ousía, a well-known term from Aristotelian philosophy,[53] occurs in the New Testament only once, in the meaning "possession, property": "And the younger of them [i.e., the two sons] said to his father, 'Father, give me the share of property [*ousía*] that is coming to me.' And he divided his property between them. Not many days later, the younger son gathered all he had and took a journey into a far country, and there he squandered his property [*ousía*] in reckless living" (Luke 15:12–13).[54] Of course, this is something very different from the Trinitarian use of the term, which involves a more literal meaning of "being" (from Gk. *eimi*, "to be," just like *essentia* comes from Lat. *esse*, "to be"). Also the Latin *substantia* can have the secondary meaning of "possession" (cf. the expression "a man of substance," that is, a wealthy man). Originally, some church fathers applied the term *ousía* to each of the three divine persons, and others applied to the one divine essence. Later, it became the reference to the being, the nature, or the essence of a matter, and thus became synonymous with *physis*; both were applied to the essence of the Deity, not (any longer) to the three hypostases.

9.7.2 *Physis*

Physis is usually rendered as "nature," whether it is the nature of plants (Rom. 11:21, 24), the nature of animals (James 3:7a), or the nature of humans (cf. the specific meaning in

---

53. Cf. Durrant (1973, chapter 2).
54. According to Ratzinger (2007, 204), "The Greek word used in the parable for the property that the son dissipates means 'essence' in the vocabulary of Greek philosophy. The prodigal dissipates 'his essence,' himself."

James 3:7b, *physis anthrōpinē* = "human species," "humanity). It may even refer to the nature of God (2 Pet. 1:4a). In the latter meaning, "nature" seems to be identical with "being." It is the incorruptible divine essence: that which characterizes God in contrast with "the corruption that is in the world because of sinful desire" (v. 4b).

Though the traditional Trinity doctrine uses the term only for the one essence or substance of God, the biblical usage hardly seems to prohibit speaking of the "nature" (natural character) of each of the divine persons. The two usages are not necessarily very different if we agree that the natures of the divine persons are essentially one and the same divine nature. When it comes to the Trinity, speaking of one nature or of three natures is as debatable, or as little debatable, as speaking alternately of the "person" of God or of the three "persons" within the Deity. It is all a matter of definition (see further below).

9.7.3 *Prosōpon*

Prosōpon originally means "face," both in the literal (e.g., Matt. 6:16–17; 17:2; 26:67) and in the more figurative sense. In the latter meaning, it is sometimes rendered as "person" (Matt. 22:16 KJV etc.). "Seeing someone's face" (Acts 20:25, 38) means seeing him or her in person; being "unknown by face" (Gal. 1:22) means being unknown in person; "accepting someone's face" (favoritism; Luke 20:21; Gal. 2:6) means "accepting" (favoring) the person. The clearest example where the rendering "person" is at place is 2 Corinthians 1:11, where the word occurs in the plural: "many persons."

The mask that ancient actors wore resembled a human face, and therefore was called *prosōpon* too. "Mask," and hence "role," was the original meaning of the Latin euivalent *persona* (cf. the verb *personare*, "to sound through," i.e., the voice through the mask). The church fathers chose the word in their Trinitarian debates because of its broad semantic range, and thus could give it the more precise sense of "person" or "hypostasis." This meaning was needed to refer to each of the three entities within the one God, although the church fathers did realize that no single term could fully express the mystery of the three divine hypostases.[55]

Yet, the term was ambiguous. Third-century theologian Sabellius said that the one divine *ousía* or *hypostasis* assumed different *prosōpa* in the sense of modes or forms of revelation, as if the one Deity put on different "faces" or "masks" at different occasions. However, the fathers answered that the three *prosōpa* in the divine essence were *prosōpa enhypostata*, that is, they existed *en hypostasei*, that is, as distinct hypostases. Therefore, the Greek term *hypostasis* was preferred to *prosōpon*, while the Latin fathers preferred *persona*.[56] Calvin emphasized the distinction between the three divine persons by describing a divine person as a hypostasis within the essence of God that distinguishes itself from the others by an incommunicable property;[57] this will be explained below.

9.7.4 *Hypostasis*

In 2 Corinthians 9:4 and 11:17, Greek *hypostasis* has the sense of "confidence." According to German-American theologian Helmut Koester (d. 2016), in Hebrews (1:3; 3:14; 11:1) the word "always denotes the 'reality' of God which stands contrasted with the corruptible, shadowy, and merely prototypical character of the world but which is paradoxically present in Jesus and is the possession of the community as faith."[58] In Hebrews 1:3, the term is rendered as "person" (KJV etc.), "nature" (ESV), "being" (NIV etc.), "substance" (DRA etc.), "essence" (CJB etc.); in short, the entire Trinitarian terminology can be found here in the translations. Yet, the common Trinitarian use of the term is not found here at all. This verse says that the Son is the "exact imprint" (Gk. *charaktēr*) of God's

---

55. Lohse (*TDNT* 6, 778).
56. Bavinck (*RD* II, 267).
57. *Institutes* I.13.6.
58. Koester (*TDNT* 8, 587–88).

hypostasis, whereas the Trinity doctrine says that the Son himself is one hypostasis, and that the Father is another one. That is, according to the traditional Trinity doctrine, God *is* not a hypostasis, nor does he *have* a hypostasis, but he *is* three hypostases in one.

Actually, Calvin wished to read this Trinitarian formulation into Hebrews 1:3,[59] wich seems to me incorrect. It is *God* who spoke to the fathers, the *Triune* God, not the *Father*. It is this God who now, in the "last days," has spoken to us *en huiōi*, that is, the One whom we hear speaking is God the Son. Calvin's objection is that, if Christ were the imprint of *God's* hypostasis, this would suggest that the entire divine being would exclusively belong to him, but this is a mistake. Just compare Colossians 1:15, where Christ is also the "image" of the invisible *God*, and compare John 1:1, where the Logos was *pros ton theon* ("with God"), and was himself *theos* ("God"), even *monógenēs theos* ("the only God"; John 1:1, 18).[60] Calvin's objection, if correct, would be true for these passages as well. Christ is the imprint of God's being, and he can perfectly be so because he himself is God—however, he is not the *Triune God*, but God the Son. Similarly, Christ is the Logos, that, the perfect expression of God's being, and he can perfectly be so because he himself is God—however, he is not the *Triune God*, but God the Son. In all these cases, Christ is the true expression of the full Deity, he himself being in his own person "just" one of the three persons within the Deity.

Notice here two exegetical details: (a) in John 1:1 the Logos was *pros ton theon* ("with God"), *theon* having the article; but in the expression *theos ēn ho logos*, *theos* does not have the article. The former refer to the (Triune) Deity, the latter to God the Son.[61]

---

59. *Institutes* I.13.2.
60. Cf. *Institutes* I.13.6, 7.
61. Quite decisive may the article not be, though: in 1 John 5:20 Jesus is called *ho alēthinos theos*, "the true God," that is, with the article; but others have argued that, strictly speaking, the Trinity is intended here.

(b) John 1:18 is highly remarkable (no wonder that later copyists changed the text): *monógenēs theos*. Perhaps we should not translate "the only God" (ESV) because, in my view, the text is not a reference to the uniqueness of God, but to the uniqueness of the Son (cf. *monógenēs* in John 1:14; 3:16, 18; 1 John 4:9); we might translate: "the only [begotten] [Son], God." That is, the Son is just as much God as the Father is, in whose bosom he is.

"Hypostasis" in the sense of one of the three persons within the Deity does not occur in the New Testament. This does not mean that the Trinity doctrine errs in this respect; it only means that it uses the term "hypostasis" in a different way than the New Testament does (which actually is not wrong, but it is not an ideal situation either). Moreover, the common Latin translation of *hypostasis* (from the Gk. verb *hyphistēmi*) is *substantia* (from Lat. *substare*), which etymologically is entirely equivalent. Yet, the term *substantia* is reserved for the one substance or essence of God. Thus, the three hypostases are distinguished from the one substance of God, although in fact the terms mean exactly the same. Here, the problem is the same as with "nature" (is/has God one nature or three natures?) and "person" (is God one person or three persons?).

It was Tatian (second half second century) who was the first to speak of God as absolute *hypostasis*, that is, "absolute, underived reality." Athanasius used *hypostasis* in more or less the same sense as *ousía*, the one essence of God, but other Greek fathers used the term to underscore the distinct existence of the three divine persons. The Eastern church emphasized in opposition to modalism (see the next chapter) the *hypostasis* of each of the three divine persons, whereas the Western church, in opposition to tritheism (the belief in three Gods), emphasized the one, common *substantia* of the three persons.[62] All this terminological confusion does not make the Trinity doctrine any more transparent.

---

62. Cf. Bavinck (*RD* II, 263–64); cf. Kettler (*RGG* 6;1029–30) on the debate concerning one or three hypostases.

9.8 Trinitarian Tension
9.8.1 Confusing Use of Terms

There is a certain tension in the traditional Trinitarian terminology that must be clearly brought to light. It may seem to be an elegant solution to speak of one essence and three hypostases, and thus to distinguish the terms: some refer to the oneness of God, others refer to his threeness. However, in practice we find that tradition has used several terms to alternately describe the one essence or the three persons. We already found several of them: *ousía*, *prosōpon*, and *hypostasis*, and I have argued that *physis* too could be used for both the one essence and the three persons. And what objection could there be, conversely, to speak of *three* essences within the Deity, or to speak of the *one* person of God?

Let me give one example of the ambiguity involved. Dutch theologian Jan van Genderen said, entirely according to tradition, that God is three persons, but just before this he said, rather surprisingly, that we call God a "person"![63] How strongly was he aware that this latter "insight" does not go back any further than the nineteenth century?

Indeed, through Immanuel Kant and Romanticism, the term "person" received quite a new content, namely, as "self-awareness" over against the objectifiable world of things. Therefore, some theologians (Friedrich Schleiermacher, David F. Strauss, Alois E. Biedermann) and philosophers (Johann G. Fichte, Georg W.F. Hegel) rejected using the term "person" with regard to God because they saw him as the absolute Reason or Mind (Spirit). However, most theologians did the reverse, and developed the notion of the "personality" of God, precisely in opposition to German Idealism as well as the new naturalist atheism. This conflict was continued in the twentieth century: especially German-American theologian Paul Tillich (d. 1965) defended the view that God is the "superpersonal" (but not entirely "unpersonal") "Being

---

63. Van Genderen (2008, 135, 143).

itself."⁶⁴ In opposition to this, we encounter various "personalists" such as Martin Buber, Philip Kohnstamm, Emil Brunner, and Heinrich Ott.⁶⁵

Those who keep to three distinct divine persons were accused by Emil Brunner of tritheism, even if such theologians explicitly claim the oneness of God.⁶⁶ But why could we not accuse Brunner himself of modalism where he said for instance: "Jesus Christ's personality is the personality of God himself,"⁶⁷ even if he xplicitly rejected the idea of the identity of the Father and the Son?⁶⁸ The same is true for Heinrich Ott, who rejected the modern personality idea in the Trinity doctrine with the following strong words: "In no way [!] is God three Persons. He is one Person."⁶⁹

This is a common phenomenon. Those tending more to the side of the oneness will always accuse those who claim keeping the balance, namely, accuse them of tritheism. And those tending more to the side of the threeness will always accuse those who claim keeping the balance, namely, accuse them of modalism. It is the same with the Christological problem: those who tend more to the divine aspect of Christ will easily accuse their opponents of stressing too strongly — "in a modernist way" — the humanity of Christ. And those who are more inclined to stressing the human aspect of Christ will easily accuse their opponents of stressing too strongly — "in a Docetist way" — the divinity of Christ.

Again, it is the same with the tension between God's sovereignty and human responsibility. This problem may seem to be very different — and in many ways it is — but still we observe the same phenomenon here. Those inclined to overem-

---

64. Tillich (1968).
65. Buber (2000), Kohnstamm (1931), Brunner (especially 1943), and Ott (1969); cf. Berkhof (1986, 135–36) and the philosophy of religion view of Brümmer (1988).
66. Brunner (1950, 241, 254).
67. Ibid., 243.
68. Ibid., 244.
69. Ott (1974, 60).

phasize God's sovereignty will easily accuse their opponents of a "free will" standpoint (whatever this may mean), and those inclined to overemphasize human responsibility will easily accuse their opponents of a form of "determinism." The theologian's life is on the razor's edge; he is always in danger of falling off at one or the other side.

9.8.2 One or Three Persons?

German theologian Werner Elert, who fully accepted the doctrine of the Trinity, assured us that, when the Holy Spirit meets us as a *personal* "you," this is the one and indivisible *person* of God, not one out of three.[70] However, if it is possible to say both that God is one person and that he is three persons, why would it not be possible as well to say that God is one essence, and at the same time three essences? Or one hypostasis as well as three hypostases? Or one substance as well as three substances? Calvin reminded us of the church father Jerome, who wrote that it is blasphemy to say that there are three substances in God. Yet, Calvin noticed, more than hundred times Hilarius did exactly that, and Anselm[71] confirmed that this is a possible way of expressing.[72] Edmund Schlink concluded that, in principle, there cannot be any objection against speaking of God as one substance in three substances, or one person in three persons[73] (or one being in three beings, or one hypostasis in three hypostases, and so on).

Elert rightly noticed that all the terms mentioned have been equally used both for the oneness and for the threeness of God, and that they are all equally inadequate and dangerous, but also all applicable, as long as they are not understood by themselves but from the coherence that is intended.[74] Thus, the heretical Arius (d. 336) did not object to referring to the Father, the Son and the Spirit as *treis hypostaseis* ("three

---

70. Elert (1956, 219).
71. *Monologion*, Prologue.
72. *Institutes* I.13.5.
73. Schlink (1983, 750).
74. Elert (1956, 210–11).

hypostases"), although he viewed them as quite unequal. And Paul of Samosata (d. 275) used the famous Nicene term *homo-ousios* in a way that was the opposite of that of the Nicene Creed, namely, to underscore the alleged subordination of the Logos. No single Trinitarian term as such is ever a guarantee against whatever heresy.[75] They have to be *defined*.

Of course, there are good (didactic) reasons to choose different terms for the one Deity and for the three persons, if even only because we wish to avoid the absurd conclusion that some have drawn from the Trinity doctrine, namely, that this doctrine implies that one equals three, and three equals one. But even if we use different terms, we constantly remind ourselves that these are only human terms in order to try to approximate that which surpasses human conceptualization. Terms such as essence, hypostasis, person, nature, substance (not to mention entity, subsistency, modes of existence, and the like) are all equally appropriate, as well as limited, to give us an idea of both the one God and the three persons. At any rate, it will hardly be possible to put an end to the custom of referring to God as a "person," and at the same time referring to the three "persons" in the Deity, as long as the latter are not understood in a modern-psychological sense as three autonomous "subjects," "personalities" or "consciousnesses," because such a view would inevitably lead to tritheism.

9.8.3 Once More: Tradition

The Augustinian tradition said quite interestingly that Father, Son and Holy Spirit are *unum*, one substance, not *unus*, one person, but *tres*, three persons. Or, the three persons are each someone else, *alius*, but not something else, *aliud*, for they partake of the one divine substance. We understand the good intentions here, but today we apparently have little difficulty referring to the divine substance as a person, that is, God is *unus*. As Galatians 3:20 put it, *ho de theos heis estin*, "God is one," in which "one" is masculine, not neuter; that is, Latin

---

75. Cf. Weber (1981, 415–19).

unus, not Greek *hen*, Latin *unum*. Does this imply a positive "development" in the doctrine of the Trinity, or only an adding to the confusion?

Paul Tillich had a point when he emphasized that we rather ought to speak of the *personae* of the Trinity, *not* the persons, apparently in order that the early-Christian term *persona* is not confused with the modern-psychological term "person."[76] This point is well taken; but I have found no one to accept this habit.

Of course, no matter how we take it, the least we can say is that the term "person" is a theological metaphor. This is self-evident because not all that can be said of human persons as such is applicable to God. This has led some to the idea that God cannot be "personal" in any literal sense, and therefore [!] is "impersonal."[77] This error makes the matter even more complicated.[78] It is the same old problem all over again: confusing concepts and ideas.

We may conclude that the doctrine of the Trinity has developed its own finite, limited, fallible techical terminology, which cannot be directly derived from the Bible. Of course, this does not mean that the Trinity doctrine is "unbiblical." But it does mean that the entire doctrine contains a large element of *theological theory building* with its own scholarly terminology. This is a common phenomenon: *all* theory building necessarily develops its own technical terminology. There is nothing wrong about it,[79] as long as the *doctrine* of the Trinity is not identified with the Bible, and people realize that such terminology and theory building is necessarily fallible. Not any Trinitarian model is "true" — only the Bible is true.

Of all Trinitarian *termini technici* it is true what Augustine

---

76. Tillich (1968,II, 166); cf. Barth (*CD* I,1, 370–372); Van Niftrik (1961, 422); Durrant (1973, chapter 5); Buri (1978, 591–95); Kasper (1983, 285–90); Durand (1985, 56–67); Van de Beek (1987, 294–308).
77. Cf. Bavinck (*RD* II, 268.
78. Also cf. Hodge (1872, 444); Chafer (*ST* 1:276).
79. Cf. Bavinck (*RD* II, 262–63).

has said of the term "person": we use the term "person" because we cannot remain silent on the subject and do have to say *something*. *Dictum est tamen tres personae, non ut illud diceretur, sed ne taceretur.*[80] Anselm even spoke of *tres nescio quid* ("three I-don't-know-whats"). We do not use the terms because they are the best, or are even adequate, but because we are forced to express ourselves on the matter; as Calvin said, too: . . . *non ut exprimeretur quod est, sed ne taceretur* ("not to express what it is, but in order not to remain silent").[81]

It is here with the doctrine of the Trinity as it is with the Christological mystery ("one person, two natures"); we may feel forced to speak of it, but sometimes it seems wiser to shut our mouths. Dietrich Bonhoeffer quoted Søren Kierkegaard in this respect: "Keep silent, for this is the absolute."[82] But it was just as correct and fitting what Dutch theologian Johannes Verkuyl (d. 2001) said,[83] "Therefore, we should not remain silent [on the Trinity], even though our speaking is so deficient." The Bible has spoken on the matter, and therefore the church must speak—and theology must undertake its own effort to speak, in order to be of service to the church.

---

80. *De Trinitate* V.9; VI.10; cf. VII.4.7; see extensively, Braun (1876); Kasper (1983, 285–90).
81. *Institutes* I.13.5.
82. Bonhoeffer (1982, 8.
83. Verkuyl (1992, 291).

Chapter 10
The Development of Trinitarianism

"There are three that bear witness in heaven: the Father, the Word, and the Holy Spirit; and these three are one."

1 John 5:7 (NKJV)

10.1 Divine Properties
10.1.1 Introduction

AT THE TOP OF THIS CHAPTER, I quoted 1 John 5:7 from the NKJV. This passage contains a phrase that is lacking in more modern translations such as ESV, which reads: "[T]here are three that testify," and continues with verse 8. What is lacking is the phrase "…the Father, the Word, and the Holy Spirit; and these three are one." Modern textual critics are generally convinced that these words, although their content is impeccable, do not belong to the original inspired text; they are lacking in the earliest manuscripts, and are obviously a later addition by one or more copyists. They form a remarkable piece of developed Trinitarianism, and this within the so-called Received Text. The development of the Trinity doctrine is the very subject of the present chapter.

The main usefulness of Trinitarian terminology and theory building has been a negative one, namely, to protect the biblical truth concerning the Trinity against all kinds of heretical approaches. On the one hand, a biblicistic theology that "wishes to stick to biblical terms only" can easily land in one of these heresies, without even realizing it. On the other hand, it is possible to imagine that a Trinitarian theology, no matter how deficient, no matter how many technical terms it may have adopted, is most in agreement with the Bible. At the same time it is possible that the doctrine of the Trinity easily goes astray in the overestimation of its theoretical potential, and goes far beyond what can be biblically accounted for. We will encounter several examples of these various mistakes.

It was for this reason that John Calvin expressed the desire that all those doubtful Trinitarian terms (*inventa nomina*, "invented names") would be buried as long as Trinitarian faith as such would be firmly maintained.[1] This is the faith that the Father and the Son and the Spirit are one God, and that yet the Son is not the Father, and the Father is not the Son. Rather, they are distinct from each other through something that is "proper" to each of them (*proprietate quadam*) — which actually does mean the introduction of another doubtful term. As soon as faith begins to *reflect* on the Trinity, it feels the necessity of a terminology that goes beyond that of Scripture, and this necessarily is inevitable but at the same time always doubtful, limited and fallible.

10.1.2 Mutual Relationships

The three divine persons do not differ in their divine being, of which they equally partake; they differ only in their mutual relationships. Their most important personal properties (sing.: Gk. *idiotēs*) in which they differ from each other precisely express these relationships. It was in particular Gregory of Nazianzus (d. 390) who has formulated them in the manner that I am following here:

(1) The *first person* in the Deity is (Gk.) *ho gennētōr*, the

---

1. *Institutes* I.13.5.

"Begetter"; he is characterized by (Gk.) *agennēsia* (i.e., he is [Lat.] *ingenitus*, "non-begotten," in comparison the Son, who was "begotten"). Or, more positively, he possesses the (Gk.) *patrotēs* (Lat. *paternitas*, "fatherhood"), the (Lat.) *generatio activa*, "active generation," namely, of the Son. Another property is the (Lat.) *spiratio activa*, that is, he makes the Holy Spirit "proceed" from him.[2]

(2) The *second person* in the Deity is (Gk.) *to gennèma*, "that which was begotten (fathered)"; he is characterized by (Gk.) *gennēsis* (i.e., he is [Lat.] *genitus*, "begotten," namely, by the Father, who was "non-begotten"), the (Lat.) *generatio passiva*, that is, his having been begotten by the Father. Another property (rejected by the Eastern church) is the (Lat.) *spiratio activa*, that is, he makes the Holy Spirit "proceed" from him. He is (Gk.) *gennētos*, "begotten," but just like the other persons of the Deity he is (Gk.) *agenētos*, "uncreated" (notice the one *n* difference between *gennētos* and *genētos*).

(3) The *third person* in the Deity is (Gk.) *to ekporeuomenon*, "that which is proceeding." He is characterized by (Gk.) *ekporeusis* (Lat. *processio*, "procession," his proceeding from the Father (and according to the Western church also from the Son) or (Gk.) *pnoē* (from Gk. *pneuma*, "spirit"), that is (Lat.), *spiratio* (from Lat. *spiritus*, "spirit"); more precisely, *spiratio passiva*, his being "breathed out" by the Father (and the Son?).

The (especially Augustinian[3]) tradition makes the following distinctions (only Latin terms to be mentioned):

I. God's *notae internae* ("internal properties," which imply his eternal, immanent works):

(a) The personal *works* of the three persons (*opera Dei ad intra*), which are eternal, both eternally completed and eternally continuing, and they are *divisa*, that is, only belong to one or two, not all three. They are:

---

2. See Ouweneel (*EDR* 2, §1.3) and Vol. II/3.
3. See *De Trinitate* V.5.6; see the summaries by Alexander (1888, 104); Weber (1981, 433–34); Trillhaas (1972, 110–11).

* for the Father: *generatio activa* and *spiratio activa*,
* for the Son: *generatio passiva* and *spiratio activa*,
* for the Spirit: *spiratio passiva*.

(b) The personal *properties* of the three persons (*appropriationes*, which are implied in God's eternal, immanent works, which are themselves implied in these properties):

* for the Father: *paternitas*,
* for the Son, *filiatio*,
* for the Spirit: *spiratio*.

II. God's *notae externae* ("external properties," which also imply his external works):

(a) God's works that are from eternity (immanent, but extravert): God's eternal counsel.

(b) God's works that are within time: the work of creation, redemption, and sanctification; these works are "undivided," that is, in each work we have to do with the full, undivided divine essence, notwithstanding a certain amount of specialization:

* the Father especially in the work of creation,
* the Son especially in the work of redemption,
* the Spirit especially in the work of sanctification.

10.1.3 Some Comments

When we take a general look at the classical picture of the Trinity, we notice that it is remarkably static. This word "static" contains the root *sta-*, which through reduplication (*si-st*) led to Latin *sistere*, and hence to English "exist." In the classical presentation, it looks as if God—to speak with what C.S. Lewis said somewhere—does not need to do anything else than "exist." Or also, the divine persons do not need to do anything else than to beget eternally, or to be begotten eternally, to breath out eternally, and to be breathed out eternally. Is this, as far as the *notae internae* ("internal properties") are concerned, really the whole story?

What is lacking in this presentation are all kinds of "internal" elements that, in our view—and also, I believe, the biblical view—makes the Trinity so dynamic, if not—if the reader allows me the term—so exciting. God is not just a Tri-unity but a Tri-community. There is the eternal communication between Father, Son, and Holy Spirit, the eternal dialogue.[4] The latter is so much more than an eternal "being," "begetting" (or "being begotten"), and "breathing out" (or "being breathed out"). We have to do with *fellowship* here. This concerns the fellowship of the Father, the Son, and the Holy Spirit, into which afterwards the believers, too, have been introduced: "... that they may all be one, just as you, Father, are in me, and I in you, that they also may be in us, so that the world may believe that you have sent me... that they may become perfectly one, so that the world may know that you sent me and loved them even as you loved me" (John 17:21, 23). "God is faithful, by whom you were called into the fellowship of [not "with," as many have it] his Son, Jesus Christ our Lord" (1 Cor. 1:9). "The grace of the Lord Jesus Christ and the love of God and the fellowship of the Holy Spirit be with you all" (2 Cor. 13:14). "[T]hat which we have seen and heard we proclaim also to you, so that you too may have fellowship with us; and indeed our fellowship is with the Father and with his Son Jesus Christ" (1 John 1:3).

This eternal Trinitarian fellowship involves the *love* between the Father and the Son (and the Holy Spirit) from before the foundation of the world, a love that is also deposited in the believers (John 17:24, 26; Rom. 5:5; 15:30, "the love of the Spirit").

Even apart from this soteriological dimension—fellowship *with people*, love *for people*, due to the salvation that is in Christ—the Trinity is more than *paternitas* ("fatherhood"), *filiation* ("sonship"), and *spiratio* (the being-breathed-out of

---
4. The Son's praying "is the dialogue of love within God himself—the dialogue that God *is*"; so Ratzinger (2007, 344).

the Spirit). It is eternal communion, communication, intimacy, sharing, belongingness, harmony, and above all, mutual *love*, affection, faithfulness, between divine persons. What is lacking in the traditional, in fact rather dull, presentation is the warmth and intimacy of the Father's *kolpos* ("bosom")"; it is the atmosphere evoked by a verse like this one: the "only begotten Son, who is in the bosom of the Father" (John 1:18 NKJV); "the only God, who is at the Father's side" (ESV; for the imagery cf. 13:23 and Luke 16:22–23).

10.2 The Two Extremes
10.2.1 Introduction

The doctrine of the Trinity, as we know it from the early church and the early Protestants, was not simply "derived" from Scripture. It took centuries full of fierce debates between the church fathers (among themselves, and with various heretics) before this doctrine received its ultimate shape, as we know it today from the Nicene-Constantinopolitan and Athanasian Creeds. Each possible alternative had been attempted, had been ardently defended, found a certain following, and sometimes for centuries led its own life. The complicated notion of one God and three divine persons was often replaced all too easily by the less complicated notion of the one God who is one person with three faces (modalism), or the notion of three Gods who are three persons (tritheism). And where the notion of one God and three persons *was* accepted, the problems often were "solved" all too easily by declaring one of the three persons, the Father, to be the one true God, and calling the Son and the Spirit only "divine," in whatever (subordinate) sense.

Roughly speaking these were the alternatives; I will now repeat them in a somewhat more elaborate form.[5]

10.2.2 Tritheism

I. *Three persons = three Gods*. This is *tritheism*. Sometimes it was

---

5. Cf. Kettler, *RGG* 6:1025–32.

even developed into a *tetratheism* or *tetradism* (the belief in four Gods), namely, when in a Platonic-realistic sense some Deity "behind" the three persons was distinguished from the latter (*quaternitas* instead of *trinitas*). Also in modalism (see the next section), the actual "essence" of God can be viewed as being hidden behind his threefold revelation in the modes of Father, Son and Spirit, and thus factually function as a "hidden fourth one."[6]

One of those who have been accused of tritheism was Damian of Alexandria (about 600). Perhaps the best known tritheist was Anselm's opponent Roscellinus (about 1100), who, in a nominalist way, declared that the three divine persons were real, whereas the "one God" was only a generic *nomen* (a reference to a group). Remarkably enough, the accusation of tritheism was also addressed to those who rejected the doctrine of the eternal generation of the Son (see the next Volume).

In modern Gnosticism and other heretical movements, the Trinity has often been compared, or even equated, with the "triads," the groups of three gods, that we encounter in various pagan religions.[7] The Babylonians knew the triad Sin, Shamash and Ishtar. Form ancient Egypt we know the triad Osiris, Isis and Horus. Among the Greeks we hear of Zeus, Hades and Poseidon (corresponding with the Roman gods Jupiter, Pluto and Neptune), among the Germanic tribes Odin (Wodan), Wele (Vili) and We (Ve), and among the Hindus Brahma, Vishnu and Shiva. A comparison of the Trinity with such triads will necessarily amount to tritheism. The biblical God who is three in one is *not* a triad but a trinity — not three Gods but one God. Christianity (and Judaism and Islam as well) does not involve a polytheism (the belief in many gods), nor a henotheism (the doctrine of a supreme deity among many gods), nor a tritheism (the belief in three gods), but a strict monotheism (the doctrine of the *one* God).

---

6. Barth (*CD* I/1, 402).
7. Verkuyl (1992, 292).

Paul says, "[There is] one God and Father of all, who is over all and through all and in all" (Eph. 4:6). And elsewhere: "[A]lthough there may be so-called gods in heaven or on earth—as indeed there are many 'gods' and many 'lords'— yet for us there is one God, the Father, from whom are all things and for whom we exist, and one Lord, Jesus Christ, through whom are all things and through whom we exist" (1 Cor. 8:5-6). Notice that this passage expresses the oneness of God, and at the same refers to Jesus Christ, according to both his divinity ("through whom are all things and through whom we exist") and his humanity (the Lord, as distinct from God the Father, where "Father" seems to be more the [Triune!] Creator than the eternal Father of the eternal Son).

10.2.3 Modalism

II. *There is one God, really, numerically and indivisibly one.* This view allowed for two alternatives: there is only one divine person (or hypostasis), or there are three divine persons (or hypostases).

A. *There is one divine person.* This view leads to *patripassianism*, which already in the second century was taught by Praxeas, about whom we only know the writings of Tertullian, who combated Praxeas' view. Tertullian coined the term *patripassianism* (from *pater*, "father," and *patior*, "to suffer") for those who asserted that the Father had suffered on the cross on the basis of the idea that the Son was only a *modus* or manifestation of God the Father. Another term is *modalist monarchianism*, in which *monarchia* refers to the exclusive rule of the one God, who during three successive world stages manifested, and manifests, himself in the *modi* ("modes [of being]," Gk. *prosōpa*) of the Father (namely, as Creator and Lawgiver in the Old Testament), the Son (namely, as Redeemer from his incarnation to his ascension), and the Holy Spirit (namely, as the One who gives life and sanctifies, since Pentecost).[8]

The chief representative of this *modalism* was Sabellius,

---
8. See extensively, Heyns (1953).

the leader of the modalist monarchians at Rome, who was excommunicated by bishop Callixtus (about 220). Through Sabellius, patripassianism or modalist monarchianism became best known as Sabellianism. Time and again it re-emerged during church history. Some scholastic theologians (John Scotus Eriugena, Peter Abelard) and some Anabaptists came very close, and it was defended in particular by Michael Servet (burned at the stake, 1553), Calvin's opponent at Geneva (see §10.6.1). It received a new form in the hands of Friedrich Schleiermacher and his school.[9] In an anti-metaphysical attitude (not necessarily wrong in itself), he placed an "economical" or "revelational Trinity" over against an "immanent" or "essential Trinity." "Economical" refers here to the various "economies" or dispensations (redemptive-historical stages) in world history; 'revelational" means here that God reveals himself as a Trinity without in essence being one.

Over against Schleiermacher, Elert rightly remarked that neither anti-metaphysical fear, nor neo-Kantian theories about the nature of human knowledge, can determine what the church must teach about the gospel.[10] Of course, we do have to acknowledge the significance of the "revelational Trinity": this is because we *know* God's eternal "essential Trinity" through his self-revelation. However, this revelation is not a revelation of some image that God wished to give of himself but a revelation of *himself*. In other words, the revelational Trinity is the image or reflection of the essential Trinity.

Especially through Karl Barth, a new appreciation of this "essential Trinity" has grown, be it in close connection with the divine revelation in Christ, and especially in the cross, to such an extent that Berkouwer even saw here a tendency to theopaschitism (the notion of the suffering *God* on the cross, mentioned above).[11] Yet, this view maintained itself in

---

9. Cf. Barth (*CD* I,1, 372, 431).
10. Elert (1956, 223).
11. Berkouwer (1954, chapter XI).

the post-Barthian German theology,[12] especially—at least to some extent—in the line of the Hegelian idealistic interpretation of the Trinity. For such authors, these seem to be the only alternatives for liberal theology: either the unitarian rejection of the "essential Trinity," or a Hegelian-historical economical interpretation of it.[13]

In the twentieth century, Gerrit Jan Heering,[14] Emil Brunner,[15] Karl Rahner,[16] Hendrikus Berkhof,[17] Fritz Buri,[18] and Hans Küng[19] came very close to the notion of an "economical" or "revelational Trinity" (as opposed to an "essential Trinity"), or defended it openly.[20] At least we may notice that traditional modalism maintained the deity of the Son and the Spirit by equating them with the Father. But in recent times, it easily developed into a "dynamic" or "adoptianist" view, which considered Christ to be a Man filled with the power of God, adopted by God as his Son, and as (only) morally "one" with God. The advocates of this adoptianism believed that, in this way, they could maintain God's "monarchy" most efficiently.[21] This led, and leads, to the views dealt with in the following sections.

10.3   Three More Models
10.3.1 Arianism

B. *There are three divine persons*. The difficulty lies here in the word "divine." Does it mean that the three persons all fully partake in the Deity, the divine essence? Or is it only the Father who in the full sense is considered to be God, where-

---

12. See Pannenberg (1964; 1988); Moltmann (1993; 1980); Jüngel (1976).
13. Cf. Berkhof (1986, 332–33); on Hegel also see Kasper (1983, 264–67).
14. Heering (1945, 111–15).
15. Brunner (1950, 213–55); vgl. Schmidt (1949.
16. Rahner (1970; 1974; 1975, 341–71).
17. Berkhof (1964; he identified the Son with the Spirit; 1986, 321, 327–33).
18. Buri (1978, 617–31).
19. Küng (1978, 699–702 Eng. ed.; 1979, 124–25).
20. Cf. the comment by Kasper (1983, 273–77, 301–03), Durand (1985, §2.3), and Pannenberg (1988, 355–64).
21. See Berkouwer (1952, 143–46).

as the Son and the Spirit allegedly only possess "divinity" (Gk. *theiotēs*, Lat. *divinitas*), but do not partake in the "deity" (Gk. *theotēs*, Lat. *deitas*)? This entails two alternatives (see this and the following sections of §10.3).

(1) *Only the Father partakes in, or rather, is, the Deity.* The Son and the Holy Spirit do not partake in the Deity; on the contrary, the Son is a created being, and the Holy Spirit is often not viewed as a person at all but as a, or the, power of God; this is the doctrine of the *pneumatomachi*.[22] Here again, we can distinguish two varieties.

(a) *The Son was pre-existent*. This was the doctrine of Arius (d. 336), called Arianism.[23] Arius claimed that the Son of God is not truly God but foreign to the being of God. He was not eternal; he is only a creature of God, be it the most supreme creature, created out of nothing. At the incarnation he adopted a body without a soul. As a creature, he was not morally perfect, though striving for moral perfection, and as such he was and is a moral example for other people.

Arius was combated by Athanasius and by the Council of Nicea (325). Ultimately, Arianism was condemned by the Council of Constantinople (381). Yet, it maintained itself for centuries, especially among the Germanic nations, until various Roman Catholic kings suppressed Arianism, and substituted Roman Catholicism for it (which also always implied acceptance of the central authority of the bishop of Rome). Arianism popped up time and again, also in Protestant theology (in the Netherlands for instance among several Arminians and in the nineteenth-century "Groningen" school). It easily developed into the doctrine to be dealt with in the next section.

10.3.2 Socinianism

(b) *The Son was not pre-existent*. This was the doctrine of

---

22. See Ouweneel (*EDR* 2:32, 97–98).
23. See the extensive study by Hanson (1988). The most conspicuous example of modern Arians are the Jehovah's Witnesses.

Socinianism, called after Lelio and Fausto Sozzini (in Latin: Laelius and Faustus Socinus), who in the sixteenth century combated the doctrine of the Trinity. Faustus Socinus founded the church of the Socinians in Poland, which became known because of many heresies. These were, besides unitarianism, especially its rejection of the two natures of Christ as well as of the doctrine of Christ's vicarious sufferings and death. Thus, this movement erred in three major dogmatic areas: theology proper, Christology, and soteriology.

Socinianism influenced many later unitarians, also among the Arminians and the Anabaptists. Its unitarianism became the common view of liberal Enlightenment theology: there was no pre-existent Son of God, therefore strictly speaking there was no "incarnation" either. There was only the birth of a special person, Jesus Christ, who at his baptism was adopted by God as his Son (adoptianism), and was filled with a special ("divine") power, but did not partake in the Deity. Insofar as he can be called "God," this name does not refer to his essence, but to his office (e.g., Albrecht Ritschl, who therefore rejected the idea of the Trinity). In this way, the impact of Socinianism has been tremendous.

Dutch theologian Cees J. den Heyer even asserted that "it cannot possibly be doubted" that certain events were the "cause of the great change that was brought about in Jesus' life around his thirtieth year."[24] Such doubt is definitely possible, if one at least rejects Den Heyer's dogmatic prejudices. In my view, the decisive change in Jesus' life was not his baptism at all, but the incarnation of the Logos.

In this respect, Enlightenment theology is often quite confusing and misleading. It uses biblical formulations, may call Christ "divine" and "God's Son," may claim that God's "incarnation" took place in the historical person of Jesus of Nazareth, and that "in him God came to us."[25] It can even speak of an "ideal" pre-existence of Christ, namely, in the mind and

---
24. Den Heyer (1986, 115).
25. Cf. examples given by Berkouwer (1952, 126–29).

counsel of God. However, it denies the eternal "ontic" pre-existence of the Son, and the *vere deus* ("true God") that the early church confessed with regard to Christ, and that we still understand to be the true biblical message: he was and is "the true God and eternal life" (1 John 5:20).

Unitarians differ on the question whether the birth of Christ was natural or supernatural, the latter involving that Christ at his conception was directly created by God. In Enlightenment theology, the supernatural standpoint was rejected. In this sense, there is a direct line running from Arianism to modernism: after the Arian stage, Christ's pre-existence was rejected (Socinianism), subsequently his supernatural origin (modernism).[26] Insofar as Jesus' "divinity" (not "deity") is still accepted at all, it is viewed in the light of an alleged successive communication of divine dignities to him at his baptism, his resurrection, and his ascension (whatever the latter two notions may really entail within modernism). German theologian Wenzel Lohff (d. 2016) rightly called this "a consistent mythologization of the way of Jesus."[27]

10.3.3 Subordinationism

(2) *Father, Son and Holy Spirit equally partake in the Deity.* The doctrine of the one God and the three divine persons entails the confession that the Son and the Spirit fully partake in the Deity. They are no created beings; rather, they are as eternal as the Father is. However, on this standpoint it is still possible to consider the Son and the Spirit as non-equal, that is, as eternally subordinate to the Father.

On this standpoint there are again two possibilities.

(a) *Subordinatianism.* This is the view that the Son is indeed eternal, not a creature, from eternity generated by the Father, yet subordinate to the Father. In fact, this was the teaching of Justin Martyr, Tertullian, Clement of Alexandria, Origen, and

---

26. Cf. Kuyper (1871, 50–51); Berkouwer (1952, 6, 13); Schlink, *RGG* 6:1033–34.
27. Lohff, *RGG* 6:123.

the semi-Arians. They all called Jesus not *homo-ousios* ("equal in being [with the Father]") but *homoi-ousios* ("resembling the being [of the Father]"). Much later we encounter similar views among the Arminians and many more recent theologians (in the Netherlands, e.g., Johannes J. van Oosterzee, and Jacobus I. Doedes; in Germany, e.g., Johann C.K. von Hofmann, Franz H.R. von Frank, and Reinhold Seeberg).

We must have some understanding for a very limited of what some might call subordination. For instance, the Father granted to the Son to have life in himself (John 5:26), not the reverse. And in the fullness of time, the Father sent his Son into the world (Gal. 4:4), not the reverse. I would avoid the term subordination here, not to confuse these points with what I consider to be far more serious forms of subordinatianism. For instance, think of the easiness with which the God of the Old Testament, YHWH, is identified with the Father of the Son in the New Testament. Think of the very reference to the Father as the first, and the Son as the second person in the Deity. Even the doctrine of the eternal "generation" of the Son—which is not based on direct statements of Scripture—easily leads to certain forms of subordinatianism (children are naturally subordinate to their parents). Think of the fact that, in the Apostolic Creed, the Father is called Creator and Almighty, but not the Son and the Spirit.[28] Think of the fact that the submission that is self-evident for the *Man* Christ Jesus, or that is involved in the fact of the incarnation, is sometimes viewed as aspects of Jesus' *deity*.

I may add here that, in a broader sense, of course Arianism and Socinianism are also forms of subordinatianism. The same is true, for instance, for the "dynamic monarchianism" of Paul of Samosata, who taught that there is only one *prosōpon*, God, that the Logos is only an attribute of God, and that the sinless Man Jesus was inspired by the Logos.

It is hard to mention orthodox dogmaticians with whom

---

28. A failure that is made up for in the Athanasian Creed.

we do *not* encounter some traces of subordinatianism, no matter how slight. Not formally, but *de facto* such traces always introduce a letter *I* into the word *homo-ousios* (turning it into *homoi-ousios*), however small. Anselm Grün said very practically,[29] "It does definitely matter whether Jesus resembles God or is identical with God ('homoi-ousios' or 'homo-ousios'). For it depends on this question how we view our humanity, and how we experience our redemption and total change. It was the endeavor of the early church to show that the initiative at incarnation and redemption proceeded from God himself [and not from a human being who resembled God. WJO], and that everything in us—our estrangement, our guilt, our mortality, our traumas, our lethal wound—is changed and healed by Jesus Christ."

In the next Volume, we will investigate this point more extensively. Let me, at present, limit myself to just one consideration. The most important cause of all forms of subordinatianism is confusing the divinity and the humanity of Christ. For instance, consider John 10:17–18, "For this reason the Father loves me, because I lay down my life that I may take it up again. No one takes it from me, but I lay it down of my own accord. I have authority to lay it down, and I have authority to take it up again. This charge I have received from my Father." In my view, the first part of verse 18 is a clear reference to Jesus' divinity: nobody could kill him, not even God took his life, no, Jesus laid it down himself, and took it up again. But then there is the sudden turn to the submission that fitted his humanity, though he spoke as the Son: "This charge I have received from my Father." We can easily understand that such passages suggest subordinatianism. But notice, for instance, Hebrews 5:8, "Although he was a son, he learned obedience through what he suffered." Not *because* he was Son, but *although* (Gk. *kaiper*) he was Son, and as such had never been in a position of obedience (on the contrary, he was the One through whom God had created the world and who upheld

---

29. Grün (2002, 127).

the world by the word of his power; 1:2–3), he had to *learn* obedience as a Man here on earth.

10.4 Orthodox Trinitarianism
10.4.1 Features

(b) *Trinitarianism* in the strict sense of the word: the Trinity doctrine of the Ecumenical Councils, of Roman Catholicism, Eastern Orthodoxy, and orthodox Protestantism. If we summarize it in the light of the heresies mentioned above, it exhibits the following characteristics:

* The Trinity doctrine is strictly *monotheistic*, that is, it rejects all forms of tri- and tetratheism. There is only one God, numerically and indivisibly one, one divine nature, one divine essence.

* The Trinity doctrine states that, in this one divine being, there are *three hypostases* or *persons*, though not "persons" in the modern psychological sense: the three are not separated individuals, are not independent of each other, yet are clearly distinct, all three with their own specific characteristics, yet all partaking in the one divine substance. This doctrine therefore rejects all patripassianism, monarchianism, or modalism.

* The Trinity doctrine emphasizes that all three divine persons are eternal and are co-equal; the Son and the Holy Spirit were not created. It therefore rejects all Arianism and Socinianism, and related heresies.

* Although the Son at, and on the basis of, his incarnation did submit to the Father, the Trinity doctrine emphasizes that he, as the eternal Son, is not subordinate but co-equal with the Father in substance and dignity. It therefore rejects all subordinatism, that is, all attempts to introduce some ontic hierarchy within the Deity.

There where the eternity and co-equality of the three divine hypostases is confessed, the doctrine of the Trinity is most threatened by, on the one hand, tritheism and, on the other hand, modalism; or, as Karl Barth put it, the denial of

God's unity on the one hand, and the denial of God's true self-revelation on the other hand. In the remainder of this Volume and in the following Volume, we will see that the Trinity doctrine is continually threatened by this dilemma.

10.4.2 Confusion

The development of the Trinity doctrine in the early church has been rightly called an (almost) miraculous event, which certainly was not due to the "orthodoxy" and faithfulness of the early (pre-Nicene) fathers.[30] Present-day Christians who are familiar with the biblical faith of the early-church Creeds can hardly imagine what heavy battles the church fathers had to go through for this proper Christian doctrine. According to our post-Nicene criteria, as we have known them for so many centuries, we would hardly call any one of them orthodox. Some of them were really godly men as far as we can assess. But in wrestling with Platonic-Stoic-Hellenistic thought, they often seemed to break down. Some shrinked away from openly proclaiming the pre-existence and perfect deity of Christ in order not to threaten the ancient view of the Deity's unity. Some did confess the biblical doctrines, but at the same time they undermined and contradicted them.

When Arius asserted that Christ was a creature, the "intuitive" faith of many Christians did resist and reject this abomination. Nevertheless, the famous *homo-ousios* with which the Arians were formally put aside had been condemned by an earlier council just as severely as a form of modalism. As a consequence, the emperor Constantine, who gave the Council of Nicea a universal character, had rehabilitated Arius under the impression of the danger of using a term that had been condemned in such a severe way. Conversely, the biblical Athanasius was dismissed by the Council of Tyre (335). Perhaps we can make an exception for the godly and faithful Irenaeus, although he did exhibit weaknesses and some forms of

---

30. Cf. Berkouwer (1952, 55).

superstition.[31] The Jesuit Denys Petau (Dionysius Petavius, d. 1652) commented upon the utter "looseness" of the pre-Nicene fathers with regard to Christ's divinity, and accused the majority of them of Arianism.[32]

10.4.3 Intuition and Speculation

I repeat, it was and is a miracle that the doctrine of the Trinity as we know and accept it could ever originate, and was moreover accepted by the early church. I venture to suggest that the biblical view was preserved in the sound Christian intuition, rooted in the intensive reading of the New Testament, rather than in much of the theological field work in the second and third century. It was only in the work of Augustine that this sound faith was linked with devoted and precise theological investigations. Besides many historical works,[33] I refer here to dogmaticians such as Herman Bavinck, Gerrit C. Berkouwer, Wolfhart Pannenberg,[34] and lexicon articles.[35]

As opponents of this orthodox development, I must mention Adolf von Harnack (1909–10), who saw in the early-Christian development especially what he called the "Hellenization" of New Testament doctrine.[36] To some extent he was right here, although his Enlightenment goals largely robbed him of perceiving the great biblical line in this development. German theologian Gotthold Hasenhüttl claimed that Athanasius and the other Nicene fathers only "transferred the late-Greek concept of God to Jesus."[37] He called all discussions about the nature or natures of Jesus *"pure speculation, which is not seriously governed by whatever experience."*[38] The most

---

31. Darby (*CW* 15, 294).
32. Ibid., 291–94.
33. E.g., Kelly (1958); Wiles (1976).
34. Bavinck (*RD* II, 246–54, 270); Berkouwer (1952, 44–56, 65–76), Pannenberg (1988, 305–26).
35. E.g., Kettler, *RGG* 6:1025–32.
36. Harnack (1909–10).
37. Hasenhüttl (1979, 75).
38. Ibid., 78; cf. 81–82, 112.

extreme was Peter Gerlitz, who did view the Trinity doctrine as a mystery of faith and as a "primoridal phenomenon," but for the rest as almost a syncretism between Christianity and paganism.[39]

As far as the early Trininiarian and Christological development is concerned, let me leave the largely negative examples largely aside (Justin Martyr, Tatian, Theophilus, Athenagoras, Origen, and even Irenaeus and Tertullian, who—it must be emphasize—at the same time taught so many good things about God and Christ). I will limit myself to some more positive examples.

10.5   The Older Tradition
10.5.1 The Big Five

Athanasius (d. 373) clearly saw the full eternal deity of the Son, co-equal with the Father. The Son was not of some lower ranking; he and the Father partook of the same divine essence. Athanasius is the church father who put the doctrine of the Trinity into the heart of Christianity, where it rightly belongs. It is interesting that he used the term *hypostasis* in the sense of the one substance of God, whereas the later Trinity doctrine reserved the term for the three persons. He left some room for subordinatianism, which was radically rejected by Augustine.

The three great *Cappadocians*, the church fathers Basil the Great (d. 379), his brother Gregory of Nyssa (d. after 394), and Gregory of Nazianzus (d. 390), have exerted great influence upon the building and development of the Trinity doctrine. We must say, though, that the middle one of them did suffer from an excess of realism; he argued that, since the Deity is one, and we thus cannot speak of three Gods, humanity is also one, and therefore we cannot speak of a multiplicity of humans![40] This kind of exaggerated realism helps us just as little as the reverse danger: nominalism, as it comes to

---
39. Gerlitz (1963).
40. Cf. chapter 9 note 34; Bavinck (*RD* II, 265–66).

expression in tritheism.

Augustine (d. 430) formulated the doctrine of the Trinity in its ultimate, classical form as it has been accepted by the Roman Catholic Church, and afterwards by the churches of the Reformation. Herman Bavinck called Augustine's extensive work *De Trinitate* ("On the Trinity") "the most profound work that has ever been written on this dogma."[41] Like Tertullian, Augustine did not "deduce" the divine persons from the Father, but from the essence of God. Like Athanasius, he taught the full deity of the Son, co-equal with the Father, and moreover rejected all traces of subordinatianism, and also all Gnosticism, which viewed the Father as invisible and concealed in contrast with the Son. He saw each divine person as equally great as the entire Trinity, and each as partaking in the same divine essence. The three persons are distinct, not in their divine attributes but in their mutual relationships.

10.5.2 Comments

Yet, "even" in the case of Augustine, some comments must necessarily be given. Like Origen, Augustine still called the Father the *fons* or the *principium deitatis* (the "source" or the "principle of the Deity"),[42] although he explains that the Father is the Father of the Son not as God (as if the Son only possessed "deduced divinity") but as a person. Augustine also defended the somewhat doubtful expression in the Nicene Creed: *Deus de Deo*, "God from God," closely related to the doctrine of the eternal generation (see next Volume), but also perhaps containing subordinatianist tendencies. Although he taught that all three persons partake in the same divine attributes, Augustine ascribed to the Father the power, to the Son the wisdom, and to the Holy Spirit the goodness or love between the two other persons (*mutuus amor*, "mutual love," or the "kiss" between Father and Son, the "bond of peace"

---

41. Bavinck (*RD* II, 253).
42. *De Trinitate* IV.20.

[cf. Eph. 4:3] between them[43]), ideas for which there is no biblical ground.

This or a similar distinction was adopted by various scholastic theologians, by Calvin,[44] by Zacharias Ursinus and Caspar Olevianus in the Heidelberg Catechism,[45] and in the newer time, for instance, by Edmund Schlink.[46] However, such famous names do not take away anything from the dangers involved in such distinctions.[47] It is the *Triune God* who is Creator, Redeemer and Sanctifier. In agreement with this, Karl Barth spoke, when referring to the Father, of "*God* the Creator," or with regard to the Son, of "*God* the Rconciler," and in the case of the Spirit of "*God* the Redeemer."[48]

The primary criticism that must be levelled at the classical Trinity doctrine is that one wonders continually whether it does not pretend to know too much. Even when reading Augustine's masterpiece *On the Trinity*, one wonders time and again whether many conclusions and claims are not rather the endless speculative products of logical thinking than that they could be biblically accounted for. This is not an appeal to biblicism; each theologian knows that a certain measure of theological theory building is inevitable, and even necessary. However, there is a limit to such theory building, and one of it is metaphysical speculation.

Helmut Thielicke wrote that, strictly speaking, the

---

43. See Ouweneel (*EDR* 2, §1.2.2) and Vol. II/3.
44. *Institutes* I.13.18: the Father as *principium* ("beginning, principle"), the Son as *sapientia* ("wisdom"), the Spirit as *virtus* ("virtue").
45. In question 24 creation is linked with the Father, redemption with the Son, and sanctification with the Holy Spirit (so also the Belgic Confession, Art. 9).
46. Schlink, *RGG* 6:1036.
47. Heyns (1988, 49) linked the Father with the creation, the Son with the redemption, and the Holy Spirit with the consummation, but he emphasized that in each work the other divine persons are involved as well. Although Weber himself (1955, 436) preferred the model of creation – redemption – sanctification, he noticed that the diversity of opinions among theologians illustrated "that the attempt as such is of more theological importance than its result."
48. Barth (*CD* I/1, 404, 419, 470).

doctrine of the Trinity does not "solve" any probleem, that is, such problems as go forth from the biblical datum of the one God and the distimct Father, Son and Spirit.[49] He rather viewed all "solutions" as unacceptable because they "dissolve" the mystery of God (as one "dissolves" sugar[50]) in presumptuous autonomy. Therefore, Thielicke called the Trinity doctrine an "auxiliary construction," though inevitable for faith,[51] and a "defensive formula" against subordinatianism, adoptianism, and modalism.[52] The consequence of these heresies was that, as soon as the Trinity doctrine began to design its own speculative "solutions," it soon did not fare any better than Arianism, modalism, Socinianism, and so on.

Let me give an example. Scholastic theologians (Bonaventura, Anselm of Canterbury, Peter Lombard, Thomas Aquinas, and so on) told us the following.

* There are *two* kinds of emanation in God: "by the way of nature" (*per modum naturae*, referring to the eternal generation of the Son) and "by the way of the will" (*per modum voluntatis*, referring to God's creative acts).

* There are *three* hypostases, each with a personal property: the non-generated but generating Father, the generated Son, and the "breathed out" Holy Spirit.

* There are *four* relational properties: *paternitas* (= active generation), *filiatio* (= passive generation), active and passive *spiratio* (see §10.1.2).

* There are *five* characteristics (*notiones*): *innascibilitas* (the not-being-born), *paternitas*, *filiatio*, active and passive *spiratio*.[53]

---

49. Thielicke (1974, 157).
50. The German verb *lösen* can be used for solving problems, but also for dissolving sugar.
51. Ibid., 156–58.
52. Ibid., 163–89.
53. Cf. Bavinck (*RD* II, 264–65).

10.5.3 Trinitarian Terminology

What was described at the end of the previous section may perhaps be called the full "development" of the theological Trinity doctrine. However, the question is whether we can still smell here the odors of the original roses. Indeed, theology must design theories in which the biblical data are accounted for. But there is no need to go beyond them in speculative imagination. Therefore, it is a relief to see that many early Protestant theologians (Johann A. Quenstedt, David Hollaz, Hieronymus Zanchius, Gijsbert Voetius, Johannes Polyander) shrinked away from doing all too explicit statements on the generation of the Son and the procession of the Spirit, and viewed the distinction between the two as not biblical and not sufficiently modest[54] (see further in the next Volume).

Although the common faith of everyday believers is not aware of essences and hypostases — not because they are dumb but because Scripture does not contain such technical terms — the early-Christian Creeds nonetheless imposed part of this terminology upon the masses of church people. In its original form, the Nicene Creed contained this phrase: "But those who say: ... 'He is of a different *hypostasis* or *ousía*,' or that the Son of God is created, or changeable, or alterable — they are condemned by the holy catholic and apostolic Church." But the later theologians spoke of *three* hypostases within the one *ousía*! Were they condemned by the church!? Of course not — the church had entangled itself here in its own terminology, with little understanding for those who could not follow her in this.

In its turn, the Athanasian Creed tells us: "[T]he catholic faith is this: that we worship [Lat. *veneremur*] one God in Trinity, and Trinity in Unity; neither confounding the Persons, nor dividing the Essence [Lat. *substantia*]." *Veneremur* is beautiful here: it is faith that is speaking here, not theology. Faith is more of a worshiping than of an analyzing character. Yet,

---

54. Bavinck (*RD* II, 281).

we wonder what the common believer knows of *substantia*, a "risky" ancient term, with all its connotations of Greek substantialism. Why not simply *deitas*, "deity"?

Further down we read of Christ: "For the right Faith is, that we believe and confess that our Lord Jesus Christ, the Son of God, is God and Man, God, of the *substantia* of the Father, begotten [*genitus*] before the worlds." This is even more dubious than the previous sentence. Was the Son "of the *substantia* of the Father"? Or is it not wiser to use the term *substantia*—if we wish to use it at all—for the *one* divine *substantia*, of which all three divine persons equally partake, instead of speaking of the distinct *substantia* of the Father (beside which we presumably must accept the *substantia* of the Son and that of the Spirit)? Moreover, why does the text not simply say that the Son was "begotten by (or from) the Father," instead of introducing doubtful terminology? This entire idea of "begetting" is already doubtful enough—it has no biblical ground (see the next Volume)—but we should not make it worse by introducing the term *substantia*.

The text of the Athanasian Creed continues with saying that Christ was "Man, of the *substantia* of his Mother, born in the world." Again, the questionably term *substantia* is introduced, now applied to Mary. As God, Jesus was of the *substantia* of the Father, as Man, he was of the *substantia* of Mary. What exactly was meant by the latter? That Jesus was truly Man? Why not simply say so? He was born of his mother, and thus he became Man as truly as he had been, and still was, God. What information does the term *substantia* add here? In other words, what contribution did some "substance" of Mary make to the humanity of Christ? Again, see the next Volume.

The text continues, "... Perfect God, and perfect Man, of a reasonable soul [*anima rationalis*] and human flesh subsisting"; and a little further, "For as the reasonable soul [*anima rationalis*] and flesh is one man; so God and Man is one Christ." This notion of the *anima rationalis* is purely ancient-Greek, and totally unbiblical.⁵⁵ And what to say of the parallel: the *anima rationalis* and the flesh in a human being relate to each other as God and Man in Christ? At the very least it is confusing because also Christ, as a Man, is a unity of a *human* spirit and a *human* soul, besides a human body (see the next Volume).

The worst part of the Athanasian Creed is that it tells us, both at the beginning and at the end, that, if we do not believe *all* this, we cannot be saved! How many Christians, from whatever century, could then indeed be saved? With all due respect for these impressive ancient Symbols, with which each Christians should agree if we follow the great lines of faith in them, is it not getting time that we clearly pronounce that *theology*, and even less a theology steeped in ancient-Greek thinking, ought not to rule over the faith of common Christians, as it occurs in these Creeds? Notice the double mistake: (a) theology should never rule faith, (b) a pagan-mixed theology even far less so.

It is quite fascinating to see that, at the outset, John Calvin refused to accept the Nicene and Athanasian Creeds as binding, whereas he, like Martin Luther, highly esteemed the more biblically speaking—and much more concise—Apostolic Creed.⁵⁶ He would have highly preferred to simply stick to the Bible, and stay far away from the philosophical terminology of fully developed Trinitarianism.⁵⁷ We can appreciate what British theologian Alfred E. Garvie (d. 1945) wrote of the Athanasian Creed:⁵⁸ "It is scholastic theology and not living religion."

10.6 Newer Examples
10.6.1 Who Is Orthodox Today?
As we saw, the doctrine of the Trinity was developed under much conflict and battle. And once it had been established,

---

55. See Ouweneel (1986, chapter 5; *EDR* 3:chapters 5–8).
56. Cf. Koopmans (1938); Berkhof (1989, 331).
57. *Institutes* 1.13.5; cf. Barth (*CD* I/1, 438–39); Weber (1981, 410, 412); Kettler, *RGG* 6:1031.
58. Garvie (1925, 127).

and Christianity in the meantime had become the state religion of the Roman Empire, it fought its own battles—often of a violent nature—to keep the heretics at a distance. Even in the beginning of the Reformation, anti-Trinitarian heresies were punished not just by the church but by the civil authorities. In 1553, the Spanish physician and theologian Michael Servet (born 1511) was condemned to death because of his heretical views. This was done by the (Reformed) Council of Geneva with the approval of John Calvin, Guillaume Farel, Theodore Beza, and Philip Melanchthon. On the basis of a wrong view of the relationship between church and state, Servet was burned at the stake, as the inscription on his statue at Geneva describes.[59] Already in his own time, Calvin was heavily criticized for his moral responsibility for Servet's gruesome death. His approval will forever be a stain on his escutcheon.

What a blessing that such things do not occur today anymore. Muslims and pagans may martyr Christians, but Christians martyring fellow-Christians is a serious matter. Even if we take as an example only Trinitarianism, who would be safe from the stake (if we still had such a thing)? We saw what verdict the Athanasian Creed proclaimed over those who were, and are, of a different opinion. What denomination or theologian is in a position today to determine who is perfectly biblical when it comes to the extremely complicated Trinity doctrine? Of course, we can have Christian fellowship only with those who confess that the Father is God, that the Son is God, and that the Holy Spirit is God, and that yet there is only one God. But when it comes to hundred details in full-fledged Trinitarianism, who is the true "orthodox"? According to what criterion or creed or confession?

10.6.2 Herman Bavinck

Let me give two examples of outstanding twentieth-century theologians, who certainly cannot be compared with Servet, but who nonetheless can be firmly criticized as well (see this

---
59. Verkuyl (1992, 291).

and the next section). Thus, in my modest opinion, the great Reformed dogmatician Herman Bavinck, sometimes stumbled over the complexity of the subject. Let me give three examples of such stumbling.

(a) He clearly confused the terms *monógenēs* ("only [begotten]") and *prōtotokos* ("firstborn") by equating them,[60] whereas they are clearly quite different. *Monógenēs* (John 1:14, 18; 3:16, 18; 1 John 4:9) is related to the *deity* of the Son; it refers to his unique position as Son of God. Only he is—not just Son of God but—God the Son. Because of his deity, no other "sons" of God (be it angels or humans) can be compared with him. The term *prōtotokos* (Rom. 8:29; Col. 1:15, 18), however, is related to the *humanity* of the Son; he is, first of all, the firstborn Son of Mary (Matt. 1:25; Luke 2:7). If *monógenēs* refers to his absolute divine uniqueness, *prōtotokos* always refers to his relationship to others: he is the firstborn of Mary; more children might follow. He is the firstborn "among many brethren" (Rom. 8:29), the "firstborn of all creation" (i.e., among all creatures, Col. 1:15 NKJV), the "firstborn from among the dead" (v. 18 NIV). *Monógenēs* refers to uniqueness, *prōtotokos* to ranking: the "firstborn" is the highest in ranking (among the brethren, among the creatures, among the dead), not necessarily the one who was literally "first" born (cf. Joseph who had the right of the firstborn [1 Chron. 5:1–2], although he was the eleventh son of his father).

(b) The term *mode of being* (cf. the Gk. *tropos hyparcheōs* of the Cappadocian fathers) is a two-edged sword. When Bavinck combated modalism, he rejected the term *modus* in agreement with the view of the church fathers "that the three [divine] persons were not *modes* but individualities"; they "are not modes but each exists in his own way." He rejected the modalistic view that "sees in the three persons only three revelational modes of the one divine being."[61] However, at other occasions he adopted the term *modi subsistendi* with

---

60. Bavinck (*RD* II, 241v.; see also Chafer (*ST* 1:316).
61. Bavinck (*RD* II, resp. 267,269,259.

regard to the divine persons, spoke of "three modes of being of one and the same essence," and stated, "The person is a mode of being of the essence; and the persons [of the Deity] thus mutually differ, like one mode of being from the other."[62] My comment to this is that it is rather confusing to say that the divine persons are not *modi* but subsistences (i.e., hypostases), but they nonetheless are *modi subsistendi*. It is just another example showing how very difficult it is to walk on the narrow path between tritheism and modalism without going astray to either side (see §10.7).[63]

Of course, Bavinck is not alone in this struggle. As we saw (§8.5.1), John of Damascus introduced the Greek term *perichōrēsis* (Lat. *circumincessio*) for the intimate fellowship between the persons of the Deity to the extent that they "pervade" each other: the one is "in" the other.[64] None of them can be, or act, apart from the other two persons.[65] The term, which literally means a continual "turning around" of the three hypostases in a kind of dance, is far from ideal, so that the Western church preferred other terms. However this may be, the terms had all been designed only to underscore the strict unity between the Deity—but it remains slippery ground. Fritz Buri had a point when he noticed that a strict *perichōrēsis* seems to leave little room for the diversity of the three persons.[66] Each attempt to emphasize the unity threatens the threeness, and is in the danger of landing in modalism. Conversely, each attempt to emphasize the threeness threatens the unity, and is in the danger of landing in tritheism (see §10.7).

(c) It is astonishing that Bavinck, with a reference to Basil the Great, can say as an argument underpinning Trinitarianism:[67] "Paul, John, Peter are all partakers of the same human

---

62. Ibid., 265, 269, 271.
63. Cf. Weber (1981, 433).
64. Cf. Barth (*CD* I/1, 390–91, 417, 509).
65. Cf. Ouweneel (*EDR* 2:38, 256).
66. Buri (1978, 593, 608–09).
67. Bavinck (*RD* II, 265).

nature, but as persons they are distinct from the essence and from each other." And with a reference to Athanasius and Gregory of Nazianzus he said,[68] "Like Adam and Eve and Abel partake in the same being, although they received it in a different way, thus, in God too, the being is one, although it exists in the three persons in a different way." However, all analogies fail here because it is clear that Adam, Eve and Abel, who partake in the same human being, *are not one human:* numerically and indivisibly they are *not* one human being. They only exhibit a generic unity because they belong to the human species, wheras the divine being is *not* a generic unity of the three persons. In other words, in using this type of analogy, Bavinck runs the danger of utlimately landing in a form of tritheism.

Of course, Bavinck was aware of such perils. Yet, he fell into the snare of using analogies; these are the so-called *vestigia trinitatis*: traces of the Trinity that supposedly can be found within the cosmos. However, they are utterly misleading, and may guide the reader into the direction of tritheism. Bavinck described many of such speculative analogies, which he criticized himself.[69] But he could not resist the temptation of using such rather senseless and misleading speculations himself.[70]

Wolfhart Pannenberg fell into the same snare, comparing the Trinity with the field theories of modern physics in such a manner as if these would form another *vestigium trinitatis*.[71] Such analogies have no argumentative power whatsoever, and, in my view, hardly possess any illustrative power.

10.6.3 Lewis Sperry Chafer

One might perhaps expect that a traditional-Reformational

---

68. Ibid., 273–74. See on this misleading comparison Seeberg (1923, 125–26).
69. Bavinck (*RD* II, 288–297); cf. Chafer (*ST* 1:289); Barth (*CD* I/1, 352–67); Weber (1981, 412–14); Rahner (1974, 81); Jüngel (1976, 5–15); Kasper (1983, 236–38, 272–73).
70. Bavinck (*RD* II, 298–99); cf. Schuler (1961, 32–42, 92–119).
71. Pannenberg (1988, 414–15).

theologian such as Bavinck would exhibit more flaws of traditional Trinitarianism than an Evangelical theologian, but this is not the case. As a second example, I mention one of the best known Evagelical dogmaticians of the twentieth century: American theologian and classical dispensationalist, Lewis Sperry Chafer (d. 1952), founder and first president of Dallas Theological Seminary.

(a) Chafer supplied his readers with a remarkable argument to give a proof "of the essential doctrine of the Trinity," "drawn from both reason and revelation." He did not seem to realize that not a single objective rational argument for the Trinity doctrine is possible or conceivable that does not already presuppose the doctrine as such. His argument — of which the content is not relevant at all for us right now — sounds very obvious and plausble. But why then, as far as we know, did no one before the incarnation ever think of this argument, and after the incarnation no one who was unfamiliar with Christianity? Why are such arguments designed only by Christians? Because the latter already know the Trinity doctrine from God's revelation, and have accepted is. This point underscores that neither in theology, nor in any other science, there is such a thing as objective rational proof. Such supposed "proofs" always depend on rational, and in particular superrational (transcendent-religious) insights that *a priori* have been accepted in faith. Please note, this does not mean that Chafer's argument is worthless; it is not. However, this argument has value only for those who already have accepted the divine revelation with regard to the Trinity.

(b) Chafer, too, seems not to be able to escape entirely from subordinatianism. At least, he quoted agreeingly American dogmatician John Miley (d. 1895), who wrote:[72] "In the divine economies [i.e., dispensations, redemptive-historical ages] of religion, particularly in the work of rdemption, there is a subordination of the Son to the Father. There is, indeed,

---

72. Miley (1892, 239); quoted by Chafer (*ST* 1:316).

this same idea of subordination in the creative and providential works of the Son." The key to such statements is always the question whether the author has carefully distinguished the Trinitarian and the Christological aspects. This is clearly seen here: Miley's former statement is correct because it involves Christ *in his humanity*; that is, as a Man, Christ was and is always subordinate to God, and obviously so. However, Miley's latter statement is incorrect because here we have to do with the pre-incarnate Christ *in his deity*, and here there can be no question of subordination. This confusion is perhaps one of the most common mistakes in Trinitarian and Christological discussions.

Generally speaking, German theologian Klaus Berger rightly wrote, especially in view of the dialogue with Judaism and Islam:[73] "Are we not inclined to view the Son and the Holy Spirit rather as two 'auxiliary assistants' of the Father, who thus is the true, only, actual God? No, the actual God cannot be pinned down to the role of the Father and Creator.[74] Rather it is true that the Christian view of the Trinity makes the actual mystery of God even more incomprehensible, more profound, more supreme than Father, Son and Holy Spirit each by himself already are" — and then continues, unfortunately, with the defence of a kind of modalism.

The path of truth is extremely narrow; and each writer on this subject, myself included, must always wonder in how far he himself has managed to avoid both the Scylla and the Charibdis. See the next sections!

10.7 Again, Tritheism and Modalism
10.7.1 The Golden Mean

The greatest challenge for the doctrine of the Trinity is to find and keep the safe middle road between tritheism and

---

73. Berger (2004, 77).
74. Thus already the Nicene Creed: "I believe in one God, the Father almighty, maker of heaven and earth," distinct from the Son and the Spirit, who are *not* called "almighty" and "maker."

modalism. On the one hand, the Trinity doctrine is explicitly *monotheistic*, and thus rejects all forms of tri-, tetra- and polytheism. There is only one God, numerically and indivisibly one, one divine nature, one divine essence. On the other hand, Trinitarianism teaches that, in this one divine being, there are *three hypostases* or *persons*, not separate, not independent of each other, but certainly distinct, all three with their own specific properties, nonetheless partaking in the one divine essence. Thus, the doctrine of the Trinity also rejects all patripassianism, monarchianism, and modalism.

So far there is hardly a problem. Many treatises of traditional Trinitarianism limit themselves to such reasonably "safe" statements. It must be clear, however, that this confession as such hardly offers sufficient warrant against both tritheism and modalism; we already saw various examples of this. If a theologian emphasizes that there is only one divine essence, that is, also one divine subject, one divine consciousness, one divine mind, one divine life—things that, taken together, justifies speaking of God as a person—he is easily accused of modalism. If a theologian emphasizes that there are three persons, and therefore also three subjects, who address each other as "I" and "you," each having his own properties (fatherhood, sonship, *spiratio*), and each doing his own work (though not independently of each other), such as creating, redeeming and sanctifying, respectively, such a theologian is easily accused of tritheism.

How can we avoid these continual dangers? Or rather, *can* we avoid them at all, or does the matter surpass the human intellect to such an extent that an unambiguous, well-balanced, and thus entirely satisfactory formulation is *a priori* impossible? Indeed, we will have to admit that the problem will never be solved to the full satisfaction of all orthodox Trinitarians. Each of them, trying to dig a little deeper and to clarify the matter, will be accused *at the same time* of tritheism (from one side of the dogmaticians' world) and of modalism (from the other side). Yet, I take the risk and concentrate again upon the term "person," endeavoring to distinguish between the ancient and the modern meanings of this term.

10.7.2 The Term *Persona*

The full-fledged doctrine of the Trinity avoided, and avoids, saying that there are three divine substances, three divine essences, or three divine natures, for fear that, in this way, it would land in tritheism. But of course people have often asked the question whether the same danger is not implied in using terms as "persons" and "hypostases." Why would they less easily lead to the danger of tritheism? One answer has been that the term "person" can be maintained as long as, in the Trinity doctrine, it is not understood in the modern-psychological way as an autonomous "subject" or "consciousness," an individual "personality." The question is, however, whether this precaution is sufficient. Does, for more modern ears, the term "person" not *necessarily always* involves notions that make tritheism unavoidable?

Perhaps the term "person" could be used without these implications in earlier centuries, but certainly not today. Actually, before 1800 the term "person" was in fact hardly ever used; theologians wrote in Latin and used *persona*, which was not yet loaded with modern psychological connotations. This is why I quoted Paul Tillich (§9.8.3), who rightly emphaszied that, also today, we should rather speak of the *personae* within the Trinity, *not* the "persons." American theologian Robert W. Jenson (d. 2017) preferred to speak of three "identities,"[75] but, according to Wolfhart Pannenberg,[76] he reckoned too little with the mutual self-distinction of Father, Son and Spirit. Such a terminology would thus tend to modalism. Please note, this does not follow only from the term "identity" as such, for terms can be explained in different ways. It can follow only from what Jenson associated with the term.

The suggestion by Albrecht Ritschl to use the "bleak"

---

75. Jenson (1982, 108 and further).
76. Pannenberg (1988, 347).

concepts of "person" or "mode of being" little or not at all in connection with the Trinity,[77] does not help very much. We cannot do without these or similar terms, and thus may use them as long as they are carefully described. But the question is whether the term "person," no matter how accurately defined, can still be used at all because of the inevitable modern connotations linked with it.

In fact, the modern-psychological term "person" can be used only in reference to the Deity as such. There can be only one divine *person*, given the fact that the modern concept of the "person" primarily implies self-consciousness and self-determination. These properties can be ascribed to the Deity equally well as to the three *personae*, or even far better. None of the divine *personae* has a consciousness strictly by himself, such as human beings who are very intimate still always have. The divine *personae* partake in one consciousness, one mind.

However, this point illustrates again how much we balance here on the razor's edge. The fact that we are not allowed to postulate three "consciousnesses," does not mean that, within this one divine consciousness, we might not postulate three *concentration points*. Roman Catholic theologian Karl Rahner (d. 1984) said that "the one consciousness exists in a threefold way: there is genuine consciousness only in God, which is possessed by the Father, Son and Spirit each in his own way."[78] Another Roman Catholic theologian, Walter Kasper, went a little further by claiming that, within the one divine consciousness there are three "centers of consciousness."[79] Each of such statements inevitably balances on the dividing line between tritheism and modalism.

10.7.3 Further Considerations

None of the three divine *personae* is self-determinating. Even a slave always remains self-determinating to a certain extent:

---

77. Ritschl (1984, 179).
78. Rahner (1975, 387).
79. Kasper (1983).

he keeps his own thoughts, his own will, his own feelings. But the three *personae* partake in the same thoughts, the same will, the same feelings. This matter becomes even more complicated if we also consider the humanity of Christ. Pure Trinitarianism is difficult enough; bringing in the two natures of Christ makes things even far more difficult, but this is inevitable. What is true for the Man Jesus might not necessarily be true for God the Son — and yet we have to do with one single person.

An example: Jesus can distinguish his own will from that of the Father by submitting his will to that of the Father (Luke 22:42; cf. John 17:24). In order to grasp this — as far as it is given to us — we must understand that Jesus as a Man possessed, and possesses, a human soul and a human spirit, which implies that, as a Man, he had his own human will, his own human thoughts, his own human feelings. This will, these thoughts and feelings, were always in perfect harmony with those of the Father — but this statement implies that Jesus' will, thoughts and feelings are at least *distinct* from the Father's will, thoughts and feelings. However, if we would say the same of the will of the eternal Son, or of the will of the Spirit, tritheism might become inevitable. This age-old question — does the Man Jesus have a will different from the will of the eternal Son of God? — will be dealt with in the next Volume.

As we saw, the three divine *personae* partake in the same divine thoughts, the same divine will, the same divine feelings. This is why traditional Trinitarians have always emphasized that the *opera Dei ad extra sunt indivisa*, that is, God's works outside himself, that is, with regard to the created world, are "undivided": the three *personae* are always equally involved in them. In these works, the three *personae* are perfectly one of mind and will; not like two people can be "of one mind," for in this case we still have always to do with two minds. Being "of one mind" only means that their two minds are in good harmony with each other — but they are still two.

However, the three *personae* act with numerically one mind and one will. The *opera ad intra*, God's works "within" himself, are indeed *divisa*, "divided," but in the traditional view these only involve the (supposed) eternal generation of the Son and the (supposed) eternal procession of the Spirit.

Even early Protestant theology often preferred to speak, not of *personae* (leave alone "persons" in any modern sense) but of *modi subsistendi*, "modes of being," or "modes of existence." As we saw, the term *modus* ("mode") does not necessarily have to lead to modalism. There is an essential difference between the "modes of manifestation," as taught by modalism, and the "modes of existence," as taught by orthodox Trinitarianism.[80] In the former case, there is only one divine hypostasis, which alternately can manifest itself in the *modus* of the Father, that of the Son, or that of the Spirit. In this view, there is no room for the personal "over against" of the Father who loves the Son and sends him into the world, of the Son who finds his delight at the side of the Father and descends into the world, and of the Spirit who proceeds from the Father (and the Son?), and glorifies the other two in the world.[81] However, in orthodox Trinitarianism, there are within the Deity three intrinsically distinct modes of *existence*, dat is, eternally existing distinct from each other, with eternal mutual relationships of love and fellowship, partaking in the same Deity.

10.8 The Three Hypostases
10.8.1 A First Pair of "Contras"

Let us try to summarize what we have found, as succinctly and accurately as possible, and with these last considerations close this Volume.

Within the one Deity there are three distinct modes of

---

80. Cf. Schleiermacher's distinction between a "revelational" and an "essential Trinity," quoted before (§10.2.3).
81. See especially John's Gospel for many examples enlightening these distinctions.

existence or hypostases. On the one hand (*contra tritheism*), these three modes of existence are not separate, not autonomous individualities, not independent of each other, not self-existing, not self-determining. Rather, they are one Deity, with one will, one feeling, one thought, one mind, one self-consciousness.

On the other hand (*contra modalism*), these three are modes of existence, not just modes of manifestation, as if the one Deity would manifest at one occasion as Father, at another occasion as Son, and at still another occasion as Holy Spirit. Even without God's self-revelation, these three modes of existence would exist within the Deity, as they indeed existed prior to any self-revelation of God. They existed, and exist, from eternity to eternity, irrespective of humanity, or God's relationships with humanity.

Even in past eternity, these three modes of existence were distinct, for the Son was in the bosom of the Father (John 1:18 NKJV etc.), not the reverse. The Father granted to the Son to have life in himself (5:26), not the reverse. And in the fullness of time, the Father sent his Son into the world (Gal. 4:4), not the reverse (see §10.3.3 in connection with the problem of subordination). And on the Day of Pentecost, the Holy Spirit proceeded from the Father and the Son (John 14:26; 15:26), not the reverse.

10.8.2 A Second Pair of "Contras"

Yet (*contra tritheism*) the Father does nothing without the Son and the Spirit; it is through the Son and in the Spirit that he performs all his works. There is not only one God, the Father, *from* whom are all things, but also one Lord, Jesus Christ, who is God the Son *through* whom are all things and *through* whom we exist (cf. 1 Cor. 8:6; cf. Col. 1:15–17). The Son does nothing of his own accord, but only what he sees the Father doing (John 5:19; cf. v. 30; 8:28), just as he does nothing without the Spirit; it is on behalf of the Father and in the power of the Holy Spirit that he performs his works. Similarly, the Holy

Spirit does nothing without the Father and Son; it is on behalf of the Father and the Son that he performs his works. Their unity of essence and counsel, of will, feelings and thoughts, is always carefully preserved.

Yet (*contra modalism*), the first person—if we may indeed use this numerical distinction—is primary in the divine counsel, and in the execution of it, not the other two. That is, all things are "from" the Father, not from the other *personae*. Colossians 1:16 goes very far in this respect: all things have been created "in" (Gk. *en*) the Son, "through" or "by means of" (Gk. *dia*) the Son, and "for" or "unto" (Gk. *eis*) the Son, but the preposition "from" (Gk. *ek*) remains reserved for "God (the Father)" (1 Cor. 1:30; 8:6; 11:12; 2 Cor. 5:18).[82]

The Son is primary in the execution of the work of redemption; that is, it was the Son who became Man and died on the cross, not the two other *personae*. The Holy Spirit is primary in the application of the results of this work to the hearts and lives of the believers, not the two others. That is, it was the Spirit who was poured out on the Day of Pentecost (Acts 2:1-4), and who chose as his dwelling-place the church (1 Cor. 3:16; 2 Cor. 6:16; Eph. 2:20-22) as well as the bodies of the individual believers (1 Cor. 6:19), not the two others.

10.8.3 A Third Pair of "Contras"

Yet (*contra tritheism*), the three *personae* are, though distinct, never separate. They are so perfectly one that the Father is "in" the Son and the Spirit, the Son is "in" the Father and the Spirit, and the Spirit is "in" the Father and the Son. It is only as the Father of the Son that the Father is eternally the Father. It is only as the Son of the Father that the Son is eternally the Son. The Holy Spirit is the Spirit of the Father (Matt. 10:20; Eph. 3:14-16), as he is also the Spirit of the Son (Gal. 4:6). They are numerically and individibly one in deity, in majesty, in bliss, in eternity, in omnipotence, in omniscience, in omni-

---

82. In Rom. 11:36, not only *ek*, but also *dia* and *eis* are used for "the Lord," who is here the Triune God (v. 34).

presence, in immutability, in sovereignty, in righteousness, in holiness, in love, and so on.

Even if it was only the Son who became Man and died on the cross, it was the Father who gave him up for all those who would believe in him (Rom. 8:32). And it was not without the "eternal Spirit" that Jesus offered himself up to God (Heb. 9:14). He rose from the dead in his own power (John 10:17–18), but he was also raised from the dead by the glory of the Father (Rom. 6:4), and "according to the Spirit of holiness" (1:4). And if it was the Holy Spirit who came to dwell in the believers, individually and collectively, this is never apart from the Father and the Son. Think of this word of Jesus: "If anyone loves me, he will keep my word, and my Father will love him, and we will come to him and make our home [abode, dwelling place] with him" (John 14:23). And the apostle Paul wishes "that Christ may dwell in your hearts through faith" (Eph. 3:17).

Yet (*contra modalism*), in spite of this unity of Father, Son and Spirit, which could be illustrated with many more biblical examples, each of the three *personae* sees the two others as "others," thus distinguishing himself from them. Jesus says with reference to the Father, "There is another who bears witness about me" (John 5:32), meaning the Father. And with reference to the Holy Spirit he says, "I will ask the Father, and he will give you another Helper" (14:16).[83] Each of the three *personae* distinguishes himself from the others as an "I" over against a "you" or a "he." In *this* respect, one might speak of three distinct "subjects."

Yet… and so on, and so forth. This summary could be continued with a long list of more contrasts. But the ones given may suffice, I trust, to make my point.

---

83. In both cases, it is Gk. *allos*, another one of the same kind, not *heteros*, another one in the sense of a different one.

Bibliography

Abbott, W. M. 1966. *The Documents of Vatican II*. New York: America Press.

Adorno, T. W et al. 1950. *The Authoritarian Personality*. New York: Harper.

Alexander, W. L. 1888. *A System of Biblical Theology*. Vol. 1. Edinburgh: T&T Clark.

Allen, R. O. and B. Spilka. 1973. "Committed and Consensual Religion: A Specification of Religion-prejudice Relationships." In *Psychology and Religion*, ed. L. B. Brown, 58–80. Harmondsworth: Penguin Books.

Allport, G. W. 1950. *The Individual and His Religion*. New York: MacMillan.

———. 1954. *The Nature of Prejudice*. Reading, Mass.: Addison-Wesley.

———. 1963. "Behavioral Science, Religion, and Mental Health." *Journal of Religion and Health* 2:187–97.

———. 1966. "Traits Revisited." *American Psychologist* 1:1–10. Reprinted in *Psychology and Religion*, ed. L. B. Brown, 54–57. Harmondsworth: Penguin Books.

——— and M. Ross. 1967. "Personal Religious Orientation and Prejudice." *Journal of Personality and Social Psychology* 5:432–43.

Althaus, P. 1952. *Die christliche Wahrheit: Lehrbuch der Dogmatik*. 3rd ed. Gütersloh: Bertelsmann.

Altizer, T. J. J. 1966. *The Gospel of Christian Atheism*. Philadelphia: Westminster Press.

_____ and W. Hamilton. 1966. *Radical Theology and the Death of God*. Indianapolis: Bobbs-Merrill.

Bakan, D. 1958. *Sigmund Freud and the Jewish Mystical Tradition*. Princeton: Van Nostrand.

Barth, K. 1956. *Church Dogmatics*. Translated by T. H. L. Parker et al. Vols. 1/1–4/1. Louisville, KY: Westminster John Knox.

_____. 1960. *Anselm: Fides Quarens Intellectum. Anselm's Proof of the Existence of God in the Context of His Theological Scheme*. London: SCM Press.

Bauer, Walter, Frederick W. Danker, William F. Arndt, and F. Wilbur Gingrich. 2000. *A Greek-English Lexicon of the New Testament and Other Early Christian Literature*. 3rd ed., revised and edited by Frederick W. Danker. Chicago: University of Chicago Press.

Bavinck, H. 2002–2008. *Reformed Dogmatics*. Edited by John Bolt. Translated by John Vriend. 4 vols. Grand Rapids, MI: Baker Academic.

Bavinck, J. H. 1956. "Elenctiek." In *Christelijke Encyclopedie*, ed. F. W. Grosheide and G. P. van Itterzon, 2:580. 2nd revised ed. 6 vols. Kampen: J. H. Kok.

_____. 1956. "Godsdienstwetenschap." In *Christelijke Encyclopedie*, ed. F. W. Grosheide and G. P. van Itterzon, 3:268–69. 2nd revised ed. 6 vols. Kampen: J. H. Kok.

_____. (1949) 1989. *Religieus besef en christelijk geloof*. Kampen: J.H. Kok

Begemann, A. W. 1963–1964. "De kerk in de Calvinistisch[e] wijsbegeerte." *Lucerna* 4:149–181.

Benton, M. A., J. Hawthorne, and D. Rabinowitz, eds. 2018. *Knowledge, Belief, and God: New Insights in Religious Episte-*

mology. Oxford: Oxford University Press.

Berger, H. 2000. *Tegen de negatieve filosofie: Dionysius, Kant, Derrida*. Leende: Damon.

Berger, K. 2004. *Jesus*. München: Pattloch.

Berkhof, H. 1960. *God voorwerp van wetenschap?* Nijkerk: Callenbach.

_____. 1964. *The Doctrine of the Holy Spirit*. Atlanta: John Knox Press.

_____. 1986. *Christian Faith: An Introduction to the Study of the Faith*. Translated by S. Woudstra. Grand Rapids, MI: Wm. B. Eerdmans.

Berkouwer, G. C. 1955. *General Revelation*. Grand Rapids, MI: Wm. B. Eerdmans. 1951. *Dogmatische Studiën: De algemene openbaring*. Kampen: J.H. Kok.

_____. 1954. *The Person of Christ*. Translated by John Vriend. Grand Rapids: Wm. B. Eerdmans. 1952. *Dogmatische Studiën: De persoon van Christus*. Kampen: J.H. Kok.

_____. 1956. *The Triumph of Grace in the Theology of Karl Barth*. Translated by H. R. Boer. Grand Rapids: Wm. B. Eerdmans. 1954. *De triomf der genade in de theologie van Karl Barth*. Kampen: J.H. Kok.

Bloesch, D. G. 1995. *God the Almighty: Power, Wisdom, Holiness, Love*. Carlisle: Paternoster Press.

Blum, E. A. 1981. *2 Peter*. EBC 12. Grand Rapids: Zondervan.

Bonhoeffer, D. (1952) 1964. *Widerstand und Ergebung: Briefe und Aufzeichnungen aus der Haft*. München: Kaiser.

Bonhoeffer, D. 1982. *Christologie*. Baarn: Ten Have.

Bouma, C. 1937. *De brieven van den apostel Paulus aan Timotheüs en Titus*. KV. Kampen: J.H. Kok.

Bray, G. L. 1993. *The Doctrine of God*. Leicester: InterVarsity Press.

Brillenburg Wurth, G. 1958. "Godsdienstpsychologie." In Grosheide and Van Itterzon, *Christelijke Encyclopedie*, ed. by F. W. Grosheide and G. P. van Itterzon, 3:262–64. 2nd revised ed. 6 vols. Kampen: J. H. Kok.

Braun, C. 1876. *Der Begriff "Person" in seiner Anwendung auf die Lehre von der Trinität und Incarnation*. Mainz: Franz Kirchheim.

Broekhuis, J. 1994. *Oriëntatie in de godsdienstwetenschap*. Zoetermeer: Boekencentrum.

Brown, C. 1971. *Philosophy and the Christian Faith: An Introduction to the Main Thinkers and Schools of Thought from the Middle Ages to the Present Day*. London: Tyndale Press.

Brown, C., ed. 1992. *The New International Dictionary of New Testament Theology*. 4 vols. Carlisle: Paternoster.

Brown, L. B., ed. 1973. *Psychology and Religion*. Harmondsworth: Penguin Books.

_____ and J. P. Forgas. 1980. "The Structure of Religion: A Multidimensional Scaling of Informal Elements." *Journal for the Scientific Study of Religion* 19:423-31.

Brown, R. E. 1994. *An Introduction to New Testament Christology*. New York: Paulist Press.

Brugger, W. 1979. *Summe einer philosophischen Gotteslehre*. München: Joh. Berchmans Verlag.

Brümmer, V. 1988. *Over een persoonlijke God gesproken: Studies in de wijsgerige theologie*. Kampen: J.H. Kok Agora.

Brunner, E. 1943. *The Divine-Human Encounter*. Translated by A. W. Loos. Philadelphia: Westminster Press.

_____. 1950. *Dogmatics*. Translated by O. Wyon. Vol. 1: *The Christian Doctrine of God*. Philadelphia: Westminster Press. 1946. Die christliche Lehre von Gott: Dogmatik, Bd. I. Zürich: Zwingli-Verlag.

Buber, M. 2000. *I and Thou*. New York: Scribner.

_____. (1953) 1989. *Eclipse of God: Studies in the Relation Between Religion and Philosophy*. Atlantic Highlands, NJ: Humanities Press International.

Bultmann, R. 1971. *The Gospel of John: A Commentary*. Translated by G. R. Beasley-Murray. Philadelphia: Westminster

Press.

Buri, F. 1956. *Dogmatik als Selbstverständnis des christlichen Glaubens. Part 1: Vernunft und Offenbarung*. Bern: Paul Haupt/Tübingen: Katzmann-Verlag.

———. 1978. *Dogmatik als Selbstverständnis des christlichen Glaubens. Part 3: Die Transzendenz der Verantwortung in der dreifachen Schöpfung des dreieinigen Gottes*. Bern: Paul Haupt/Tübingen: Katzmann.

Buytendijk, F. J. J. (1951) 2008. *De vrouw: Haar natuur, verschijning en bestaan*. Utrecht: Het Spectrum.

Caputo, J. D. 2006. *Philosophy and Theology*. Nashville, TN: Abingdon Press.

——— and G. Vattimo (ed. by J. W. Robbins). 2007. *After the Death of God*. New York: Columbia University Press.

Carson, D. A. 1984. *Matthew*. EBC 8. Grand Rapids: Zondervan.

Cassirer, E. 1954. *Philosophie der symbolischen Formen*. 2nd ed. Vol. 2. Darmstadt: Wissenschaftliche Buchgesellschaft.

Chafer, L. S. 1983. *Systematic Theology*. 15th ed. 8 vols. Dallas, TX: Dallas Seminary Press.

Charnock, S. (1853) 1996. *The Existence and Attributes of God*. Grand Rapids: Baker Books.

Clack, B. and B. R. Clack. 2008 (rev. ed.). *The Philosophy of Religion: A Critical Introduction*. Cambridge: Polity Press.

Clark, W. H. 1958. "How Do Social Scientists Define Religion?" *Journal of Social Psychology* 47:143–47.

Cobb, J. B. 1966. *A Christian Natural Theology*. Philadelphia: Westminster Press.

Cornwall, M., S. L. Albrecht, P. H. Cunningham, and B. L. Pitcher. 1986. "The Dimensions of Religiosity: A Conceptual Model with an Empirical Test." *Review of Religious Research* 27.3:226–44.

Crabtree, T. 1984. "The Analyst Analysed." *New Scientist* 101.1393:24–27.

Cremer, H. (1897) 1917. *Die christliche Lehre von den Eigenschaften Gottes*. 2nd ed. Gütersloh: C. Bertelsmann.

Davidson, J. D. 1972a. "Religious Belief as an Independent Variable." *Journal for the Scientific Study of Religion* 11:65–75.

———. 1972b. "Patterns of Belief at the Denominational and Congregational Levels." *Review of Religious Research* 13:197–205.

———. 1972c. "Religious Belief as a Dependent Variable." *Sociological Analysis* 33:81–94.

De Boer, T. 1984. "De filosofie van Dooyeweerd." *Algemeen Nederlands Tijdschrift voor Wijsbegeerte* 76:247–61.

———. 1989. *De God van de filosofen en de God van Pascal: Op het grensgebied van filosofie en theologie*. 's-Gravenhage: Meinema.

De Groot, J. and A. R. Hulst. 1952. *Macht en wil: De verkondiging van het Oude Testament aangaande God*. Nijkerk: Callenbach.

Den Heyer, C. J. 1986. *De messiaanse weg*. Vol. 2. Kampen: J.H. Kok.

Dennison, J. T., Jr., ed. 2008–2014. *Reformed Confessions of the 16th and 17th Centuries in English Translation*. Grand Rapids, MI: Reformation Heritage Books.

Derrida, J. 1991. *Circumfession*. Paris: Éditions du Seuil.

Diestel, L. 1859. "Die Heiligkeit Gottes." *Jahrbuch für protestantische Theologie* 1859:3–62.

Dittes, J. E. 1969. "Psychology of Religion." In *Handbook of Social Psychology*, ed. G. Lindzey and E. Aronson. 5:602–45. Reading, Mass.: Addison-Wesley.

Dooyeweerd, H. 1926. *De beteekenis der wetsidee voor rechtswetenschap en rechtsphilosophie*. Kampen: J.H. Kok.

———. 1928a. "Het juridisch causaliteitsprobleem in 't licht der wetsidee." *Antirevolutionaire Staatkunde* (driemaand. org.) 2:21–121.

―――. 1928b. "Beroepsmisdaad en strafvergelding in 't licht der wetsidee: Een bijdrage tot de dogmatiek van de beroepsmisdaad de lege ferenda." *Antirevolutionaire Staatkunde* (driemaand. org.) 2:233–309, 389–436.

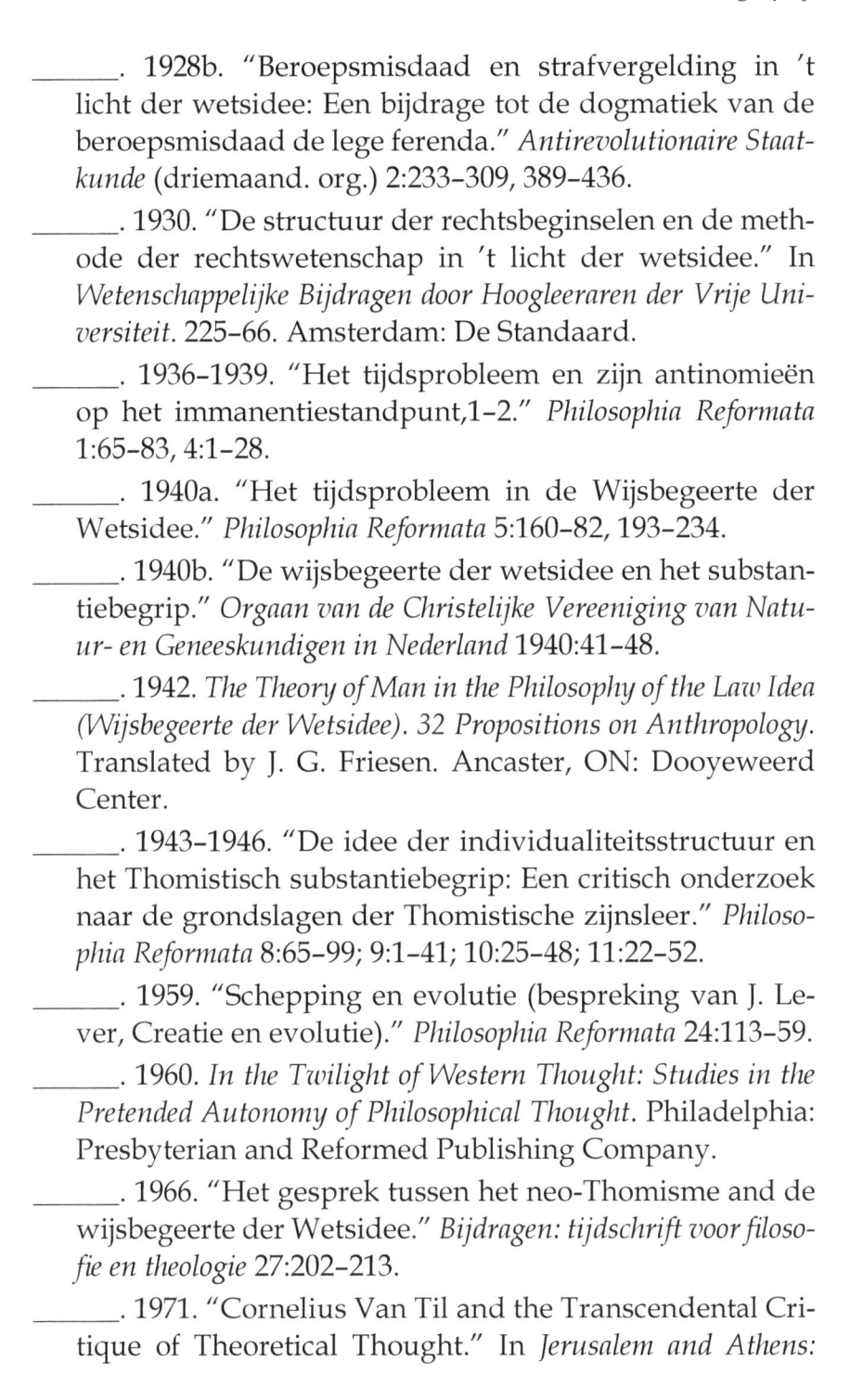

―――. 1930. "De structuur der rechtsbeginselen en de methode der rechtswetenschap in 't licht der wetsidee." In *Wetenschappelijke Bijdragen door Hoogleeraren der Vrije Universiteit*. 225–66. Amsterdam: De Standaard.

―――. 1936–1939. "Het tijdsprobleem en zijn antinomieën op het immanentiestandpunt,1–2." *Philosophia Reformata* 1:65–83, 4:1–28.

―――. 1940a. "Het tijdsprobleem in de Wijsbegeerte der Wetsidee." *Philosophia Reformata* 5:160–82, 193–234.

―――. 1940b. "De wijsbegeerte der wetsidee en het substantiebegrip." *Orgaan van de Christelijke Vereeniging van Natuur- en Geneeskundigen in Nederland* 1940:41–48.

―――. 1942. *The Theory of Man in the Philosophy of the Law Idea (Wijsbegeerte der Wetsidee). 32 Propositions on Anthropology.* Translated by J. G. Friesen. Ancaster, ON: Dooyeweerd Center.

―――. 1943–1946. "De idee der individualiteitsstructuur en het Thomistisch substantiebegrip: Een critisch onderzoek naar de grondslagen der Thomistische zijnsleer." *Philosophia Reformata* 8:65–99; 9:1–41; 10:25–48; 11:22–52.

―――. 1959. "Schepping en evolutie (bespreking van J. Lever, Creatie en evolutie)." *Philosophia Reformata* 24:113–59.

―――. 1960. *In the Twilight of Western Thought: Studies in the Pretended Autonomy of Philosophical Thought*. Philadelphia: Presbyterian and Reformed Publishing Company.

―――. 1966. "Het gesprek tussen het neo-Thomisme and de wijsbegeerte der Wetsidee." *Bijdragen: tijdschrift voor filosofie en theologie* 27:202–213.

―――. 1971. "Cornelius Van Til and the Transcendental Critique of Theoretical Thought." In *Jerusalem and Athens:*

Critical Discussions on the Philosophy and Apologetics of Cornelius Van Til, ed. E. R. Geehan, 74–89. Nutley, NJ: Presbyterian and Reformed Publishing Company.

———. 1984. *A New Critique of Theoretical Thought*. Vol. 1: *The Necessary Presuppositions of Philosophy* (1953). Vol. 2: *The General Theory of the Modal Spheres* (1955). Vol. 3: *The Structures of Individuality of Temporal Reality* (1957). Jordan Station: Paideia Press.

Dorner, I. A. (1856–1858) 1883. "Über die richtige Fassung des dogmatischen Begriffs der Unveränderlichkeit Gottes." In *Gesammelte Schriften*, 188–377.

Durand, J. J. F. and W. D. Jonker, eds. (1976) 1985. *Wegwysers in die Dogmatiek*. Vol. 1: *Die lewende God*. 2nd ed. Pretoria: N.G. Kerkboekhandel.

Durrant, M. 1973. *The Logical Status of "God": The Function of Theological Sentences*. London: Macmillan.

Ebeling, G. 1979. *Dogmatik des christlichen Glaubens*. Vol. 1: *Prolegomena, Der Glaube an Gott, den Schöpfer der Welt*. Tübingen: Mohr (Siebeck).

Eichrodt, W. 1962. *Theologie des Alten Testaments*, Bd. I. Stuttgart: Klotz.

Elert, W. 1974. *The Christian Faith: An Outline of Lutheran Dogmatics*. Translated by M. A. Bertram and W. R. Bouman. [Columbus]:[Lutheran Theological Seminary].

1956. *Der christliche Glaube: Grundlinien der lutherischen Dogmatik*. 3rd ed. Hamburg: Furche-Verlag.

Erickson, M. J. 1998. *Christian Theology*. Grand Rapids: Baker Book House.

Fee, G. D. 1987. *The First Epistle to the Corinthians*. NICNT. Grand Rapids: Wm. B. Eerdmans.

Feuerbach, L. 1957. *The Essence of Christianity*. Translated by G. Eliot. New York: Harper.

Fontana, D. 2003. *Psychology, Religion and Spirituality*. Oxford: Wiley-Blackwell.

Ford, D. F. and M. Higton, eds. 2002. *Jesus*. Oxford: Oxford University Press.

Fortman, E. J. 1972. *The Triune God: A Historical Study of the Doctrine of the Trinity*. Grand Rapids: Baker Book House.

Freud, S. 2011. *Sigmund Freud – The Complete Works*. E-book. Available at https://holybooks-lichtenbergpress.netdna-ssl.com/wp-content/uploads/Sigmund-Freud-The-Complete-Works.pdf.

Frick, H. 1928. *Vergleichende Religionswissenschaft*. (Sammlung Göschen). Berlin: W. de Gruyter.

Ganssle, G. E., ed. 2001. *God and Time: Four Views*. Downers Grove, IL: InterVarsity Press.

Garvie, A. E. 1925. *The Christian Doctrine of the Godhead*. London: Hodder and Stoughton.

Geisler, N. L. 1974. *Philosophy of Religion*. Grand Rapids: Zondervan.

Geldenhuys, N. 1951. *Commentary on the Gospel of Luke*. NICNT. Grand Rapids: Wm. B. Eerdmans.

Gerlitz, P. 1963. *Ausserchristliche Einflüsse auf die Entwicklung des christlichen Trinitätsdogmas*. Leiden: E.J. Brill.

Gispen, W. H. 1932. *Het boek Exodus*. Vol. 1. KV. Kampen: J.H. Kok.

Glock, C. Y. 1965. "On the Study of Religious Commitment." In *Religion and Society in Tension*, ed. C. Y Glock and R. Stark, 18–38. Chicago: Rand McNally.

Graafland, C. 1990. *Gereformeerden op zoek naar God: Godsverduistering in het licht van de gereformeerde spiritualiteit*. Kampen: De Groot Goudriaan.

Green, J. B. 1997. *The Gospel of Luke*. NICNT. Grand Rapids: Wm. B. Eerdmans.

Grenz, S. J. and J. R. Franke. 2001. *Beyond Foundationalism: Shaping Theology in a Postmodern Context*. Louisville, KY: Westminster John Knox Press.

Grosheide, F. W. and G. P. van Itterzon, eds. 1956–1961. *Christelijke Encyclopedie*. 2nd revised ed. 6 vols. Kampen: J. H. Kok.

Grün, A. 2002. *Beelden van Jezus*. Tielt: Lannoo/Baarn: Ten Have.

Guarino, T. G. 2005. *Foundations of Systematic Theology*. New York: T&T Clark.

Hanson, R. P. C. 1988. *The Search for the Christian Doctrine of God*. Edinburgh: T&T Clark.

Harnack, A. von 1909–1910. *Lehrbuch der Dogmengeschichte*. 4th ed. 3 vols. Tübingen: Mohr (Siebeck).

Harrison, V. S. 2007. *Religion and Modern Thought*. London: SCM.

Hart, H. 1983. "The Articulation of Belief: A Link Between Rationality and Commitment." In *Rationality in the Calvinian Tradition*, ed. H. Hart et al., 209–48. Lanham: University Press of America.

Hartshorne, C. E. 1964. *The Divine Relativity: A Social Conception of God*. New Haven: Yale University Press.

Hasenhüttl, G. 1979. *Kritische Dogmatik*. Graz: Styria.

Hauerwas, S. 2001. *With the Grain of the Universe: The Church's Witness and Natural Theology*. Grand Rapids: Brazos Press.

Heering, G. J. 1945. *De christelijke godsidee*. Arnhem: Van Loghum Slaterus.

Heidegger, M. 1972. *On Time and Being*. New York: Harper & Row. (1927) 1967. Sein und Zeit. Tübingen: Max Niemeyer Verlag.

Heidegger, M. 2009. *Vorträge und Aufsätze*. Stuttgart: Klett-Cotta.

Helm, P. 1988. *Eternal God: A Study of God Without Time*. Oxford: Clarendon Press.

Hendrikse, K. 2007. *Geloven in een God die niet bestaat: Manifest van een atheïstische dominee*. Amsterdam: Nieuw Amsterdam.

Hengel, M. 1995. *Studies in Early Christology*. Edinburgh: T&T Clark.

Henry, C. F. H. 1976a/b. *God, Revelation and Authority: God Who Speaks and Shows*. 2 vols. Waco, TX: Word Books.

Herrmann, W. 1925. *Dogmatik: Vorlesungsdiktate*. Gotha: F. A. Perthes.

Hodge, C. A. 1872. *Systematic Theology*. Vol. 1. New York: Scribner, Armstrong and Co.

Heschel, A. J. 1936. *Die Prophetie*. Krakow: Verlag der Polnischen Akademie der Wissenschaften.

Heschel, A. J. 1965. *Who Is Man?* Stanford: Stanford University Press.

Heyns, J. A. 1953. *Die grondstruktuur van die modalistiese Triniteitsbeskouing*. Kampen: J.H. Kok.

_____. 1977. "Grondlyne van 'n Algemene Wetenskapsleer," and "Teologie as Wetenskap." In *Op weg met die teologie*, ed. J. A. Heyns and W. D. Jonker, 13–228. Pretoria: N.G. Kerkboekhandel.

_____. 1988. *Dogmatiek*. Pretoria: N.G. Kerkboekhandel.

Holwerda, B. 1971. *Oudtestamentische voordrachten*. Vol. 1: *Historia Revelationis Veteris Testamenti*. Kampen: Van den Berg.

Hood, R. W., P. C. Hill, and B. Spilka. 2009. *The Psychology of Religion: An Empirical Approach*. 4th ed. New York: Guilford Press.

Honig, A. G. 1910. *De persoon van den Middelaar in de nieuwere Duitsche dogmatiek*. Kampen: J.H. Kok.

Houtepen, A. W. J. 1997. *God, een open vraag: Theologische perspectieven in een cultuur van agnosme*. Zoetermeer: Meinema.

Hubbeling, H. G. 1983/4. Het kosmologisch Godsbewijs. *Wijsgerig Perspectief* 24:163–167.

Hughes, P. E. 1962. *The Second Epistle to the Corinthians*. NICNT. Grand Rapids: Wm. B. Eerdmans.

Huxley, J., Barry, G., Bronowsky, and J. Fisher, eds. 1965. *Growth of Ideas: The Evolution of Thought and Knowledge.* London: Macdonald.

Ice, J. L. and J. J. Carey, eds. 1967. *The Death of God Debate.* Philadelphia, PA: Westminster Press.

Immink, F. G. 1987. *Divine Simplicity.* Kampen: J.H. Kok.

Jacob, B. 1974. *Das erste Buch der Tora: Genesis übersetzt und erklärt.* New York: Ktav.

Jaffé, A., ed. 1962. *Erinnerungen, Träume, Gedanken von C. G. Jung.* Zürich: Rascher.

James, W. 1902. *The Varieties of Religious Experience.* New York: Longmans.

Janssen, J. 2007. *Religie in Nederland: kiezen of delen?* Tilburg: KSGV.

Janssen, J., J. van der Lans, and M. Dechesne. 2001. "Fundamentalism: The Possibilities and Limitations of a Social-psychological Approach." In *Religious Identity and the Invention of Tradition*, ed. J. W. van Henten. Assen: Van Gorcum.

Jenson, R. W. 1982. *The Triune Identity: God According to the Gospel.* Philadelphia: Fortress Press.

Joest, W. 1984. *Die Wirklichkeit Gottes. Dogmatik.* Vol. 1. Göttingen: Vandenhoeck and Ruprecht.

Jones, E. 1953–1957. *Sigmund Freud: Life and Work.* 3 vols. London: Hogarth Press.

Jung, C. G. 1931. *Seelenprobleme der Gegenwart.* Zürich: Rascher.

_____. 1944. *Psychologie und Alchemie.* Zürich: Rascher.

_____. 1948. "Über das Selbst." *Eranos-Jahrbuch.* 16:285–315. Zürich: Rhein-Verlag.

_____. 1976. *Mysterium Coniunctionis.* Princeton: Princeton University Press.

Jüngel, E. 1976. *The Doctrine of the Trinity: God's Being is in Becoming.* Translated by H. Harris. Grand Rapids, MI: Wm.

B. Eerdmans.

———. 1983. *God as the Mystery of the World*. Grand Rapids: Wm. B. Eerdmans.

———. 2003. "Thesen zum Verhältnis von Existenz, Wesen und Eigenschaften Gottes." In *Ganz werden: Theologische Erörterungen* V. Tübingen: Mohr (Siebeck).

Kalsbeek, L. 1970. *De Wijsbegeerte der Wetsidee*. Amsterdam: Buijten and Schipperheijn.

Kamphuis, J. 1982. *Aantekeningen bij J. A. Heyns' Dogmatiek*. Kampen: Van den Berg.

Kärkkäinen, V.-M. 2004. *The Doctrine of God: A Global Introduction*. Grand Rapids: Baker Academic.

Kasper, W. 1983. *The God of Jesus Christ*. London: SCM Press.

Kelly, J. N. D. 1958. *Early Christian Doctrines*. New York: Harper.

Kittel, G. et al., eds. 1964–1976. *Theological Dictionary of the New Testament*. Translated by G. W. Bromiley. 10 vols. Grand Rapids, MI: Eerdmans.

Koopmans, J. 1938. *Het oudkerkelijk dogma in de reformatie, bepaaldelijk bij Calvijn*. Wageningen: Veenman.

Kohnstamm, P. 1931. *De heilige*. Haarlem: Tjeenk Willink.

Kolakowski, L. 1981. "Die Sorge um Gott in unserem scheinbar gottlosen Zeitalter." In *Der nahe und der ferne Gott: Nichttheologische Texte zur Gottesfrage im 20. Jahrhundert. Ein Lesebuch*, ed. H. Rössner. Berlin: Severin and Siedler.

König, A. 1975. *Hier is ek! Gelovig nagedink*. Vol. 1: *Oor God*. Pretoria: N.G. Kerkboekhandel.

———. 1982. *Hy kan weer en meer*. Pretoria: N.G. Kerkboekhandel.

Korff, F. W. A. 1940. *Christologie: De leer van het komen Gods*. Vol. 1. Nijkerk: Callenbach.

Kreeft, P. 1990. *A Summa of the Summa: The Essential Philosophical Passages of St. Thomas Aquinas' Summa Theologica*. San Francisco: Ignatius Press.

Kuitert, H. M. 1962. *De mensvormigheid Gods: Een dogmatisch-hermeneutische studie over de anthropomorphismen van de Heilige Schrift*. Kampen: J.H. Kok.

———. 1993. *I Have My Doubts: How to Become a Christian without Becoming a Fundamentalist*. Translated by J. Bowden. London: SCM Press. *Het algemeen betwijfeld christelijk geloof: een herziening*. Baarn: Ten Have.

Küng, H. 1970. *Menschwerdung Gottes: Eine Einführung in Hegels theologisches Denken als Prolegomena zu einer künftigen Christologie*. Freiburg: Herder.

———. 1978. *Does God Exist? An Answer for Today*. London: Collins.

———. 1979. *24 Thesen zur Gottesfrage*. München: R. Piper and Co. Verlag.

Kuyper, A. 1871. *Het modernisme een fata morgana op Christelijk gebied*. Amsterdam: H. de Hoogh and Co.

Kuyper, A. 1898. *Encyclopedia of Sacred Theology: Its Principles*. Translated by J. H. De Vries. New York: Charles Scribner's Sons.

———. 1908–1909. *Encyclopaedie der heilige godgeleerdheid*, 2nd rev. ed. 3 vols.: vol. 1 (1908): *Inleidend deel*; vol. 2 (1909): *Algemeen deel*; vol. 3 (1909): *Bijzonder deel*. Kampen: J.H. Kok.

Kuyper, A. n.d. *Dictaten Dogmatiek*. Vol. 2: *Locus de Sacra Scriptura, Creatione, Creaturis*. Kampen: J.H. Kok.

Lamont, J. R. T. 2004. *Divine Faith*. Aldershot: Ashgate.

Levin, J. 2001. *God, Faith and Health: Exploring the Spirituality-Healing Connection*. New York: Wiley.

Lewis, C. S. 1944. *Beyond Personality: The Christian Idea of God*. London: Geoffrey Bles.

———. 1960. *The Four Loves*. Glasgow: Collins Fount Paperbacks.

———. (1950) 2009. *The Lion, the Witch and the Wardrobe*. New York: HarperCollins Children's Books.

Lewis, H. D. 1959. *Our Experience of God*. London: Allen and

Unwin.

Lightfoot, J. B. 1880. *Saint Paul's Epistles to the Colossians and to Philemon*. London: Macmillan.

Loewenthal, K. M. 2000. *Psychology of Religion: A Short Introduction*. Oxford: Oneworld Publications.

Lonergan, B. 1976. *The Way to Nicea: The Dialectical Development of Trinitarian Theology*. London: Darton, Longman and Todd.

Loonstra, B. 2003. *God schrijft geschiedenis: Disputaties over de Eeuwige*. Zoetermeer: Boekencentrum.

Lyotard, J.-F. 1979. *La Condition postmoderne*. Paris: Éditions de Minuit.

McFague, S. 1983. *Metaphorical Theology*. London: SCM Press.

———. 1987. *Models of God*. London: SCM Press.

MacGregor, G. 1960. *Introduction to Religious Philosophy*. New York: MacMillan.

Macquarrie, J. 1975. *Thinking about God*. London: SCM Press

MacLeod, D. 1998. *The Person Of Christ: Contours of Christian Theology*. Downers Grove, IL: InterVarsity.

Marx, K. 1975. *Karl Marx, Frederick Engels: Collected Works*. Translated by R. Dixon et al. Moscow: Progress Publishers. *Einleitung zur Kritik der Hegelschen Rechtsphilosophie*.

Maslow, A. H. 1954. *Motivation and Personality*. New York: Harper & Row.

Milbank, J., C. Pickstock, and G. Ward. 1999. *Radical Orthodoxy: A New Theology*. London: Routledge.

Miley, J. 1892. *Systematic Theology*. Vol. 1. New York: Methodist Book Concern.

Miskotte, K. H. 1941a. *Bijbelsch ABC*. Nijkerk: Callenbach.

———. 1941b. "Halt bij Chalcedon?" *Woord en Wereld* 1941:23-42.

Moltmann, J. 1993. *The Crucified God: The Cross of Christ as the Foundation and Criticism of Christian Theology*. Translated by

R. A. Wilson and J. Bowdon. Minneapolis: Fortress Press. 1972. *Der gekreuzigte Gott: Das Kreuz Christi als Grund und Kritik christlicher Theologie*. München: Kaiser.

_____. 1981. *The Trinity and the Kingdom: The Doctrine of God*. Translated by M. Kohl. New York: Harper & Row. 1980. *Trinität und Reich Gottes*. München: Chr. Kaiser.

Montgomery, J. W. 1966. *The "Is God Dead?" Controversy*. Grand Rapids, MI: Zondervan.

Morris, L. 1971. *The Gospel According to John*. NICNT. Grand Rapids: Wm. B. Eerdmans.

Morris, T. V. 1976. *Francis Schaeffer's Apologetics: A Critique*. Chicago: Moody Press.

Muis, J. 2010. "The Truth of Metaphorical God-Talk." *Scottish Journal of Theology* 63.2:146–62.

Murchland, B. 1967. *The Meaning of the Death of God*. London: Random House.

Murray, J. 1968. *The Epistle to the Romans*. NICNT. Grand Rapids: Wm. B. Eerdmans.

Nietzsche, F. 1974. *The Gay Science, With a Prelude in Rhymes and an Appendix of Songs*. Translated by W. Kaufmann. New York: Vintage Books. 1999. *De vrolijke wetenschap*. Utrecht: Arbeiderspers.

Nygren, A. 1930–1937. *Eros und Agape: Gestaltwandlungen der christlichen Liebe*, Bd. I,II. Gütersloh: C. Bertelsmann.

Ogletree, T. W. 1966. *The Death of God Controversy*. Nashville, TN: Abingdon Press.

Oswalt, J. N. 1986. *The Book of Isaiah*. Vol. 1: Chapters 1–39. New International Commentary on the Old Testament. Grand Rapids: Wm. B. Eerdmans.

Ott, H. 1969. *Wirklichkeit und Glaube*. Vol. 2: *Der persönliche Gott*. Göttingen: Vandenhoeck and Ruprecht.

_____. 1972. *Die Antwort des Glaubens: Systematische Theologie in 50 Artikeln*. Stuttgart: Kreuz Verlag.

_____. 1974. *God*. Edinburgh: St. Andrew Press.

Otto, R. 1958. *The Idea of the Holy*. Oxford: Oxford University Press.

Ouweneel, W. J. 1973. *Het Hooglied van Salomo*. Winschoten: Uit het Woord der Waarheid.

———. 1982. *"Wij zien Jezus": Bijbelstudies over de brief aan de Hebreeën*. 2 vols. Vaassen: Medema.

———. 1984. *Psychologie: Een christelijke kijk op het mentale leven*. Amsterdam: Buijten and Schipperheijn.

———. 1986. *De leer van de mens: Proeve van een christelijk-wijsgerige antropologie*. Amsterdam: Buijten and Schipperheijn.

———. 1987a. *Woord en wetenschap: Wetenschapsbeoefening aan de Evangelische Hogeschool*. Amsterdam: Buijten and Schipperheijn.

———. 1988/1990. *De Openbaring van Jezus Christus*. 2 vols. Vaassen: H. Medema.

———. 1989a. "De mens als religieus wezen." *Philosophia Reformata* 54:44–64.

———. 1989b. "Is het hart tijdelijk of niet-tijdelijk?" *Philosophia Reformata* 54:103–108.

———. 1991a. "Korrespondensie of koherensie? Diskussie, veral na aanleiding van J. Botha: Semeion (1990)." *Koers* 56:167–84.

———. 1993. "Supratemporality in the Transcendental Anthropology of Herman Dooyeweerd." *Philosophia Reformata* 58:210–20.

———. 1994. *Godsverlichting: De evocatie van de verduisterde God: Een weg tot spiritualiteit en gemeenteopbouw*. Amsterdam: Buijten and Schipperheijn.

———. 1995. *Christian Doctrine: I. The External Prolegomena*. Amsterdam: Buijten and Schipperheijn.

———. 1998. *De zevende koningin: Het eeuwig vrouwelijke en de raad van God. Metahistorische triologie*. Vol. 2. Heerenveen: Barnabas.

———. 2003. *De negende Koning: Het laatste der hemelrijken: De triomf van Christus over de machten*. 3rd ed. *Metahistorische triologie*. Vol. 1. Soesterberg: Aspekt.

———. 2005. *De God die is, of: Waarom ik geen atheïst ben*. Vaassen: Medema.

———. 2007. *De Geest van God: Ontwerp van een pneumatologie*. Vaassen: Medema (abbrev.: EDR 1).

———. 2008. *De schepping van God: Ontwerp van een scheppings-, mens- en zondeleer*. Vaassen: Medema (abbrev.: EDR 3).

———. 2012. *Het Woord van God: Ontwerp van een openbarings- en schriftleer*. Heerenveen: Medema (abbrev.: EDR 11).

———. 2013. *De glorie van God: Ontwerp van een godsleer en van een theologische vakfilosofie*. Heerenveen: Medema (abbrev.: EDR 12).

———. 2014a. *Wisdom for Thinkers: An Introduction to Christian Philosophy*. St. Catharines: Paideia Press.

———. 2014b. *What Then Is Theology? An Introduction to Christian Theology*. St. Catharines: Paideia Press.

———. 2015. *Searching the Soul: An Introduction to Christian Psychology*. St. Catharines: Paideia Press.

———. 2016. *The Heidelberg Diary: Daily Devotions on the Heidelberg Catechism*. Jordan Station, ON: Paideia Press.

———. 2017. *The World Is Christ's: A Critique of Two Kingdoms Theology*. Toronto: Ezra Press.

———. 2018. *Adam, Where Are You? – And Why This Matters: A Theological Evaluation of the New Evolutionist Hermeneutics*. Jordan Station, ON: Paideia Press.

———. 2019 (forthcoming). *The Eternal Word*. Jordan Station, ON: Paideia Press.

Pailin, D. A. 1986. *Groundworks of Philosophy of Religion*. London: Epworth Press.

Paloutzian, R. F. and C. L. Park, eds. 2005. *Handbook of the Psychology of Religion and Spirituality*. New York: Guilford

Press.

Pannenberg, W. 1964. *Grundzüge der Christologie*. Gütersloh: Gerd Mohn.

_____. 1971. *Grundfragen systematischer Theologie*. Göttingen: Vandenhoeck and Ruprecht.

_____. 1988/91a/93. *Systematische Theologie*, Bd. I-III. Göttingen: Vandenhoeck and Ruprecht.

Pascal, Blaise. n.d. *Pensées*. Translated by W. F. Trotter. Grand Rapids, MI: Christian Classics Ethereal Library. http://www.ccel.org/ccel/pascal/pensees.pdf.

Peterson, M., W. Hasker, B. Reichenbach, and D. Basinger. (1991) 2009. *Reason and Religious Belief: An Introduction to the Philosophy of Religion*. 4th ed. New York/Oxford: Oxford University Press.

Plantinga, A. 2000. *Warranted Christian Belief*. New York: Oxford University Press.

_____ and M. Tooley. 2008. *Knowledge of God*. Malden, MA: Blackwell Publishing.

_____ and N. Wolterstorff, eds. 2009. *Faith and Rationality: Reason and Belief in God*. Notre Dame, IN: University of Notre Dame Press.

Pike, N. 1970. *God and Timelessness*. London: Routledge and Kegan Paul.

_____. 2002. *God and Timelessness*. Publisher: Eugene, OR: Wipf and Stock.

Plessner, H. 1928. *Die Stufen des Organischen und der Mensch: Einleitung in die philosophische Anthropologie*. Berlin: W. de Gruyter.

Prenter, R. 1971. Der Gott der Liebe ist: Das Verhältnis der Gotteslehre zur Christologie. *Theologische Literaturzeitung* 96:401-413.

Rahner, K. 1970. *The Trinity*. New York: Herder and Herder.

_____. 1972. "The need for a 'short formula' of Christian faith." TI IX:117-126 (orig.: ST VIII, 1967).

———. 1974. "Remarks on the dogmatic treatise 'De Trinitate'." TI IV:77–102 (oorspr.: ST IV, 1960).

———. 1975. "Der dreifaltige Gott als transzendenter Urgrund der Heilsgeschichte." In *Mysterium Salutis*, ed. J. Feiner and M. Löhrer, 317–401. Vol. 2. Einsiedeln: Benziger.

———. 1961-1992. *Theological Investigations*. London: Darton, Longman and Todd.

———. 1979. "The hiddenness of God." TI XVI:227–43 (orig.: ST XII, 1975).

Ratzinger, J. (Benedict XVI). 2007. *Jesus of Nazareth*. Vol. 1: *From the Baptism in the Jordan to the Transfiguration*. New York: Doubleday.

Richards, J. W. 2003. *The Untamed God: A Philosophical Exploration of Divine Perfection, Simplicity and Immutability*. Downers Grove, IL: InterVarsity Press.

Ridderbos, H. N. 1967. *De Pastorale brieven. Commentaar op het Nieuwe Testament*. Kampen: J.H. Kok.

Ridderbos, J. 1958. *Psalmen*. Vol. 2: *Psalm 42–106. Commentaar op het Oude Testament*. Kampen: J.H. Kok.

Ritschl, A. 1881. *Theologie und Metaphysik*. Zur Verständigung und Abwehr. Bonn: A. Marcus.

———. 1889–1890. *Die christliche Lehre von der Rechtfertigung und Versöhnung*, Bd. I-III. Bonn: A. Marcus and E. Weber.

Ritschl, D. 1986. *The Logic of Theology: A Brief Account of the Relationship between Basic Concepts in Theology*. London: SCM Press.

Robinson, J. A. T. 1963. *Honest to God*. London: SCM Press.

Rokeach, M. 1969. "Religion, values, and social compassion." *Review of Religious Research* 11:3–39.

Rouse Ball, W. W. (1908) 2003. *A Short Account of the History of Mathematics*. 4th ed. Dover: Dover Publications.

Runia, D. T. 1986. *Philo of Alexandria and the Timaeus of Plato*. Leiden: Brill.

Rushdoony, R. J. 1965. *Freud*. Philadelphia: Presbyterian and Reformed Publ. Co.

Saroglou, V., ed. 2013. *Religion, Personality, and Social Behavior*. Abingdon: Routledge.

Sarot, M. 1992. *God, Passibility and Corporeality*. Kampen: J.H. Kok.

Sartre, J.-P. 1943. *L'être et le néant: Essai d'ontologie phénoménologique*. Paris: Gallimard.

Schaeffer, F. 1968. *The God Who Is There*. Downers Grove, IL: InterVarsity Press.

Schilder, K. n.d. *Kompendium dogmatiek*. 2 vols. Kampen: Van den Berg.

Schillebeeckx, E. 1974. *The Understanding of Faith: Interpretation and Criticism*. Translated by N. D. Smith. New York: Seabury Press.

———. 1989. "Elke theologie heeft haar eigen filosofie." In *Geloof dat te denken geeft: Opstellen aangeboden aan Prof. dr. H. M. Kuitert*, ed. K. U. Gäbler et al., 221–34. Baarn: Ten Have.

Schleiermacher, F. D. E. (1799) 1996. *On Religion: Speeches to its Cultured Despisers*. Translated by R. Crouter. Cambridge: Cambridge University Press.

———. (1830) 1977. *Kurze Darstellung des theologischen Studiums zum Behuf einleitender Vorlesungen*. Hildesheim: Georg Olms.

———. (1831) 1999. *The Christian Faith*. London: T & T Clark.

Schlink, E. 1983. *Oekumenische Dogmatik: Grundzüge*. Göttingen: Vandenhoeck and Ruprecht.

Schmidt, M. 1949. "Der Ort der Trinitätslehre bei Emil Brunner." *Theologische Zeitschrift* 5:46–66.

Scholem, G. 1976. *On the Mystical Shape of the Godhead*. New York: Schocken Books.

Schuler, B. 1961. *Die Lehre von der Dreipersönlichkeit Gottes*. Paderborn: Ferdinand Schöningh.

Schwöbel, C. 2006. "Gott im Gespräch: Die Gottesfrage im Dialog der Kulturen." *Neue Zeitschrift für systematische Theologie und Relgionsphilosophie* 49:516-33.

Scobie, G. E. W. 1975. *Psychology of Religion*. London/Sydney: B. T. Batsford.

Seeberg, R. (1895-1898) 1923. *Lehrbuch der Dogmengeschichte*, Bd. I,II. Leipzig: Deichert.

Shakespeare, S. 2007. *Radical Orthodoxy: A Critical Introduction*. London: SPCK.

Shults, F. L. 1999. *The Postfoundationalist Task of Theology: Wolfhart Pannenberg and the New Theological Rationality*. Grand Rapids: Wm. B. Eerdmans.

Smit, J. H. 1980. "Skeppingsopenbaring en wetenskap." *Tydskrif vir Christelike Wetenskap* 16:174-200.

Söderblom, L. O. J. 1942. *Der lebendige Gott im Zeugnis der Religionsgeschichte*. München: Reinhardt.

Sölle, D. 1967. *Christ the Representative: An Essay in Theology after the "Death of God."* Translated by D. Lewis. London: SCM Press.

_____. 1968. *Atheistisch an Gott glauben: Beiträge zur Theologie*. Freiburg: Walter-Verlag.

Sperna Weiland, J. 1966. *Oriëntatie: Nieuwe wegen in de theologie*. Baarn: Wereldvenster.

_____. 1971. *Voortgezette oriëntatie: Nieuwe wegen in de theologie*. Baarn: Wereldvenster.

Springer, J. L. 1969. *Waar, wat en wie is God?* Wageningen: H. Veenman and Zonen.

Spykman, G. J. 1992. *Reformational Theology: A New Paradigm for Doing Dogmatics*. Grand Rapids, MI: Eerdmans.

Steenbergen, W. 1990. "Godsverduistering (1-4)." *De Wekker* Oct. 19-Nov. 9.

Stephan, H. 1941. *Glaubenslehre: Der evangelische Glaube und sein Weltverständnis*. Berlin: Töpelmann.

Stern, P. J. 1976. *C. G. Jung: The Haunted Prophet*. New York:

George Braziller.

Stone, H. W. and J. O. Duke. 2006. *How to Think Theologically.* 2nd ed. Minneapolis: Fortress Press.

Strauss, D. F. M. 1983. "The Nature of Philosophy." TCW 19:40–55.

———. 1988. "Begripsvorming in die sistematiese teologie." TCW 24:124–61.

———. 1989. *Die wysgerige grondslae van die moderne natuurwetenskappe.* Bloemfontein: VCHO.

———. 1990. "Enkele grondprobleme van en denkrigtings in die wiskunde." *South African Journal of Philosophy* 9.1:28–42.

———. 1991. "Hoe kan ons wetenskaplik oor God praat?" TCW 27.2:23–43.

———. 2009. *Philosophy: Discipline of the Disciplines.* Grand Rapids: Paideia Press.

———. 2010. "God in Himself" and "God As Revealed to Us": The Impact of the Substance Concept." *Acta Theologica* 30.1:123–44.

——— and P. J. Visagie. 1984. "Die verhouding tussen nie-teologiese wetenskappe en die teologie." TCW 20.3/4:51–79.

Strommen, M. P., ed. 1971. *Research on Religious Development: A Comprehensive Handbook.* New York: Hawthorn Books.

Tate, E. D., and G. R. Miller. 1971. "Differences in the value systems of persons with varying religious orientations." *Journal for the Scientific Study of Religion* 10:357–65.

Taylor, C. 2007. *A Secular Age.* Cambridge, MA: Belknap Press.

Ter Linden, N. 1996–2003. *Het verhaal gaat . . . .* 6 vols. Amsterdam: Rubinstein Media.

Teubal, S. J. 1984. *Sarah the Priestess: The First Matriarch of Genesis.* Athens, OH: Ohio University Press.

Thiel, J. 2000. *Nonfoundationalism.* Minneapolis, MN: Fortress Press.

Thielicke, H. 1974. *The Evangelical Faith*. Translated by G. W. Bromiley. Vol. 2: *The Doctrine of God and Christ*. Grand Rapids: Wm. B. Eerdmans. 1973. *Der evangelische Glaube, Bd. II: Gotteslehre und Christologie*. Tübingen: Mohr (Siebeck).

Tillich, P. 1964. *Theology of Culture*. New York: Oxford University Press.

_____. 1968. *Systematic Theology*. 2 vols. Digswell Place: Nisbett and Co.

Tisdale, J. R. 1966. Selected correlates of extrinsic religious values. *Review of Religious Research* 7:78–84.

Towner, P. H. 2006. *The Letters to Timothy and Titus*. NICNT. Grand Rapids: Wm. B. Eerdmans.

Trillhaas, W. 1972. *Dogmatik*. 3rd ed. Berlin: W. de Gruyter.

Troost, A. 1978. "De relatie tussen scheppingsopenbaring en woordopenbaring." *Philosophia Reformata* 43:101–29.

_____. 1983. *The Christian Ethos: A Philosophical Survey*. Bloemfontein: Patmos.

_____. 1992. "Kritiek op art. 1 van de Nederl. Geloofsbelijdenis." *Opbouw* 36.8:147–49.

_____. 2004. *Vakfilosofie van de geloofswetenschap: Prolegomena van de theologie*. Budel: Damon.

_____. 2005. *Antropocentrische totaliteitswetenschap: Inleiding in de "reformatorische wijsbegeerte" van Herman Dooyeweerd*. Budel: Damon.

Van de Beek, A. 1984. *Waarom? Over lijden, schuld en God*. Nijkerk: Callenbach.

_____. 1987. *De adem van God: De Heilige Geest in kerk en kosmos*. Nijkerk: G.F. Callenbach.

Van den Brink, G. 1993. *Almighty God: A Study of the Doctrine of Divine Omnipotence*. Kampen: J.H. Kok Pharos.

_____. 2000. *Oriëntatie in de filosofie*. Zoetermeer: Boekencentrum.

_____ and M. Sarot, eds. 1995. *Hoe is uw Naam? Opstellen over de eigenschappen van God*. Kampen: J.H. Kok.

Vander Goot, H., ed. 1981. *Life is Religion: Essays in Honor of H. Evan Runner*. St. Catharines: Paideia Press.

Van der Hoeven, J. 1986. "Na 50 jaar: philosophia reformata - philosophia reformanda." *Philosophia Reformata* 51:5–28.

———. 1991. "Schepping en redding." In *De God van de filosofen en de God van de Bijbel*, ed. H. M. Vroom, 20–39. Zoetermeer: Meinema.

Van der Lans, J. 1978. *Religieuze ervaring en meditatie*. Nijmegen: Dissertation University of Nijmegen.

Van der Leeuw, G. 1956. *Phänomenologie der Religion*. 2nd ed. Tübingen: Mohr (Siebeck).

Van Genderen, J. and W. H. Velema. 2008. *Concise Reformed Dogmatics*. Translated by G. Bilkes and E. M. van der Maas. Phillipsburg, NJ: Presbyterian and Reformed Publishing Company.

Van Herck, W. 1999. *Religie en metafoor: Over het relativisme van het figuurlijke*. Leuven: Peeters.

Van Huyssteen, J. W. V. 1997. *Essays in Postfoundationalist Theology*. Grand Rapids: Wm. B. Eerdmans.

Van Niftrik, G. C. 1961. *Kleine dogmatiek*. Nijkerk: Callenbach.

———. 1971. *Het bestaan van God in de kentering van deze tijd*. Den Haag: J. N. Voorhoeve.

Van Til, C. 1955. *The Defense of the Faith*. Philadelphia: Presbyterian and Reformed Publishing Company.

———. 1969. *In Defense of the Faith*. Vol. 2: *A Survey of Christian Epistemology*. n.p.: Den Dulk Christian Foundation.

Van Uden, M. and J. Pieper, eds. 2009. *Zichtbare en onzichtbare religie: Over de varianten van religieuze zin*. Nijmegen: Valkhof Pers.

Van Woudenberg, R. 1992. *Gelovend denken: Inleiding tot een christelijke filosofie*. Amsterdam: Buijten and Schipperheijn/Kampen: Uitg. J.H. Kok.

Vergote, A. 1967. *Godsdienstpsychologie*. Den Haag: Lannoo.

Verkuyl, J. 1992. *De kern van het christelijk geloof.* Kampen: J.H. Kok.

Visagie, P.J. 1979. "Humanistiese invloede in die teologie en die soeke na 'n Bybelse Godsleer." TCW 15:141–60.

_____. 1982. "Some basic concepts concerning the idea of Origin in Reformational philosophy and theology." TCW 18:1–13.

Von Gall, A. 1900. *Die Herrlichkeit Gottes.* Giessen: J. Ricker.

Von Rad, G. 1957. *Theologie des Alten Testaments*, Bd. I. München: Kaiser.

Wainwright, A.W. 1969. *The Trinity in the New Testament.* London: SPCK.

Wainwright, W., ed. 2004. *The Oxford Handbook of Philosophy of Religion.* Oxford: Oxford University Press.

Weber, O. 1981. *Foundations of Dogmatics.* Translated by D. L. Guder. Vol. 1. Grand Rapids: Wm. B. Eerdmans. 1955. *Grundlagen der Dogmatik*, Bd. I. Neukirchen: Verlag der Buchhandlung des Erziehungsvereins.

Weima, J. 1981. *Reiken naar oneindigheid: Inleiding tot de psychologie van de religieuze ervaring.* Baarn: Ambo.

Wentsel, B. 1970. *Natuur en genade. Een introductie in en confrontatie met de jongste ontwikkelingen in de Rooms-katholieke theologie inzake dit thema.* Kampen: J.H. Kok.

_____. 1987. *Dogmatiek.* Vol. 3a: *God en mens verzoend: Godsleer, mensleer en zondeleer.* Kampen: J.H. Kok.

Whitehead, A. N. (1929) 1969. *Process and Reality.* New York: Free Press.

Wiles, M. 1976. "Some Reflections on the Origins of the Doctrine of the Trinity." *Working Papers in Doctrine.* 1–17. London: SCM Press.

Wiskerke, J. R. 1978. *De strijd om de sleutel der kennis.* Groningen: De Vuurbaak.

Wolterstorff, N. 1995. *Divine Discourse: Philosophical Reflections on the Claim that God Speaks*. Cambridge: Cambridge University Press.

Scripture Index

OLD TESTAMENT
Genesis
1   285, 291
1:1   191
1:22   291
1:26   124
1:26–27   72
1:28   124, 291
1:28–29   129
2:1   285
2:7   249
2:22   129
3:8   131
3:8–9   291
4:1   19
4:17   19
4:25   19
5:3   72
6:3   129
6:6   187, 251
6:7   234
8:1   128
8:21   128, 251
9:6   72, 124
9:9–17   292
11:5   233, 269
12:7   149
14:18–22   215, 230
15   292
15:1   246
15:2   254
16:14   256
17   292
17:1   149, 246
17:5   129
17:15   129
17:22   233
18   20
18:1–2   129
18:14   242
18:19   19
18:21   128, 269
18:23–32   234
18:25   268, 311
21:1   129
21:33   165, 167
22:2   280
22:12   280
24:27   328
24:63   256
25:11   256
26   292
26:24   149
28:3   246
28:16–17   229
30:33   309
32:29   207
35   292
35:7   149
35:11   246
35:13   233
38:7   205
38:26   309
43:30   248
46   292
49:10   311
49:25   246

Exodus
2:2   301
2:24   128
2:25   19, 197, 198, 270
3   238
3:5   323
3:6   2, 294
3:8   233, 293
3:14   167, 172, 188, 237, 291, 292
3:15   294
3:15–16   2
3:18   129
4   238
4:5   2
4:14   236
4:22   280, 320
5:1   294

6:1–13	292	33:11	129	4:6	325
6:2–3	292	33:12	19	4:7	230
8:10	214	33:18–19	301	4:13	286
9:12	280	33:19	277	4:20	293
9:14	214	33:20	251, 254	4:24	196, 246
9:16	280	33:23	251, 254	4:35	213, 341
9:27	306	34:1	129	4:37	314
12:12	214	34:5	149, 233	4:39	213, 341
12:27	299	34:6	254, 318, 328	5:24	251
13:15	205	34:6–7	238	5:26	247
13:21–22	303	34:28	286	6:4	213, 219, 341
14:24	303	40:34–35	301, 303	6:5	313, 315
15:3	285			7:7–8	314
15:8	128	**Leviticus**		7:9	328
15:11	121, 207	11:44–45	202	7:13	314, 315
15:13	293	19:2	202, 324	8:2	128, 269
15:17	293	19:18	315	8:5	21, 129, 320
15:26	250	20:3	323	10:4	286
17:15	246	22:2	323	10:15	314
18:10–11	214	25:23	315	10:17	207, 215, 348
18:21	328	26:12	131	10:18	314
19:5	292			11:2	21
19:16	300	**Numbers**		13:3	269, 313
19:20	233	4:18	318	13:4	313
20:4	121	7:89	301	15:17	164
20:5	121	10:32	317	19:10	280
20:7	285	11:1	236	23:5	314
23:7	280, 309	11:25	233	23:18	322
24:1–8	292	11:33	236	25:1	311
24:9–10	254	12:5	233	26:15	224
24:10	301	14:14	303	27:25	280
24:10–11	251	16:5	26	28:11	129
24:15–16	300	20:12–13	323	29:5–6	21
24:15–17	301	21:18	311	29:26	344
24:16	229	21:29	348	32:4	196, 235, 245, 306, 328, 331
25:8	293	23:19	243	32:6	250, 320
29:42–46	229, 293	24:16	215, 230	32:8	215, 230
31:17	128	24:17	246	32:11	259
32	40	31:18	19	32:15	245, 266
32–33	20	31:35	19	32:17	348
32:10	257	33:4	214	32:18	245, 250, 320
32:10–14	187, 234			32:27	128, 256
32:11	128	**Deuteronomy**		32:30–31	245
32:14	205, 234, 256	1:17	309	32:36	256
32:32–33	288	1:31	314, 320		

Scripture Index

32:37	245	23:10–13	270	19:19	213
32:39	213, 247, 348	24:15	267	19:22	324
32:40	167	24:16	268	19:31	256
33:2	268, 299, 300	24:18	309		
33:5	236	28:6	205	**1 Chronicles**	
33:12	314			5:1–2	397
33:16	229, 293	**2 Samuel**		10:14	205
33:27	165	6:2	301	16:10	323
33:29	261	7:14	250, 320	16:34	317
		7:21	251	16:35	323
Joshua		7:22	348	17:19	251
3:11	247	7:23	214	17:20	348
5:15	323	7:24	236	17:23–24	328–329
11:20	280	7:28	328	29:3	323
22:22	348	12:24–25	314		
		16:10	280	**2 Chronicles**	
Judges		22:3	299	1:9	329
5:4–5	300	22:9	128	2:6	224
6:24	305	22:10	233	2:11	314
10:15	234	22:16	128	5:13	317
10:16	236	22:33	196	6:1	228
11:23–24	348	22:47	266	6:14	348
11:27	268			6:17	329
13:18	207	**1 Kings**		7:16	251
13:20	233	1:6	301	12:6	306
13:22	251, 254	3:9–12	20, 325	16:9	270
15:2	301	3:26	248	19:4	247
21:12	19	8:10–11	303	19:16	247
		8:12–13	229	33:13	234
1 Samuel		8:23	193, 213, 348		
1:3	285	8:26	328	**Ezra**	
1:11	128	8:27	224, 228, 229	9:15	306
2:12	21	8:39	270		
2:35	251	9:3	251	**Nehemiah**	
13:14	251	19	20	7:2	328
15	189	19:11–12	301	9:8	306
15:11	188, 189, 205, 234, 243	20:23	246	9:12	303
		20:28	246	9:13	233
15:29	189, 234, 237, 243	22:19	285	9:17	318
		22:19–20	128	9:19	303
15:35	189, 234, 243	22:21–22	254	9:32	295
16:12	301			9:33	328
17:26	247	**2 Kings**		11:1	323
17:36	247	5:15	348	11:18	323
17:45	285	10:30	251	13:22	299

13:26	314	9:9	230	40:7	288
		9:9–10	21	42:2	247
Job		10:1	7	42:4	7
5:8	267	10:4	7	42:11	7
5:17	261	11:4	131, 224	43:1	267
6:10	324	11:5	205	43:4	202, 305, 340
7:17	251	11:7	306	45:4	328
9:3	277	18:2	230	45:6–8	337
9:4	277	18:7–9	303	46:7	230, 285
9:14–15	309	18:9	233	46:11	230, 285
9:15	268	18:15	129	47:5	233
9:19–20	309	18:31	213	50:1	348
9:32–33	309	19:1	301	50:1–2	268
10:5	167	19:2	20	50:9–13	296
10:9	277	19:7	325	51:6	328
10:13	251	19:9	328	51:11	323, 324
11:7–9	266	22:1	204, 225, 230	54:6	317
11:10	277	22:2–3	7	57:3	328
13:3	254, 267	22:11	204, 225, 230	59:9	230
13:18–19	267	22:19	204, 225, 230	59:17	230
18:21	22	23:1	250	60:7	311
23:4–7	267	24:8	285	60:8	131
28:28	20, 325	25:7	317	61:4	230
30:27	248	25:10	328	61:7	328
31:35	254	25:14	295	62:1–2	340
33:13	277	26	317	62:6–7	340
34:14	247, 251	27:1	246, 268, 340	62:8	230
36:5	251	27:4	301	63:2	7
36:22	49	29	300	65:11	317
36:26	167, 266	29:3	264, 304	68:5	336
42:2	242	31:5	328, 331	68:18	233
		32:1–2	261	69:5	270
Psalms		32:12	261	69:16	317
1:1	261	33:4	328	69:28	288
2:4	128	33:11	173, 251	73:1	317
2:12	261	33:21	323	75:1	230
3:4	128	34:8	251, 317	75:7	268, 311
4:1	202	35:23	267	77:13	348
4:6–7	268	36:5	328	77:14	20
4:7	337	36:7–9	268	77:19	228
5:5	205	36:9	246, 247	78:40	128, 256
5:7	323	36:10	21	78:41	324
7:9	128, 202, 306	37:13	128	78:65	285
7:11	202, 268, 306	38:23	340	78:68	315
9:2	254	40:5	266	79:1	323

Reference	Pages
79:6	22
80:1	268, 301
80:1–2	229
84:2	247
84:4	21
84:11	245, 246
86:5	317
86:8	207
86:15	318
87:1	166
87:2	315
88:1	340
88:2	340
88:15	7
89:8	207
89:14	328
89:18	324
89:26	266
89:27	340
89:28	295, 329
90	169
90:2	163, 167, 169, 187, 197
90:3	169
90:4	169
90:17	301
91:1	246
92:1–5	200
92:5	266
93:3	167
94	300
94:1	268
94:2	311
94:9	128, 129, 131
94:9–11	270
94:22	230
95:1	266
95:10	24
97:11	268
98:1–2	309
98:2	20
100:5	317
102:15	300
102:25–27	167
103:1	21, 323
103:8	318
103:13	314, 320, 336
104:1	224
104:1–2	304
104:7	129
104:24	276
104:29–30	247
105:42	323
106:1	317
106:8	20
106:21	299
107:1	317
108:8	311
109:21	317
111:7	328
111:10	325
112:4	306
113:4–6	1
115:3	173, 224, 228, 229, 242, 277, 279
115:16	228, 229
116:5	306
118:1	317
118:27	300
118:29	317
119:68	317
119:86	328
119:105	266
119:114	230
119:137	306
119:142	328
119:151	328
119:154	267
127:2	314
129:4	306
135:3	317
136	205, 318
136:1	317
136:2	215, 348
138:2	323
139:2–3	270
139:7–10	225
139:8	228
139:11–12	228
139:16	288
139:17	222
139:17–18	266
139:23–24	269
144:3	197
144:5	233
145	200
145:5	299
145:8	318
145:9	317
145:17	306
146:8	314
147:3	128
147:5	222, 224
150	223
150:2	223, 224

Proverbs

Reference	Pages
1:4	19
1:7	325
2:6	19
3	325
3:12	314, 336
3:19–20	276, 325
4:23	100
5:2	19
6:16–19	205
6:17	280
6:34	257
8	325
8:14	145
8:22–31	325
9:10	325
15:9	314
15:33	325
16:4	278, 280
18:10	230
21:1	277
27:4	257

Ecclesiastes

Reference	Pages
1:18	19
3:11	179
4:4	257
12:13–14	20

Song of Solomon
5:4	248
8:6–7	314

Isaiah
1:3	21
1:18	266
1:24	285
2:10	299
2:19	299
2:21	299
4:3	288
5:4	256
5:13	22
5:16	323
6:1	254
6:3	254, 321, 323
6:3–4	303
7:15	325
7:18	250
7:20	250
8:18	229
9:2	268, 300
9:6	158, 207
10:15	277
11:2	20
11:4	129
11:9	20, 323
13:6	246
14:25	315
16:11	248
19:1	214
22:14	149
26:13	22
29:16	277
30:14	277
30:27	128, 225
31:3	252
31:4	260
31:5	259, 299
33:22	268, 311
37:4	247
37:17	247
40:13	25
40:13–14	270
40:26	225, 242
40:28	167
40:28–29	296
41:4	167
41:14	324
41:20	21
41:22–23	270
42:1	129
42:9	270, 288
43:3	197, 299, 324
43:4	314
43:9	309
43:10	348
43:11	299
43:14	324
43:26	309
44:6	167, 213, 348
44:8	348
45:5	348
45:7	280
45:9	277
45:15	299
45:21	299, 348
45:21–22	213
46:10	173, 242, 270, 288
46:13	309
47:4	324
48:2	323
48:3	288
48:12	167
48:14	314
48:17	324
49:7	328
49:11	315
49:15	129, 314
49:16	129
49:18	247
49:26	299
50:1–2	314
50:8–9	309
51:4	311
51:5–8	309
52:1	323
53:7	260
54:5	324
54:5–8	314
54:17	309
55:3	329
55:8	232
55:8–9	265
56:1	309
56:7	323
57:15	167, 229
58:8	302
59:7	280
59:8	24
59:19	300
60:1	300
60:1–2	302
60:16	299
60:19	268
61:10	314
61:10–11	309
62:1	309
62:4–5	314
63:4	129, 251
63:8	299
63:9	128, 203, 256, 257, 293, 314
63:10–11	323, 324
63:15	224, 248
63:15–16	336
63:16	250, 254, 320
64:1	233
64:3	233
64:4	348
64:8	250, 277, 320, 336
64:10	323
65:9	315
65:19	128, 256
66:1	131, 224
66:13	129, 314

Jeremiah
1:5	19
2:8	21
2:13	246
3:4	250, 320, 336

Scripture Index

3:6–13	314	33:16	312	**Daniel**	
3:15	251	42:10	234	1:4	301
3:19	250, 320, 336	44:21	251	2:47	215, 348
4:19	248	50:14	129	3:25	293
7:6	280			4:17	280
7:31	251	**Lamentations**		4:25	280
9:3–6	21	1:18	306	4:32	280
10:10	166, 247, 328, 330	1:20	248	4:35	173, 277, 280
		2:11	248	4:37	328
10:12	276	3:10	260	6:20	247
10:25	22	3:25	317	6:26	247
11:20	128, 267, 268	3:58	267	7:9	129, 166, 254, 302
13:14	299				
14:8	299	**Ezekiel**		7:9–10	311
16:21	20	1	300	7:13	166
17:9–10	270	1:22	235	9:14	306
17:10	128	1:26–28	254, 302	11:36	215, 348
18:6	277	8:6	225	12:1	288
18:8–10	234	10:4	302		
19:15	251	10:18	302	**Hosea**	
20	20	11:5	270	1:10	247
20:12	267, 270	11:22–23	302	2:1–13	314
21:7	299	16:8	314	2:15	314
22:3	280	16:11	129	2:17	311
22:16	20, 21	16:15–58	314	2:18–19	314
22:17	280	18:23	280	3:1	314
23:6	312	18:32	280	4:1	20, 21
23:20	251	20:17	299	4:6	19, 20, 21
23:23–24	225	20:41	323	5:9	329
23:24	224	22:30	234	6:3	19
23:36	247	24:14	299	6:6	20, 21
23:29	43	28:2	251	11:1	314
24:7	22	28:6	251	11:1–4	314
30:24	251	28:22	323	11:3	21
31:3	314	28:25	323	11:4	314
31:9	250, 320, 336	33:11	280	11:8	319
31:20	128, 248, 313, 319	36:20–23	323	11:8–9	314
		36:23	323	11:9	323, 324
31:34	22, 24, 128	38:16	323	13:4	348
32:17	242	38:21	315	13:5	19
32:19	270	39:27	323	13:8	260
32:27	242	43:2	299	14:4	314, 315
32:35	251	43:2–5	302	14:9	20
32:41	251				
33:11	317				

Joel
1:15	246
2:13	188, 234, 318
2:17	299
2:18	236

Amos
3:2	19, 270
3:3	4
3:6	280
4:2	323
5:15	313
5:21	256
6:8	323
7:3	188, 234
7:6	188, 234
7:8	299
8:2	299
9:2	228

Jonah
3	40
3:9–10	188
3:10	205, 234
4:2	188, 318
4:11	299

Micah
1:3	233
5:2	349
6:5	21
7:9	267
7:18	265

Nahum
1:3	318
1:7	197, 317

Habakkuk
1	20
1:13	243, 280
3:3–6	300

Zephaniah
3:5	306

3:17	205, 285, 314

Zechariah
2:8	131
8:6	242
11:6	299
13:7	259
14:4	131
14:9	213

Malachi
1:2–3	314
1:6	336
2:7	20
2:10	250, 320, 336
2:14	128
3:17	299
4:2	245, 302

NEW TESTAMENT

Matthew
1:18	324
1:25	19, 397
3:9	242
3:11	296
4:3	349
4:4	43
5:3–11	261
5:16–7:11	250
5:32	276
5:34	224
5:48	202, 295, 296
6:8	270
6:9	229, 323
6:10	280
6:16–17	361
6:32	270
7:21	279
7:23	26
8:8	296
9:36	248
9:38	311
10:20	408
10:29	277
11:6	345

11:27	27, 149
11:29	305
12:50	279
13:11	24
13:21	169
13:44–46	299
14:14	248
15:1–20	60
15:32	248
16:16	247, 342
16:16–17	28
16:17	342
17:2	299, 302, 361
17:5	303
17:22–23	280
17:24	295
17:25	295
19:17	317
19:26	242
20:15	277
20:18–19	280
20:28	299
20:34	248
22:16	361
22:32	2, 294
22:42	342
22:43–45	342
23:23	327
23:37	205, 259
26:42	277, 280
26:63	247
26:67	361
27:19	312
27:24	312
27:50	251
28:18	241, 242
28:19	333, 345, 347

Mark
1:7	297
1:24	23, 324
1:34	23
1:41	248
4:17	169
5:7	230

Scripture Index

5:17	9	**John**		6:20	291, 345
6:20	322	1:1	191, 276, 285,	6:35	292, 345
12:6	313		356, 363	6:41	292
12:29	213	1:1–2	236, 288	6:46	254
12:30	313	1:3	240	6:48	292
		1:5	66, 300	6:51	164, 292
Luke		1:9	292	6:57	247
1:32	230	1:10	25	6:63	85, 247
1:33	164	1:11	322	6:69	324
1:35	230, 324	1:13	256	7:17	279, 345
1:37	242	1:14	236, 249, 276,	7:28–29	23
1:47	299		285, 288, 298,	7:29	23
1:68	294		299, 356, 364,	8:12	292, 345
1:70	163		397	8:14	23
1:76	230	1:18	158, 254, 276,	8:19	23
1:77	24		286, 356, 363,	8:23	23
2:7	397		364, 376, 397,	8:24	291, 344
2:9	299		407	8:28	291, 407
4:34	23, 324	1:25	322	8:42	291
4:41	23	1:26	23	8:44	191
6:36	202, 264, 296	1:29	260	8:54–55	23
7:13	248	1:31–34	23	8:55	23
9:14	9	1:36	260	9:5	292
10:2	311	2:11	303	9:29	23
10:20	288	3:8	251	9:32	164
10:22	27, 149	3:16	314, 316, 364,	10:7	292, 345
11:2	323		397	10:9	292
11:52	26	3:18	364, 397	10:11	292, 317, 345
12:20	247	3:19	292	10:14	26, 292, 317
13:34	280, 314	3:19–20	268	10:17–18	385, 409
15:11–32	7	3:33	331	10:18	385
15:12–13	360	4:10	23	10:27	26
15:13	7	4:22	23, 344	10:33	337
15:14	8	4:24	126, 196, 251,	10:34–36	349
15:17	8		253, 254, 325	10:38	24, 216
16:15	270	4:34	279	11:9	292
16:22–23	376	5:17	129	11:25	292, 345
18:1–8	234	5:18	337, 356	11:27–28	197, 270
18:27	242	5:19	407	12:46	292
19:18	313	5:20	315	13:3	23
19:34	313	5:21	247	13:8	164
19:42	24	5:26	247, 249, 384,	13:19	291
19:44	24		407	13:23	376
20:21	361	5:30	407	14:1–3	42
22:42	405	5:32	409	14:6	246, 292, 345

447

14:7	23	3:14	312, 322, 324	1:19–21	105
14:9	251, 255	3:15	247	1:20	105, 106, 254
14:10	229	3:18	280	1:21	25, 28, 104, 105, 107
14:10–11	216	3:21	163		
14:16	409	4:24	311	1:21–23	106
14:16–17	23	4:28	280	1:22	105
14:23	229, 314, 409	7:2	264, 304	1:22–23	325
14:26	407	7:32	2, 294	1:23	105, 167, 179
14:27	305	7:34	233	1:24–26	280
14:31	313	7:52	312	1:28	25, 28
15:1	250, 292, 345	10:29	276	1:29	273
15:5	292	13:22	251	2:4	318
15:9–10	313	13:33	337	2:12	247
15:26	407	14:11	233	2:14–16	105
15:27	191	14:15	247	2:15	106
16:7	23	14:15–17	105	2:17–29	60
16:8	51	14:17	317	2:27	247
16:25–27	23	15:18	163	3:3	327
16:27	314, 315	16:14	96	3:4	328, 331
17:3	19, 213, 331	17:11	351	3:7	328
17:5	187, 271	17:23	344	3:17	24
17:6	149	17:24	224	3:26	306, 308, 310
17:11	323	17:26–27	134	3:30	213
17:11–16	230	17:26–28	105	5:5	28, 151, 314, 375
17:21	375	17:27	106		
17:23	314, 375	17:27–28	225	5:8	314, 316
17:24	187, 263, 271, 313, 375, 405	17:28	71, 106	6:4	303, 409
		18:14	276	7:12	322
17:25	306	18:21	277	8:4–14	85
17:26	149, 375	19:24	306	8:9	229
18:5	345	20:25	361	8:11	229
18:5–6	291	20:38	361	8:27	270
18:8	291, 345	22:11	303	8:29	397
20:17	4, 250	22:14	24, 312	8:29–30	271
20:27	337	26:13	302	8:32	299, 310, 409
				8:39	314
Acts		**Romans**		9:5	214, 356
1:9–11	232	1	102, 105, 106	9:15–18	277
1:18	248	1:4	166, 409	9:16	264
1:24	270	1:8	25	9:18	205, 280
2:1–4	408	1:17	307, 310	9:18–19	280
2:23	280	1:18	107	9:19	173
2:37	96	1:18–19	28, 105	9:21	277
2:46	34	1:19	25	9:22	318
3:13	2, 294	1:19–20	134	9:22–23	277

9:23	271		408		299
9:25	316	4:19	277	4:8	186
9:26	247	6:12–20	27	4:17	303
9:29	206, 207	6:19	229, 408	4:18	169
10:9–10	96	6:20	299	5:16	23
11:21	247, 360	7:22	299	5:18	408
11:22	299, 318	8	26	6:16	42, 229, 247,
11:24	247, 360	8:1–6	27		293, 408
11:26	165	8:3	26, 197, 270	6:18	246
11:29	243	8:4	25, 341	8:9	24, 345
11:33	135, 154, 276	8:4–6	26	9:4	362
11:34	25, 408	8:5–6	215, 378	10:1	318
11:34–35	173	8:6	25, 213, 214,	11:3	34
11:36	240, 408		240, 407, 408	11:13	19
12:1	75	8:10–11	26	11:17	362
12:2	279	8:13	164	13:4	205, 244
13:7	295	9:16	342	13:11	264, 305
14	202	10:13	326, 330	13:13	214
14:11	247	10:20	348	13:14	346, 347, 348,
14:17	202	11:7	72		375
14:18	202	11:12	408		
15:30	263, 375	12:4–6	346, 348	**Galatians**	
15:32	277	12:4–7	214	1:22	361
15:33	202, 264, 305	12:8	26	2:6	361
16:20	202, 305	12:11	277	2:15	247
16:26	166, 167	13:8	27	3:7	26
16:27	325	13:12	26	3:20	368
		14:6	26	4:4	308, 384, 407
1 Corinthians		14:33	305	4:6	408
1:9	19, 326, 330,	15:9	297	4:8	22
	375	15:28	215	4:8–9	25
1:17–31	27	15:45	247, 250	4:9	26
1:18–31	325			5:16–22	85
1:21	25	**2 Corinthians**		5:22	327
1:23	336	1:3	264, 320, 348		
1:24	325	1:9	247	**Ephesians**	
1:30	325, 408	1:11	361	1:4	187
2:2	23	1:12	34	1:4–5	271
2:6	325	1:18	326, 330	1:5	173, 277, 280
2:7	164	2:14	25	1:9	277, 280
2:10	27	3:3	247	1:11	271, 277, 280
2:10–11	214	3:5	297	1:17	22, 26, 348
2:16	25	3:17	214	1:17–18	251, 342
3:9	294	4:4	72, 299	1:19	225
3:16	42, 229, 293,	4:6	25, 31, 268,	1:19–20	243

1:20	224		363, 397	2:4	25, 205, 280, 282
1:23	215	1:15–17	407		
2:3	247	1:16	408	2:5	213, 214, 259
2:7	225, 318	1:16–17	241	2:6	299
2:19–22	293	1:17	245	3:15	42, 247, 293
2:20–22	42, 229, 408	1:18	240, 397	3:16	214, 232, 249, 325
3:8	225	1:19	229		
3:9	164	1:23	27	4:3	26
3:10	276	1:26	164	4:10	247
3:11	164, 191	1:26–27	27	6:15	246, 261, 262, 311
3:14–16	408	1:28	27		
3:17	409	2:2	24	6:16	154, 167, 203, 247, 251, 254, 268
3:19	26, 255	2:3	27		
3:20	223	2:9	229, 255, 359		
3:21	164	2:18	27	6:20	27, 129
4:3	391	3:4	249		
4:4–6	214	3:10	26, 72	**2 Timothy**	
4:6	215, 341, 378	3:15	305	1:9	165, 308
4:13	24	3:22	34	2:10	166
4:24	202, 322			2:13	243, 327
4:26	257	**1 Thessalonians**		2:19	26
5:1	202	1:9	247	3:7	24
5:8–14	268	4:3	279	4:8	268, 306
6:5	34	4:5	22		
6:17	43	5:23	305	**Titus**	
		5:24	326, 330	1:2	165, 243, 308
Philippians				1:3	299
1:9–10	26	**2 Thessalonians**		1:16	22
2:1	19	1:8	22	2:11	327
2:6–11	345	1:9	225, 304	2:13	214, 260, 261, 299, 356
2:13	277	2:8	251		
3:8	26	2:11	280	3:4	299, 315, 318
3:10	26	2:13	314		
3:12–14	26	2:16	314	**Philemon**	
4:3	288	3:2	327	6	26
4:7	255	3:3	327	7	248
4:9	305	3:16	305	12	248
4:11	278			15	164
4:19	296	**1 Timothy**		20	248
		1:1	299		
Colossians		1:11	256, 261, 262	**Hebrews**	
1:6	24	1:16	318	1:2	166
1:9–10	26	1:17	134, 154, 166, 176, 213, 254	1:2–3	386
1:11	303			1:3	203, 232, 245, 285, 288, 303,
1:15	72, 154, 254,	2:3	299		

	362, 363	1:13	243	2:21	26
1:5	337	1:17	154, 188, 264	3:1	318
1:7	251	1:18	277	3:8	169, 186
1:8	164	1:27	75	3:9	205, 280, 282
2:10	296	2:7	317	3:18	26, 165, 169
2:14	249, 251	2:19	23		
2:17	327	2:20	26	**1 John**	
3:2	327	3:7	247, 360, 361	1	300
3:6	42	3:9	124	1:1	191, 288, 289
3:10	24	4:12	268, 311	1:1–4	28
3:12	247	4:15	247, 277	1:2–3	19
3:14	362	5:4	206, 207	1:3	289, 375
4:12	43	5:6	312	1:5	196, 218, 253,
4:13	270	5:9	268		254, 300, 304,
4:14	232	5:17	232		325
5:5	337			1:5–6	268
5:8	385	**1 Peter**		1:9	306, 308, 310,
5:9	296	1:2	271		327, 330
5:14	20, 325	1:15–16	202, 323	1:18	289
6:3	277	1:19	260	2:1	312
6:18	243	1:20	271, 288, 309	2:3–5	26
7:26	324	1:22–2:1	85	2:20	324
7:28	296	1:23	43, 167	2:25	308
8:11	22, 24	2:2	43	2:28	256
9:14	1, 166, 247,	2:3	251	2:29	256, 306
	409	2:5	42, 43, 293	3:1	256
9:24	232	2:9	195	3:2	251, 256
10:5	288	2:9–10	268	3:3	256
10:23	326, 330	2:23	259	3:6	26
10:31	6, 247	3:15	93, 96	3:7	306
11:1	362	3:17	277	4:6	24
11:3	166	3:18	312	4:7–8	26
11:10	306	3:20	318	4:8	73, 157, 196,
11:11	326	3:22	232		218, 253, 254,
11:25	169	4:11	164		287, 312, 316,
11:27	154, 254	4:17	293		317, 325
11:40	296	4:19	327, 330	4:9	364, 397,
12:5–11	314	5:10	166	4:9–10	314, 316
12:22	247			4:12	254
12:23	268, 288, 296	**2 Peter**		4:16	73, 157, 196,
12:29	6, 246	1:1	299, 356		218, 253, 254,
13:20	305	1:4	247, 249, 361		287, 312, 313,
		1:5–6	26		316, 317, 325
James		1:17	303	4:20	254
1:5	219	2:4–5	299	5	249

5:7	288, 371	15:8	303
5:8	371	16:5	306, 324
5:11–12	249	16:7	254
5:11–13	336	16:19	257
5:20	1, 24, 166, 249, 250, 331, 356, 363, 383	17:8	288
		19:6	254
		19:11	330
		19:13	288
2 John		20:12	268, 288
1:9–10	345	20:15	288
		21:3	294
Jude		21:5	330
20	324	21:6	240
25	192, 299	21:22	246
		21:23	246, 303
Revelation		22:6	330
1:4	167, 188	22:13	167, 240
1:8	167, 188, 240, 246	22:16	246
1:16	302		
1:17	247		
2:18	349		
2:23	24		
2:24	27		
3:7	324		
3:14	240		
4:1–2	224		
4:2–3	254		
4:8	167, 188, 246, 254, 321		
4:9–10	247		
4:11	173, 277, 280		
5:5	260		
5:6–14	260		
6:10	311, 322, 323		
7:2	247		
9:2	303		
9:20	348		
10:6	167, 168, 247		
11:17	188, 254		
13:8	288, 308		
14:10	128, 256		
14:11	303		
15:4	324		
15:7	167, 247		

Subject Index

A
Abbott, W. M. 12
Abelard, Peter 379
Abraham 2, 4, 8, 20, 32, 70, 149, 233, 242, 280, 294
Adam 17, 249, 250, 252, 291, 399
Adoptianism 337, 380, 382, 392
Adorno, Theodor W. 83, 86
Aesthetic modality 199, 295, 299, 300, 301, 303, 305
Albert the Great 154
Alexander, W. L. 373
Alexander the Great 134

Allah 320
Allen, Russell O. 82, 83, 89
Allport, Gordon W. 83, 84, 85, 86
Alsted, Johann Heinrich 103
Althaus, Paul 130, 132, 133, 137, 187, 209, 226, 241, 260, 262, 263, 298, 299, 308, 314, 316, 320, 321, 322, 335
Altizer, T. J. J. 9, 113, 114
Ambrosiaster 307
America 6, 59
Anabaptists 379, 382
Ananias 312

Ancient of Days 166, 311
Ancient philosophy 134, 233, 337, 343
Angels 126, 171, 207, 233, 254, 348, 397
Anselm of Canterbury 100, 111, 112, 116, 145, 154, 227, 351, 370, 392
Anthropology 12, 13, 14, 57, 73, 77, 100, 139, 252
Apologetics 50, 93, 94, 95, 96, 97, 98, 99, 101, 107
Apologists 3, 94, 99, 135, 226, 307, 353
Apostasy 15, 16, 63,

64, 106
Apostolic Creed
    353, 384,
    395
Apostolic Fathers
    321, 353
Aquinas, Thomas
    15, 33,
    112, 128,
    144, 154,
    155, 156,
    170, 175,
    179, 281,
    297, 307,
    320, 351,
    392
Arianism   380, 381,
    383, 384,
    386, 388,
    392
Arians   381, 384,
    387
Aristotle   112, 173,
    175, 220,
    234, 277
Arius   367, 381,
    387
Arminians   216, 273,
    274, 281,
    381, 382,
    384
Arnoldi, Nicolaus
    103
Artificial intelligence
    8, 14
Aslan the Lion
    6
Athanasian Creed
    3, 127,
    137, 358,
    376, 384,
    393, 394,
    395, 396
Athanasius   154, 351,
    364, 381,
    387, 388,
    389, 390,
    399
Atheism   6, 9, 10, 12,
    113, 144,
    226, 365
Athenagoras
    389
Athenians   344
Augustine   11, 74,
    100, 117,
    152, 154,
    155, 173,
    175, 186,
    220, 222,
    227, 237,
    243, 263,
    273, 274,
    280, 301,
    307, 317,
    351, 369,
    388, 389,
    390

B
Baals   62, 63
Babel   233, 269
Babylonians
    377
Bakan, David
    63
Barth, Karl   58, 116,
    118, 124,
    152, 172,
    185, 187,
    196, 201,
    203, 209,
    213, 215,
    219, 225,
    227, 231,
    234, 235,
    238, 241,
    244, 259,
    290, 299,
    308, 315,
    318, 319,
    321, 325,
    335, 340,
    344, 346,
    359, 369,
    377, 379,
    386, 391,
    395, 398,
    399
Barth, P.   103
Basil the Great
    389, 398
Basinger, David
    244
Basinger, Randall
    244
Bavinck, Herman
    30, 31, 45,
    47, 50, 103,
    124, 128,
    135, 144,
    145, 149,
    153, 154,
    159, 160,
    163, 172,
    174, 175,
    185, 189,
    208, 209,
    214, 215,
    218, 226,
    227, 229,
    239, 242,
    251, 252,
    254, 263,
    268, 271,
    272, 273,
    275, 276,
    277, 278,
    279, 280,
    282, 289,
    295, 297,
    299, 301,
    303, 306,
    309, 311,
    316, 317,

320, 323, 329, 359, 362, 364, 369, 388, 389, 390, 392, 393, 396, 397, 398, 399, 400
Bavinck, Johan Herman 50, 51, 55, 56
Begemann, A. W. 182
Belgic Confession 126, 142, 193, 219, 391
Believers 3, 4, 8, 21, 23, 27, 28, 34, 42, 43, 115, 149, 150, 151, 202, 216, 242, 249, 250, 254, 255, 256, 267, 277, 296, 305, 308, 313, 314, 316, 341, 342, 375, 393, 408, 409
Benjamin 314
Benton, M. A. 59
Bereans 351
Berger, H. 132
Berger, Klaus 401
Bergson, Henri 180

Berkhof, Hendrikus 32, 125, 132, 201, 231, 235, 236, 238, 244, 307, 347, 366, 380, 395
Berkouwer, Gerrit C. 102, 105, 259, 340, 342, 343, 344, 354, 359, 379, 380, 382, 383, 387, 388
Bethel 229
Beza, Theodore 396
Bible 3, 6, 11, 17, 21, 22, 25, 26, 33, 36, 37, 38, 39, 40, 46, 47, 58, 72, 87, 89, 95, 98, 105, 109, 111, 112, 115, 127, 128, 129, 134, 143, 154, 155, 157, 158, 159, 160, 161, 165, 167, 168, 169, 176, 179, 186, 188, 189, 190, 191, 194, 195, 200, 214, 215, 216, 219, 223,

224, 226, 228, 231, 232, 236, 241, 243, 244, 247, 248, 251, 254, 256, 257, 261, 265, 268, 275, 282, 294, 298, 300, 306, 309, 311, 314, 316, 317, 318, 319, 321, 322, 324, 326, 327, 341, 343, 344, 346, 347, 348, 356, 369, 370, 372, 395
Biblicism 94, 338, 350, 391
Biedermann, Alois E. 57, 132, 365
Biotic Modality 247, 259
Blasphemy 235, 337, 367
Bloesch, Donald G. 210, 211, 241, 321
Blum, E. A. 169
Boehme, Jakob 303
Boethius 127, 170, 175
Bonaventura 392
Bonhoeffer, Dietrich 8, 10, 244,

455

Bouma, C. 327
Brahma 377
Braun, C. 370
Bray, Gerald
  210
Brillenburg Wurth, G.
  59
Broekhuis, J.
  74
Brown, Colin
  18, 117,
  118, 163
Brown, Laurence B.
  90
Brown, R. E.
  354
Brücke, Ernst
  Wilhelm von,
  62, 63
Brugger, Walter
  103, 146,
  210
Brümmer, V.
  41, 366
Brunner, Emil
  36, 130,
  134, 135,
  137, 146,
  147, 152,
  172, 196,
  201, 205,
  206, 209,
  226, 236,
  238, 241,
  242, 257,
  262, 284,
  304, 308,
  316, 321,
  322, 326,
  339, 366,
  380
Buber, Martin
  8, 15, 67,
  68, 122,
  370
  129, 238,
  291, 366
Bultmann, Rudolf
  25, 27, 134,
  152
Buri, Fritz 105, 147,
  156, 209,
  210, 335,
  369, 380,
  398
Buytendijk, F. J. J.
  34

C
Cabbala 63
Callixtus 379
Calvin, John
  71, 72,
  103, 106,
  149, 243,
  281, 309,
  351, 362,
  363, 367,
  370, 372,
  391, 395,
  396
Calvinists 274
Cantor, Georg
  220, 221
Cappadocian fathers
  397
Cappadocians
  389
Caputo, John D.
  10, 11
Carey, J. J. 114
Carson, D. A.
  27
Cassirer, Ernst
  72
Catechisms 351, 353
Causa sui 238, 239,
  240
Chafer, Lewis Sperry
  159, 287,
  289, 336,
  357, 369,
  397, 399,
  400
Chalcedon 350, 354,
  356
Charnock, Stephen
  207
Cherubim 301
Christ's divinity
  355, 388
Christian theology
  53, 135,
  137, 173,
  186, 333,
  339
Christian thinkers
  10, 74,
  116, 359
Christianity
  3, 7, 8, 10,
  45, 47, 52,
  53, 58, 65,
  96, 97, 98,
  117, 118,
  134, 149,
  335, 353,
  377, 389,
  396, 400
Christians 2, 34, 45,
  62, 87, 89,
  95, 114,
  116, 125,
  253, 319,
  326, 335,
  336, 337,
  347, 353,
  354, 356,
  387, 395,
  396, 400
Christology
  200, 334,
  344, 350,
  353, 354,
  382

Subject Index

Church fathers 172, 216, 271, 307, 356, 357, 360, 361, 362, 376, 387, 389, 397
Cicero 74
Clack, Beverley 211
Clack, Brian R. 211
Clark, Gordon H. 94
Clark, Walter H. 84
Clement of Alexandria 154, 383
Clement of Rome 135, 226, 321
Cobb, J. B. 201, 235
Commandments 20, 28, 121, 269, 286, 318, 325
Constantine 387
Constantinople 350, 354, 356, 381
Cornwall, Marie 90
Cosmology 94, 113, 176
Cosmos 30, 32, 44, 112, 113, 144, 148, 166, 168, 169, 177, 180, 185, 192, 226, 227, 399
Council of Chalcedon 350, 354
Council of Constantinople 350, 354, 381
Council of Florence 290
Council of Geneva 396
Council of Nicea 350, 354, 381, 387
Council of Tyre 387
Cowper, William 232
Crabtree, Adam 62
Creator 35, 44, 47, 125, 137, 139, 140, 141, 147, 174, 185, 189, 190, 227, 257, 279, 330, 335, 336, 349, 378, 384, 391, 401
Creeds 59, 135, 151, 351, 353, 356, 376, 387, 393, 395
Cremer, Hermann 150, 200, 201, 203, 208, 323
Cusanus, Nicolaus 215, 220, 222
Cyrillus 253
Cyrus 314

D

D'Alembert, Jean-le-Rond 5
Dallas Theological Seminary 400
Damian of Alexandria 377
Darby, John N. 105, 166, 237, 388
Darwin, C. 63
David 225, 269
Davidson, James D. 89
Day of Pentecost 407, 408
De Boer, Theo 5, 10, 70, 113, 114, 118, 245
De Brès, Guido 219
De Groot, J. 220
Decalogue 126, 278
Deity of Christ 334, 337, 341, 387
Den Heyer, Cees J. 382
Dennison, J. T., Jr. 39
Derrida, Jacques 10, 11
Descartes, René 5, 111, 112, 139, 277
Diestel, L. 321
Dittes, James E. 80, 81, 83

457

Divine attributes 124, 143, 146, 147, 150, 156, 194, 197, 198, 200, 201, 202, 211, 216, 289, 311, 326, 358, 390
Divine revelation 16, 51, 52, 59, 88, 379, 400
Doctrine of God 1, 2, 3, 4, 12, 13, 17, 18, 20, 21, 49, 93, 101, 123, 136, 141, 142, 152, 202, 252, 320, 352
Doedes, Jacobus I. 384
Dogmaticians 322, 335, 384, 388, 400, 402
Dogmatics 21, 30, 31, 32, 58, 123, 135, 137, 144, 149, 151, 152, 196, 200, 201, 282, 320, 335
Dooyeweerd, Herman 14, 15, 36, 52, 68, 69, 70, 71, 72, 73, 74, 76, 77, 78, 81, 94, 100, 103, 136, 139, 141, 170, 172, 177, 178, 179, 180, 181, 182, 183, 211, 218, 221, 295
Dorner, Isaak A. 57, 235
Du Bois-Reymond, Emil 63
Dualism 3, 47, 51, 102, 103, 141, 142, 153, 154, 182, 183, 184, 217, 226, 231, 252
Duke, J. O. 34
Durand, J. J. F. 6, 357, 369, 380
Durrant, M. 206, 359, 360, 369
Dutch States' Translation 232, 237, 260

E
Early Church 135, 195, 333, 337, 338, 350, 376, 383, 385, 387, 388
Earth 1, 163, 167, 193, 213, 224, 225, 228, 254, 259, 265, 266, 270, 277, 280, 288, 300, 303, 350, 378, 386, 401
Eastern church 364, 373
Ebeling, Gerhard 133, 202
Ecclesiology 200
Economic modality 174, 295, 298
Ecumenical Councils 338, 386
Ego 7, 61, 66, 67, 68, 72, 73, 118, 133, 237, 287, 344, 345
Egypt 214, 233, 293, 377
Egyptians 252
Eichrodt, W. 307, 308
Einstein, Albert 180
Election 39, 275
Elert, Werner 126, 147, 150, 152, 153, 204, 367, 379
Elihu 267
Elijah 20
Enlightenment 5, 6, 7, 8, 59, 112, 154, 343,

Subject Index

350, 355, 388
Enlightenment theology
103, 339, 382, 383
Ephesus 354
Ephraim 248, 324
Epistemology
13, 34, 94, 108
Erickson, Millard J.
145, 294
Eriugena, John Scotus
379
Eschatology
200
Essenes 27
Eternal life 1, 19, 28, 166, 248, 249, 250, 263, 308, 383
Eternal One
176, 188, 237
Eternity 5, 136, 147, 148, 158, 159, 163, 164, 165, 166, 167, 168, 169, 170, 171, 172, 174, 175, 176, 177, 178, 179, 180, 181, 183, 184, 185, 186, 187, 188, 189, 190, 191, 192, 197, 202, 207, 208, 209,

210, 211, 220, 224, 226, 235, 236, 237, 239, 247, 255, 287, 288, 289, 290, 294, 296, 298, 308, 312, 314, 374, 383, 386, 407, 408
Ethical modality
157, 199, 312, 313, 315, 317, 320, 324
Ethnocentrism
82, 86, 88
Eusebius 154
Existentialism
95, 116

F
Faith knowledge
18, 28, 29, 30, 33, 34, 35, 36, 44, 115, 344
False religion
16, 17, 50, 56, 57, 60, 82, 83, 85, 89, 91
Farel, Guillaume
396
Fee, G. D. 27
Feuerbach, Ludwig
7, 68, 132, 144, 312
Fichte, Johann G.
132, 133, 154, 365
Fideism 108, 116

First Vatican Council
102, 119
Fontana, D. 59
Ford, D. F. 344
Forgas, Joseph P.
90
Fortman, Edmund J.
127, 128, 357
Franke, J. R.
94
Freud, Sigmund
7, 60, 61, 62, 63, 65, 68, 144
Frick, Heinrich
50
Fundamentalism
118, 338

G
Galileo Galilei
138, 233
Ganssle, G. E.
136
Garvie, Alfred E.
395
Geisler, Norman L.
107, 108, 109, 110, 111, 112, 114, 115
Geldenhuys, N.
318
Geneva 379, 396
Gentiles 22, 25, 155, 336
Gerber, Uwe
133
Gerhard, Johann
144, 147
Gerhardt, Johann
307
Gerhardt, Paul
304

459

Gerlitz, Peter 389
Germans 49, 119
Germany 10, 384
Gideon 305
Gilgal 323
Gispen, W. H. 237
Glock, C. Y. 86
Gnosticism 26, 27, 134, 377, 390
God's attributes 123, 141, 142, 143, 151, 193, 194, 199, 200, 201, 203, 204, 206, 207, 212, 213, 216, 217, 248, 265, 290, 298, 305, 312, 330, 335
God's being 29, 30, 122, 133, 142, 143, 144, 148, 151, 152, 153, 155, 156, 196, 203, 206, 207, 217, 218, 236, 252, 279, 284, 292, 300, 304, 305, 310, 312, 319, 322, 329, 363
God's eternity 136, 167, 170, 172, 174, 175, 178, 179, 180, 181, 183, 184, 185, 186, 188, 189, 190, 191, 197, 211, 224, 226, 237
God's faithfulness 238, 326, 327, 329
God's Fatherhood 39, 46, 47, 158, 159
God's foreknowledge 271, 272, 273, 274, 275
God's glory 197, 203, 295, 299, 300, 301, 322
God's holiness 196, 202, 206, 218, 320, 321
God's immutability 136, 174, 175, 189, 233, 234, 235, 257
God's love 113, 154, 158, 202, 203, 235, 262, 263, 284, 286, 312, 313, 314, 315, 316, 317, 318, 319, 320, 330, 354
God's omnipresence 200, 225, 226, 227, 228, 229
God's omniscience 202, 269, 270, 272
God's perfection 203, 209, 257, 295, 296, 298, 299, 312, 321
God's personality 122, 126, 127, 131, 133
God's revelation 16, 17, 25, 29, 31, 36, 58, 60, 77, 105, 115, 208, 335, 400
God's sovereignty 38, 275, 277, 283, 334, 366, 367
God's Word 1, 30, 32, 33, 37, 41, 57, 99, 113, 116, 286
Godhead 2, 113, 165, 206, 215, 216, 220, 251, 344, 358, 359

Subject Index

Graafland, Cornelis 10
Grace 3, 4, 51, 65, 102, 103, 148, 201, 202, 208, 209, 211, 225, 308, 310, 312, 313, 316, 318, 319, 320, 347, 375
Greek-Orthodox Church 303
Greek philosophy 79, 135, 173, 220, 360
Greek thought 134, 168, 216, 317
Greeks 2, 377
Green, J. B. 318
Gregory of Nazianzus 372, 389, 399
Gregory of Nyssa 389
Grenz, S. J. 94
Griffin, David R. 244
Grün, Anselm 385
Guarino, T. G. 156

H
Hades 228, 377
Hamilton, W. 9, 114
Hanson, R. P. C. 381
Harris, Samuel 357
Harrison, V. S. 56
Hartshorne, Charles 111, 201, 235, 244
Hasenhüttl, Gotthold 388
Hauerwas, S. 11
Heaven 28, 43, 167, 193, 213, 224, 225, 227, 228, 229, 232, 233, 246, 265, 277, 301, 302, 371, 378, 401
Heering, Gerrit Jan 380
Hegel, Georg W. F. 57, 125, 132, 224, 277, 365, 380
Heidegger, Martin 7, 70, 114, 180
Heidelberg Catechism 339, 391
Hellenism 134, 237
Helm, Paul 187
Hendrikse, Klaas 12, 113
Hengel, M. 338
Henle, Robert J. 112
Henry, C. F. H. 105
Heraclitus 134
Heresies 63, 216, 372, 382, 386, 392, 396
Herrmann, W. 335
Heschel, Abraham J. 124, 258
Heyns, Johan A. 31, 32, 101, 106, 151, 171, 193, 216, 218, 229, 230, 252, 255, 340, 378, 391
Higton, M. 344
Hilarius 367
Hinduism 80
Hindus 87, 377
Hobbes, Thomas 180
Hodge, C. A. 369
Hölderlin, Friedrich 7
Holiness 41, 121, 123, 148, 166, 194, 196, 197, 201, 202, 203, 204, 206, 208, 209, 210, 211, 216, 217, 218, 234, 268, 279, 313, 320, 321, 322, 323, 324, 325, 327, 330, 358, 409
Hollaz, David 56, 57, 146, 393

Holwerda, Benne 238
Holy Land 315
Holy Spirit 16, 17, 19, 23, 42, 49, 51, 72, 96, 98, 99, 108, 109, 116, 117, 123, 166, 202, 206, 251, 288, 290, 322, 324, 333, 334, 335, 337, 338, 339, 340, 341, 345, 347, 354, 357, 359, 367, 368, 371, 373, 375, 378, 381, 383, 386, 390, 391, 392, 396, 401, 407, 408, 409
Honig, Anthonie G. 355
Hood, R. W. 59
Horus 377
Houtepen, A. W. J. 11
Hubbeling, H. G. 113
Hughes, P. E. 24
Hughes, Tim 304
Hulst, A. R. 220

Human nature 15, 40, 57, 58, 121, 259, 354, 355
Human personality 14, 15, 122, 127, 131, 133
Human reason 14, 97, 102, 103, 104, 116, 118
Human responsibility 38, 272, 274, 275, 282, 334, 366, 367
Humanism 55, 68, 94
Humanity 8, 10, 14, 15, 16, 30, 37, 45, 47, 49, 51, 57, 60, 64, 66, 70, 72, 74, 75, 93, 100, 103, 107, 108, 119, 122, 124, 125, 126, 133, 139, 140, 141, 145, 147, 148, 156, 157, 165, 177, 199, 208, 235, 236, 244, 259, 290, 292, 294, 319, 325, 326, 334, 336, 349, 355, 361, 366, 378, 385, 389, 394, 397, 401, 405, 407
Hume, David 6, 110, 111, 112, 155
Huxley, Julian S. 55
Hypostases 276, 334, 357, 358, 359, 360, 362, 363, 364, 365, 367, 368, 378, 386, 392, 393, 398, 402, 403, 406, 407
Hypostasis 3, 5, 136, 334, 357, 358, 359, 362, 363, 364, 365, 367, 368, 378, 389, 393, 406

I

Ice, J. L. 114
Idealism 143, 159, 365
Idolatry 27, 79, 106
Ignatius 135, 136, 257
Immink, F. Gerrit 215
India 56
Institutes of the Christian Religion 71, 72, 106, 149,

Subject Index

Irenaeus 173, 387, 389
Irrationalism 108, 116
Isaac 2, 4, 8, 32, 70, 149, 292, 294
Ishtar 377
Isis 377
Islam 377, 401
Israel 21, 22, 24, 62, 66, 95, 121, 193, 207, 213, 222, 233, 254, 270, 285, 292, 293, 294, 295, 314, 315, 323, 324
Israelites 266, 280, 293

J
Jacob 2, 4, 8, 32, 70, 149, 233, 292, 294
Jacob, Benno 291
Jaffé, A. 65
James, William 59, 60
Janssen, J. 71
Jehovah's Witnesses 240, 381
Jenson, Robert W. 403
Jerome 239, 367
Jerusalem 303, 315, 362, 363, 367, 370, 372, 391, 395
Jesus Christ 4, 19, 23, 25, 31, 51, 58, 117, 137, 199, 229, 232, 240, 249, 255, 259, 260, 289, 324, 325, 327, 333, 347, 349, 351, 352, 356, 357, 375, 378, 382, 385, 394, 407
Jewish tradition 166, 188
Jews 95, 136, 237, 335, 336, 337
Joest, W. 126
John of Damascus 290, 398
John the Baptist 297
Josephus, Flavius 278, 302
Judaism 134, 168, 377, 401
Jung, Carl G. 64, 65, 66, 67, 68
Jüngel, Eberhard 46, 119, 122, 236, 312, 380, 399
Junius, Franciscus 234
Jupiter 377
Juridical modality 197, 199, 268, 306, 308
Justification 202, 309, 310

K
Kalsbeek, L. 139, 279
Kamphuis, J. 252
Kant, Immanuel 6, 10, 103, 110, 111, 112, 137, 154, 180, 365
Kärkkäinen, V.-M. 11
Kasper, Walter 8, 15, 102, 119, 127, 131, 142, 335, 369, 370, 380, 399, 404
Kelly, J. N. D. 388
Kettler 364, 376, 388, 395
Kierkegaard, Søren 95, 370
Kinematic Modality 138, 174, 230, 233
Kingdom of God 138, 202, 261
Kittel, Gerhard 302
Knowledge of God 13, 17, 18, 19, 20, 21, 23, 24, 25, 26, 28, 29,

30, 31, 32, 33, 34, 35, 36, 44, 45, 49, 57, 69, 71, 72, 105, 106, 117, 118, 131, 132, 134, 146, 149, 150, 160, 197, 198, 224, 229, 255
Koester, Helmut 362
Kohnstamm, Philip 366
Kolakowsky, Leszek 8
König, Adrio 31, 130, 252, 258, 259
Koopmans, J. 395
Koran 320
Korff, Frederik W.A. 354, 355
Kreeft, P. 15
Kuitert, Harry 104, 105, 155, 201, 252
Küng, Hans 12, 75, 119, 130, 258, 259, 380
Kuyper, Abraham 29, 30, 31, 47, 103, 145, 177, 208, 209, 383

L
La Mettrie, Julien Offray de 5
Lactantius 74, 239
Lamont, J. R. T. 11
Laplace, Pierre-Simon 7
Leibniz, Gottfried W. 111, 112, 114
Lessing, Gotthold E. 5
Leuven 71
Levin, J. 82
Levinas, Emmanuel 114
Lewis, C. S. 6, 99, 110, 121, 122, 316, 374
Lewis, H. D. 55
Liberal theology 5, 380
Lightfoot, J. B. 27
Lingual modality 285, 289
Locke, John 5
Loewenthal, K. M. 59
Logical modality 198, 265, 269, 270
Logos 96, 134, 268, 276, 285, 286, 288, 289, 326, 337, 338, 363, 368, 382, 384
Lohff, Wenzel 383

Lohse, E. 362
Lombard, Peter 320, 392
Lonergan, B. 357
Loofs, Friedrich 343
Loonstra, B. 11
Luther, Martin 103, 154, 173, 219, 220, 227, 237, 307, 316, 340, 351, 395
Lutheran theology 173, 304
Lutheranism 344
Lutherans 254, 273, 281, 355
Lyotard, Jean-François 245

M
MacGregor, Geddes 78
MacLeod, D. 358
Macquarrie, John 115, 125, 155
Mann, William E. 244
Manoah 207, 233, 254
Marcion 273
Marck, Johannes à 103
Martyr, Justin 136, 154, 307, 383, 389
Marx, Karl 7, 60, 68

Subject Index

Mary 276, 354, 355, 394, 397
Mary Magdalene 337
Maslow, A. H. 85
McFague, S. 46
Melanchthon, Philip, 103, 173, 344, 396
Melito 253
Mercy 38, 41, 113, 123, 148, 160, 201, 203, 205, 208, 209, 210, 211, 262, 264, 280, 301, 312, 313, 316, 317, 318, 319, 320
Merleau-Ponty, Maurice 114
Messiah 63, 165, 207, 337, 342, 349, 350
Meyer, Frederick B. 309, 346
Milbank, John 10
Miley, John 400
Miller, G. R. 86
Miskotte, Kornelis H. 200, 354, 355
Modalism 359, 364, 366, 376, 377, 378, 380, 386, 387, 392, 397, 398, 401, 402, 403, 404, 406, 407, 408, 409
Modernism 10, 11, 102, 383
Molina, Luis de 273
Moltmann, Jürgen 10, 258, 259, 355, 357, 380
Monarchianism 378, 379, 384, 386, 402
Monotheism 61, 377
Montgomery, J. W. 114
Mormons 334
Morris, Leon 27
Morris, Thomas V. 94
Moses 20, 40, 61, 62, 63, 233, 254, 257, 269, 293
Mount Paran 300
Mount Sinai 229, 233, 286, 293, 301
Mount Zion 315
Muis, J. 46
Murchland, B. 114
Murray, John 309, 310
Musculus, Wolfgang 281
Muslims 87, 335, 336, 337, 396
Mysticism 26, 44, 45, 55, 63, 80, 88, 132, 147, 278

N
Natural reason 4, 6, 52, 102, 103, 105, 117
Natural theology 4, 5, 94, 101, 102, 103, 104, 105, 106, 107, 108, 113, 134, 143, 144, 146,
Nature–grace dualism 3, 51, 102, 103
Neo-Platonism 47, 155
Netherlands 2, 9, 215, 381, 384
New Testament 2, 19, 20, 22, 24, 26, 134, 135, 163, 166, 206, 250, 261, 262, 284, 293, 302, 305, 312, 315, 316, 323,

465

324, 330,
336, 345,
346, 347,
348, 349,
350, 352,
356, 360,
364, 384,
388
Nicea 350, 354,
356, 357,
381, 387
Nicene-Constantino-
politan Creed
151, 335,
376
Nicene Creed
351, 368,
390, 393,
401
Nietzsche, Friedrich
6, 7
Nihilism 7, 14
Nijmegen 71
Nineveh 40
Noah 17, 292

O
Odin 377
Oedipus complex
61, 62, 63
Ogletree, T. W.
114
Old Testament
2, 18, 19,
24, 163,
168, 206,
237, 250,
260, 300,
303, 309,
318, 320,
322, 323,
324, 328,
336, 349,
350, 378,
384

Olevianus, Caspar
391
Ontology 94, 109,
237, 343,
347
Open Theists
273
Origen 3, 135,
154, 220,
257, 274,
383, 389,
390
Orthodox theology
5, 199
Osiris 377
Ott, Heinrich
9, 16, 93,
117, 118,
119, 129,
130, 133,
236, 366
Otto, Rudolf
55, 58, 321
Ousia 3, 5, 358,
360, 362,
364, 365,
393

P
Pack, E. A. 357
Pagan religions
65, 377
Paganism 57, 90,
106, 389
Pagans 28, 396
Pailin, D. A.
41, 109
Paloutzian, R. F.
59
Pannenberg, Wolfhart
7, 10, 12,
54, 56, 57,
58, 76,
105, 119,
126, 134,

135, 142,
143, 148,
153, 170,
172, 187,
200, 210,
214, 215,
222, 227,
234, 239,
244, 252,
266, 307,
312, 314,
326, 346,
380, 388,
399, 403
Pantheism 174, 226,
230, 231,
277, 314
Park, C. L. 59
Parmenides 2
Pascal, Blaise
3, 4, 79,
109, 117
Patriarchs 256, 292,
314
Patripassianism
378, 379,
386, 402
Paul 23, 24, 25,
96, 166,
214, 225,
242, 249,
297, 302,
303, 305,
348, 351,
378, 398,
409
Paul of Samosata
337, 368,
384
Pelagians 282
Pensées 79, 117
Pentecost 378, 407,
408
Perceptive modality
250, 254

Petau, Denys 388
Petavius, Dionysius 388
Peterson, M. 41, 88, 110
Pharaoh 280
Phenomenology of religion 50, 53, 59, 77
Philippi, Friedrich A. 309
Philo 134, 136, 151, 155, 168, 172, 173, 229
Philolaus 173
Philosophers 3, 4, 5, 11, 12, 32, 70, 78, 103, 112, 115, 122, 132, 133, 134, 136, 154, 215, 277, 365
Philosophical anthropology 14, 73
Philosophy 3, 4, 10, 11, 50, 53, 64, 68, 70, 73, 74, 79, 81, 103, 105, 107, 108, 134, 135, 168, 170, 173, 177, 195, 220, 226, 233, 234, 283, 284, 337, 338, 343, 350, 360, 366
Philosophy of religion 50, 53, 81, 105, 107, 284, 366
Physical Modality 238, 240, 241
Physics 139, 399
Pickstock, Catherine 10
Pieper, J. 71
Pike, Nelson 136, 186
Pilate 312
Pistical modality 28, 41, 81, 88, 178, 199, 326, 329, 330
Plantinga, A. 11, 12, 60
Plato 112, 137, 143, 168, 258, 277
Plessner, H. 139
Plotinus 33, 153, 155, 172, 216, 220, 229, 277, 315
Pluto 377
Poland 382
Polanus, Amandus 174, 281
Polyander, Johannes 393
Polycarp 257
Polytheism 377, 402
Poseidon 377
Postmodernism 10, 11
Postmodernists 10
Praxeas 378
Prayer 26, 29, 89, 202, 250, 280, 325
Pre-Nicene fathers 387, 388
Predestination 271, 273, 274
Prenter, Regin 312
Presuppositionalism 94
Presuppositionalists 98
Prophets 3, 24, 258, 266
Protestant dogmatics 137, 144, 196
Protestant scholasticism 29, 174
Protestant theologians 321, 354, 393
Protestant theology 56, 125, 136, 143, 146, 153, 173, 307, 338, 381, 406
Protestantism 146, 386
Protestants 12, 119, 351, 376
Providence 56, 135, 202, 226, 283
Pseudo-Dionysius 143, 145, 147, 150

Psychoanalysis 61, 63
Psychology 50, 53, 59, 63, 67, 71, 77, 78, 80, 87, 91, 139, 355
Pye Smith, J. 357

Q
Quenstedt, Johannes Andreas 152, 393

R
Radical Orthodoxy 10
Rabbis 245, 326
Rahner, Karl 12, 75, 119, 151, 153, 200, 340, 380, 399, 404
Rational knowledge 38, 43, 45, 46, 76, 126, 130, 131, 132, 185, 224, 234, 248, 283
Rationalism 43, 55, 107, 116, 118, 143
Rationality 119, 126, 127, 128, 265, 266, 267, 268
Ratzinger, J. 338, 360, 375
Redeemer 336, 378, 391
Redemption 36, 37, 41, 51, 56, 66, 86, 102, 188, 200, 248, 277, 283, 292, 310, 323, 324, 325, 329, 374, 385, 391, 408
Reformation 307, 390, 396
Reformational theology 31, 103
Reformed theologians 254, 281
Reformed theology 154, 273, 294
Reformers 340, 344, 357, 359
Regeneration 16, 17, 104, 108, 181, 277
Religiosity 49, 52, 53, 54, 55, 56, 57, 59, 60, 73, 77, 81, 83, 84, 85, 86, 87, 89, 90, 91
Remonstrants 274
Reprobation 39, 275
Richard of Saint Victor 127
Richards, Jay W. 11, 236, 237
Ridderbos, H. N. 327
Ridderbos, Jan 169
Ritschl, Albrecht 133, 152, 262, 309, 343, 382, 403, 404
Ritschl, D. 152
Robinson, John A. T. 9
Rokeach, M. 83
Roman Catholic Church 390
Roman Catholicism 102, 146, 381, 386
Roman Catholics 12, 281
Roman Empire 396
Romanticism 365
Rome 135, 226, 321, 379, 381
Rosenzweig, Franz 238, 291
Ross, M. 84, 86
Rouse Ball, W. W. 7
Rousseau, Jean-Jacques 5
Runia, D. T. 168
Rushdoony, R. J., 62, 63

S

Sabbatai Zvi 63
Sabellianism 379
Sabellius 362, 378, 379
Salt Lake City 334
Samaritans 344
Sanctification 277, 323, 324, 325, 374, 391
Sardis 253
Saroglou, V. 59
Sarot, M. 11, 215, 228, 234, 258, 273
Sartre, Jean-Paul 114, 239
Sasse, Hermann 166, 167
Satan 27
Schaeffer, Francis A. 94, 97, 98, 99
Scheeben, Matthias J. 128
Schelling, Friedrich 277
Schilder, Klaas 155, 172, 207, 209, 215, 252
Schillebeeckx, Edward 9, 10, 105
Schleiermacher, Friedrich 57, 58, 59, 95, 132, 152, 172, 214, 222, 365, 379
Schlink, Edmund 21, 151, 152, 210, 229, 287, 335, 344, 367, 383, 391
Scholastic theology 3, 151, 170, 273, 395
Scholasticism 29, 31, 94, 99, 144, 145, 173, 174, 280, 338, 343
Scholastics 173, 239, 307
Scholem, G. 303
Schopenhauer, Arthur 277
Schrenk, Gottlob 306
Schuler, Bertram 204, 399
Schwöbel, C. 12
Science of religion 29, 49, 50, 51, 52, 53, 54, 56, 58, 68, 70, 71, 80, 87, 93
Scientific knowledge 13, 18, 29, 30, 33, 35, 77
Scientism 35, 107, 109
Scobie, G. E. W. 78
Scripture 3, 4, 16, 25, 26, 30, 31, 32, 33, 34, 35, 36, 39, 40, 57, 58, 75, 98, 103, 190, 191, 195, 225, 257, 258, 263, 269, 271, 272, 273, 275, 277, 283, 284, 293, 297, 337, 338, 343, 347, 350, 351, 353, 356, 372, 376, 384, 393
Scriptures 245, 326, 351
Second Vatican Council 12
Sectarianism 88
Seeberg, Reinhold 384, 399
Segond, Louis 219, 237
Seir 300
Semi-Arians 384
Sensitive modality 199, 256, 260
Septuagint 18, 22, 206, 214, 237, 246, 261, 284, 285, 316, 324
Seraphim 254, 321
Servet, Michael 379, 396

Subject Index

469

Shakespeare, S. 10
Shamash 377
Sheol 225, 266
Shiva 377
Shults, F. L. 94
Siger of Brabant 170
Simon Bar-Jonah 28
Smit, J. H. 125
Socinianism 381, 382, 383, 384, 386, 392
Socinians 216, 253, 273, 382
Socinus, Faustus 382
Söderblom, Nathan 54
Sölle, Dorothee 9
Solomon 224, 314, 325
Son of God 137, 249, 255, 256, 296, 337, 342, 349, 381, 382, 393, 394, 397, 405
Soteriology 124, 200, 201, 320, 382
Sozzini, Fausto 382
Spatial Modality 174, 223, 224, 225, 226
Spengler, Oswald 180
Sperna Weiland, Jan 9, 10
Spilka, Bernard 82, 83, 89
Spinoza, Baruch 111, 220, 245, 266
Springer, Johannes L. 9, 10
Spykman, Gordon 125, 149
Stafleu 221
Steenbergen, W. 9
Stephan, Horst 196, 335
Stephen 312
Stern, Paul J. 65, 66
Stoa 226, 258, 277
Stoic thought 226
Stoics 134
Stone, H. W. 34
Strauss, Daniel F. M. 32, 45, 46, 136, 138, 150, 155, 156, 160, 194, 220, 221, 233, 240
Strommen, Merton P. 80
Subordinationism 383
Substantialism 136, 137, 138, 139, 140, 141, 142, 144, 152, 234, 297, 312, 359, 394
Supra-rational knowledge 35, 45, 46, 132
Synesius 239
Systematic theology 1, 2, 12, 18, 31, 35, 36, 37, 40, 49, 93, 124, 156, 343

T

Tanakh 238, 337
Tate, E. D. 86
Tatian 364, 389
Taylor 11, 12
Teleology 109, 110
Ter Linden, Nico 12
Tertullian 136, 253, 280, 378, 383, 389, 390
Teubal, Savina J. 246
Theists 8, 109, 113, 273
Theologians 3, 12, 19, 29, 34, 38, 39, 40, 46, 56, 57, 78, 96, 118, 119, 121, 122, 125, 128, 132, 133, 134, 137, 152, 174, 175, 187, 206, 211, 215, 254, 274, 275, 281,

282, 283,
309, 320,
321, 334,
337, 344,
351, 352,
353, 354,
355, 356,
365, 366,
379, 384,
391, 392,
393, 396,
403
Theopaschitism
379
Theophilus 389
Thiel, J. 94
Thielicke, Helmut
130, 238,
341, 391,
392
Thomism 47, 101,
125, 234
Thomists 102
Thyatira 27
Tilburg 71
Tillich, Paul
54, 125,
130, 187,
232, 335,
343, 365,
366, 369,
403
Tisdale, J. R.
85
Tooley, M. 11, 12
Torah 1, 2, 63,
276, 286,
326
Towner, P. H.
327
Traditional theology
134, 151,
155, 172,
173, 195,
199, 214,

215, 218,
229, 253,
254, 270,
272, 275,
276, 299,
320
Trillhaas, Wolfgang
147, 150,
201, 202,
226, 346,
373
Trinitarianism
341, 343,
344, 347,
350, 353,
357, 359,
371, 386,
395, 396,
398, 400,
402, 405,
406
Trinitarians
402, 405
Trinity 3, 4, 40,
102, 123,
137, 149,
150, 151,
198, 200,
204, 206,
214, 263,
276, 286,
287, 290,
294, 298,
308, 313,
314, 319,
333, 334,
335, 336,
337, 338,
339, 340,
341, 342,
343, 344,
345, 346,
347, 348,
351, 352,
354, 356,

357, 358,
359, 361,
363, 364,
366, 367,
368, 369,
370, 371,
372, 374,
375, 376,
377, 379,
380, 382,
386, 387,
388, 389,
390, 391,
392, 393,
395, 396,
399, 400,
401, 402,
403, 404,
406
Tritheism 355, 358,
359, 364,
366, 368,
376, 377,
386, 390,
398, 399,
401, 402,
403, 404,
405, 407,
408
Triune God 251, 255,
288, 289,
335, 340,
343, 344,
346, 363,
391, 408
Troeltsch, Ernst
57
Troost, Andree
38, 53, 54,
79, 83, 98,
106, 126,
150, 215,
219, 339
True religion
16, 21, 56,

Turnell 79, 57, 58, 60, 71

U
Ulpian 307
Unitarians 336, 337, 382, 383
United States 59
Ursinus, Zacharias 281, 391

V
Van de Beek, Bram, 234, 369
Van den Brink, Gijsbert 11, 73, 74, 215, 228, 234, 241, 244, 258, 273
Van den Brom, L. J., 228
Van der Hoeven, J. 70
Van der Lans, J. 71
Van der Leeuw, G. 53
Van Genderen, Jan 103, 185, 186, 219, 234, 237, 238, 244, 252, 290, 307, 348, 365
Van Herck, W. 46
Van Huyssteen, J. W. 94
Van Niftrik, Gerrit C. 9, 10, 199, 335, 340, 369
Van Oosterzee, Johannes J. 384
Van Til, Cornelius 44, 94
Van Uden, M. 71
Van Woudenberg, René 70, 182
Vander Goot, H. 52
Vattimo, G. 11
Ve 377
Venema, Hermannus 357
Vergote, A. 71
Verkuyl, Johannes 370, 377, 396
Vili 377
Visagie, Johan 136, 194, 215, 220, 221, 233
Vishnu 377
Voetius, Gisbertus 279, 393
Vollenhoven, Dirk H. 70, 103, 211
Voltaire, François-Marie Arouet 5, 128
Von Frank, Franz H. 384
Von Gall, A. 299
Von Harnack, Adolf 343, 388
Von Hartmann, Eduard 277
Von Hofmann, Johann 384
Von Rad, G. 322
Vos, A. 234

W
Wainwright, Arthur 347
Wainwright, W. 59
Ward, Graham 10
Weber, Otto 32, 103, 105, 124, 144, 147, 152, 196, 200, 201, 206, 209, 214, 229, 232, 243, 273, 308, 320, 359, 368, 373, 391, 395, 398, 399
Wegscheider, Julius 257
Weima, J. 71
Weiser, Alfons 329
Wele 377
Wentsel, Ben 6, 7, 102, 130, 157, 229, 230, 234, 238, 244, 252, 294, 304, 308, 313, 326, 348
Western church 290, 364, 373, 398

Western thought 5, 109, 220
Westminster Confession 39
Whitehead, A. N. 235
Wiles, M. 388
William of Ockham 112, 243, 278
Wisdom 19, 25, 26, 123, 145, 148, 154, 193, 198, 199, 208, 209, 210, 211, 216, 217, 234, 276, 313, 321, 324, 325, 342, 390, 391
Wiskerke, Jelier R. 252
Wodan 377
Wolterstorff, Nicholas 11, 12
Word of God 36, 40, 43, 56, 57, 98, 123, 167, 275, 286, 288, 335, 356

X
Xenophanes 2, 79, 215, 216

Y
YHWH 66, 123, 172, 188, 205, 206, 207, 213, 214, 219, 220, 225, 233, 237, 238, 254, 284, 285, 291, 292, 300, 301, 302, 303, 305, 311, 322, 330, 331, 336, 348, 349, 384

Z
Zanchius, Hieronymus 174, 393
Zarathustra 6
Zeus 377
Zion 229, 315
Zurvan 67
Zwingli, Ulrich 227

Milton Keynes UK
Ingram Content Group UK Ltd.
UKHW011621130624
444093UK00018B/181/J